Introductory
Visual
IFPS/Plus
Release 5 for Windows®

Roger Hayen

Central Michigan University

CTI

A DIVISION OF COURSE TECHNOLOGY
ONE MAIN STREET, CAMBRIDGE, MA 02142

an International Thomson Publishing company I(T)P®

Cambridge • Albany • Bonn • Boston • Cincinnati • London • Madrid • Melbourne • Mexico City
New York • Paris • San Francisco • Singapore • Tokyo • Toronto • Washington

© 1997 by CTI.
A Division of Course Technology – I⊤P®

For more information contact:

Course Technology
One Main Street
Cambridge, MA 02142

International Thomson Editores
Campos Eliseos 385, Piso 7
Col. Polanco
11560 Mexico D.F. Mexico

International Thomson Publishing Europe
Berkshire House 168-173
High Holborn
London WCIV 7AA
England

International Thomson Publishing GmbH
Königswinterer Strasse 418
53227 Bonn
Germany

Thomas Nelson Australia
102 Dodds Street
South Melbourne, 3205
Victoria, Australia

International Thomson Publishing Asia
211 Henderson Road
#05-10 Henderson Building
Singapore 0315

Nelson Canada
1120 Birchmount Road
Scarborough, Ontario
Canada M1K 5G4

International Thomson Publishing Japan
Hirakawacho Kyowa Building, 3F
2-2-1 Hirakawacho
Chiyoda-ku, Tokyo 102
Japan

Trademarks
Course Technology and the open book logo are registered trademarks and CourseKits is a trademark of Course Technology. Custom Editions is a registered trademark of International Thomson Publishing, Inc.

I⊤P® The ITP logo is a registered trademark of International Thomson Publishing, Inc.

Some of the product names and company names used in this book have been used for identification purposes only and may be trademarks or registered trademarks of their respective manufacturers and sellers.

Disclaimer
CTI reserves the right to revise this publication and make changes from time to time in its content without notice.

ISBN 0-7895-0112-0

Printed in the United States of America

10 9 8 7 6 5 4 3 2 1

Contents

Preface

Organization and Coverage

Introductory Visual IFPS/Plus contains twelve tutorials that present hands-on instruction. In these tutorials, students learn how to plan, build, and solve models. Moreover, this books harnesses the power of Visual IFPS by emphasizing the Toolbar buttons and other Windows features for creating models, reports, and datafiles. Students using this book will learn how to do more advanced tasks sooner than they would if they used other texts. As an examination of the table of contents affirms, by the end of the book, student will have learned such "advanced" tasks as creating a model with a balance sheet, cash flow statement, and statement of financial position.

Approach

The unique two-pronged approach of *Introductory Visual IFPS/Plus* sets it apart from other Windows books. Initially, students see *why* they need to learn the concepts and skills. This book teaches the concepts of Visual IFPS using a task-driven rather than a feature-driven approach. By working through the tutorials (each motivated by a realistic case), students learn how to use Visual IFPS in typical workplace situations , rather than learn out-of-context features one by one. Second, the book's content, organization, and pedagogy make full use of the Windows environment. What content is presented, when it is presented, and how it is presented capitalize on the power of Visual IFPS to perform complex analyses. This supports effective decision making more easily than earlier releases of IFPS/Plus did.

Features

The following features testify to the exceptional appeal of *Introductory Visual IFPS/Plus:*

- **Tutorial Case.** Each tutorial includes the same business-planning problem with changing topics in each tutorial. This problem-solving process will be meaningful to students as the cases expand to encompass new features and applications.

- **Step-by-Step Methodology.** The unique methodology keeps students on track. They click or press keys *always* within the context of solving the problem presented in the Tutorial Case Problems. The text consistently guides students, informing them of when they are in the problem-solving process. Numerous screen shots throughout the text include callouts that direct students' attention to important information on the screen.

- **TROUBLE?** TROUBLE? paragraphs anticipate students' likely mistakes and recommend ways to recover from these errors. This feature facilitates independent learning and frees the instructor to focus on substantive conceptual issues rather than on common procedural errors.

- **Reference Window and Task Reference.** Reference Windows provide short, generic summaries of frequently used procedures. The Task Reference appears at the end of the book and summarizes how to accomplish tasks using the buttons, menus, and keyboard. Both of these features are designed and written so that students can continue to use the book as a reference manual after completing the course.

- **Questions and Case Problems.** Each tutorial concludes with conceptual Questions that test students' understanding of what they learned in the tutorial. The Questions are followed by Case Problems that have approximately the same scope as the Tutorial Case.

- **Installation.** The appendix contains the directions on how to install Visual IFPS/Plus on your computer.

Acknowledgments

I would like to thank the many people who contributed to the successful completion of *Introductory Visual IFPS/Plus*.

I am grateful for the many suggestions and valuable insight provided by my colleagues. Kim Hayen, an undergraduate student, contributed in many ways, including the development of the tutorials layout, the case problems, and the innumerable repeated screen shots. The faculty and staff in the Business Information Systems Department at Central Michigan University encouraged and supported the book's formulation and development in a variety of ways.

And, lastly, but certainly not least, I would like the thank my family. During this project, the book overshadowed many family activities, but their encouragement, support, and, most of all, perseverance enabled me to complete this project.

Roger Hayen

PART I: USING VISUAL IFPS

Tutorial 1

Fundamentals of Visual IFPS and Business Modeling

Buffalo Computer Systems, owned and operated by Herbert and Patricia Wattsun, is a full-service microcomputer outlet. They provide total system support, selling turnkey systems to businesses and government. Each system includes hardware, software, installation, and training. Herbie and Pattie specialize in the Byte line of computers manufactured by Gat Computer Inc. of Citrus Grove Valley, California. The Wattsuns opened Buffalo Computer Systems in the middle of the year. They expect to sell 12 systems, at an average price of $7,500 per system, during their first half-year of operation. Herbie and Pattie are preparing their financial plan for next year. They expect to sell 49 systems next year but could sell as many as 56 without hiring any additional staff or increasing the size of their current facility in the Tumble Weed Shopping Mall. Working with their accountant, Herbie and Pattie estimate the following costs for next year:

Planning Items	Calculations
Sales	343000
Cost of Sales	77% of Sales
Salaries	49000
Benefits	19% of Salaries
Admin Expenses	2.3% of Sales
Depreciation	8000
Interest	1600

Herbie thinks that Buffalo Computer Service may not make sufficient profit at his expected level of sales, and he may have to consider other alternatives to make Buffalo more profitable. To evaluate the profit potential, Herbie wants to construct a business model using Visual IFPS/Plus.

Using the Tutorials Effectively

This book is divided into three parts; each part has a series of computer tutorials. First read the text that explains the concepts. Then, when you come to the number steps, follow the steps as you work at your computer. Read each step carefully and completely before you try it.

As you work, compare your screen with the screen illustrations in the book. to verify your results. Your screen might vary slightly from the book, depending on what printer or monitor you are using. The important parts of the screen display are labeled in each figure. Just make sure that the labeled parts appear on your screen.

Do not worry about making mistakes: That is part of the learning process. **TROUBLE?** paragraphs identify common problems and explain how to get back on track. Complete the steps in the **TROUBLE? paragraph** *only* if you are experiencing the problem described.

After you read the conceptual information and complete the steps, you can do the exercises found at the end of each tutorial in the sections entitled Questions and Case Problems. The exercises are carefully structured to help you review what you learned in the tutorials and apply your knowledge to new situations.

As you work through the exercises, refer to the Reference Window boxes. These boxes, found throughout the tutorials, provide short summaries of frequently used procedures. You can also use the Task Reference at the end of the book; which summarizes how to accomplish tasks using the mouse, menus, and keyboard.

Your Student Disk

To complete the tutorials and exercises in this book, you should have a Student Disk, on which you store your IFPS files. If your instructor or lab manager provides your Student Disk, you are ready to Launch Visual IFPS. If your instructor asks you to make your Student Disk, you need to format a disk for your computer.

Before you begin working to assist Herbie and Pattie with their model, you need to understand what IFPS is as well as a few important modeling terms and concepts.

What Is IFPS/Plus?

The first question to ask is, what is **IFPS**? Starting from the back of the name, PS stands for Planning System. IFPS is a planning and budgeting language. It is a fourth-generation language (4GL) specifically designed as a problem-oriented language that you can use for any planning or analysis problem that fits its tabular presentation of information as *spreadsheet* type reports. Equations and logic, usually referred to collectively as the *model*, express how each row and column, or cell, in the IFPS spreadsheet is calculated. Users can readily attack production-planning, engineering, and other analytical problems that fit a spreadsheet structure with the help of IFPS.

The F stands for Financial. IFPS includes some shortcut means for performing financial calculations such as net present value, internal rate of return, depreciation, and loan amortization. This built-in capability gives IFPS its financial focus. You can perform many analyses, however, without using these financial features.

The I represents Interactive. IFPS is designed for hands-on operation, rather than running in a batch mode. Because all planning systems are now interactive, this is an expected feature. However, in the early days of IFPS (the mid-1970s), the interactive aspect, of IFPS set it apart from other systems. IFPS can still run in batch mode, which is preferable for some very large jobs.

Finally, the Plus refers to the built-in database capabilities for IFPS. This supports the management of large data sets that are frequently used in advanced applications with IFPS models.

What Is a Model?

Models come in all different sizes and shapes. For example, there are fashion models, model cars, airplanes, trains, and spacecraft. Model homes let prospective buyers see what is available from a builder. Model citizens are ones whose behavior and actions are the most outstanding. Automobiles come in two-door, four-door, or sports models. A 924 is a specific model of a Porsche, whereas a 300 is a sports model from Nissan. Webster's defines a **model** as follows:

Model:
1. a) A small copy or imitation of an existing object, such as a ship, building, etc., made to scale.
   b) Preliminary representation of something, serving as the plan from which the final, usually larger, object is constructed.
2. A person or thing considered as a standard of excellence to be imitated.
3. A style or design; as, last year's model of an automobile.
4. a) A person who poses for an artist or photographer.
   b) A person, especially a woman, employed to display clothes by wearing them; mannequin.

Models can be classified as physical and mathematical. (For a more in-depth description of physical and mathematical models, see *Decision Support And Expert Systems: Management Support Systems* by Efrain Turban, Third Edition, Macmillan Publishing Co., 1993, p. 44.) A physical model can be scaled down, but the model behaves as though it has characteristics that mirror those of the larger object. For example, consider a scale model of an airplane that is tested in a wind tunnel. It is considerably more cost effective to build a scale model of a Boeing 777 and test it in a wind tunnel than it is to build a wind tunnel large enough to accommodate a full-size 777.

A mathematical model is a set of equations whose solution explains changes in the state of an entity. Mathematical models frequently used in businesses include projected business plans or budgets. These mathematical models permit managers to explore "what if" alternatives without the actual experience. For example, consider the situation in which a company is exploring the feasibility of building a large petrochemical plant. Before building the plant, the managers need to determine the financial consequences that will result from a decision to build the plant. Of course, they could just build the plant and hope that everything goes well. However, to assure the viability of the plant, a projected financial analysis that considers a variety of "what if" situations will allow a better, more informed decision to be made. In other words, cause and effect relations can be examined through various scenarios providing the model contains the correct assumptions describing the phenomenon.

IFPS is a tool for creating mathematical models that take on the form of a spreadsheet. In a planning language such as IFPS, a model can be defined as: A mathematical description of a problem such as a business system; a description of the assumptions and relationships among variables; and the logic describing a business problem.

Since the mathematical equations in an IFPS model represent the logical interrelationships of business activities, these equations of the IFPS model are known as "model logic" or simply as "logic." So, IFPS modelers use the terms *model logic* and *logic* interchangeably.

A computer program written in BASIC, FORTRAN, C++ (or whatever your favorite computer dialect may be) is a mathematical model consisting of the logic used to perform the required calculations. An IFPS model is very similar to a program. However, the analyst who uses IFPS would much rather be known as a financial modeler than a programmer. Hence, in IFPS your logic is a model, *not* a program. (If, however, it helps you to understand the uses of IFPS in solving your problem by calling your IFPS model a program, go right ahead and call it an IFPS program.) An IFPS model is useful when the decision process is not clearly defined; contains many variables; involves complex relationships; and includes uncertainties.

A model is a vehicle for providing information that allows an analyst to assess impacts of potential decisions; evaluate alternate courses of action; measure trade-offs among different situations; and allocate resources to meet objectives. An IFPS model is an English-like description of your problem, which is easily constructed and readily understood. You can easily include the unique characteristics of the structure of your company, business unit, division, group, or product line in your IFPS model. Your model can start small and then grow as your understanding of the problem increases and requires more complexity. When your environment changes, the model can evolve as well.

The Automated Spreadsheet

IFPS is a modeling language specifically designed to solve a variety of simple and complex spreadsheet-type problems. IFPS lets you create spreadsheet reports or solutions such as the planning solution illustrated in Figure 1-1. The arrangement of this report is identical to that shown on an accounting spreadsheet in Figure 1-2. For years, accountants have used big green spreadsheets such as this for preparing budgets and performing other analyses.

BUFFALO COMPUTER SYSTEMS
PROJECTED INCOME STATEMENT

	YEAR1	YEAR2	YEAR3	YEAR4	YEAR5
SALES	$343,000	$411,600	$493,920	$592,704	$711,244
COST OF SALES	264,110	316,932	380,318	456,382	547,658
GROSS PROFIT	78,890	94,668	113,602	136,322	163,586
SALARIES	49,000	52,920	57,153	61,725	66,663
BENEFITS	9,310	10,055	10,859	11,728	12,666
ADMIN EXPENSE	7,889	9,467	11,360	13,632	17,738
DEPRECIATION	8,000	8,000	9,000	9,000	8,000
INTEREST	1,600	1,600	1,600	1,600	1,600
TOTAL EXPENSES	75,799	82,042	89,972	97,685	106,667
EARNINGS BEFORE TAX	$ 3,091	$ 12,626	$ 23,630	$ 38,637	$ 56,919

Figure 1-1
Planning
Solution

BUFFALO COMPUTER SYSTEMS
PROJECTED INCOME STATEMENT

	YEAR1	YEAR2	YEAR3	YEAR4	YEAR5
SALES	$343,000	$411,600	$493,920	$592,704	$711,245
COST OF SALES	264,110	316,932	380,318	456,382	547,658
GROSS PROFIT	78,890	94,668	113,602	136,322	163,586
SALARIES	49,000	52,920	57,154	61,726	66,663
BENEFITS	9,310	10,055	10,859	11,728	12,666
ADMIN EXPENSE	7,889	9,467	11,360	13,632	17,738
DEPRECIATION	8,000	8,000	9,000	9,000	8,000
INTEREST	1,600	1,600	1,600	1,600	1,600
TOTAL EXPENSES	75,799	82,042	89,973	97,686	106,667
EARNINGS BEFORE TAX	$3,091	$12,626	$23,629	$38,637	$56,919

Figure 1-2
Accounting
Spreadsheet

In Figure 1-2, the spreadsheet "rows" are the planning items, accounts, or line items that are considered. The "columns" are years. All spreadsheets have this row and column organization, which is also known as a two-dimensional matrix or simply as a **matrix**. A column and row intersection is called a **cell**. A spreadsheet and a matrix have identical cell structures.

How do you arrange the rows and columns of the solution matrix in IFPS? Any way you want! Be creative! Figure 1-3 portrays the general organization of the IFPS solution matrix or spreadsheet. In the most common situation, the rows are line items or accounts and the columns are time. In IFPS though, *none* of the rows and columns are predetermined. It is just like a blank spreadsheet. You can let the rows and columns be anything you want.

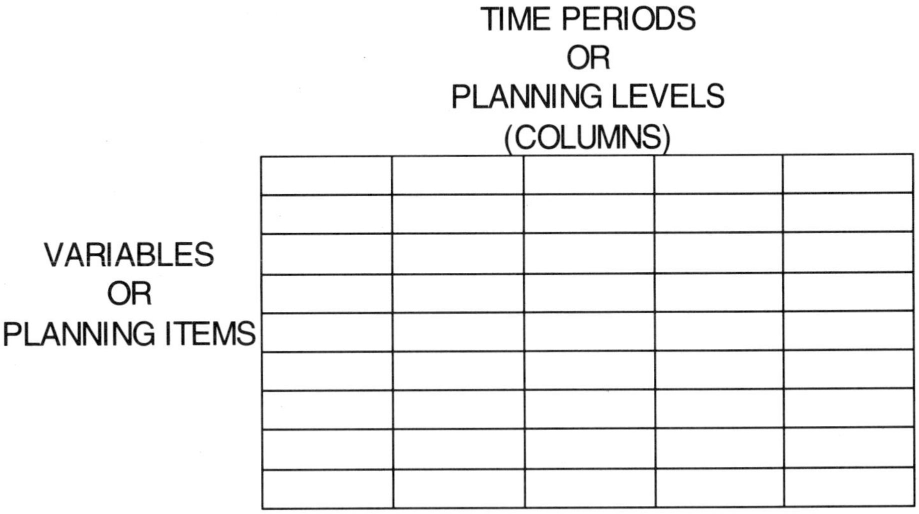

TIME PERIODS
OR
PLANNING LEVELS
(COLUMNS)

VARIABLES
OR
PLANNING ITEMS

Figure 1-3
Planning Model
Solution Matrix
View

IFPS does not have a predefined row and column organization as Lotus 1-2-3, Microsoft Excel, and other spreadsheets do. You determine the names for the rows and columns that best describe your problem. One reported case of a creative solution matrix organization was for budget planning in a large corporation. The company in question had 1,000 departments, with each department's budget including about 25 line items. Each column represented a department's budget for the next year. The solution matrix was arranged as 25 rows, for the 25 line items, and 1,000 columns for the 1,000 departments.

In another company, the most useful organization of the solution matrix was to let each row represent a department and each column a variable. There were 60 departments and 9 variables. This arrangement allowed easier data input for each department. After you have laid out your initial arrangement of rows and columns, give the matrix a 90-degree turn and determine if it might be better to interchange your rows and columns.

Since an accounting big green spreadsheet is organized identically to an IFPS matrix, a spreadsheet is a great IFPS design tool, which you can use as a springboard in designing and creating your IFPS model.

Decision Support Systems

So far, IFPS has been described as a computer tool used to build decision support systems. What, then, is a **Decision Support System (DSS)?** It is the use of the computer to assist managers with their decision process in semistructured tasks; to support, rather than replace managerial judgment; and to improve the effectiveness rather than efficiency of decision making.

The key concept of DSS is to focus on the use of the computer to support managers in their decision making. Clearly, managers *not* IFPS models, make decisions. An IFPS model allows a manager to gain insight into a situation so that an informed decision can be made.

A DSS provides information for decision making. The DSS should provide information as portrayed in Figure 1-4. The "what has been" and "what is" represent data on current and past conditions and the "what if" provides insight into alternative courses of action evaluated for decision makers.

Figure 1-4
Past,
Present,
and Future

"WHAT HAS BEEN"	"WHAT IS"	"WHAT IF"

As Figure 1-5 shows, the computer-based components of a DSS provide for three primary functions: database management, statistical analysis, and modeling. Each of these components is *not* a DSS. Rather, they are computer tools that allow you to create a DSS for your particular situation. Therefore, IFPS is *not* a DSS, but, instead, a DSS generator or tool that facilitates the development of a DSS for your specific situation.

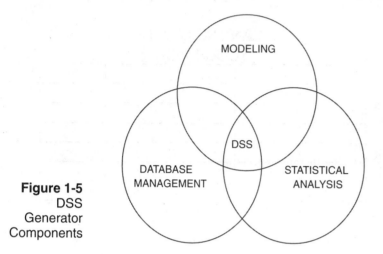

Figure 1-5
DSS
Generator
Components

The "what is" component is frequently implemented with a database management system (DBMS) that permits access to data from a database, whereas the "what if" is approached through modeling.

Structure of IFPS

IFPS is organized into several major components. Each component part allows you to perform a different task. Think of each major task as a "vice president." Then, the organization chart of IFPS is as shown in Figure 1-6. The "president" level is known as the Executive System. All other "vice president" level functions are known as Subsystems. Although there are several subsystems, three of the primary ones, which are described here, are model, report, and datafile. You are introduced to other subsystems as you begin working with them. IFPS lets you move from the Executive System to each of the Subsystems with considerable ease—like an automobile with an automatic transmission.

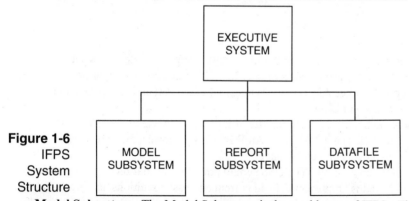

Figure 1-6
IFPS
System
Structure

Model Subsystem. The Model Subsystem is the workhorse of IFPS. This is where you create your model by entering your logic into IFPS. It is where the calculations are performed to produce your solution. Model interrogations through "what if" and "goal seeking" are all performed in the Model Subsystem. A number of other activities take place in the Model Subsystem such as analyzing and explaining model results.

Report Subsystem. This is the report-writer component of IFPS. With the Report Subsystem, you *describe* a professional looking report, but you do not produce the report itself. It is a mechanism for creating the report. In this subsystem, you can specify titles to be centered, headings and data that should be underlined, and many other stylistic operations to improve the appearance of your output report. The solution values that go into a report *always* come from a *model* that was *solved* in the Model Subsystem. In this subsystem, you merely describe or define the appearance of a management style report.

Datafile Subsystem. The Datafile Subsystem lets you store and work on data separately from a model. Datafiles are data stored external to a model. They let you have one departmental model, which you can use with a half-dozen different datafiles. Each datafile can represent a separate department, a different "what if," or a case scenario.

Overview of Visual IFPS for Windows

Visual IFPS/Plus is a software tool that functions in the Windows environment and is marketed by Comshare, Incorporated. Visual IFPS is **client/server** software with Visual IFPS as the user friendly **client** that runs in a Windows environment and IFPS/Plus that functions as the **server**. The Visual IFPS client runs on you personal computer with DOS and Windows or with Windows95. The IFPS/Plus server runs on a computer with Windows NT, UNIX, or other mainframe computer operating system. Figure 1-7 portrays the client/server computer configuration and interaction. With the Windows95 and Windows NT operating systems, you can configure a single, standalone installation of Visual IFPS/Plus with the client and server running on the same computer. (Also, the Student version is a single-machine installation that runs under DOS and Windows or under Windows95.) In addition to running Visual IFPS, you can run the IFPS/Plus server as an interactive terminal session. This capability is used with the more advanced features of IFPS/Plus. Think of IFPS/Plus as the main calculating engine. Visual IFPS prepares input for and receives output from the IFPS/Plus engine. In a client/server environment, one IFPS/Plus server can act as the calculating engine for a number of Visual IFPS clients. The IFPS/Plus server must be running before Visual IFPS clients can access it.

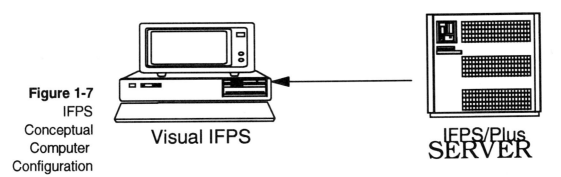

Figure 1-7
IFPS
Conceptual
Computer
Configuration

Visual IFPS

IFPS/Plus
SERVER

Typical application features of Visual IFPS/Plus include:

Creating Models	Variance from Solution
Solving Models	Variable Dictionary
Doing What-if	Templates
Goal Seeking	Side-by-Side Solutions
Generating Reports	Windows Style On-line Help
Creating Graphs	Using Datafiles

Launching Visual IFPS

The first step in working with Visual IFPS/Plus is to **launch**, or start, the software package. Launching Visual IFPS/Plus is similar to starting other Windows applications. Both the server and client must be running, however. Let's launch Visual IFPS from Windows NT with a single computer installation. (The same procedure is used to launch the Student version of Visual IFPS.)

To launch Visual IFPS:

❶ Start Windows NT. Or, if you are using another operating system, then boot that operating system.

TROUBLE? If Windows NT does not start, turn off the computer and try again. If working from Windows 3.1 or Windows 95, launch Windows and proceed with Step 3.

❷ Log onto Windows NT using your user name and password.

TROUBLE? If you forget your user name and password, then you cannot access Windows NT. See your instructor for your user name and password.

❸ Look for an icon or window titled "Visual IFPS/Plus." See Figure 1-8.

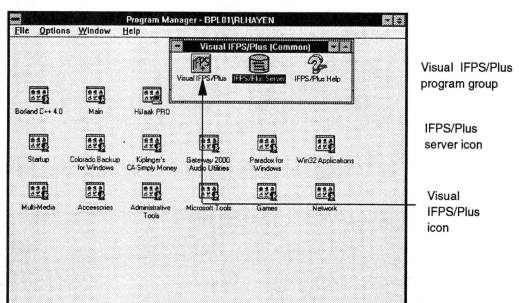

Visual IFPS/Plus program group

IFPS/Plus server icon

Visual IFPS/Plus icon

Figure 1-8
Visual IFPS/Plus
Program Group

❹ If you see the Visual IFPS/Plus group icon, doubleclick the **Visual IFPS/Plus group** icon to open the program group. If you see the Visual IFPS/Plus *program icon* instead of the *group icon,* go to Step 5.

❺ Doubleclick the **Visual IFPS/Plus** program icon. After a short pause, the IFPS/Plus Server is automatically launched, then the Visual IFPS/Plus copyright information appears in a box and remains on the screen until you complete the next step. See Figure 1-9.

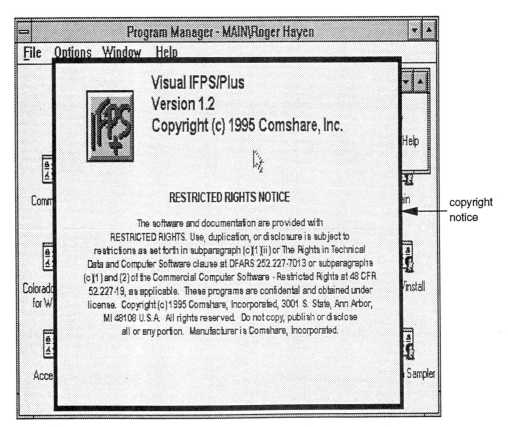

Figure 1-9
Visual IFPS/Plus
Copyright Box

❻   Click the mouse button on the **Visual IFPS/Plus copyright notice.** After a
short pause, the application window of Visual IFPS/Plus appears.

❼   Click the **OK button** in the Server Setting dialog box to display the
Desktop. See Figure 1-10. (The Server Setting dialog box may not be
displayed in the Student version.)

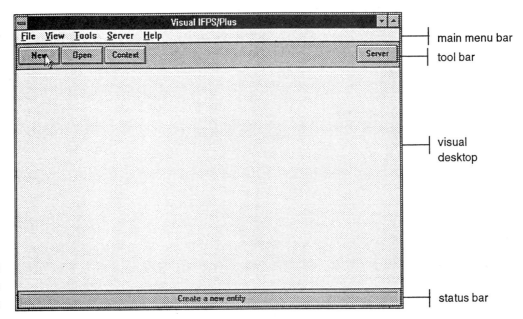

Figure 1-10
Visual IFPS/Plus
Blank Desktop

TROUBLE? If the IFPS copyright information does not appear on the screen, log off by clicking the File and Log off. Now repeat Steps 1 through 7.

TROUBLE? If the message "Sorry, either your comm path descriptors are wrong or the server is not running." displays, then you have an older version of Visual IFPS/Plus that requires you to manually launch the server. First, doubleclick the IFPS/Plus Server icon to start the server, then doubleclick the Visual IFPS/Plus icon. Now repeat Steps 6 and 7.

The Visual IFPS Desktop

The Desktop is where you begin all your work in Visual IFPS. When you first start Visual IFPS, the Desktop is empty. However, as you work with Visual IFPS, objects, such as models, reports, and datafiles appear on the Desktop in separate windows. Figure 1-10 shows the main components of the Visual IFPS Desktop. Let's take a look at these components so you are familiar with their function and location on the Desktop.

Main Menu Bar

The Visual IFPS **main menu bar**, located at the top of the screen, is similar to that of other Windows applications (Figure 1-10). **File** is the same as other Window applications. **View** displays the status bar and the toolbar. **Tools** add micros and sets that are advanced IFPS features. **Server** switches you to a terminal session in the IFPS/Plus server. **Help** is similar to other Windows help features.

Toolbar

The **toolbar** contains buttons that provide immediate and easy access to all commonly used Visual IFPS commands, allowing you to perform tasks more quickly. For example, instead of accessing first File on the main menu bar and then Open from the file menu, you can click the Open button on the toolbar to open a model.

Status Bar

The **status bar** contains two status indicators that advise you of active files. The first one tells you what model and report file is active. The other indicates what database is available for use with your models, if any. The status bar displays a description for a button in the toolbar, when you move the mouse over any button (Figure 1-10).

Working with Visual IFPS

Now that you have a basic understanding of modeling terms and are familiar with the Visual IFPS Desktop, you are ready to use Visual IFPS to build the model for Buffalo Computer Service. First, you will begin by creating a new **model and report file** (or M&R) file. One model and report file can contain a number of different models and reports. Visual IFPS arranges them by whether they are either a model or a report. An M&R file functions as a project notebook or folder where all your models and reports for a particular application in Visual IFPS are saved and stored as a single computer file (Figure 1-11).

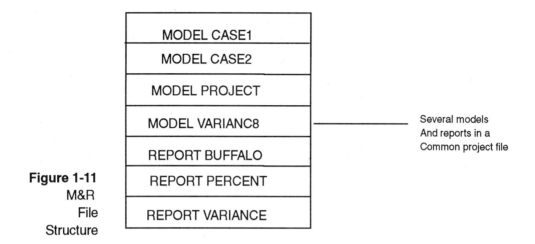

Figure 1-11
M&R
File
Structure

Several models
And reports in a
Common project file

Changing the Working Entity Context Directory

In Visual IFPS, the current models and reports file is called the working Entity Context Directory. You click the Context button to established where the M&R file will be stored.

Reference Window

Changing the Working Entity Context Directory
■   Click the Context button.
■   Type the name of the desired directory in the Directory text box and press [Enter].
■   Click the Save Context button.

When you are working on a project, it is best to put all your related models and reports into one M&R file. So that you can save all the models and reports on your Student disk for future use, you need to change the working Entity Context. Let's change the working Entity Context now.

To change the working entity context to A:\:

❶   Make sure your formatted Student Disk is in drive A.

TROUBLE? If you do not have a Student Disk, you need to get one before proceeding. You make your own by formatting a blank disk.

❷   Click the **Context button**, which is located on the toolbar, to display the Set Entity Context dialog box.

❸   Type **A:** in the Directories text box and press [**Enter**]. See Figure 1-12.

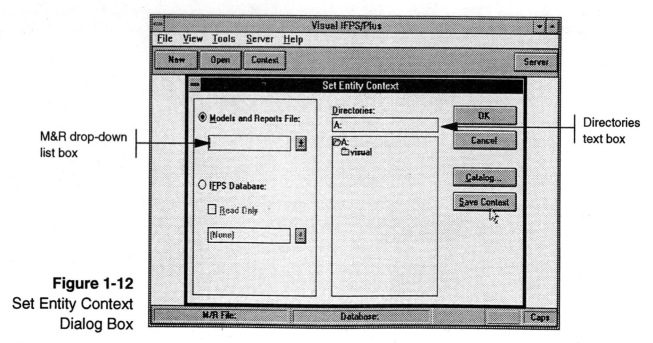

M&R drop-down list box

Directories text box

Figure 1-12
Set Entity Context
Dialog Box

❹   Click the **Save Context button** to establish this as your default disk.

Now that Visual IFPS can locate the files in your directory, you can create an M&R file for Herbie and Pattie.

Creating a Models and Reports File

Before you create a model or a report, you need to create an M&R file where it will be stored. A convenient method of naming files that helps you recognize your IFPS model and report file from other files is to use "MR" as the first two characters of the file name. An M&R file name of MRBCS is a convenient name for the Buffalo Computer Services business planning file.

Reference Window

Creating a New M&R File
■   Click Context in the toolbar to display the Set Entity Context box.
■   Type the M&R file name in the Models and Reports File drop-down list box.
■   Click the OK button to accept that M&R file.
■   Click the OK button when the message box appears to confirm that you want a new M&R file.

Let's create an M&R file for Herbie named MRBCS.

To create a new M&R file:

❶   Make sure the Set Entity Context box is displayed.

TROUBLE? If it is not displayed, then redo the steps for setting the entity context.

❷   Type **MRBCS** in the Models and Reports File drop-down list box, then click the **OK button** to accept this as the M&R file name. A message such as the following displays "Specified M&R file does not exist. To actually create this M&R file you need to create and save a model or report."

❸   Click the **OK button** in the message box to return to the Visual IFPS Desktop. The M&R file name appears in the status bar indicating the M&R file is established and ready for storing your model.

Now that an M&R file is created for storing models and reports, Herbie and Pattie are ready to create a model.

Creating a Model in Visual IFPS

A well-designed model should clearly identify the overall goal of the business plan for a particular company or organization, present information in a clear and well-organized format, include all the necessary data, and produce the results that address the management questions. As envisioned by Herbie and Pattie, they would like a five-year plan similar to the model solution in Figure 1-13. The first step in creating a model is to prepare a plan for it.

	YEAR1	YEAR2	YEAR3	YEAR4	YEAR5
SALES	343,000	411,600	493,920	592,704	711,244
COST OF SALES	264,110	316,932	380,318	456,382	547,658
GROSS PROFIT	78,890	94,668	113,602	136,322	163,586
SALARIES	49,000	52,920	57,153	61,725	66,663
BENEFITS	9,310	10,055	10,859	11,728	12,666
ADMIN EXPENSE	7,889	9,467	11,360	13,632	17,738
DEPRECIATION	8,000	8,000	9,000	9,000	8,000
INTEREST	1,600	1,600	1,600	1,600	1,600
TOTAL EXPENSES	75,799	82,042	89,972	97,685	106,667
EARNINGS BEFORE TAX	3,091	12,626	23,630	38,637	56,919

Figure 1-13
Solution
for Model

Planning the Model

When you plan a model, you analyze the problem you are trying to solve. By analyzing the problem, you define the overall goal of the model and determine the information you need to include in it. This information consists of the data and the calculations you need to gather and enter in the model to produce the desired results.

Herbie and Pattie have already defined their problem. They want to determine the overall profitability of Buffalo Computer Services by creating a five-year plan of their operations. They collected all the data they need for projecting their income and created a planning analysis sheet. A planning analysis sheet answers the following questions:

1.   What is the goal of the model? The goal defines the problem you need to solve.
2.   What results do I want to see? This is the output or the information that solves the problem you have defined.
3.   What information do I need to build the model to produce the results I want to see? This information is the input or the data you enter in the model to solve the problem.
4.   What calculations will I need to perform to produce the output? These calculations are the formulas you use in your worksheet. Because IFPS is English-like, you can write these formulas directly as IFPS model statements.

Herbie's completed planning sheet is shown in Figure 1-14. Because an IFPS model is an English-like description of your problem, IFPS model logic is used directly in specifying the calculations that are needed.

Planning Analysis Sheet

My goal:
Develop a model for the projected income statement of Buffalo Computer Systems for the next five years.

What results do I want to see?
Revenues and expenses for the next five years with appropriate subtotals.

What information do I need?
Columns are YEAR1, YEAR2, YEAR3, YEAR4, YEAR5
Sales [Year1] = 343000
Sales growth rate = 20%
Cost of sales percent = 77%
Salaries[Year1] = 49000
Salary growth rate = 8%
Benefits ratio = 19%
Admin expense ratio = 2.3%
Depreciation (each year) = 8000, 8000, 9000, 9000, 8000
Interest (each year) = 1600

What calculations will I perform?
(Written in IFPS model statements)
COLUMNS YEAR1, YEAR2, YEAR3, YEAR4, YEAR5
SALES = 343000, PREVIOUS SALES * 1.20
COST OF SALES = SALES * .77
GROSS PROFIT = SALES - COST OF SALES
SALARIES = 49000, PREVIOUS * 1.08
BENEFITS = SALARIES * 19%
ADMIN EXPENSE = SALES * .023
DEPRECIATION = 8000, 8000, 9000 FOR 2, 8000
INTEREST = 1600
TOTAL EXPENSES = SUM(SALARIES THRU INTEREST)
EBT = GROSS PROFIT - TOTAL EXPENSES

Figure 1-14 Herbie's Planning Analysis Sheet

Herbie wrote the calculations to be performed directly in the syntax of IFPS. Let's examine the IFPS model statements that produce the results shown previously in Figure 1-13.

COLUMNS YEAR1, YEAR 2, YEAR3, YEAR4, YEAR5

This column statement describes the width of the spreadsheet. The columns statement sets aside the desired number of columns. It says there will be five columns that will be labeled YEAR1, YEAR2, and so on.

The English-like feature of IFPS is clearly illustrated by several selected lines from the model. First let's consider how they are calculated and then examine the other lines of the model individually.

GROSS PROFIT = SALES - COST OF SALES

Here, GROSS PROFIT is calculated by subtracting COST OF SALES from SALES. Of course, you could read that directly. This shows some of the rules used in writing IFPS models. First, the row name or account name goes on the left side of the equal. The equal sign is a separator. It separates the row name from the equation. The equation to be calculated goes on the right side of the equation sign.

EBT = GROSS PROFIT - TOTAL EXPENSES

EBT or EARNINGS BEFORE TAX is another straightforward calculation. Notice how the variable or row names are written out so you can easily understand what is being calculated.

The other IFPS modeling statements are described as follows:

SALES = 343000, PREVIOUS SALES * 1.20

The account SALES, whose name appears on the left side of the equal sign, is calculated by the equations specified on the right side of the equal sign. The value assigned to YEAR1 is 343000. It was necessary for the 343000 to be input in YEAR1 in order to provide a beginning value of the logic used in YEAR2 through YEAR5. The 343000 could also represent last year's history on which the projection is based. In many business models, the first year or column is either historical data or a base starting point, which is input directly into the model.

You calculate the value for YEAR2 by taking the value for the previous column (that is the column immediately to the left–in this case, YEAR1) and multiplying it by 1.20. With this logic a 20-percent growth rate is applied to the YEAR1 value to obtain 411600 in YEAR2. The asterisk (*) in this case means to multiply. In IFPS, as in many computer programming languages, arithmetic operators are used to specify mathematical manipulation. The IFPS arithmetic operators are shown in Figure 1-15.

OPERATORS	SYMBOLS
Add	+
Subtract	-
Multiply	*
Divide	/
Percent	%
Group Calculations	()

Figure 1-15 Arithmetic Operators

Returning to the calculation of SALES, the comma between 343000 and PREVIOUS means to move over to the next column to the right before calculating the expression following the comma. As a result, commas may not appear in any numbers that consist of input data in an IFPS model. You should note, however, that it is possible (and simple) to have commas appear in numeric values output from an IFPS model. This is similar to the input of numbers with other computer tools.

In continuing with the SALES calculation, let's turn to how the values will be calculated for YEAR3 through YEAR5. IFPS *automatically* repeats or replicates logic in all remaining columns as you proceed from left to right across the row, using the logic of the last column in which logic was specified. Because no new equations or logic has been entered, PREVIOUS SALES * 1.20 is used to calculate a value in each of YEAR3 through YEAR5 columns. The value 411600 in YEAR2 is multiplied by 1.20 to obtain 493920 for YEAR3. IFPS continues using the same logic for YEAR4 and YEAR5, producing the values shown in Figure 1-13.

COST OF SALES = SALES * .77

The COST OF SALES is calculated as a percentage of SALES. Here, COST OF SALES are 77 percent of SALES in each and every column (YEAR1 through YEAR5). Notice that the percentage was input as a decimal.

SALARIES = 49000, PREVIOUS * 1.08

SALARIES are 49000 in YEAR1 and increase at 8 percent per year. Notice the PREVIOUS operator used by itself refers to the prior value in the *same* row. It is equivalent to entering PREVIOUS SALARIES. The automatic logic replication works here just like in the calculation for SALES.

BENEFITS = SALARIES * 19%

BENEFITS are calculated as a percentage of SALARIES. There is no question about how BENEFITS are calculated. You may not agree with the assumption used here for the benefit rate. If you don't like this percent, try your own. This demonstrates how IFPS gets you to focus on the issues (in this case, the benefit rate). You don't get bogged down in how the calculation was performed. The benefit rate of 19 percent could have been entered as the decimal value of .19.

ADMIN EXPENSE = SALES * .023
Similarly, ADMIN EXPENSE is calculated as a percent of SALES.

DEPRECIATION = 8000, 8000, 9000 FOR 2, 8000
The DEPRECIATION amount is input for each year. Recall that the comma signals the separation between columns. The use of FOR allows logic (in this case, constants) to be repeated *for* the number of columns specified. Here, "9000 FOR 2" is equivalent to "9000, 9000." The actual values are therefore 8000 in YEAR1, 8000 in YEAR2, 9000 in YEAR3, 9000 in YEAR4, and 8000 in YEAR5, as Figure 1-13 shows.

INTEREST = 1600
INTEREST of 1600 is input in YEAR1. Since no logic appears for YEAR2, YEAR3, and so on , this constant is replicated across all five columns.

TOTAL EXPENSES = SUM(SALARIES THRU INTEREST)
TOTAL EXPENSES are calculated by adding up SALARIES, BENEFITS, ADMIN EXPENSE, DEPRECIATION, and INTEREST. The SUM function in IFPS is a shorthand method to specify a group of rows that are to be added. Notice the first and last rows are specified in the SUM function. THRU is a key or reserved word used as part of the SUM function and must be surrounded by one blank space on each side. You may use ".." in the place of "THRU" in IFPS. The parentheses are part of the syntax or rules for writing a function. All IFPS functions are enclosed in parentheses, with the name of the function preceding the left parenthesis. You will learn about other IFPS functions later. As you have just seen, IFPS is very English-like. In fact, you probably could have read the model and understood the logic with little coaching. If it seems easy, that is because it *is*. It will get a little more complex, but not much more difficult than this example. Now that you know how to plan a model, let's enter the model from Figure 1-14 in Visual IFPS.

Building the Model

Building the model involves entering the model logic in a Visual IFPS window. The model window is a workspace where you type and edit your model logic. For a new model, you need to open a new model window before you begin typing your model. For an existing model, you need to open its window before making any edit changes.

Reference Window

Opening a New Model Window
■ Click the New button in the toolbar.
or
Click the File menu, then click the New option in that menu.
■ Click Model in the list box.
■ Click the OK button.

Let's open a new model window and enter Herbie's projected income statement model for BCS.

To create a new model:

❶   Click **File**, then click **New** to display the New dialog box. See Figure 1-16.

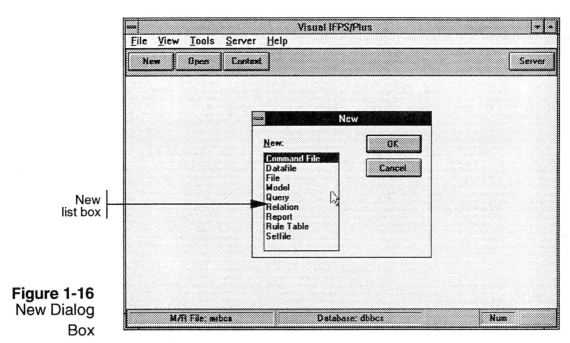

Figure 1-16
New Dialog
Box

❷   Doubleclick **Model** to select this type of entity. The model window appears. See
Figure 1-17.

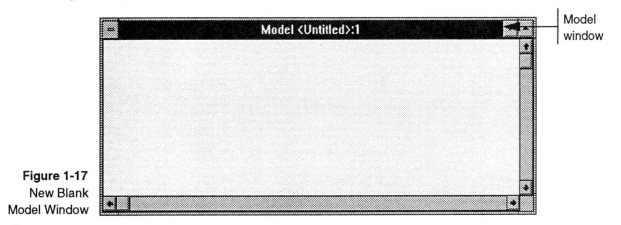

Figure 1-17
New Blank
Model Window

❸   Type the model from Figure 1-14 in the Model window. If you make any typing
mistakes use the [Delete] or [Backspace] key to remove the unwanted characters
and retype them.

Now that you have entered the model, let's save it in the MRBCS M&R file.

Saving a New Model

The Save command copies the model to the M&R file using the correct model name. You use the Save
command to update the current file with changes you have made. Because you created the model as an
"untitled" model, you need to give this model a name. To do that, you must have your Student Disk in the
disk drive. Herbie wants you to edit this model later, so it is a good idea before editing the model to save
the model so you can go back to the original model if you make a number of mistakes in editing.

Using Save to Save a New Model
■   Click File, then click Save to display the Save As dialog box. ■   In the Entity Name text box, type your model name. ■   Make sure the A:\ is specified in the Directories text box. ■   Click the OK button.

Let's save the new model for future use.

To save a new model using Save:

❶   Click **File** to display the file menu.

❷   Click **Save** to display the Save As dialog box. Notice that the Entity name text box contains the default model name "*." This default is the name Visual IFPS gives the model until you specify a different name. See Figure 1-18.

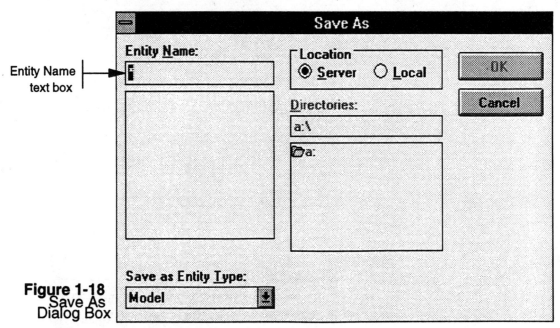

Figure 1-18
Save As
Dialog Box

TROUBLE? If you click the Location Local option button, next click the Location Server button. Make sure that Figure 1-18 looks like your screen before you go on to Step 3.

❸   Type **PROJECT** in the Entity Name text box as the model name.

       TROUBLE? If the model name you type doesn't replace the default model name, doubleclick the Entity name text box and repeat Step 3.

❹   Click the **OK button** to accept the model name and save it to your M&R file MRBCS. Notice that PROJECT now appears in the title bar of the model window. See Figure 1-19. Note that Visual IFPS does not assign an extension to the model name because the model is a member of the M&R file rather than being stored as a separate computer file.

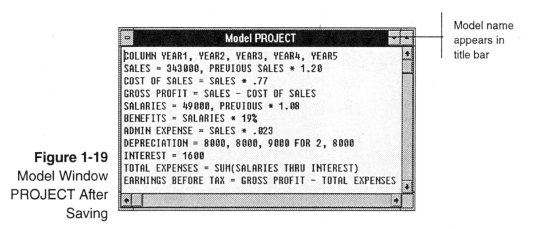

Figure 1-19
Model Window
PROJECT After
Saving

Model name
appears in
title bar

Now that you have built and saved the model, let's explore obtaining a solution to the model.

Exploring a Model Solution

Pattie wants to review the solution with Herbie before he returns to the accountant. When you entered the model, you typed the equations that are used to produce the solution. A model is solved to display the calculations for your review.

Reference Window

Solving a Model for All Variables
■ Click the Solve button in the toolbar.
■ Click the OK button in the Solve dialog box to accept the default for the solution.

Let's solve Herbie's model.

To solve a model:

❶   Click the **Solve button** in the toolbar to display the Solve dialog box. See Figure 1-20.

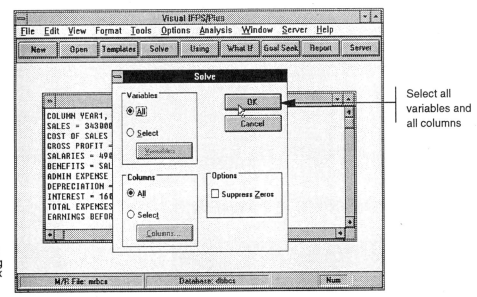

Figure 1-20
Solve Dialog
Box

Select all
variables and
all columns

TROUBLE? If you click the Solve button and an error message box appears, click the model PROJECT window, then compare your model with the model shown in Figure 1-14. Make any necessary changes to your model, then save your model. You can now repeat Step 1.

❷ Click the **OK button** in the Solve dialog box to accept the solve default of all variables and all columns and to produce the solution. The solution displays in its window. See Figure 1-21.

[Model PROJECT Solution:1]	YEAR1	YEAR2	YEAR3	YEAR4	YEAR5
SALES	343,000.00	411,600.00	493,920.00	592,704.00	711,244.80
COST OF SALES	264,110.00	316,932.00	380,318.40	456,382.08	547,658.50
GROSS PROFIT	78,890.00	94,668.00	113,601.60	136,321.92	163,586.30
SALARIES	49,000.00	52,920.00	57,153.60	61,725.89	66,663.96
BENEFITS	9,310.00	10,054.80	10,859.18	11,727.92	12,666.15
ADMIN EXPENSE	7,889.00	9,466.80	11,360.16	13,632.19	16,358.63
DEPRECIATION	8,000.00	8,000.00	9,000.00	9,000.00	8,000.00
INTEREST	1,600.00	1,600.00	1,600.00	1,600.00	1,600.00
TOTAL EXPENSES	75,799.00	82,041.60	89,972.94	97,686.00	105,288.74
EBT	3,091.00	12,626.40	23,628.66	38,635.92	58,297.56

Figure 1-21
Solution for
Model PROJECT

Printing Models and Solutions

Herbie wants a printed copy of his model and its solution to take with him to the accountant. Let's first explore how to print a model and then how to print the solution to the model.

Reference Window

Printing Models and Solutions
■   Click the window that contains the model or the solution you want to print.
■   Click **File**, then click **Print** to print the model or solution.

To print the model:

❶ Click the **Model PROJECT window** to select it as the active window.

TROUBLE? If you do not have the model open, reopen the model by clicking the Open button and selecting PROJECT from the Open dialog box.

❷ Click **File**, then click **Print** to print the model.

Next, print the model's solution.

To print a model solution :

❶ Click the **Solution window** to make it the active window.

TROUBLE? If you do not have the model open and solved, you will not be able to print the solution. Reopen the model and then solve it before you continue with the next step.

❷   Click **File**, then click **Print** to print the model solution.

Editing the Model

After discussing it with Pattie, Herbie decides that the benefits percent should be 20 percent and depreciation should be 4000 for all five years. Herbie wants to revise their model for these changes. You can change a model by editing it to insert or delete characters.

Reference Window

Editing the Model
■   Move the edit cursor to where you want to remove or insert characters. ■   Use either the [Backspace] or [Delete] key to remove unwanted characters; then type the appropriate characters. *or* Drag the edit pointer over the unwanted characters to select them, then type the appropriate characters.

Herbie's changes are made by editing their existing model. Let's see how you can change these equations.

To edit the contents of the BENEFITS equation:

❶   Click the **Model PROJECT window** to make it the active window.

❷   Place the I-beam pointer after the **19%** in the **BENEFITS** formula. See Figure 1-22.

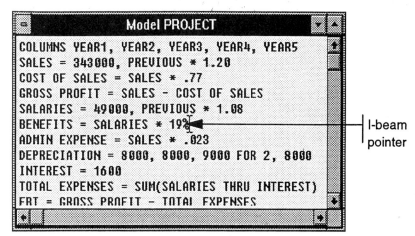

Figure 1-22

Placement of the I-beam Pointer

❸   Press **[Backspace]** three times to remove 19%, then replace it by typing **20%**.

TROUBLE? If you delete the wrong characters, type the characters you deleted. Then start again at Step 2.

❹   Click and drag the I-beam pointer to select 8000, 8000, 9000 FOR 2, 8000 in the **DEPRECIATION** formula. This highlights the selection.

❺   Type **4000** to replace the selected text with this new value.

❻   Click the **Solve button** on the toolbar to display the Solve dialog box, then click the **OK button** to display a solution for the revised model.

Closing Entities

Congratulations on completing Tutorial 1! Now that you have finished exploring Herbie's model and solution, you need to close them. This removes it from the model or report window and from RAM, but the file remains stored on your Student Disk. Let's close the model window.

To close the PROJECT model window:

❶   Click the **Model PROJECT window** to make it the active window.

❷   Click the **Control menu box** located at the left side of that window.

❸   Click **Close**. A message box will display asking if you wish to save the correction to the model.

❹   Click **No** in the message box so that the last changes to the model are not saved.

TROUBLE? If you click Yes instead of No in the message box, then the changes you have made are saved. You will need to edit the model so the logic matches that from Figure 1-14. Then save the model and repeat Steps 2 and 3.

Let's close the solution window.

To close the Solution model window:

❶   Click the **Solution window** to make it the active window.

❷   Click the **Control menu box** located at the left side of the window.

❸   Click **Close** to close the solution.

If there are any other windows still open in the Visual IFPS desktop, close those windows by following the directions above. When you have closed all the windows, your Visual IFPS desktop should look empty as shown earlier in Figure 1-10.

Exiting Visual IFPS

You may now exit from Visual IFPS.

To exit from Visual IFPS/Plus:

❶   Click **File**, then click **Exit** to return to the Program Manager. See Figure 1-23.

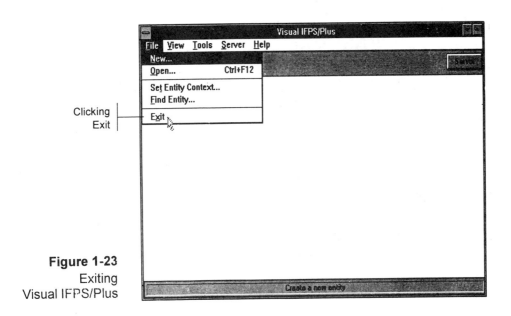

Figure 1-23
Exiting
Visual IFPS/Plus

Now you may leave Windows NT.

To Exit Windows NT:

❶   Click **File**.

❷   Click **Logoff** to log off the computer.

> **TROUBLE?** If you are in Windows 3.1, click the **control menu box** and then
> the **Close button** to exit windows. If you are in Windows95, click the **Start
> button,** then click **Shut Down**.

What IFPS Is Not Designed to Do

The model in this tutorial demonstrates that IFPS is *not* a transaction processing language. It is *not*
designed to create a transaction driven computer processing system. Finally, it is *not* designed for
processing payroll, accounts receivable, accounts payable, general ledger, inventory, and so on. Of course,
some users might be using IFPS for these purposes. But one disadvantage of using IFPS for this type of
application is that it does not readily accommodate the master file updating required in payroll, receivables,
and so forth. In most cases, COBOL, PL/1, or some other procedural programming language would work
much better than IFPS.

IFPS is *not* a discrete event simulation modeling tool and it is *not* a set of subroutines used with a
standard procedural programming language such as FORTRAN, BASIC, COBOL, PL/1, C++, etc. Finally,
it is *not* a "form-driven" system that utilizes predetermined account names or assumptions about the
interaction of various accounts.

IFPS is a 4GL that is a problem-oriented language that addresses spreadsheet calculations. If your
problem does *not* have this orientation, IFPS is probably not the most appropriate choice of a language.
Think of IFPS as an adjustable crescent wrench. If you want to loosen or tighten variously shaped and
sized bolts, this type of wrench works wonderfully, but it makes a poor hammer and is a terrible saw. The
point is that you should choose the right tool for the job. If you have a spreadsheet problem such as that
explored in this tutorial, then IFPS is likely to be the right tool for your task. Remember, though, that IFPS
is *not* a panacea for all data-processing problems.

Questions

1. What does the abbreviation IFPS stand for?
   a. International Financial Planning System
   b. Interactive Funding Planning System
   c. Interactive Financial Planning System
   d. International Financial Plumbing System

2. A cell is a:
   a. row and column intersection
   b. row and row intersection
   c. column and column intersection
   d. a column

3. Which of the following is *not* a characteristic of a decision support system (DSS):
   a. assists managers with their decision process in a semistructured task
   b. supports, rather than replaces, managerial judgment
   c. improves the effectiveness of decision making rather than its efficiency
   d. automates the decision process in structured tasks

4. M&R stands for:
   a. models are read
   b. model and report
   c. music and report
   d. music and read

5. The SUM function is a shorthand method for specifying a group of rows to be:
   a. multiplied
   b. divided
   c. added
   d. subtracted

6. To create a new model, you:
   a. Click File, click New, and select Model in the new entity dialog box
   b. Click Options, click New
   c. Click Server, click New
   d. Click File, click Save

7. To close an entity, you:
   a. Click File, click Exit
   b. Click File, click Save
   c. Click the Control Menu box, click Close
   d. Click Server, click Close

8.   IFPS is *not* a _____ processing language.
   a. solving
   b. timing
   c. moving
   d. transaction

Case Problems

1. Good Morning Products

Good Morning Products is an international bottler and distributor of the Liquid Gold brand of fresh orange juice. Good Morning Products, located in Citrus Grove Valley, California, was established in 1919 by Charles "Frosty" Frost. Frosty now serves as the chairman of the board of Good Morning Products. The business is family-owned and -operated with Matthew "Crush" Frost as President, Kimberly Frost-Moore as Vice President and General Manager, Christopher Frost as Treasurer, and Jennifer Frost-Krone as Secretary. Sales for this year are expected to be 530,000 liters of orange juice in 1,060,000 bottles at $3.19 per bottle. Good Morning's plant in Citrus Grove Valley has a production capacity of 1,200,000 bottles per year. Kimberly and Christopher are in the midst of preparing next year's budget for Good Morning (GM) for presentation to Frosty and Crush. They anticipate next year's sales will be the same number of bottles as this year's. Kim and Chris have reviewed this year's expenditures and have estimated the following costs next year for GM:

Fixed Costs		Variable Costs	
General and Admin	$ 98,000	Labor per Bottle	$ .89
Advertising	79,000	Oranges per Bottle	1.21
Interest	64,000	Packaging per Bottle	.57
Depreciation	102,000		

Kim and Chris want you to prepare GM's next year's budget in the following arrangement Jenny developed:

Good Morning Products' Budget

	NEXT YEAR
Bottles	XXXXXXXXX
Price	XXXXX.XXX
Sales	XXXXXXXXX
Fixed Costs:	
General and Admin	XXXXXXXXX
Advertising	XXXXXXXXX
Interest	XXXXXXXXX
Depreciation	XXXXXXXXX
Fixed Costs	XXXXXXXXX
Variable Costs:	
Labor per Bottle	XXXXX.XXX
Oranges per Bottle	XXXXX.XXX
Packaging per Bottle	XXXXX.XXX
Variable Costs	XXXXXXXXX
Total Costs	XXXXXXXXX
EBT	XXXXXXXXX
ROS	XXXXX.XXX

In this arrangement of the results, the variable costs for Labor, Oranges, and Packaging are entered and displayed as costs per bottle. EBT is Earnings Before Tax, which is calculated by subtracting Total Costs from Sales. ROS is Return On Sales, which Kim wants calculated as EBT / SALES * 100. Here, the multiplication by 100 places the decimal point in the desired position. Your task is to create this one-column model in IFPS for presentation to Frosty and Crush at tomorrow's board meeting. In creating this model, only include the variables you want to calculate and let IFPS handle the decimal places. You will learn how to include headings and control decimal places in the next tutorial.

Quick Check Answers:	EBT	$ 208200
	ROS	6.157

2. The Woodcraft Furniture Company

The Woodcraft Furniture Company is an established manufacturer of home furniture. Founded in 1955, Woodcraft is located in the heart of the hardwood forest country. The company's initial market was local, but it has since expanded into a 15-state regional market. Woodcraft's president, Joe Birch, an MBA graduate from Harvest University, has repositioned his company from the 20th to the largest furniture maker in the region. Joe has achieved this remarkable task within his 3-year tenure at Woodcraft. He attributes his success to his fine staff and their proactive management style. To further improve operations, he recently hired you to head the strategic planning department. Your primary task is to coordinate the financial planning and budgeting operations. Joe has asked you to prepare a financial forecast of next year's income before tax (IBT).

Woodcraft produces three products: tables, chairs, and sofas. Martha Goodguess, the director of marketing, has compiled the results of her market research for next year. She expects 10,600 tables to be sold. For each table sold, on the average, five chairs are sold. She expects the sale of 7,067 sofas as well. The price schedule for these is as follows:

Product	Price
Tables	$ 450
Chairs	100
Sofas	300

Martha has planned an advertising expenditure of 10 percent of total sales.

Ray Jointer, production manager, expects to produce these units with 157 production line employees at an average salary of $9.60 per hour. Last year, the average hours worked per employee were 2,080. Ray expects the same number of hours this year. A check of Ray's records indicates that raw material costs are 26 percent of total sales. The factory overhead charge is 71.4 percent of the cost of raw material.

In the finance department, Talbert "Tall" Pine, the treasurer of Woodcraft, has reviewed the production forecast and feels no new external financing is required. A review of last year's financial statements with "Tall" produces the following estimates:

1. Total debt is $1,836,000 at a weighted average interest rate of 8 percent.
2. Insurance expense is 2 percent of total sales.
3. Management salaries will be $675,000.
4. General and Administrative will be $290,000.

After meeting with Joe, you've settled on a planning report format like the one below:

Woodcraft, Inc.
Pro Forma Income Statement

	NEXT YEAR
Production:	
(In units)	
Tables sold	XXXXX
Chairs sold	XXXXX
Sofas sold	XXXXX
Revenues:	
Table sales	XXXXX
Chair sales	XXXXX
Sofa sales	XXXXX

Total sales	XXXXX
Cost of sales:	
Raw materials	XXXXX
Labor	XXXXX
Overhead	XXXXX

Cost of sales	XXXXX
Gross profit	XXXXX
Operating expenses:	
Advertising	XXXXX
Insurance	XXXXX
Management Salaries	XXXXX
General and Admin	XXXXX

Operating expenses	XXXXX
Operating profit	XXXXX
Interest expense	XXXXX
Income before taxes	XXXXX
	======
Return on sales	XXXXX

You now have all the preliminary data required to prepare a forecast for next year. Even though it is past 6 p.m., you can't wait to try out your modeling skills on IFPS. You call your spouse to let him/her know you'll be late for dinner. You are certain this model won't take more than 30 minutes to construct, and you begin at once. In creating this model, only include the variables you want to calculate and let IFPS handle the decimal places. Ignore the underlines for your model solution. You will learn how to do headings and control decimal places in the next tutorial. Tutorial 6 explains how underlining is included in a report. Develop a planning analysis sheet to help in designing your model.

3. The Last National Bank of Broken Spoke

The Last National Bank of Broken Spoke is a full-service bank that services a variety of commercial and individual customers. The Last National Bank was founded in 1804 by John J. Green. Today, John J. Green, III is the bank's chairman and chief operating officer. The innovation of the three J. J. Greens has kept Last National profitable when other banks fell on hard times. To keep the bank more competitive, J. J. has decided better information is required to assist in managing the asset and liability portfolio of the bank. He had recently attended a bank executives meeting where he had learned about financial modeling from a Dr. G. R. Wagner. When J. J. returned to Broken Spoke, he was convinced his bank should create an asset and liability model to better manage its funds.

J. J. called in his controller, Carrie Campbell, and assigned her the project of creating a funds management asset and liability financial planning model. The model would be used by J. J. and other top-level bank managers to establish policy and direction for the bank.

Carrie decided to create a model that would calculate the net interest margin on the bank's portfolio of assets and liabilities for next year. That is, she decided to create a one-column model that would contain next year's projection. (*Note:* This will later be expanded to a quarterly model.) In entering data, Carrie decided all dollar amounts would be entered in thousands. The balances for the asset and liability planning accounts would be entered directly into the model. Because the daily balances can vary significantly from one day to the next, she decided to make use of an average daily balance for each asset and liability account. After considerable discussion with J. J. and the other bank officers, Carrie selected the following asset and liability accounts and established their expected average daily balance:

Assets:
(Amounts in Thousands)

Real Estate Mortgages	----->	35000
Installment Loans	----->	10000
Commercial Loans	----->	25000
Other Investments	----->	2000

Liabilities:
(Amounts in Thousands)

Regular Savings	----->	10000
Interest Plus Checking	----->	15000
Money Market Certificates	----->	40000
Other Borrowed Funds	----->	5000

The bank's officers have estimated that the prime rate will be an average of 15 percent for the next year. The interest income or interest expense of each asset and liability account is to be determined from these estimates for interest rates:

Real Estate Interest	----->	10%
Installment Loan Interest	----->	Prime + 1%
Commercial Loan Interest	----->	Prime + 2%
Other Investment Interest	----->	Prime + 1%
Regular Savings Interest	----->	5.5%
Interest Plus Checking Interest	----->	6%
Money Market Interest	----->	Prime - 3%
Other Borrowed Funds Interest	----->	Prime - 4.5%

As the above interest rates show, some are fixed rate accounts whereas others are variable rate with the variable rate stated as a premium over or under the prime rate.

In creating the model, Carrie decided to include a line item for the total interest on earning assets and for total interest expense. Also, she wants the net interest margin percent calculated where the net interest margin percent is the net interest margin divided by the total interest on earning assets and multiplied by 100 to transform it to a percent. Your task as an aspiring young banker is to create this model for Carrie and J. J. in IFPS. Only include the variables you want to calculate and let IFPS handle the decimal places. (You will learn how to include headings and control decimal places in the next tutorial.) Develop a planning analysis sheet in preparation for creating this model.

4. Harvest University

Harvest University (HU) is an internationally recognized private college located in Great Plains. HU currently enrolls 19,700 students in both its undergraduate and graduate degree programs. As the chief financial officer of Harvest, it is your responsibility to prepare a budget for next year. You determine your planning items and formulate a means for calculating each item as follows:

Students	----->	20000
Credit Hours	----->	Credit Hours Per Student * Number of students
Credit Hours per Student	----->	44
FTE Faculty	----->	Credit Hours / Credit Hour Ratio
Credit Hour Ratio	----->	600
Administrative Salaries	----->	4550000
Secretarial Salaries	----->	3250000
Full-Time Faculty Salaries	----->	FTE Faculty * Full to FTE Ratio * Average Full-Time Faculty Salary
Part-Time Faculty Salaries	----->	FTE Faculty * (1 - Full to FTE Ratio) * Average Part-Time Faculty Salary
Average Full-Time Faculty Salary	----->	35000
Average Part-Time Faculty Salary	----->	5000
Full to FTE Ratio	----->	.90
TA's Salaries	----->	285000
Other Salaries	----->	1050000
Fringe Benefits	----->	25 percent of salaries
Utilities	----->	2200000
Other Operating Expenses	----->	800000
Tuition per Credit Hour	----->	90
Tuition	----->	Credit Hours * Tuition per Credit Hour
Lab Fee Percent	----->	20
Lab Fees	----->	Tuition * Lab Fee Percent
Endowment Income	----->	2500000
Other Income	----->	100000

Your task is to create this financial plan for next year. (This will be a one-column model.) All dollar amounts in expenses and revenues should be specified in thousands. Include Total Expenses and Total Revenue as line items in your model. Calculate the Reserve as the difference between Total Revenue and Total Expenses. Develop a planning analysis sheet in preparation for creating this model.

5. Midwest Universal Gas

Midwest Universal Gas (MUG) is a diversified energy company serving the energy needs of business and industry throughout mid-America. Recently, the company has experienced a shift in demand for natural gas. This is due partly to changing economic activity, climatic conditions, and energy conservation. The director of MUG's gas division, Mary Derrick, has just called you to her office. Mary is concerned that her division's after tax return on investment might fall below 12 percent. She instructs you to coordinate the pro forma compilation of next year's income for the gas division. Your first task is to establish a demand forecast for natural gas in your markets for next year. Francis Foresight, the director of marketing, said last year's production and sales were 715 billion cubic feet (BCF). He also reported that this year's demand has decreased to an annual rate of 700 BCF because of economic and conservation activities. Francis feels that, given the proper budget, his department will be able to add several accounts to the 325 communities currently being served. Traditional marketing and selling expenses have been between 10 to 14 percent of sales. Francis has asked for an increased level of 14.4 percent of sales to support a more aggressive marketing effort. In addition to the predicted new accounts, Francis anticipates an expansion in industrial accounts. After considering all these conditions, he expects next year's volume to be 720 BCF. Based on an analysis of prior years' sales, he expects revenues to be generated in this manner:

Volume Sold	Next Year's Rate
22% Retail	$3,500 per million cubic feet
78% Wholesale	$2,859 per million cubic feet

Given this forecast of demand for next year, you decide to check with the production department to insure Midwest's ability to meet the demand. Petro Newgas, or "Pete," reports no problem in satisfying this demand since the proven reserves are nine times the forecasted demand and they have sufficient pipeline capacity to transport the gas. Pete discusses a variety of sources and costs for next year's production with you. After three hours of reviewing reports and tables, the numbers almost become a blur. Pete finally indicates he expects the weighted average cost of the gas to be 63 percent of total revenues.

Having secured the demand and production forecast, your next encounter is with Sam Wright, the division comptroller. Sam has reviewed the operating budget and concludes that with anticipated salary increases and other price adjustments, next year's administrative expenses will be $162,500,000. Also, Sam expects to be able to charge off 8.6 percent of the division's investments to depreciation. With the adjustment for new plant and equipment, next year's divisional investments will total $1,204,000,000. Midwest has $492,000,000 in long-term debt at a weighted average interest rate of 9 percent. In addition to this long-term debt, Midwest holds $139,333,000 on a short-term basis with a weighted average interest rate of 12 percent. Sam expects the current and carryforward investment tax credits applicable to next year's income would be $84,000,000. Finally, federal, state, and local taxes after all tax credits are expected to be at the rate of 40 percent. Sam works with you in laying out this format for the pro forma statement:

```
REVENUES ('000)      NEXT YEAR
Retail Sales           XXXXXX
Wholesale Sales        XXXXXX
                      ------------
Total Sales            XXXXXX
Cost of Sales          XXXXXX
                      ------------
Gross Profit           XXXXXX

EXPENSES ('000)
Selling                XXXXXX
General Admin          XXXXXX
Depreciation           XXXXXX
                      ------------
Total Expenses         XXXXXX
Operating Income       XXXXXX
Interest Expense       XXXXXX
                      ------------
Income Before Tax      XXXXXX
Investment Tax Credits XXXXXX
Income Taxes           XXXXXX
                      ------------
Net Income             XXXXXX
Return on Investment    XX.XX
```

In creating this model, only include the variables you want to calculate. Let IFPS handle the decimal places. You will learn how to include headings and control decimal places in the next tutorial. Ignore the underlines in your model solution. You will learn how to include them in your output in Tutorial 6. Write out a planning analysis sheet to help organize your solution.

6. General Memorial Hospital

General Memorial Hospital, which has 100 beds, is one of ten hospitals serving a community of one million. The hospital administrator, Berry Wellman, has called you into his office to discuss the compilation of next year's forecasted income. Berry has been instructed by the hospital's board to increase the return on investment so that General Memorial can begin to build its reserve for future expansions.

Berry's directive to you is to forecast next year's income based on the administration's operational expectations.

You meet with the hospital's accountant and chief financial officer, Gloria Vander Balance, and review bed utilization. Last year, the bed utilization rate was 75 percent of capacity. Gloria sees no reason to expect a change in next year's rate. The hospital's gerontology service served 2 percent of all patients admitted during last year, and this is expected to remain at the same rate for next year.

Gloria advises you that revenues are divided into three categories: in-patient services, nursing services, and professional services. In-patient revenues are $200 per day for each patient day. Patient days are calculated by multiplying the bed capacity by the utilization rate by 365 days per year. Nursing revenues result from gerontology services. Gerontology services, or the "gerontology load," is calculated as an additional 2 percent of the patient days. Nursing revenue for gerontology services are $100 per patient day. Professional services revenues consist of all the lab tests, medicines, and other services provided to patients during their stay. These professional revenues have been and are expected to continue to be 80 percent of in-patient revenues.

Nursing service costs are the personnel costs for the required nursing staff, which has been equal to the bed capacity. Nurses will be paid an average salary of $20,500 next year. There are 5 staff doctors who will receive an average salary of $75,000 next year. General Memorial employs two technicians for each staff doctor. Next year, the technicians' salary will be $22,000 each. Administrative expenses are personnel costs. Berry expects to have a staff of 10 administrators next year with an average salary of $25,000. Benefits are based on 13 percent of personnel cost. Even though General Memorial Hospital is a nonprofit organization, Gloria will show a $500,000 charge for depreciable assets in order to disclose all the costs of operations and because this is allowable for cost reimbursements.

Last year, bad debts were 3.95 percent of total revenues. For the forecast, Gloria has recommended using a 5-percent allowance for bad debts. The cost of medical supplies and other charges for the professional revenues has been and is expected to continue at 67 percent of the professional revenues. Although utilities are somewhat variable, they have been 25 percent of professional revenues and are expected to continue at that rate even though Midwest Universal Gas has announced a significant rate increase for next year. Interest expense is 11 percent on an outstanding balance of $2,000,000. The total investment in plant and equipment is expected to be $5,000,000 next year. Berry and Gloria want you to arrange the projection of revenues and expenditures following this format:

	NEXT YEAR
REVENUES ('000)	
In-patient Revenue	XXXXXX
Nursing Revenue	XXXXXX
Professional Revenue	XXXXXX

Total Revenue	XXXXXX
EXPENSES ('000)	
Nursing Services	XXXXXX
Doctor Staff	XXXXXX
Technicians	XXXXXX
Administration	XXXXXX
Benefits	XXXXXX
Bad Debts	XXXXXX
Medicines	XXXXXX
Utilities	XXXXXX

Total Expenses	XXXXXX
Income from Operations	XXXXXX
Interest Expense	XXXXXX

Net Income	XXXXXX
Return on Investment	XX.XX

In creating this model, only include the variables you want to calculate and let IFPS handle the decimal places. You'll learn how to include headings and control decimal places in the next tutorial. Ignore the underlines in your model solution for now. Tutorial 6 explains how to include them in your output.

7. River City

River City is a midwestern city with a population of approximately 400,000. The local economy has an enviable balance of high-tech manufacturers, light fabrication for consumer products, and a solid agrarian base. Your position with the mayor's planning department requires political sensitivity and financial astuteness. Mayor Lisa Goodnight has summoned you to her office to discuss the compilation of the next fiscal year's city budget. Lisa's instructions are concise: "go see Frank Frugal in the finance department and make sure he submits a budget that I can live with."

Frank has been busy comparing the revenue forecast for this year against actual performance. The city's revenues are generated from three major sources: property tax, sales tax, and permits. Property taxes are levied at a rate of $0.7141 per $100 of actual value. Last year, property values were $5,137,648,000. The assessor, Al Roundup, reports new construction valued at $50,000,000 will be added to next year's property base. The city collects a sales tax of $0.01 per $1 on all retail sales. Frank expects retail sales to increase with price levels that he has estimated to be 6 percent for next year. Last year's retail sales were $3,272,639,000. Permit revenues last year were $4,048,000. Frank expects this to vary directly with population levels that are expected to increase by 2 percent.

Having compiled all the necessary data for next year's revenue forecast, you turn to a line-item budget of last year's actual performance. You recall Lisa's directive and express her concerns with respect to expanding the city government. Last year, the city spent $4,090,000 for city government, and Lisa wants this increased by 10 percent. After all, this was an election year, and she has many political debts to repay. Law-enforcement costs came to $2,314,000. You noticed a high correlation between past increases and the incidence of crime. Crime statisticians estimate the level for next year's crime rate to increase by 8 percent. This appears to be a reasonable increase over last year's law-enforcement expenditure.

Public safety last year was $30,636,000, which is composed to a large extent of labor. As a campaign promise to secure the police and firefighters vote, Lisa pledged a 10-percent increase in pay. This rate should be applied against last year's expenditure to ensure that Lisa's promise is kept. Public works, which is the water and gas service, is not labor intensive; however, it is sensitive to price increases so the price level that Frank predicted is sufficient for next year's operations. Last year, public works spent $3,774,000. Park expenditures are related to the cost of fuel required to mow and operate the equipment. With the recent drop in fuel prices, Frank expects a short-term trend downward by 5 percent for fuel cost. Lisa wants to restrict the budget in places where people will notice it least. Park personnel will not be replaced if they quit or retire, so, you expect an overall drop in park expenditures by 5 percent from last year's level of $10,000,000.

Housing moneys have recently become available from the federal government based on a one-to-one match. Lisa wants to take advantage of this new money before it dries up. She feels an 11-percent increase over last year's level of $2,200,000 is all she can presently afford. Benefits are expected to be 20 percent of city government, law enforcement, public safety, public works, parks, and housing. The libraries spent $2,735,000 last year; their allowance for next year will increase by 6 percent. Finally, the miscellaneous category is composed of numerous small expenditures; these will grow by price levels and with population or by 8 percent over last year's level of $5,475,000. The format of the budget is as follows:

```
                              NEXT YEAR
REVENUES ('000)
Property tax                  XXXXXXX
Sales tax                     XXXXXXX
Permits                       XXXXXXX
                              ---------------
Total Revenue                 XXXXXXX
EXPENDITURES ('000)
City government               XXXXXXX
Law enforcement               XXXXXXX
Public safety                 XXXXXXX
Public works                  XXXXXXX
Parks                         XXXXXXX
Housing                       XXXXXXX
Benefits                      XXXXXXX
Libraries                     XXXXXXX
Miscellaneous                 XXXXXXX
                              ---------------
Total Expenditures            XXXXXXX
                              ---------------
Surplus or Deficit            XXXXXXX
```

In creating this model, only include the variables you want to calculate and let IFPS handle the decimal places. You will learn how to include headings and control decimal places in the next tutorial. Ignore the underlines in your model solution for now. Tutorial 6 describes how to include underlines in your reports. Prepare a planning analysis sheet to help in designing your model logic.

Notes:

Tutorial 2

Modifying Models

When Herbie and Pattie returned from their accountant, they knew they had to get busy and revise their model. Although the accountant liked Herbie's budget alternatives, he had some questions about how Herbie and Pattie determined their sales figures. He suggested they show the quantity of Byte computers sold per year and the price for each sale. Herbie wants to make this change to the model. Let's see how you can make the model revisions. First, you need to open an existing model. Then you edit it.

Opening an Existing Model

When you want to use a model that has already been saved, you must first open it. When the model is open, it is both in the computer's memory and stored on your Student Disk. Any changes that are made *affect only the copy in the computer's memory.* The file must be *saved* to your Student Disk before the file on disk is changed. You can view, edit, print, solve, or save your model once it is open. Let's open Herbie's model file for the business plan, which he saved as PROJECT in the MRBCS M&R file.

Herbie and Pattie already have a model containing their plan. Herbie would like you to open that particular model so that you can change it. First, let's select your M&R file.

To select an existing M&R file:

❶   Make sure your are in Visual IFPS.

        TROUBLE? If you get an error message box before getting the copyright notice, click the OK button in the error message box.

❷   Make sure your Student Disk is in drive A.

❸   Click the **Context button**, located in the toolbar, to display the Set Entities Context dialog box.

❹   Select MRBCS in the drop-down list box, then click the **OK button** in the Set Entity Context box to establish this as your working M&R file.

Opening an Existing Model
■ Click the Open button in the toolbar to display the Open dialog box.
■ Click the desired model name in the drop-down list box.
■ Click the OK button to complete selecting the model.

Now open the model.

To open the existing model PROJECT:

❶ Click the **Open button** in the toolbar to display the Open dialog box. See Figure 2-1.

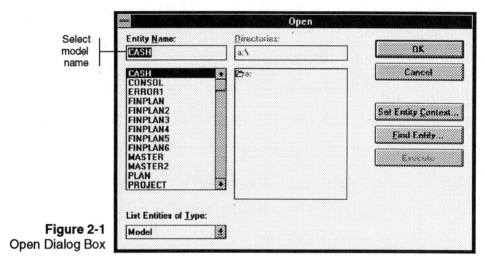

Figure 2-1
Open Dialog Box

❷ Click **PROJECT** to select this model, then click the **OK button**. The model appears in its window. See Figure 2-2.

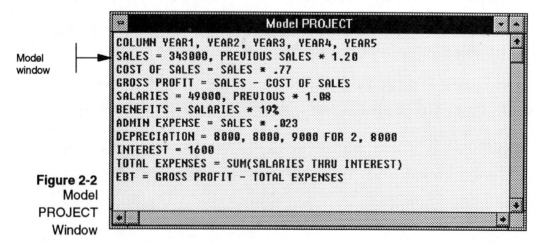

Figure 2-2
Model
PROJECT
Window

TROUBLE? If you selected the wrong model, doubleclick the Control Menu box for the Model window to remove the unwanted model. Repeat Steps 2 through 5 to select the PROJECT model.

Using Help

If you experience trouble with a model, solution, or other activity, the Visual IFPS HELP feature can provide an explanation.

Reference Window

Using Help
■   Click Help, then click the Contents option.
■   Click the Help topic you want displayed.
■   Scroll the Help window to read the Help information.
■   Click the Help window Control Menu box and click Close to exit from the On-line Help.

Let's explore the use of the on-line Visual IFPS Help feature.

To access Visual IFPS/Plus On-line Help:

❶   Click **Help** in the main menu bar**,** then click the **Contents button** to view the list of available Help topics. See Figure 2-3.

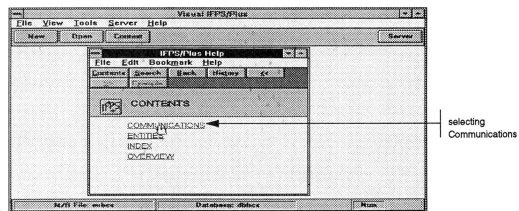

selecting
Communications

Figure 2-3
Help Window

❷   Move the pointer to **Entities**. The pointer changes to a hand shape. In the Help window, you can select the text that appears in green and is underlined.

❸   Click **Entities** to select this Help topic and display the entities used in IFPS.

TROUBLE? If you selected the wrong Help topic, click the Back button to back up one screen and click the desired topic.

After you find the information you want, you can exit from Help. Do that now.

To exit from Help:

❶   Click the Help window **Control Menu box**.

❷   Click **Close** to close the Help window and return to the Model window.

Equation Reordering

Equation reordering is the nonprocedural feature of IFPS. It means you can enter your variables in whatever sequence you like, and IFPS will determine the correct sequence in which they must be calculated. IFPS does the sequencing and performs the calculations in the correct order. You could have reorganized your model, but then the variables would not have been arranged in the order you normally think about them. With some business models, even if you organized your variables so the equations are in the appropriate calculation sequence, the equations are so complex that some may still be in the wrong order. Of course, with IFPS you need not be concerned. Just write your model in the sequence that is easiest for you and let IFPS do the rest of the work. To help you understand the concept of a nonprocedural language, the best way to manually reorder an equation is to cut the equation to the Windows clipboard. A **clipboard** is a Windows area where you can temporarily store data that you cut or copy so you can paste the same data elsewhere.

Reference Window

Moving an Equation
■ Move your cursor to the equation you wish to relocate.
■ Select that entire line by highlighting it.
■ Click Edit, then click Cut to place the line in the Windows clipboard.
■ Move your cursor to the line where you wish to relocate the equation.
■ Press the [Enter] key to insert a blank line.
■ Click Edit, then click Paste to complete moving the equation.

Equation reordering is explored by relocating Herbie's formula for EBT to the top of his model. Although EBT becomes the first variable in the model, you still must calculate it last. Consider how Herbie would like to move the EBT equation to the top of the model.

To move an equation in a model:

❶   Click the **Model PROJECT window** to make it the active window.

❷   Move the edit cursor to the line that defines **EBT** and drag it across the line to select it. See Figure 2-4.

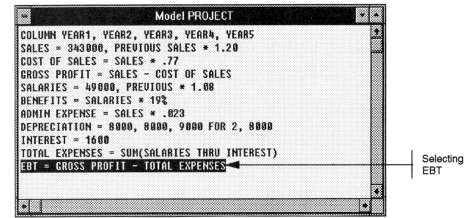

Figure 2-4
Selecting the
EBT Line

❸   Click **Edit**, then click **Cut** to place the selection in the Windows clipboard.

❹   Move the edit cursor to the beginning (left side) of the **SALES** line.

❺   Press the **[Enter]** key to insert a blank line, then move the cursor to the blank line.
See Figure 2-5.

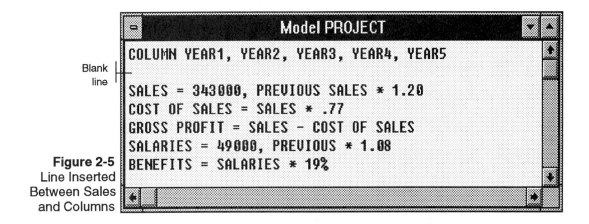

Figure 2-5
Line Inserted
Between Sales
and Columns

❻   Click **Edit**, then click **Paste** to place the equation from the Windows clipboard
into the model definition. See Figure 2-6.

EBT
relocated

```
Model PROJECT

COLUMN YEAR1, YEAR2, YEAR3, YEAR4, YEAR5
EBT = GROSS PROFIT - TOTAL EXPENSES
SALES = 343000, PREVIOUS SALES * 1.20
COST OF SALES = SALES * .77
GROSS PROFIT = SALES - COST OF SALES
SALARIES = 49000, PREVIOUS * 1.08
BENEFITS = SALARIES * 19%
ADMIN EXPENSE = SALES * .023
DEPRECIATION = 8000, 8000, 9000 FOR 2, 8000
INTEREST = 1600
TOTAL EXPENSES = SUM(SALARIES THRU INTEREST)
```

Figure 2-6
Placing EBT
Before SALES

❼   Click the **Solve button** in the toolbar, then click the **OK button** in the Solution
dialog box to accept the default solution. See Figure 2-7.

EBT
calculated
last

Model PROJECT Solution:1	YEAR1	YEAR2	YEAR3	YEAR4	YEAR5
EBT	3,091.00	12,626.40	23,628.66	38,635.92	58,297.56
SALES	343,000.00	411,600.00	493,920.00	592,704.00	711,244.80
COST OF SALES	264,110.00	316,932.00	380,318.40	456,382.08	547,658.50
GROSS PROFIT	78,890.00	94,668.00	113,601.60	136,321.92	163,586.30
SALARIES	49,000.00	52,920.00	57,153.60	61,725.89	66,663.96
BENEFITS	9,310.00	10,054.80	10,859.18	11,727.92	12,666.15
ADMIN EXPENSE	7,889.00	9,466.80	11,360.16	13,632.19	16,358.63
DEPRECIATION	8,000.00	8,000.00	9,000.00	9,000.00	8,000.00
INTEREST	1,600.00	1,600.00	1,600.00	1,600.00	1,600.00
TOTAL EXPENSES	75,799.00	82,041.60	89,972.94	97,686.00	105,288.74

Figure 2-7
Re-ordering of the
Model PROJECT
Solution

The same solution is calculated for EBT. Although the EBT variable is calculated last, it appears in the
solution in the sequence in which the logic is entered, rather than its sequence of calculation. This is a key
feature that makes IFPS a 4GL. Equation reordering is a temporary, internal activity performed
automatically by IFPS in calculating a solution. As you can see, the variables are not rearranged in your
model listing or its solution.

Using Save As to Change a Model Name

There are two ways to save a model or a report. You can use the Save command (explained in Tutorial
1) or the Save As command. The Save command copies the model to the M&R file. If you want to give it
a different model name, you use the Save As command. Figure 2-8 shows the decision process that occurs
when you want to save a model or a report. Herbie wants to save model PROJECT as model PLAN so he

that he has a backup of the model in case he makes unwanted changes and wants to start over using his backup.

Reference Window

Using Save As to Save the Model
■   Click File, then click the Save As option to display the Save As dialog box.
■   In the Entity Name text box, type the desired model name.
■   Make sure the Directories text box displays A:\.
■   Click the OK button.

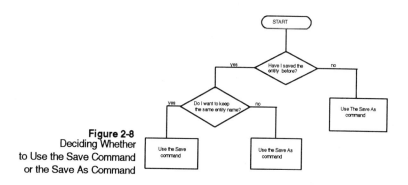

Figure 2-8
Deciding Whether
to Use the Save Command
or the Save As Command

Save a copy of model PROJECT as model PLAN.

To save a copy of a model using Save As:

❶   Click **File**, then click **Save As** to display the Save As dialog box.

❷   Type **PLAN** in the entity name text box.

TROUBLE? Make sure when you use the Save As command that you rename the model. If you do not enter a new name, you wipe out your original model.

❸   Click the **OK button** to accept the model name and save it to your Student Disk..

Copying Model Statements

Herbie wants to make a copy of the current model by using the Windows clipboard. With Visual IFPS, you can create a copy of a model by renaming it or by copying it using the Windows clipboard. Using the clipboard, you open a new Model window, copy the entire model, and place it into a new Model window.

Reference Window

Copying Model Statements
■ Click the New button, then select Model and click the OK button.
■ Click the Model window that you will copy from.
■ Highlight the statements you wish to copy.
■ Click Edit, then click Copy to place the selection in the Windows clipboard.
■ Click the Model window where you want to place the copied information.
■ Click Edit, then click Paste to insert the contents of the clipboard at the location of the edit cursor.

Let's create a new model from an existing model definition by copying the entire PROJECT model.

To create a new model from an existing model:

❶   Click the **New button** in the toolbar.

❷   Select **Model**, then click the **OK button** to display a new Model window. This Model window is blank and ready to receive the copy.

❸   Click the **model PROJECT window** to make it the active window.

❹   Select all the statements in model PROJECT by clicking **Edit** in the main menu, then click **Select All**. See Figure 2-9.

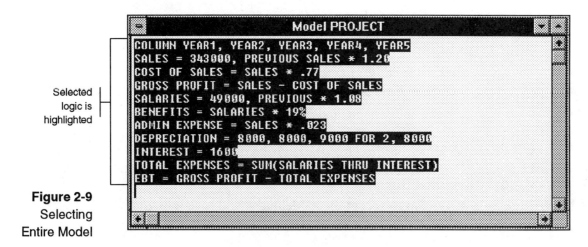

Selected logic is highlighted

Figure 2-9
Selecting
Entire Model

TROUBLE? If the model PROJECT window is not available, reopen the model.

❺   Click **Edit**, then click **Copy** to copy the selection to the Windows clipboard.

❻   Click the untitled Model window to make it the active window.

❼   Click **Edit**, then click **Paste** to insert the contents of the clipboard at the location of the edit cursor. See Figure 2-10.

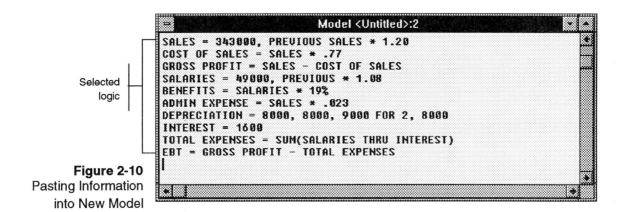

Selected
logic

Figure 2-10
Pasting Information
into New Model

```
Model <Untitled>:2
SALES = 343000, PREVIOUS SALES * 1.20
COST OF SALES = SALES * .77
GROSS PROFIT = SALES - COST OF SALES
SALARIES = 49000, PREVIOUS * 1.08
BENEFITS = SALARIES * 19%
ADMIN EXPENSE = SALES * .023
DEPRECIATION = 8000, 8000, 9000 FOR 2, 8000
INTEREST = 1600
TOTAL EXPENSES = SUM(SALARIES THRU INTEREST)
EBT = GROSS PROFIT - TOTAL EXPENSES
```

TROUBLE? If you click anything instead of PASTE, repeat Steps 3 through 7.

Now all the information that is in Model PROJECT is also in the new Model window. Herbie wants you to change the logic for SALES from 343000 to BYTES SOLD * PRICE PER BYTE as suggested by his accountant. Let's see how to change the logic for sales.

To change SALES:

❶   Select the entire formula to the right of the equal sign, then press **[Delete]**. By pressing the [Delete] key, you remove the selected text.

❷   Type the new formula: **BYTES SOLD * PRICE PER BYTE**

Adding Variables to a Model

The next step in revising the model is to add new variables. Variables or planning accounts are readily added to an existing model, which will improve Herbie's sales projections. The new variables and formulas Herbie wants added to the model are described as follows:

Bytes = 44, then increase by 8 per year
Price per Byte = 8000 with no expected increase
ROS = Earnings Before Tax divided by Total Sales times 100
Let's add these variables to the model.

Reference Window

Adding Variables to the Model
■   Click the location where you want to insert the variable.
■   Press [Enter] to insert a blank line.
■   Type the variable you wish to add.

To insert new variables into an existing model:

❶   Click the beginning (left side) of the SALES line for inserting the new variable.

❷   Press **[Enter]** to insert a blank line.

❸   Type **BYTES SOLD = 44, PREVIOUS + 8** into the blank line.

❹   Press **[Enter]**, then type **PRICE PER BYTE = 8000**. A second line is added to the model. See Figure 2-11.

Added variable ▸

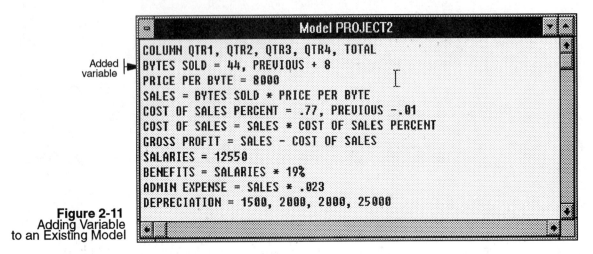

COLUMN QTR1, QTR2, QTR3, QTR4, TOTAL
BYTES SOLD = 44, PREVIOUS + 8
PRICE PER BYTE = 8000
SALES = BYTES SOLD * PRICE PER BYTE
COST OF SALES PERCENT = .77, PREVIOUS -.01
COST OF SALES = SALES * COST OF SALES PERCENT
GROSS PROFIT = SALES - COST OF SALES
SALARIES = 12550
BENEFITS = SALARIES * 19%
ADMIN EXPENSE = SALES * .023
DEPRECIATION = 1500, 2000, 2000, 25000

Figure 2-11
Adding Variable
to an Existing Model

❺   Click the end of the model to position the edit cursor.

❻   Press **[Enter]** and type **ROS = EBT / TOTAL SALES * 100**. See Figure 2-12. This adds the ROS variable at the bottom of the model.

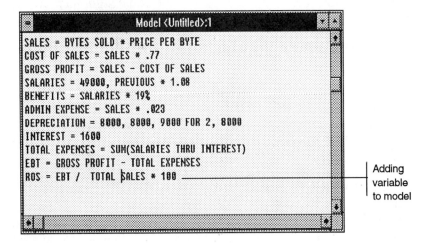

SALES = BYTES SOLD * PRICE PER BYTE
COST OF SALES = SALES * .77
GROSS PROFIT = SALES - COST OF SALES
SALARIES = 49000, PREVIOUS * 1.08
BENEFITS = SALARIES * 19%
ADMIN EXPENSE = SALES * .023
DEPRECIATION = 8000, 8000, 9000 FOR 2, 8000
INTEREST = 1600
TOTAL EXPENSES = SUM(SALARIES THRU INTEREST)
EBT = GROSS PROFIT - TOTAL EXPENSES
ROS = EBT / TOTAL SALES * 100 ──── Adding variable to model

Figure 2-12
Adding the
ROS Line

❼   Click **File**, click **Save**, then type **PROJECT2** in the Entity Name text box to save the new model with this name.

Correcting Undefined Variables

When IFPS solves a model, it compiles the model before doing the actual calculations. A **compile** is a line-by-line check of the model to make sure that all the variable names are defined on the left side of an equal sign, that arithmetic operators are used correctly, and that function names are valid. If any errors are detected an error message is displayed; otherwise, the solution is calculated. An **undefined variable** is a misspelled or unspecified name for a variable that appears on the right side of an equal sign but is not specified on the left side of an equal sign. This situation is detected when the model is solved causing an undefined variable error message to appear. Herbie specified one of his variables incorrectly. Let's solve the model and detect this undefined variable.

Reference Window

Correcting Undefined Variables
- Click the Solve button.
- Click the Cancel button when the message displays.
- Click the Model window and move the cursor to the error's location.
- Fix the error.
- Click the Solve button, then click the OK button for the default solution.

To detect undefined variables:

❶   Click the **Solve button** in the toolbar and the Error Message dialog box appears. See Figure 2-13.

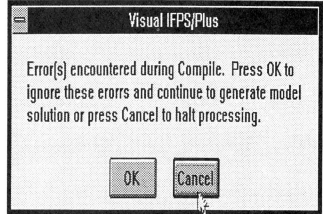

Figure 2-13
Error Message
Dialog Box

❷   Click **Cancel** to remove the Error Message dialog box. The error messages are displayed for your review. See Figure 2-14.

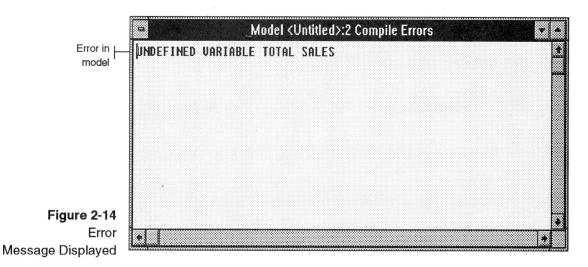

Error in
model

Figure 2-14
Error
Message Displayed

TROUBLE? If you clicked OK, then the model was solved with the undefined variables set to zero. Select the Model window and repeat Steps 1 and 2.

It looks like Herbie misspelled a variable name in the formula for ROS. The correct equation should be ROS = EBT / SALES * 100. Let's correct his error.

To correct an undefined variable error:

❶   Click the **Model PROJECT2 window** to make it the active window.

❷   Click **Edit**, then click **Find** to display the Find dialog box. See Figure 2-15.

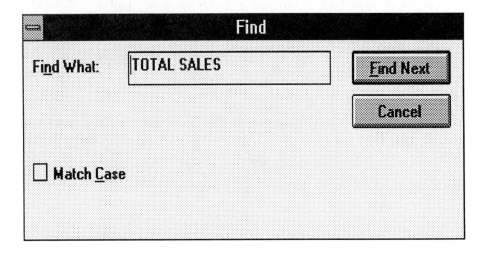

Figure 2-15
Find Dialog Box

❸   In the text box, type **TOTAL SALES** and click the **Find Next button**, then click the **Cancel button**. This will highlight the line that contains **TOTAL SALES**.

❹   Scroll the Model window, as necessary, until you locate the highlighted TOTAL SALES.

❺   Press **[Delete]**, then type **SALES.** See Figure 2-16.

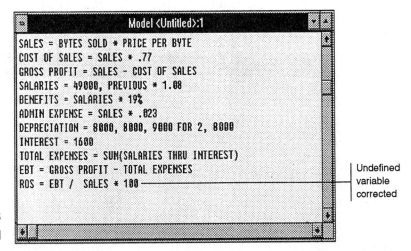

Figure 2-16
Corrected Model

Now that the error is fixed, Herbie wants the model solved once more to make sure all the errors have been removed. Let's resolve the model.

To resolve the model:

❶   Click the **Solve button** in the toolbar.

❷ Click the **OK button** to accept the solve defaults. See Figure 2-17.

	YEAR1	YEAR2	YEAR3	YEAR4	YEAR5
BYTES SOLD	44.00	52.00	60.00	68.00	76.00
PRICE PER BYTE	8,000.00	8,000.00	8,000.00	8,000.00	8,000.00
SALES	352,000.00	416,000.00	480,000.00	544,000.00	608,000.00
COST OF SALES	271,040.00	320,320.00	369,600.00	418,880.00	468,160.00
GROSS PROFIT	80,960.00	95,680.00	110,400.00	125,120.00	139,840.00
SALARIES	49,000.00	52,920.00	57,153.60	61,725.89	66,663.96
BENEFITS	9,310.00	10,054.80	10,859.18	11,727.92	12,666.15
ADMIN EXPENSE	8,096.00	9,568.00	11,040.00	12,512.00	13,984.00
DEPRECIATION	8,000.00	8,000.00	9,000.00	9,000.00	8,000.00
INTEREST	1,600.00	1,600.00	1,600.00	1,600.00	1,600.00
TOTAL EXPENSES	76,006.00	82,142.80	89,652.78	96,565.81	102,914.11
EBT	4,954.00	13,537.20	20,747.22	28,554.19	36,925.89
ROS	1.41	3.25	4.32	5.25	6.07

Model PROJECT2 Solution:1

Figure 2-17
Solution of
Model

❸ Click the **Model PROJECT2 window** to make it the active window.

❹ Click **File**, then click **Save**.

Creating a Total Column

When Herbie and Pattie returned from their accountant, they realized that they should revise their plan. Buffalo Computer Services is expected to undergo considerable growth and change during the upcoming year. Because of the company's anticipated rapid growth, the accountant suggests that Herbie and Pattie create a model for just next year to provide more detail for their budget. They need to make it through this critical first year; and a one-year budget helps them with this planning. The accountant wants Pattie and Herbie to prepare a quarterly budget with an annual total. Because the same variables are included in the quarterly budget, Herbie thinks a good approach is to revise a copy of his annual model. He wants a report with each quarter numbered for appropriate identification, as Figure 2-18 shows:

	QTR1	QTR2	QTR3	QTR4	TOTAL
BYTES SOLD	8	10	12	14	44
PRICE PER BYTE	7500	7750	8000	8250	7931
SALES	60000	77500	96000	11550	349000
COST OF SALES PERCENT	.77	.76	.75	.74	
COST OF SALES	46200	58900	72000	85470	262570
GROSS PROFIT	13800	18600	24000	30930	86430
SALARIES	12250	12250	12250	12250	49000
ADMINISTRATIVE EXPENSE	2327	2327	2327	2327	9310
DEPRECIATION	1500	2000	2000	2500	8000
INTEREST	400	400	400	400	1600
TOTAL EXPENSES	17857	18759	19185	20134	75937
EBT	-4057	-160	4815	9896	10493
ROS	-6.76	-.21	5.02	8.57	3.01

Figure 2-18
Quarterly Model Solution
with Annual Total

To produce this result, we must lay out the IFPS solution matrix, as Figure 2-19 shows. The five columns are divided into two types: regular columns and special columns. Columns one through four are regular columns, whereas column five is a special column. Special-column calculations must be specified separately. For most of the line items, the TOTAL column is the sum of columns one through four. Therefore, all regular columns in the IFPS solution matrix must be calculated *before* the special columns can be calculated.

	1ST QTR (1)	2ND QTR (2)	3RD QTR (3)	4TH QTR (4)	TOTAL (5)
	← REGULAR COLUMNS →				SPECIAL COLUMNS

Figure 2-19 Solution Matrix Organization for Total Column Calculations

Figure 2-20 shows the planning analysis sheet for this model. This model produces the report shown in Figure 2-18. Let's look at selected lines to see how the regular and special calculations are defined along with several other modeling features.

Planning Analysis Sheet

My goal:
Develop a model for the projected income statement of Buffalo Computer Systems for the next year by quarter with an annual total.

What results do I want to see?
Revenues and expenses for the next year by quarter with appropriate subtotals and totals.

What information do I need?
Columns are Quarter1, Quarter2, Quarter3, Quarter4, Total
Bytes Sold [Quarter1] = 8
Bytes Sold [increase per Quarter] = 2
Price Per Byte [Quarter1] = 7500
Price Per Byte [increase per Quarter] = 250
Sales growth rate = 20%
Cost of sales percent [Quarter 1] = 77%
Cost of sales percent [change per Quarter] = -1%
Salaries [each quarter] = 12250
Benefits ratio = 19%
Admin expense ratio = 2.3%
Depreciation [each quarter] = 1500, 2000, 2000, 2500
Interest [each quarter] = 400

Figure 2-20 Revised Planning Analysis Sheet *(continued)*

<u>What calculations will I perform?</u>
COLUMNS QTR1, QTR2, QTR3, QTR4, TOTAL
BYTES SOLD = 8, PREVIOUS + 2
PRICE PER BYTE = 7500, PREVIOUS + 250
SALES = BYTES SOLD * PRICE PER BYTE
COST OF SALES PERCENT = .77, PREVIOUS - .01
COST OF SALES = SALES * COST OF SALES PERCENT
GROSS PROFIT = SALES - COST OF SALES
SALARIES = 12250
BENEFITS = SALARIES * 19%
ADMIN EXPENSES = SALES * .023
DEPRECIATION = 1500, 2000, 2000, 2500
INTEREST = 1600 / 4
TOTAL EXPENSES = SUM(SALARIES through INTEREST)
EBT = GROSS PROFIT - TOTAL EXPENSES
ROS = EBT / SALES * 100
* SPECIAL COLUMN COMPUTATIONS
COLUMN TOTAL FOR BYTES SOLD, SALES, COST OF SALES, '
    GROSS PROFIT THROUGH EBT = SUM(C1 THROUGH C4)
COLUMN TOTAL FOR PRICE PER BYTE = SALES / BYTES SOLD
COLUMN 5 FOR ROS = EBT/ SALES * 100

Figure 2-20 Revised Planning Analysis Sheet

COLUMNS QTR1, QTR2, QTR3, QTR4, TOTAL

The column statement sets up all the columns, including regular and special. Your columns may be named or numbered. Here, TOTAL becomes a special column because it is defined by special-column computations starting after the equation for ROS. If these special column computations were not there, then TOTAL would be a regular column.

BYTES SOLD = 8, PREVIOUS + 2
PRICE PER BYTE = 7500, PREVIOUS + 250
SALES = BYTES SOLD * PRICE PER BYTE
COST OF SALES PERCENT = .77, PREVIOUS - .01
COST OF SALES = SALES * COST OF SALES PERCENT
GROSS PROFIT = SALES - COST OF SALES
SALARIES = 12250
BENEFITS = SALARIES * 19%
ADMIN EXPENSES = SALES * .023
DEPRECIATION = 1500, 2000, 2000, 2500
INTEREST = 1600 / 4
TOTAL EXPENSES = SUM(SALARIES THRU INTEREST)
EBT = GROSS PROFIT - TOTAL EXPENSES
ROS = EBT / SALES * 100

These are the calculations performed in the regular columns of the solution matrix. Notice that SALES starts at 8 units in the first quarter and increase by 2 units each quarter. DEPRECIATION is input for each quarter. INTEREST is input as "1600 / 4," allowing IFPS to divide the annual amount into a quarterly amount of 400 for each quarter. You can input your data in either form. Let's examine the TOTAL column for the four quarters.

* SPECIAL COLUMN COMPUTATIONS

A comment statement identifies where the special column computations are placed in the model. This comment statement does not cause the calculation of the special column. It merely serves as a notation in the model of where you intend to place these calculations. As a result, the same calculations are performed, regardless of whether this statement is included in your model. A comment statement can be used to add any comments to your model.

Special columns are created by specifying calculations in COLUMN statements. It is the specification in the column statements that conditions a column, making it a special column in IFPS. Thus, if *no* column calculation statements exist, there will be *no* special columns. When column calculation statements are entered, the use of a column is switched from regular to special usage.

COLUMN TOTAL FOR BYTES SOLD, SALES, COST OF SALES, '
GROSS PROFIT..EBT = SUM(C1..C4)

In Herbie's model, the special column TOTAL is calculated for eleven of the variables that are addable. The SUM function is used to specify the addition of column 1 through column 4, where the "C" means column and the "1" is the column number. You could use THRU instead of the two dots. The apostrophe at the right end of the first line indicates the statement continues on the following line. In IFPS, this is known as the **line continuation**. You can continue an IFPS statement for as many lines as needed. Simply use an apostrophe at the end of each line that is continued, and do *not* split variable names between lines.

COLUMN TOTAL FOR PRICE PER BYTE = SALES / BYTES SOLD

This line calculates one cell, that is, one row and column intersection, in the solution matrix. It works as follows: IFPS gets the value in the TOTAL column for SALES and the value in the TOTAL column for BYTES SOLD and uses them to calculate the PRICE PER BYTE in the TOTAL column. This is a *weighted average* calculation, which adjusts for the fact that the units were *not* all sold for the same price. IFPS operates procedurally on special column computations so that the calculations for the TOTAL column of SALES and BYTES SOLD had to appear in the model before this calculation of the PRICE PER BYTE.

·COLUMN 5 FOR ROS = EBT/ SALES * 100

Here, column five represents the TOTAL column since columns can be identified by either number or name. IFPS column numbers always start with one and are numbered from left to right across the solution matrix, as expected. Since the Return On Sales (ROS) is calculated differently than any other variables, its method of calculation is specified here. Also, notice that this is exactly the same logic as is used in the regular columns. Since TOTAL is a special column, though, the regular logic was automatically turned off by IFPS. Let's add the special column statements to Herbie's quarterly model.

To add special column statements to a model:

❶   Click the **Model PROJECT2 window** to make it the active window.

❷   Position the edit cursor at the end of the model and press **[Enter]** to insert a blank line.

❸   Enter: *** SPECIAL COLUMN COMPUTATIONS**
         COLUMNS TOTAL FOR BYTES SOLD, SALES, COST OF SALES,'
             GROSS PROFIT..EBT = SUM (C1..C4)
         COLUMN TOTAL FOR PRICE PER BYTE = SALES/ BYTES SOLD
         COLUMN 5 FOR ROS = EBT/SALES * 100

See Figure 2-21 for the completed model.

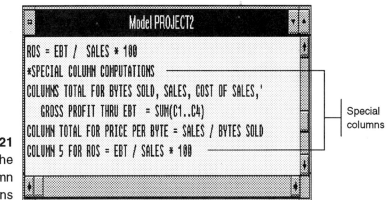

Figure 2-21
Adding the
Special Column
Computations

TROUBLE? To avoid possible pitfalls with IFPS column, computation statements, it is recommended that you place *all* column computation statements at the *end* of your model.

Herbie looks at the model and notices that some formulas must be revised from annual values to quarterly values as indicated in Figure 2-20. Let's see how to make those changes.

To modify equations for quarterly calculations:

❶   Move the cursor to the COLUMNS line and change it to **COLUMNS QTR1, QTR2, QTR3, QTR4, TOTAL**.

❷   Position the cursor at the beginning of the row containing COST OF SALES and press the **[Enter]** key to insert a line.

❸   Type: **COST OF SALES PERCENT = .77, PREVIOUS -.01** in the blank line to insert this variable in your model.

❹   Move the cursor to the COST OF SALES line and change the formula to **SALES * COST OF SALES PERCENT.**

❺   Move the cursor to the SALARIES line and change the formula to the constant amount of **12250**.

❻   Move the cursor to the DEPRECIATION line and change the amounts to **1500, 2000, 2000, 2500**.

❼   Move the cursor to the INTEREST line and add **/4** to the end**.**

❽   Change the rest of the model so it matches the Planning Analysis Sheet in Figure 2-20. See Figure 2-22.

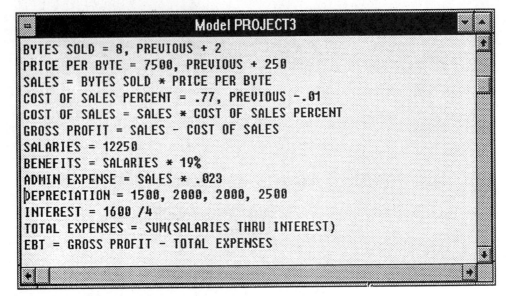

Figure 2-22
Revised Model
with Quarterly
Calculations

Now that the modifications are complete, Herbie wants to save the model and look at the solution.

To save the model and view the solution:

❶   Click **File,** then click **Save As** to display the Save As dialog box.

❷   Type **PROJECT3** in the Entity Name text box.

❸   Click the **Solve button** in the toolbar, then click the **OK button** to accept the default solution variables. See Figure 2-23.

Model PROJECT3 Solution:2	QTR1	QTR2	QTR3	QTR4	TOTAL
BYTES SOLD	8.00	10.00	12.00	14.00	44.00
PRICE PER BYTE	7,500.00	7,750.00	8,000.00	8,250.00	7,931.82
SALES	60,000.00	77,500.00	96,000.00	115,500.00	349,000.00
COST OF SALES PERCENT	0.77	0.76	0.75	0.74	0.00
COST OF SALES	46,200.00	58,900.00	72,000.00	85,470.00	262,570.00
GROSS PROFIT	13,800.00	18,600.00	24,000.00	30,030.00	86,430.00
SALARIES	12,250.00	12,250.00	12,250.00	12,250.00	49,000.00
BENEFITS	2,327.50	2,327.50	2,327.50	2,327.50	9,310.00
ADMIN EXPENSE	1,380.00	1,782.50	2,208.00	2,656.50	8,027.00
DEPRECIATION	1,500.00	2,000.00	2,000.00	2,500.00	8,000.00
INTEREST	400.00	400.00	400.00	400.00	1,600.00
TOTAL EXPENSES	17,857.50	18,760.00	19,185.50	20,134.00	75,937.00
EBT	-4,057.50	-160.00	4,814.50	9,896.00	10,493.00
ROS	-6.76	-0.21	5.02	8.57	3.01

Figure 2-23
Solution of
Model PROJECT3

Pattie wants a print out of both the model and its solution so that she and Herbie can take them to the accountant for another review.

To print the model:

❶   Click the **Model PROJECT3 window** to make it the active window.

❷   Click **File,** then **Print** to print the model.

Now, print the solution.

To print the solution:

❶   Click the **Solution window** to make it the active window.

❷   Click **File**, then **Print** to print the solution.

Changing Column Widths

Changing column width is one way to improve the appearance of a model's solution.

Reference Window

Changing Column Width
▪ Move the pointer to the solution frame and point to the line that separates the columns you want to change from the next column. The pointer changes to <-|->.
▪ Drag the pointer left to narrow the column or right to widen it.
▪ Release the mouse button when the column width is correct.

Herbie wants to increase the width of the column for QTR1. Let's change the column width for QTR1.

To change the column width:

❶   Move the pointer to the solution frame and point to the line that separates QTR1 from QTR2. The pointer should change to <-\|->. See Figure 2-24.

Change of pointer

	QTR1	QTR2	QTR3	QTR4	TOTA
Model PROJECT3 Solution:1					
BYTES SOLD	8.00	10.00	12.00	14.00	4
PRICE PER BYTE	7,500.00	7,750.00	8,000.00	8,250.00	7.93
SALES	60,000.00	77,500.00	96,000.00	115,500.00	349.00
COST OF SALES PERCENT	0.77	0.76	0.75	0.74	
COST OF SALES	46,200.00	58,900.00	72,000.00	85,470.00	262.57
GROSS PROFIT	13,800.00	18,600.00	24,000.00	30,030.00	86.43
SALARIES	12,250.00	12,250.00	12,250.00	12,250.00	49.00
BENEFITS	2,327.50	2,327.50	2,327.50	2,327.50	9.31
ADMIN EXPENSE	1,380.00	1,782.50	2,208.00	2,656.50	8.02
DEPRECIATION	1,500.00	2,000.00	2,000.00	2,500.00	8.00

Figure 2-24
Positioning the
Pointer for
Changing
Column Width

TROUBLE? If the solution is not open, resolve model PROJECT3, and then repeat Step 1.

❷   Click the mouse and drag the pointer right to increase the width of column QTR1.

❸   Release the mouse button when the column is the desired width. See Figure 2-25.

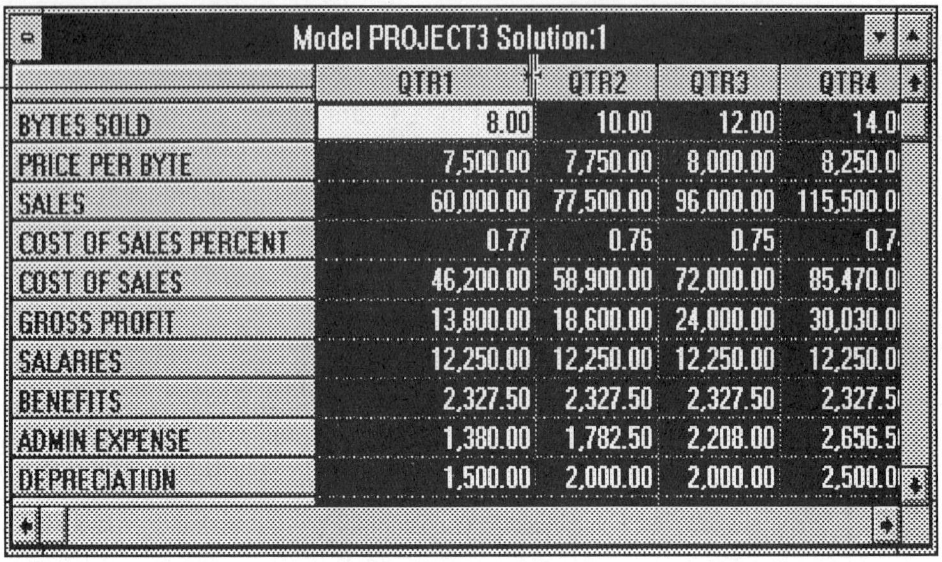

Increase
column width |

Figure 2-25
Increasing Width
of Column QTR1

Changing Appearance with Number Formats

Herbie wants the solution to appear with currency symbols. To do this, he must format the numbers in the solution. Let's see how to change the appearance of the solution.

Reference Window

Changing the Entire Solution Appearance with the Number Format
■   Click the upper-left corner of the solution to select all the solution values.
■   Click Format, then click Numbers.
■   Select the number format you want displayed.

To change the appearance of the numbers:

❶   Click the **Model PROJECT3 Solution window** to make it the active window.

❷   Click the upper-left corner of the solution to select all the solution values. See Figure 2-26.

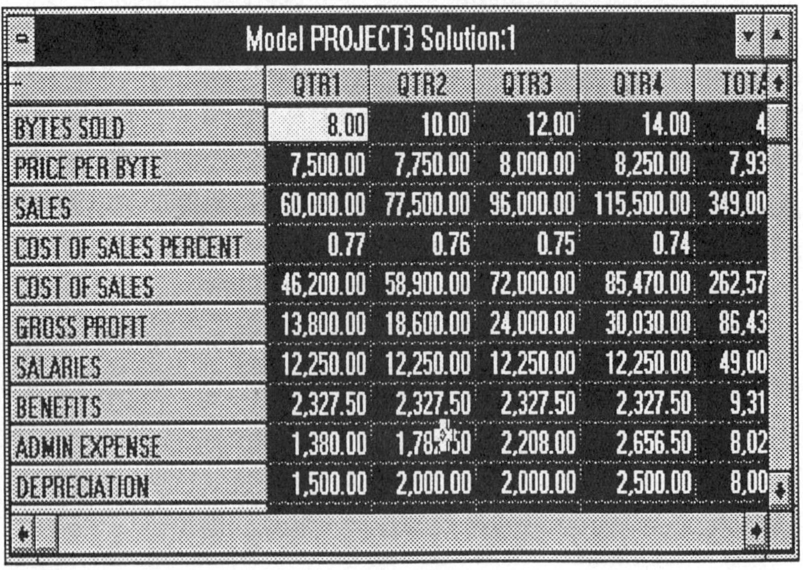

Click here
to select
entire
solution

Figure 2-26
Solution Selected
for Formatting

❸   Click **Format** to display the menu. See Figure 2-27.

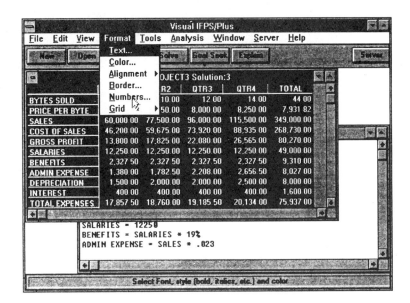

Figure 2-27
Format Menu

❹   Click **Numbers** to display the Format Numbers dialog box. See Figure 2-28.

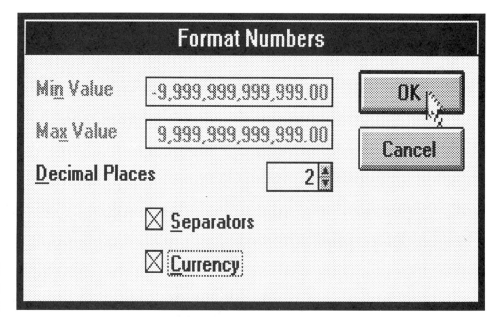

Figure 2-28
Format Numbers
Dialog Box

❺   Click the **Currency** check box to specify this format, then click the **OK button** in
the Format Numbers dialog box to accept currency. See Figure 2-29.

Figure 2-29
Currency Format
Added to the Solution

Model PROJECT3 Solution:1	QTR1	QTR2	QTR3	QTR4
BYTES SOLD	$8.00	$10.00	$12.00	$14.00
PRICE PER BYTE	$7,500.00	$7,750.00	$8,000.00	$8,250.00
SALES	$60,000.00	$77,500.00	$96,000.00	$115,500.00
COST OF SALES PERCENT	$0.77	$0.76	$0.75	$0.74
COST OF SALES	$46,200.00	$58,900.00	$72,000.00	$85,470.00
GROSS PROFIT	$13,800.00	$18,600.00	$24,000.00	$30,030.00
SALARIES	$12,250.00	$12,250.00	$12,250.00	$12,250.00
BENEFITS	$2,327.50	$2,327.50	$2,327.50	$2,327.50
ADMIN EXPENSE	$1,380.00	$1,782.50	$2,208.00	$2,656.50
DEPRECIATION	$1,500.00	$2,000.00	$2,000.00	$2,500.00

You can set the format for an individual row in the solution separately. Because it is not appropriate to display the currency symbol for the number of bytes sold, it should be removed from this row. Let's turn off the currency format for just BYTES SOLD.

To select a format for a single row:

❶ Click **BYTES SOLD** in the Solution window to select just this variable's row.

❷ Click **Format** to display the menu.

❸ Click **Numbers** to display the Format Numbers dialog box.

❹ Click the **Currency** check box to specify this format is now turned off, then click the **OK button** to complete this specification. See Figure 2-30.

Figure 2-30
Currency Format
Turned Off
for BYTES SOLD

Model PROJECT3 Solution:1	QTR1	QTR2	QTR3	QTR4
BYTES SOLD	8.00	10.00	12.00	14.00
PRICE PER BYTE	$7,500.00	$7,750.00	$8,000.00	$8,250.00
SALES	$60,000.00	$77,500.00	$96,000.00	$115,500.00
COST OF SALES PERCENT	$0.77	$0.76	$0.75	$0.74
COST OF SALES	$46,200.00	$58,900.00	$72,000.00	$85,470.00
GROSS PROFIT	$13,800.00	$18,600.00	$24,000.00	$30,030.00
SALARIES	$12,250.00	$12,250.00	$12,250.00	$12,250.00
BENEFITS	$2,327.50	$2,327.50	$2,327.50	$2,327.50
ADMIN EXPENSE	$1,380.00	$1,782.50	$2,208.00	$2,656.50
DEPRECIATION	$1,500.00	$2,000.00	$2,000.00	$2,500.00

Rounding Results

With the ROUND function, you can round off numbers in your solution. ROUND performs rounding in the manner you would expect. If a fractional part is one-half or greater, it rounds up to the next-higher number, whereas if it is less than one-half it rounds down to the next lower number. Two companion functions also aid in obtaining well-rounded numbers. Let's look at how Herbie may have used the ROUND function in Model PROJECT4 for his five-year plan (Figure 2-31).

Figure 2-31
Model PROJECT4
with the
ROUND Function

MODEL PROJECT4 VERSION OF 11/11/83 9:00
COLUMNS YEAR1, YEAR2, YEAR3, YEAR4, YEAR5
SALES = 343000, **ROUND**(PREVIOUS SALES * 1.20)
COST OF SALES = **ROUND**(SALES * .77)
GROSS PROFIT = SALES - COST OF SALES
SALARIES = 49000, **ROUND**(PREVIOUS * 1.08)
BENEFITS = **ROUND**(SALARIES * .19)
ADMIN EXPENSE = **ROUND**(SALES * .023)
DEPRECIATION = 8000, 8000, 9000 FOR 2, 8000
INTEREST = 1600
TOTAL EXPENSES = SUM(SALARIES THRU INTEREST)
EARNINGS BEFORE TAX = GROSS PROFIT - TOTAL EXPENSES

Here, Herbie uses the ROUND function on any arithmetic that might possibly produce a fractional result. IFPS automatically rounds off numbers in a solution matrix when they are printed. If you do the solution manually with a calculator, the EARNINGS BEFORE TAX might be off by one dollar because of rounding errors. This apparent error could cast suspicion on Herbie's entire plan when his banker reviews it. To avoid this problem, Herbie has rounded all his variables as they are calculated. If you want all your numbers to cross-check and foot, then you will likely need to round your numbers. Now, Herbie wants to include rounding in model PROJECT and save it under model PROJECT4. Let's see how you can accomplish rounding in a model.

To include rounding in a model:

❶   Click the **Open button** and select **PROJECT** from the Entity Name list box.

❷   Edit the model, changing all of the lines that need the **ROUND** function added to the model by moving your cursor to that line and positioning it where you are going to type **ROUND**.

❸   Type **Round(** and then the **)** at the end of the line. Repeat Steps 2 and 3 until all the lines are changed.

❹   Click **File**, click **Save As**, then type **PROJECT4** in the Entity Name text box to save the model under its new name.

❺   Click the **Solve button** in the toolbar, then click the **OK button** to accept the default solution variables. Finally, click the upper-left corner of the solution.

❻   Click **Format**, click **Numbers**, then type **0** (zero) in the Decimal Places text box. Click the **OK button** to complete the format specification with all numbers displayed as integers. See Figure 2-32.

	YEAR1	YEAR2	YEAR3	YEAR4	YEAR5
SALES	343,000	411,600	493,920	592,704	711,245
COST OF SALES	264,110	316,932	380,318	456,382	547,658
GROSS PROFIT	78,890	94,668	113,601	136,321	163,586
SALARIES	49,000	52,920	57,154	61,726	66,664
BENEFITS	9,310	10,055	10,859	11,728	12,666
ADMIN EXPENSE	7,889	9,467	11,360	13,632	16,359
DEPRECIATION	8,000	8,000	9,000	9,000	8,000
INTEREST	1,600	1,600	1,600	1,600	1,600
TOTAL EXPENSES	75,799	82,042	89,973	97,686	105,289
EARNINGS BEFORE TAX	3,091	12,626	23,628	38,635	58,297

Model PROJECT4 Solution:2

Figure 2-32
Solution Using
the ROUND Function

Adding Comments

Any model line that begins with a backslash (\) or with an asterisk (*) constitutes a comment line. The two lines below are additional comment lines that could be included in the four-quarter model examined in a previous section. Comment lines let you enter whatever text or descriptive information you want in your model. They allow you to include subheadings in your solution. Comments provide documentation that makes the model more easily comprehensible, as shown previously with the column computation statements. Let's add these comment lines to Herbie's model:

    * BUFFALO COMPUTER SYSTEMS
    * PROJECTED PROFIT AND LOSS STATEMENT

To add comment lines to a model:

❶   Click the **Open button** and select **PROJECT3** from the Entity Name list box.

❷   Move the cursor to insert a line immediately below the columns statement.

❸   Press the **[Enter]** key twice to insert two blank lines.

❹   Position your cursor at the first blank line and type:
    * BUFFALO COMPUTER SYSTEMS

❺   Move your cursor to the next blank line and type:
    * PROJECTED PROFIT AND LOSS STATEMENT
    See Figure 2-33.

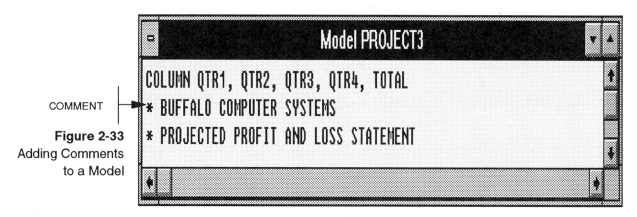

COMMENT

Figure 2-33
Adding Comments
to a Model

Herbie and Pattie are ready to take the quarterly model to their accountant. You can exit Visual IFPS until they return with any revisions.

Questions

1.   Variables are used in _____ in the IFPS model.
      a. equations
      b. values
      c. titles
      d. areas

2.   A _____ is a check of the model line by line to make sure that all the variable names are defined.
      a. variable
      b. equation
      c. compile
      d. walk through

3.   An undefined variable is a:
      a. misspelled variable
      b. defined equation
      c. specified name for an equation
      d. bad model

4.   The special column statements should be placed at:
      a. the beginning of the model
      b. the middle of the model
      c. in another model
      d. at the end of a model

5.   Comments let you enter _____ into your model.
   a. numbers
   b. variables
   c. equations
   d. text

Case Problems

1. Good Morning Products

Frosty and Crush have requested Kim and Chris to extend the Good Morning Products budgeting and planning model to be a projection by quarter with a total for the year. Frosty knows that drinking orange juice (OJ) is seasonal and would like to see this factor included in the budget. In creating this quarterly model, be sure to sum those variables that are additive in computing the annual total. For those variables that are *not* additive, calculate their weighted average for the quarter. In expanding GM's model, use this data provided by Chris and Kim:

	1st Quarter	2nd Quarter	3rd Quarter	4th Quarter
Bottles	330000	310000	260000	300000
Price	3.19	3.19	3.39	3.39
General and Administrative	23000	23000	26000	26000
Advertising	18000	19000	21000	21000
Interest	16000	16000	16000	16000
Depreciation	25500	25500	25500	25500

The variable costs per bottle are expected to be the same for all four quarters. Include comment statements for the subheadings shown in the design section in Tutorial 1.

Quick Check Answers: Total
   Price $3.283
   EBT $393000
   ROS   9.975

2. The Woodcraft Furniture Company

Extend the Woodcraft income model to a monthly projection with a column for quarterly totals. Be certain to sum only those variables that are additive. For those variables that cannot be summed, calculate their weighted average for the quarter. In extending the model, use the following data:

	July	August	September
Table Price	450	450	450
Chair Price	100	100	100
Sofa Price	300	300	300
Employees	157	160	165
Hourly Rate	9.60	9.60	9.60
Hours Worked	174	174	174
Tables Sold	850	900	950
Management Salaries	47250	47250	47250
General and Admin	24000	25000	26000

The percents and ratios used to determine Cost of Sales, Overhead, Advertising, Insurance, and Interest are the same for this monthly projection as they were in the annual projection. Include comment statements for the subheadings shown in the design section in Tutorial 1.

3. The Last National Bank

Extend the Last National Bank to be a monthly projection for the quarter. That is, the analysis will be for three months with a quarterly total. Planning items that can be summed for the quarter should have their total in the quarterly total column. Those items that cannot be summed should have their weighted average calculated as appropriate. In extending the model, use the following data as input assumptions:

Assets:	January	February	March
(Amounts in Thousands)			
Real Estate Mortgages	32000	31000	29500
Installment Loans	11000	12000	14200
Commercial Loans	27000	29000	33000
Other Investments	2000	2500	3500
Liabilities:			
(Amounts in Thousands)			
Regular Savings	11000	12000	12500
Interest Plus Checking	16000	17800	18200
Money Market Certificates	40000	42000	43300
Other Borrowed Funds	3000	2500	3800
Interest Rates:			
Prime Rate Interest	14%	14.5%	14%
Real Estate Interest	10%	10.1%	10.2%
Installment Loan Interest*	1%	1.1%	1.1%
Commercial Loan Interest*	2%	1.9%	1.9%
Other Investment Interest*	1%	1.1%	1.2%
Regular Savings Interest	5.5%	5.5%	5.5%
Interest Plus Checking Interest	6%	6%	6%
Money Market Interest*	- 3%	-2.5%	-2.5%
Other Borrowed Funds Interest*	-4.5%	-4.0%	-4.0%

* Amount above or below the prime interest rate.

Include comment statements for the subheadings shown in the design section in Tutorial 1.

4. Harvest University

Harvest University operates on the quarter system with four quarters per year. As the chief financial officer, you want to extend your projection to be a quarterly projection with an annual total. Those planning items that can be summed for the annual total such as the expenses and revenues should be summed. Those items that cannot be added should have a weighted average calculated in the total column, if it is appropriate. Data for each quarter are as follows:

	Fall	Winter	Spring	Summer
Students	6200	6000	4800	3000
Credit Hours per Student	14	14	11	5
Credit Hour Ratio	150	150	150	150
Administrative Salaries	1137500	1137500	1137500	1137500
Secretarial Salaries	850000	850000	850000	700000
Full to FTE Ratio	.85	.90	.90	.95
Average Full-Time				
Faculty Salary	9000	9000	9000	9000
Average Part-Time				
Faculty Salary	2000	2000	2000	2000
Teaching Assistant Salaries	73250	73250	73250	73250
Other Salaries	262500	262500	262500	262500

Utilities	550000	700000	550000	400000
Other Operating Expenses	200000	200000	200000	200000
Endowment Income	625000	625000	625000	625000
Other Income	250000	250000	250000	250000

Other parameters for Credit Hour Ratio, Fringe Benefits, and so on are the same for the quarterly projection as for the annual projection. Include comment statements for the subheadings shown in the design section in Tutorial 1.

5. Midwest Universal Gas

Midwest Universal Gas (MUG) operates and plans their fiscal year by quarter. Revise the MUG projection to be a quarterly projection with an annual total. Those planning items that can be summed for the annual total such as expenses and revenues should be summed. Those items that cannot be added should have a weighted average calculated in the total column, as is appropriate. Input data (as dollar in thousands) for each quarter are as follows:

	1st Quarter	2nd Quarter	3rd Quarter	4th Quarter
Demand	220	210	80	210
General Admin	40625	40625	40625	40625
Tax Credits	21000	21000	21000	21000

Demand is the total amount of gas sold (also referred to as just Total Gas Sold). Other planning items are calculated based on the same assumptions as in the annual projection. Remember to divide the interest rate and other appropriate rates by four (4) to obtain the quarterly rate. Include comment statements for the subheadings shown in the design section in Tutorial 1.

6. General Memorial Hospital

Berry Wellman at General Memorial Hospital wants you to revise the projection to be a monthly projection for the quarter. That is, the plan will be for three months with a quarterly total. Planning items that are additive should be summed for the quarter. Those that are not additive should have a weighted average calculated, as appropriate. Use the following information in revising the model:

	April	May	June
Daily Charges	200	210	190
Nursing Charges	105	95	100
Bed Utilization Rate	.65	.80	.75
Days per Month	30	31	30

Days per Month is a new parameter that needs to be added to the model. Other planning items are calculated based on the same assumptions used in the annual projection. Remember to divide wages and salaries and other annual amounts and rates by twelve (12) to obtain the monthly value. Include comment statements for the subheadings shown in the design section in Tutorial 1.

7. River City

River City's financial officer is preparing the revised operating budget for next quarter. Revamp the annual projection model creating a quarterly model by month with a total for the quarter. For those planning items that can be added, provide a total for the quarter. For other planning items calculate a weighted average, as appropriate. Frank Frugal has prepared the following data for input to the model:

	July	August	September
Property Tax	18522	0	0
Permits	2500	100	120
Parks	1500	1750	1000

Other expenses are based on the same assumptions as those used in the annual model. The annual amounts should be adjusted to monthly amounts by dividing by twelve (12) as required. Include comment statements for the subheadings shown in the design section in Tutorial 1.

8. Good Morning Product

Chris and Crush have decided they would like you to revise their quarterly model from Case Problem 1 so the row and column total will foot correctly. Jenny suggests you use the ROUND function on those calculations with multiplication or division that have the potential for producing a fractional result. Copy the quarterly model and revise it to include rounding. Save the model using a name you select.

9. The Woodcraft Furniture Company

After Joe Birch reviewed the model, he asked for some revisions to the quarterly model from Case Problem 2. To make sure that the quarterly totals add and report correctly, Joe wants all revenue and expense amounts, which are calculated by multiplying by a rate or ratio, to be rounded to the nearest whole dollar. Make a copy of the quarterly model for including rounding. Save the copy using a name you give it, then make your revisions.

10. The Last National Bank

After J. J. reviewed the model, he requested several changes to the quarterly model from Tutorial 2 Case Problem 3. To insure that the quarterly totals added up correctly, J. J. wants all interest income and interest expense amounts, which are calculated by multiplying by an interest rate, to be rounded to the nearest whole dollar. Copy the quarterly model and save it with a new name of your choice. Then revise the copy to include rounding.

11. Harvest University

Revise the Harvest University quarterly model from Case Problem 4 so the number of FTE Faculty and other appropriate line items are rounded to the nearest integer. Apply rounding to those line items that can potentially produce a fractional result. Make a copy of the model from Tutorial 2 and include your revisions in this copy. Give this model a name you select.

12. Midwest Universal Gas

Francis Foresight of Midwest Universal Gas has requested the application of rounding to the quarterly model from Case Problem 5. Use rounding on those line items which might produce fractional results. Copy the quarterly model and save it under a new name of your choice. Include rounding in this copy of the model.

13. General Memorial Hospital

Berry Wellman wants you to add rounding to the quarterly model from Case Problem 6 of General Memorial Hospital. He knows from prior experience that his board of directors will question the plan unless all the numbers foot correctly. Copy the monthly model and save it under a new name of your choice. Then make your revisions to the copy of the model.

14. River City

Before Frank Frugal presents the revised River City quarterly budget from Case Problem 7 to Lisa Goodnight, he wants all the numbers to foot correctly. Add rounding to the model to facilitate this rounding. Make a copy of the quarterly budget model and make your revisions to this copy. Give the new model a name you select.

Notes:

Tutorial 3

Creating and Printing Graphs

Introduction to Graphs

With graphs, you can present data in a visually appealing and easily understood format. Presentations that include graphs are more effective and persuasive than those that consist of text only. Some examples of what a graph can do are:

- Make your message more powerful, clear, and persuasive
- Help viewers grasp your point of view faster and remember it longer
- Summarize large quantities of complex data
- Discover new relationships among data

Once you create a solution for a model, you can graph any data that the solution contains. Each single set of data from a solution that you can graph is known as a **data series**.

Once you know what data you want to graph, you must determine the relationship you want to see between the various data series. The graphs used in business often deal with two basic situations:

- Showing trends (that is, How do conditions change over time?)
- Comparing components and relative amounts (that is, What proportion is each component to the total amount?) .

The type of relationship you want your graph to illustrate determines the graph type you need to use. Visual IFPS includes a variety of graph types: bar graphs, line graphs, pie graphs, and other graphs. Figure 3-1 summarizes the application of graphs to typical situations.

Figure 3-1
Selecting a Graph Type

Situation	Graph Type
Showing trends	Bar and line graph
Comparing components	Pie chart

Figure 3-2 summaries the types of graphs Visual IFPS has to offer.

Graph Type	Purpose
Area	Shows the magnitude of change over time.
Bar	Shows comparison among the data series represented by bars. Most useful with a limited number of data series.
Line	Shows trends or changes over time. Most useful for showing trends with many data values in each data series.
Pie	Shows the proportion of parts to a whole for a single data series.
Symbol	Shows trends or changes over time by symbols and not by lines.
3-D Bar	Similar to a 2-D bar graph, but bars appear three-dimensional.
3-D Pie	Shows the proportion of parts to a whole, with emphasis on the data value in the front wedges, for a single data series.

Figure 3-2 Visual IFPS Graph Types

It is important to understand Visual IFPS graph terminology so that you can successfully construct and edit graphs. Let's examine the elements of Herbie's bar graph shown in Figure 3-3.

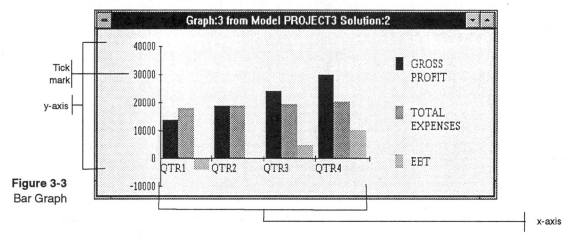

Figure 3-3 Bar Graph

The horizontal axis of the graph is referred to as the *x-axis*. The vertical axis is referred to as the *y-axis*. The y-axis labels show the scale for the y-axis. A tick mark indicates the location for each value on the scale. Visual IFPS automatically generates this scale based on the values selected for the graph. The x-axis labels usually correspond to the columns for your model. A *data series* is a group of related data points from a range of cells in the model's solution. Let's see how Visual IFPS creates different graph types for a data series.

Creating a Bar Graph

Before creating any graph, you first have to open and solve a model. Herbie wants a bar graph like that shown in Figure 3-3. Let's see how this graph is created after opening and solving the model.

To open and solve a model in preparation for creating a graph:

❶ Click the **Model PROJECT3 window** to make this the active window.

> **TROUBLE?** If model PROJECT3 is not opened, then open the model by clicking Open in the toolbar and selecting PROJECT3 from the Entity Name list box.

❷   Click the **Solve button**, then click the **OK button** to solve the model. See Figure 3-4.

Model PROJECT3 Solution:1	QTR1	QTR2	QTR3	QTR4	TOTAL
BYTES SOLD	8.00	10.00	12.00	14.00	44.00
PRICE PER BYTE	7,500.00	7,750.00	8,000.00	8,250.00	7,931.82
SALES	60,000.00	77,500.00	96,000.00	115,500.00	349,000.00
COST OF SALES	46,200.00	59,675.00	73,920.00	88,935.00	268,730.00
GROSS PROFIT	13,800.00	17,825.00	22,080.00	26,565.00	80,270.00
SALARIES	12,250.00	12,250.00	12,250.00	12,250.00	49,000.00
BENEFITS	2,327.50	2,327.50	2,327.50	2,327.50	9,310.00
ADMIN EXPENSE	1,380.00	1,782.50	2,208.00	2,656.50	8,027.00
DEPRECIATION	1,500.00	2,000.00	2,000.00	2,500.00	8,000.00

Figure 3-4
Solution for
Model PROJECT3

Now that there is a solution for the model, let's create a graph like the one in Figure 3-3 that displays the GROSS PROFIT, TOTAL EXPENSES, and EBT.

To create the bar graph for selected variables:

❶   Move the cell pointer to the **QTR1** values in the **GROSS PROFIT** line, then hold down the mouse button and drag it to select the values for quarter one through quarter four.

❷   Move the cell pointer to the **QTR1** values in the **TOTAL EXPENSES** line, then press and hold down the **[Ctrl]** key while holding down the mouse button and dragging it to select the values for quarter one through quarter four for the graph.

       TROUBLE? If the data for GROSS PROFIT is not highlighted, then you did not hold down the **[Ctrl]** key while selecting the quarterly data with the mouse button. To highlight the desired data for GROSS PROFIT, repeat Steps 1 and 2.

❸   Move the cell pointer to the **QTR1** values in the **EBT** line, then press and hold down the **[Ctrl]** key while holding down the mouse button and dragging it to select the values for quarter one through quarter four. See Figure 3-5.

       TROUBLE? If the data GROSS PROFIT and EBT are not highlighted, then you did not hold the **[Ctrl]** key while selecting the quarterly data with the mouse button. To highlight the appropriate data for GROSS PROFIT and EBT, repeat Steps 1 through 3.

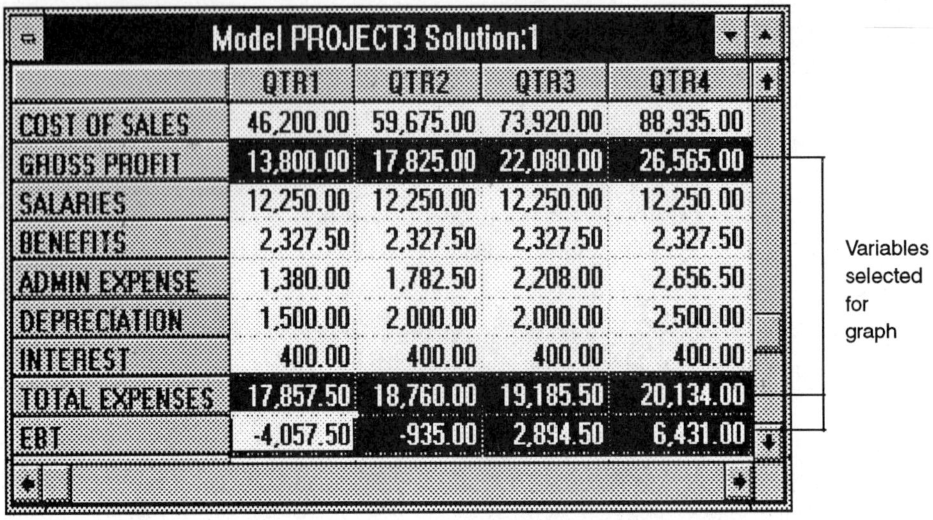

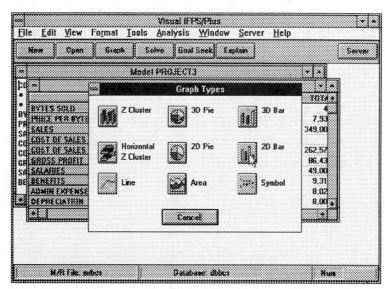

Figure 3-5
Selecting the
Variables

TROUBLE? If you select the variable name, then you select the data series for all four quarters *and* the total. To select the four quarters, you need to select the values for the four quarters and not all columns of the variable. If you selected the variable name, repeat Steps 1 through 3.

❹ Click the **Graph button** in the toolbar to display the Graph Types dialog box. See Figure 3-6.

Figure 3-6
Graph Types
Dialog Box

❺ Click the **2-D Bar button** in the Graph Types dialog box to open a window containing the 2-D bar graph. See Figure 3-7.

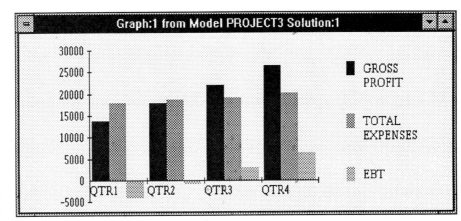

Figure 3-7
Bar Graph of
Model PROJECT3

Selecting a Graph Type

After obtaining an initial Visual IFPS graph, you can select another graph type from the toolbar displayed for the graph window. This toolbar is context-sensitive and changes to match the type of your currently active window (Figure 3-8).

Figure 3-8
Toolbar for
Graph Mode

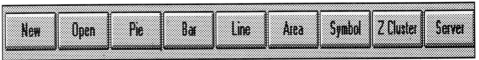

You might have to experiment with different graph types to find the one that best represents your data. Sometimes, the graph you planned isn't the right type for the information you want to plot. As you work through this tutorial, you will find that the procedure for changing from one graph type to another is easy.

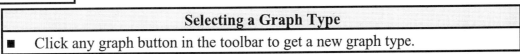

You might have to experiment with different graph types to find the one that best represents your data.

Reference Window

Selecting a Graph Type
■   Click any graph button in the toolbar to get a new graph type.

Herbie needs to change the graph type from a bar graph to a line graph. Let's change the graph type.

To change the graph type:

❶   Verify that the Graph window is your currently active window.

TROUBLE? If the Graph window is not the currently active window, either click the Graph window to make it the active window or follow the steps in the section entitled "Creating a Bar Graph" to display the bar graph.

❷   Click the **Line button** in the toolbar to display a line graph. See Figure 3-9.

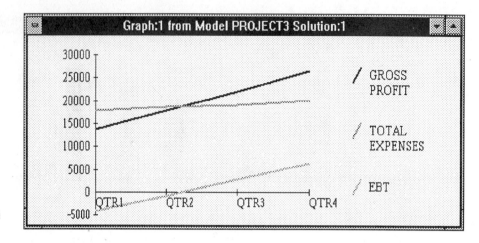

Figure 3-9
Line Graph
of Model PROJECT3

Herbie thinks his line graph appropriately displays the data, but Pattie wonders how it would look as a 3-D bar graph. Let's change Herbie's line graph to a 3-D bar graph to see this arrangement of the data.

To select a 3-D bar graph type:

❶　　Verify that the Graph window is your currently active window.

❷　　Click the **Bar button** in the toolbar to display a 3-D bar graph. See Figure 3-10.

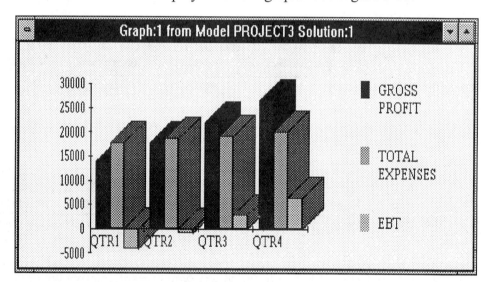

Figure 3-10
3-D Bar Graph
of Model PROJECT3

Adding Titles

Herbie likes the appearance of the 3-D bar graph, but he wants to include a title with his company's name at the top of the graph. Let's see how you can add a title to the graph.

Reference Window

Adding Graph Titles
■　Click Options, then click Titles. Select the position of the desired title.
■　Type the desired title in the Title text to use box.
■　Click the OK button to add the title(s) to the graph.

To add a title to a graph:

❶   Click **Options**, then click **Title** to display the title menu.

❷   Click **Top** from the title menu to display the Chart Title text box.

❸   Type **Buffalo Computer Systems** as the desired title.

❹   Click the **OK button** in the Chart Title text box to complete specifying the title. See Figure 3-11.

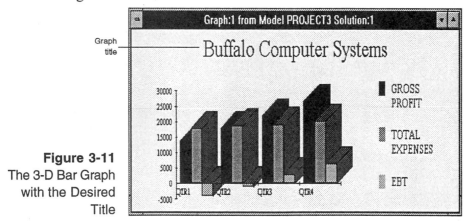

Figure 3-11
The 3-D Bar Graph with the Desired Title

Herbie wants a title at the left side of the graph describing the y-axis. Let's see how to add a title for the y-axis.

To add a title for the y-axis of a graph:

❶   Click **Options**, then click **Title** to display the title menu.

❷   Click **Left** from the title menu to display the Chart Title text box.

❸   Type **Dollars** as the y-axis title.

❹   Click the **OK button** in the Chart Title text box to place the title on the graph. See Figure 3-12.

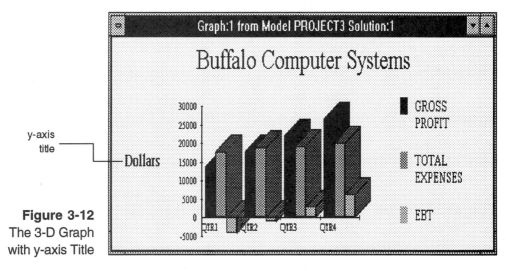

Figure 3-12
The 3-D Graph with y-axis Title

Printing a Graph

Herbie wants to print the graph with the titles. Let's see how you print a graph.

To print a graph:

❶   Click **File** to display the File menu.

❷   Click **Print** to produce a hardcopy of the graph in the active window.

Creating a Pie Chart

Pattie thinks a pie chart of all the expenses for the year would help her and Herbie better understand these expenses. Let's see how to create a pie chart that compares these expenses from the TOTAL column.

To create a pie chart:

❶   Click the **Solution window** to make it the active window.

❷   Select the values from **SALARIES** to **INTEREST** in the **TOTAL column**. See Figure 3-13.

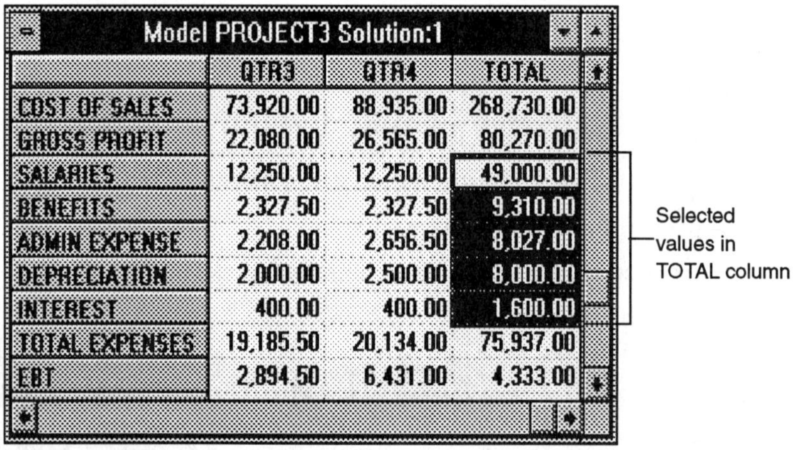

Model PROJECT3 Solution:1	QTR3	QTR4	TOTAL	
COST OF SALES	73,920.00	88,935.00	268,730.00	
GROSS PROFIT	22,080.00	26,565.00	80,270.00	
SALARIES	12,250.00	12,250.00	49,000.00	
BENEFITS	2,327.50	2,327.50	9,310.00	
ADMIN EXPENSE	2,208.00	2,656.50	8,027.00	
DEPRECIATION	2,000.00	2,500.00	8,000.00	
INTEREST	400.00	400.00	1,600.00	
TOTAL EXPENSES	19,185.50	20,134.00	75,937.00	
EBT	2,894.50	6,431.00	4,333.00	

Selected values in TOTAL column

Figure 3-13
Selecting Column
of Total Expenses

❸   Click the **Graph button** to display the Graph Types dialog box.

❹   Click the **2-D Pie Chart button** in the Graph Types dialog box. A pie chart of Total Expenses appears. See Figure 3-14.

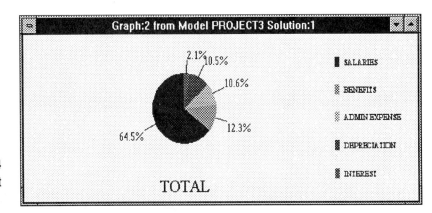

Figure 3-14
The Pie Chart
of Total Expenses

Graphing a What If

Herbie wants to produce a graph depicting a what-if scenario. (You will learn more about what-if alternatives in the next tutorial.) He wants to know what happens when SALARIES are 7500 each quarter. Let's see how to do the what-if scenario and graph it.

To do a what-if scenario:

❶   Click the **Model PROJECT3 window** to make it the active window.

❷   Click the **What If button** on the toolbar.

❸   Type **SALARIES = 7500**

❹   Click the **Solve button** on the toolbar.

   TROUBLE? If you do not click Solve, then you cannot create a graph of the what if. Click the Solve button in the toolbar.

❺   Click the **OK button** to display the solution. See Figure 3-15.

Figure 3-15
Solution of the
What If for Model
PROJECT3

Case <Untitled>:1 of Model PROJECT3 Solution:2

salaries = 7500

	QTR1	QTR2	QTR3	QTR4
BYTES SOLD	8.00	10.00	12.00	14.00
PRICE PER BYTE	7,500.00	7,750.00	8,000.00	8,250.00
SALES	60,000.00	77,500.00	96,000.00	115,500.00
COST OF SALES	46,200.00	59,675.00	73,920.00	88,935.00
GROSS PROFIT	13,800.00	17,825.00	22,080.00	26,565.00
SALARIES	7,500.00	7,500.00	7,500.00	7,500.00
BENEFITS	1,425.00	1,425.00	1,425.00	1,425.00

Herbie looks at the solution. He wants a pie chart of all expenses for the TOTAL column to compare it to the chart you already created and printed in the previous sections. Let's see how to graph a what-if solution.

To graph the What if solution:

❶   Select the values from **SALARIES** to **INTEREST** in the **TOTAL column**.

❷   Click the **Graph button** to display the Graph Types dialog box.

❸   Click **2-D Pie Chart** in the Graph Types dialog box. See Figure 3–16.

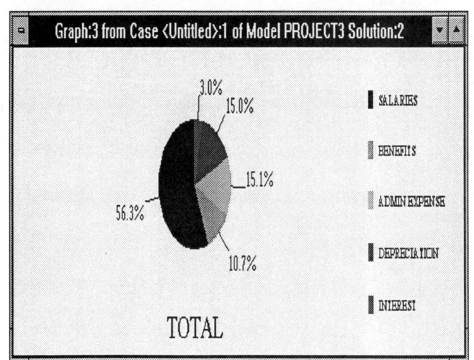

Figure 3-16
Pie Chart of
Total Expenses
after What If

Herbie and Pattie have finished graphing their expected performance and are ready for the next meeting with their accountant. The graphs will help them make an informed decision on what actions they should take in expanding Buffalo Computer Services.

Questions

1.   _____ are used to present data in a visually appealing way.
   a. Graphs
   b. Pictures
   c. Photos
   d. Drawings

2.   _____ are best used to compare components.
   a. Bar charts
   b. Line charts
   c. Z charts
   d. Pie charts

3.   The x-axis is the:
    a. vertical axis of a graph
    b. width of the graph
    c. horizontal axis of a graph
    d. length of the graph

4.   The y-axis is the:
    a. vertical axis of a graph
    b. width of the graph
    c. horizontal axis of a graph
    d. length of the graph

5.   A _____ is a group of related data points from a range of cells in a model's solution.
    a. data
    b. data series
    c. graph series
    d. graph points

6.   The _____ bar is context-sensitive and changes to match the type of active window.
    a. model
    b. report
    c. tool
    d. main

Case Problems

1. Good Morning Products

Frosty, Crush, Kim, and Chris would like to graphically represent their quarterly budgeting and planning model. Frosty has reviewed the model solution but is wondering what the numbers graphically represent. Crush wants to see a graph of only the Total Fixed Costs and Total Variables Costs of the four quarters with the title Good Morning Products at the top and Costs as the y-axis. Kim wants to see a graph comparing the Fixed Costs for the year. Create the graphs for Kim and Crush. After you have created these graphs, Frosty would like you to create another graph of what ever you want and explain what the graph represents to their company.

2. The Woodcraft Furniture Company

Joe and Martha would like to graphically represent there quarterly budgeting and planning model. Joe has reviewed the solution of the model but wants to see what the numbers graphically represent. Martha wants to see two graphs. The first graph shows sales for the three months. The graph should include the title Woodcraft at the top and Sales as the y-axis. The second graph represents all operation expenses for the quarter. After you have created these graphs, Joe wants you to create another graph of your choice and explain what the graph represents to their company.

3. The Last National Bank

Carrie wants to graphically represent the quarterly budgeting and planning model. After reviewing the solution to the model, she wants to see two graphs. The first graph compares total assets and total liabilities by month. This graph should include the title Last National Bank at the top and Dollars as the y-axis. The second graph is of all liabilities at the end of the quarter. After you have created these graphs, Carrie wants you to create another graph of your choice and explain what the graph represents to the bank.

4. Harvest University

Harvest University wants to graphically represent the quarterly budgeting and planning model. The administrators have examined the solution to the model but wish to view the numbers graphically. They want to see two graphs. The first graph shows Students and Reserve for the four terms. This graph should include the title Harvest University at the top and Dollars as the y-axis. The second graph demonstrates salaries by term for the year. After you have created these graphs, they want you to create another graph of your design and explain what the graph represents.

5. Midwest Universal Gas

Mary and Pete want to graphically represent their quarterly budgeting and planning model. Pete wants to see two graphs. The first graph is total revenue, total expenses, and income before tax for the four quarters. This graph should include the title Midwest Universal Gas at the top and Dollars as the y-axis. The second graph is of the same planning items except they are just the totals for the year. After you have created these graphs, Mary wants you to create another graph that you design and explain what the graph represents to MUG.

6. General Memorial Hospital

Berry wants to graphically represent the solution of their quarterly budgeting and planning model. He wants two graphs. The first graph is of all revenues items for the three months. This graph should include the title General Memorial Hospital at the top and Revenue as the y-axis. The second graph is of the total of each expense for the quarter. After you have completed these graphs, create another graph of your choice and explain what the graph represents to the hospital.

7. River City

Frank Frugal, River City's financial officer, wants to graphically represent the solution of their quarterly budgeting and planning model. After reviewing the solution to the model, the mayor wants to see two graphs. The first graph is total revenues and total expenses for each of the three months. This graph should include the title River City at the top and Revenues versus Expenses as the y-axis. The second graph is for total revenues and total expense quarterly totals. After you have created these graphs, create another graph of your choice and explain what the graph represents to the city.

Tutorial 4

Preparing and Examining What If Alternatives

Explaining Model Results

Herbie and Pattie completed their budget for next year. As they review the budget with their accountant, several questions arise. Herbie writes out a planning analysis sheet for these questions (Figure 4-1).

```
                          Planning Analysis Sheet

   My goal:
   Why do the ROS and EBT vary in different quarters?
   What if the number of Bytes Sold increased or decreased?
   What quantity of Bytes do I need to sell in order to just break-even?

   What results do I want to see?
   Revenues and expenses that explore the model's solution for gaining insight into
   the interactions among the planning variables.

   What information do I need?
         EXPLAIN WHY DID ROS GO UP IN QTR4?
         EXPLAIN WHY DID EBT GO DOWN IN QTR3?
         ANALYZE GROSS PROFIT
         ANALYZE EBT
         OUTLINE ROS
         OUTLINE SALES

   What calculations will I perform?
   Calculations in quarterly model with annual total.
```

Figure 4-1 Planning Analysis Sheet of Questions

In this tutorial you examine the quarterly model for BCS and gain a better understanding of it by using the what if, goal seeking, and expert system capabilities of Visual IFPS. **Expert systems** are computerized advisory programs that attempt to imitate the reasoning processes and knowledge of experts in solving specific types of problems, where an IFPS model represents one method for experts to specify problem solutions. One of the key features of an expert system is that the system can *explain* how a particular result was produced. The explanation commands of IFPS are advanced tools for interpreting and explaining the results of a business model, with the explain commands providing a *natural language explanation* of how a selected result is calculated by a model. In the next tutorial, you will examine other expert system features of Visual IFPS.

There are several different ways of examining model results. The different methods are: explain, analyze, and outline. Each of these methods provides a different look at the model solution. Before you learn about these, you first need to open and solve the model. Herbie and Pattie want to gain a better understanding of results of model PROJECT3. Let's open and solve model PROJECT3.

To open and solve Model PROJECT3:

❶   Open model **PROJECT3**.

        TROUBLE? If model PROJECT3 is not available to be opened, then you need
        to open your M&R file. Click Context and select the appropriate M&R file, then
        repeat Step 1.

❷   Click the **Solve button**, then click the **OK button** to select all the variables and
        columns.

Let's explore the EXPLAIN, ANALYZE, and OUTLINE commands as sketched out in Herbie's planning analysis sheet (Figure 4-1).

The EXPLAIN Command

The **EXPLAIN** command provides a natural language interpretation of the changes in data values between adjacent columns in a solution. The model is analyzed, and a narrative of the results is displayed on the screen. When several variables are used in a calculation, the most significant variables are described in the narrative and selected for display.

Reference Window

Using the EXPLAIN Command
■ Click the cell of the variable and column that you want explained, then click the Explain button in the toolbar.   *or*   Doubleclick the cell of the variable and column that you want explained.   ■ Click the Explain alternative button in the Explain dialog box for the situation you wish to explore.

Herbie wants you to use the EXPLAIN command to answer the question, **EXPLAIN WHY DID ROS GO UP IN QTR4?** Let's see how to use the EXPLAIN command to answer the question, why did ROS go up in QTR4?

To use the EXPLAIN command:

❶   Click **ROS** in column **QTR4** of the solution to position the cell pointer at this
        location. See Figure 4-2.

Model PROJECT3 Solution:1	QTR1	QTR2	QTR3	QTR4	TOTAL
COST OF SALES	46,200.00	58,900.00	72,000.00	85,470.00	262,570.00
GROSS PROFIT	13,800.00	18,600.00	24,000.00	30,030.00	86,430.00
SALARIES	12,250.00	12,250.00	12,250.00	12,250.00	49,000.00
BENEFITS	2,327.50	2,327.50	2,327.50	2,327.50	9,310.00
ADMIN EXPENSE	1,380.00	1,782.50	2,208.00	2,656.50	8,027.00
DEPRECIATION	1,500.00	2,000.00	2,000.00	2,500.00	8,000.00
INTEREST	400.00	400.00	400.00	400.00	1,600.00
TOTAL EXPENSES	17,857.50	18,760.00	19,185.50	20,134.00	75,937.00
EBT	-4,057.50	-160.00	4,814.50	9,896.00	10,493.00
ROS	-6.76	-0.21	5.02	8.57	3.01

Figure 4-2
Selecting
ROS in
Column QTR4

Selecting
the cell

TROUBLE? If you selected the wrong cell in the solution, repeat Step 1.

❷   Click the **Explain button** in the toolbar to display the Explain dialog box. See
Figure 4-3.

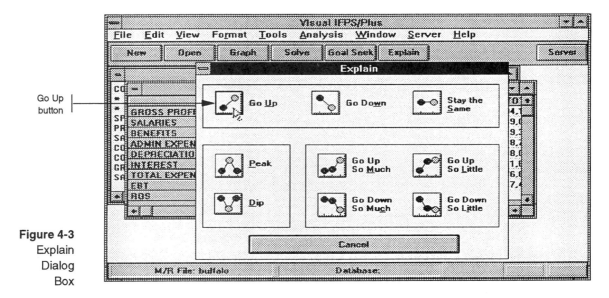

Go Up
button

Figure 4-3
Explain
Dialog
Box

❸   Click the **Go Up button** in the Explain dialog box to produce an explanation of
why ROS went up in QTR4. See Figure 4-4.

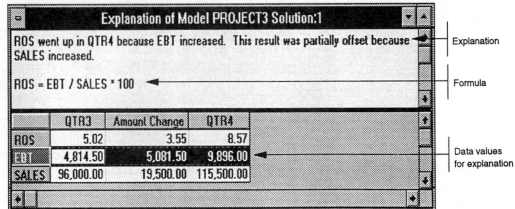

Figure 4-4
Explanation
of ROS

TROUBLE? If you clicked the wrong explain option, Visual IFPS still gives you the correct explanation. "Actually" indicates you requested a wrong direction of change.

Pattie has a better understanding of the results for ROS so, she wants you to use the EXPLAIN command again. This time, use the EXPLAIN command to **EXPLAIN WHY DID EBT GO DOWN IN QTR3?** Let's see how to change the EXPLAIN command to answer that question.

To change the EXPLAIN command:
❶   Click the **Solution window** to make it the active window.
❷   Position the cursor at column **QTR3** and row **EBT**.
❸   Click the **Explain button** to display this dialog box.
❹   Click the **Go Down button** in the Explain dialog box to display an explanation of why EBT went down in QTR 3. See Figure 4-5.

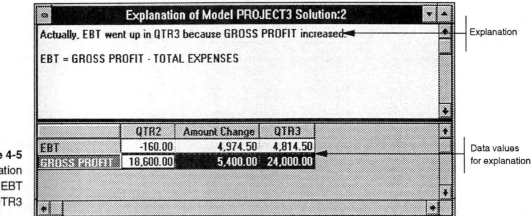

Figure 4-5
Explanation
of EBT
in QTR3

Although the Go Down explanation was selected, IFPS detects that EBT increased. IFPS uses the word *actually* to indicated the direction is different than your selection. The data are used to determine the direction of the change.

The ANALYZE Command

The **ANALYZE** command provides a means for gaining insight into the components that produced the results of a particular variable. Thus, as the ANALYZE name indicates, you can analyze or gain an understanding of the interactions that take place among variables. The ANALYZE command is also useful in debugging your model because it allows you to study the calculation of possibly erroneous variables. When the variables do not look right, you should investigate them further.

The ANALYZE command causes the following output to be displayed:

1. The model statement containing the logic used in performing the calculation.
2. The solution values of the variable being analyzed.
3. The solution values of all the variables that appear on the right-hand side of the equal sign in the equation being calculated. *Note:* This includes only the solution values, not the logic.

Reference Window

Using the Analyze Command
■ Click the Solution window.
■ Click the variable name or solution value of the variable you wish to analyze.
■ Click Analysis, then click Analyze to view the logic and solution values for that variable.

The ANALYZE command is useful for Pattie and Herbie because they want to know the values of the variables that were used in calculating GROSS PROFIT and EBT. Let's see how to analyze GROSS PROFIT so Herbie can examine the variables used in its calculation.

To analyze GROSS PROFIT:

❶ Click the **Solution window** to make it the active window.

TROUBLE? If there is not a Solution window on the desktop, make sure model PROJECT3 is active, then solve the model.

❷ Click **GROSS PROFIT** to select this variable. See Figure 4-6.

Entire row selected

Model PROJECT3 Solution:1	QTR1	QTR2	QTR3	QTR4	TOTAL
COST OF SALES	46,200.00	58,900.00	72,000.00	85,470.00	262,570.00
GROSS PROFIT	13,800.00	18,600.00	24,000.00	30,030.00	86,430.00
SALARIES	12,250.00	12,250.00	12,250.00	12,250.00	49,000.00
BENEFITS	2,327.50	2,327.50	2,327.50	2,327.50	9,310.00
ADMIN EXPENSE	1,380.00	1,782.50	2,208.00	2,656.50	8,027.00
DEPRECIATION	1,500.00	2,000.00	2,000.00	2,500.00	8,000.00
INTEREST	400.00	400.00	400.00	400.00	1,600.00
TOTAL EXPENSES	17,857.50	18,760.00	19,185.50	20,134.00	75,937.00
EBT	-4,057.50	-160.00	4,814.50	9,896.00	10,493.00
ROS	-6.76	-0.21	5.02	8.57	3.01

Figure 4-6
Selecting
Gross Profit

TROUBLE? If you selected the wrong variable, then change the selected variable to GROSS PROFIT by repeating Step 2.

❸   Click **Analysis** to display the Analysis menu. See Figure 4-7.

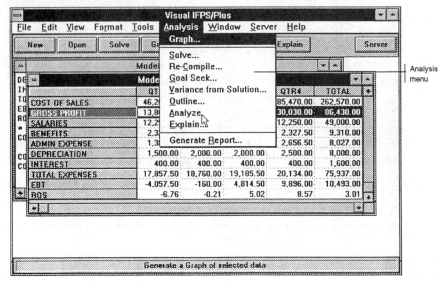

Figure 4-7
Analysis
Options

❹   Click **Analyze** to view the model logic for GROSS PROFIT and the data values
     used in its calculation. See Figure 4-8.

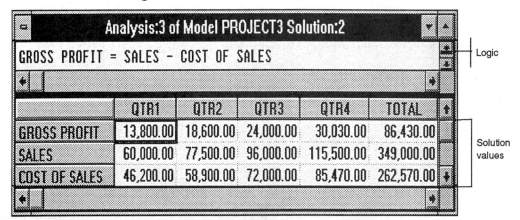

Figure 4-8
Analysis
of Gross Profit

Herbie wants to examine EBT rather than GROSS PROFIT. Let's see how to ANALYZE EBT so that
Pattie can see the variables used in calculating this variable.

To analyze EBT:

❶   Click the **Solution window** to make it the active window.

❷   Click **EBT** to select this variable.

❸   Click **Analysis** to display the Analysis menu, then click **Analyze** from the
     Analysis menu to analyze EBT. See Figure 4-9.

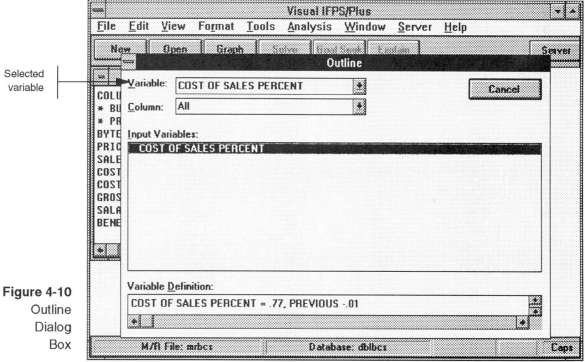

Figure 4-9
Analysis
of EBT

The OUTLINE Command

The **OUTLINE** command causes both direct and indirect input variables to be displayed for a selected variable. This allows you to outline all the variables used in calculating the selected variable. The OUTLINE command is useful in helping you understand which variables are used in calculating other variables in your model. A review of an OUTLINE provides a quick method for checking on the use of appropriate formulas in your model. Herbie wants to see the outline of ROS to verify its formula. Let's see how to outline ROS so Pattie can examine the outline of this variable to make sure that ROS is being calculated correctly.

To outline ROS:

❶   Click the **Solution window** to make it the active window.

❷   Click **Analysis** to display the Analysis menu.

❸   Click **Outline** to display the Outline dialog box. See Figure 4-10.

Figure 4-10
Outline
Dialog
Box

❹   Click the **Variable** drop-down list box arrow to display a list of variables.

❺   Click **ROS** to select this variable.

TROUBLE? If you selected the wrong variable from the drop-down list box, redo Step 5.

❻   Verify that **All** is in the Column drop-down list box and review the outline displayed for ROS. See Figure 4-11.

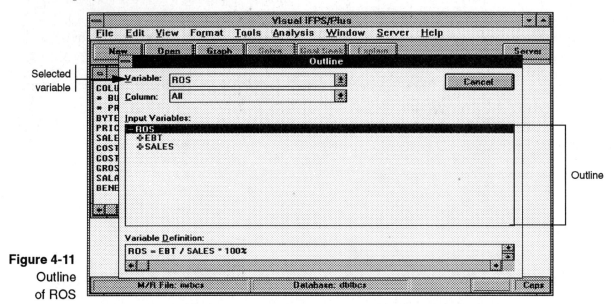

Figure 4-11
Outline
of ROS

TROUBLE? If All does not appear, then click the column drop-down list box arrow and select All.

Pattie thinks the OUTLINE command is interesting. She wants to review the outline for SALES by changing the variable from ROS to SALES. Let's see how to change the variable in the outline command from ROS to SALES.

To change the OUTLINE variable to SALES:
❶   Click the **Variable** drop-down list box arrow to display a list of variables in the Outline dialog box.
❷   Click **SALES** to select this variable and review the outline. See Figure 4-12.

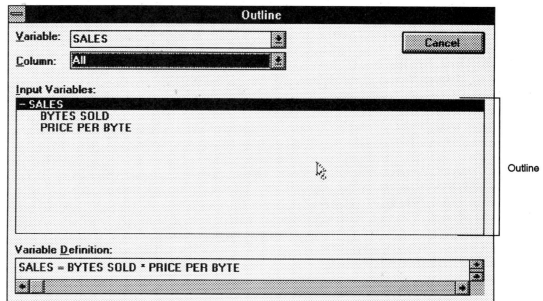

Figure 4-12
Outline
of SALES

❸   Click the **CANCEL button** to leave the outline mode.

Now that Herbie and Pattie have a better understanding of the interactions among the variables in their model, they are ready to explore changes to their key assumptions.

Performing a What If Analysis

What if allows you to *temporarily* change your model so you can quickly see their effect. Whenever you are performing a what if, you get a solution that contains changes dictated by what if statements. What if statements are similar to the statements you enter in your original model. When you enter your what if statement, you may refer to a variable in your original model by its name. You may even decide to create new variables. When performing a what if, you can enter as many what if statements as you like.

A what if statement can contain a **circular definition** with the same variable, in the same column, appearing on both sides of the equal sign, in one statement. In the solution of the original model, this causes simultaneous equations. In **simultaneous equations,** two or more variables are defined in terms of each other. In a what if, a circular definition merely says to use the solution value from the proceeding solution. Whenever this occurs in a what if statement, IFPS has a special way of performing the calculations. It means that IFPS will go look at the last solution of the model, get the value from that solution, and use it in calculating the what if.

Herbie and Pattie decide to explore several what if scenarios to evaluate the following potential courses of action:

1. The EBT and ROS with maximum sales before another salesperson needs to be hired with 14 units sold each quarter.
2. The EBT and ROS at maximum sales as in 1 above and an average selling price per unit of $1500 *more* than their initial estimate.

Creating a What If

In creating a what if, you use a Case window. A **Case window** is a window in which you place the equations you wish to apply to your model for a what if scenario that you obtain from the solution for that scenario. Pattie writes out a planning analysis sheet for the what if scenario they would like to explore (Figure 4-13).

Planning Analysis Sheet

My goal:
To see what the maximum number of units for Bytes sold would be before adding
an employee.

What results do I want to see?
EBT and ROS for the quarterly model.

What information do I need?
Bytes sold [each quarter] = 14

What calculations will I perform?
BYTES SOLD = 14

Figure 4-13 Planning Analysis Sheet for What If

Reference Window

Creating a What If Analysis
■   Click the Model window to select the desired model.
■   Click the What If button in the toolbar.
■   Type the equation you want for the what if analysis.   *or*   Copy the variable from the Model window and edit the equation to revise it for your what if.
■   Click the Solve button in the toolbar, then click the OK button to accept the solution of all the variables and columns.

Let's see how to create a what-if scenario for 14 units sold each quarter to examine the ROS and EBT.

To create a what if scenario:

❶   Click the **Model PROJECT3 window** to make it the active window.

TROUBLE? If the window is not in the desktop then, reopen the window.

❷   Click the **What If button** in the toolbar.

❸   Type **BYTES SOLD = 14** in the Case window. Since this is the only what if statement, you can obtain a solution.

TROUBLE? If you use the wrong variable in the Case window, you will get the wrong answer. So, make sure that BYTES SOLD is the variable. If it is not the variable, then change the Case window so it contains the desired formula.

❹   Click the **Solve button**, then click the **OK button** to accept the solution of all variables and columns that is displayed in the Case window. See Figure 4-14.

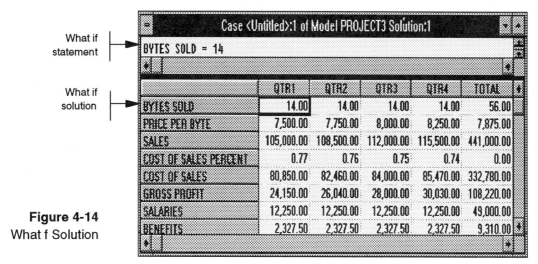

What if statement

What if solution

Figure 4-14
What f Solution

❺   Scroll the window to view the **EBT** and **ROS** for the what if solution.

Now that you have the basics of creating and solving a what if, let's try solving the other alternative. Herbie wants the sales level to be the same as in his first what if case, but he wants to increase the selling price per unit by 1500. This what if continues from the prior what if because another formula is added to the what-if case. Let's see how to continue the what if from the last scenario so the selling price per unit is $1500 *more* than their initial estimate.

To continue a what if:

❶   Position the edit cursor after the last statement in the Case window and press the **[Enter]** key to insert a blank line in the Case window.

❷   Type: **PRICE PER BYTE = PRICE PER BYTE + 1500**
That is, the price is increased by 1500 from the original solution value.

❸   Click the **Solve button** in the toolbar, then click the **OK button** to display all variables and columns for the continued what if solution. See Figure 4-15.

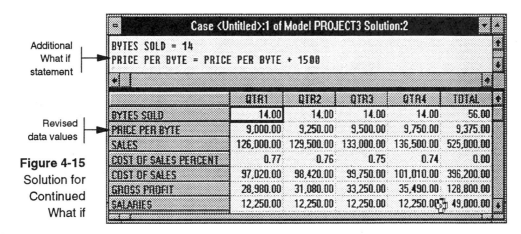

Additional What if statement

Revised data values

Figure 4-15
Solution for Continued What if

Saving the What If Case

Herbie thinks the last what if case should be saved for future reference because he expects additional alternatives will be investigated from this scenario. He decides to save it as **WHATIF1**. Visual IFPS saves this what if as a **CASE** in the models and reports files. It can be accessed for further use with the Get Case button in the toolbar.

Reference Window

Saving a What if Case
■ Click File, then click Save As to display the Save As dialog box.
■ Type the name you want for the what if case in the Entity Name text box.
■ Click the OK button to save the what if statements as a case.

Save the what if case as WHATIF1.

To save a what if:

❶ Click the **Control box** of the Case window, then click **Close**.

❷ Click the **Yes button** in the dialog box to save the what if case.

❸ Type **WHATIF1** in the Entity Name text box, by entering a name in the text box you are automatically saving the what if as a case.

❹ Click the **OK button** to complete saving the what if statements as a case.

Using Variance to Compare Solutions

After saving the what if, Herbie wants to review and compare the what if solution against that of the base solution. A **variance** is the difference between two model solutions. Let's see how a variance is calculated.

To calculate the variance between the what if and base solutions:

❶ Click the **Variance button** in the toolbar to display the Variance from Solution dialog box. See Figure 4-16.

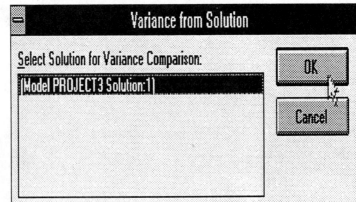

Figure 4-16
Variance from
Solution Dialog
Box

TROUBLE? If Visual IFPS will not allow you to do the variance solution, click the Model window title bar for PROJECT3, click Solve, and click the OK button.

Click the Case window, then click Solve. Click the OK button. Now, repeat Step 1.

❷   Click the **OK button** to calculate the variance. Only those variables that have changed are displayed in the variance window. Notice that SALARIES, BENEFITS, INTEREST, and DEPRECIATION are not shown because they remain unchanged. See Figure 4-17.

Variance Model PROJECT3 Case ⟨Untitled⟩:1 Solution:2 vs Solution:3	QTR1	QTR2	QTR3	QTR4	TOTAL
BYTES SOLD	6.00	4.00	2.00		12.00
PRICE PER BYTE	1,500.00	1,500.00	1,500.00	1,500.00	1,443.18
SALES	66,000.00	52,000.00	37,000.00	21,000.00	176,000.00
COST OF SALES	50,820.00	39,520.00	27,750.00	15,540.00	133,630.00
GROSS PROFIT	15,180.00	12,480.00	9,250.00	5,460.00	42,370.00
ADMIN EXPENSE	1,518.00	1,196.00	851.00	483.00	4,048.00
TOTAL EXPENSES	1,518.00	1,196.00	851.00	483.00	4,048.00
EBT	13,662.00	11,284.00	8,399.00	4,977.00	38,322.00
ROS	14.39	8.80	4.92	2.33	6.29

Figure 4-17
Variance
Solution

❸   Click **File**, then click **Print** to print the variance calculation.

Examining Alternatives with Goal Seeking

Goal seeking lets you solve your model *backwards*. You can specify a "goal" value that you want a particular variable to have and then select a variable that you want to allow to take on whatever values are necessary. This will allow your first variable to have the values you specified when the model is solved. So, with goal seeking, you are focusing your analysis on two variables. For one of these variables, you specify the values you want in your solution. The other variable is varied by whatever values that are required so that the first variable's values can be attained.

Column-by-Column Goal Seeking

Herbie and Pattie created a planning analysis sheet of their goal seeking alternatives for their quarterly model (Figure 4-18).

Planning Analysis Sheet

My goal:
Examine alternatives that produce these outcomes:
1. Earnings Before Tax of 1000 in each quarter.
2. Earnings Before Tax of 0 in each quarter.
3. Earnings Before Tax of 0 in the second quarter.
4. Return On Sales of 10% in the fourth quarter.

What information do I need?
1. Number of Bytes Sold
2. Price per Byte
3. Price per Byte
4. Price per Byte

What results do I want to see?
Revenues and expenses for the next four quarters and their annual total.

What calculation will I perform?
Backward solution of formulas in my quarterly model.

Figure 4-18 Planning Analysis Sheet for Goal Seeking

Herbie and Pattie want IFPS to determine the number of Byte computers sold for each quarter such that the EBT is 1000. Once this has been determined for the first quarter, it is then determined for each of the other three quarters, one at a time. In IFPS, this is a column-by-column goal seek because a goal is achieved in each individual column. As Figure 4-19 illustrates, IFPS sets the EBT in the first column and solves for the BYTES SOLD. After finishing column one, IFPS proceeds in turn to each of the other columns.

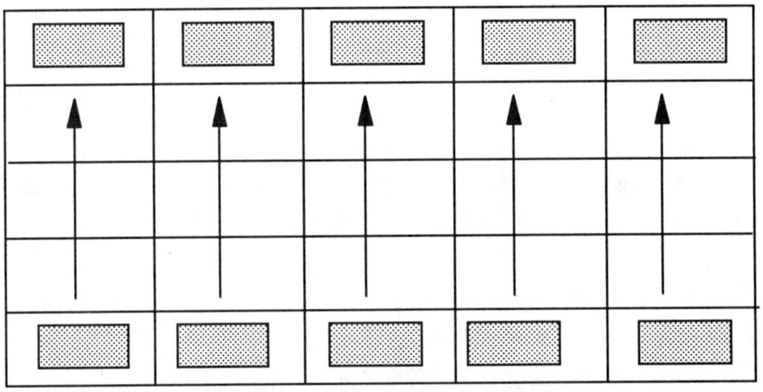

Figure 4-19
Column-by-Column
Goal Seeking

Herbie wants to see how many Byte computers need to be sold to achieve an EBT of 1000 in each quarter. Let's see how to do a column-by-column goal seek, in which Herbie wants the value for the EBT formula to be 1000.

Reference Window

Performing a Goal Seek Analysis

- Click the Goal Seek button in the toolbar.
- Click the Goal Variable drop-down list arrow and select the variable whose value you know.
- Click the Column drop-down list arrow and select the desired column(s).
- Click the Goal Expression box and type the goal value.
- Click the Adjust Variable drop-down list and select the variable you what to find.
- Click the Column drop-down list arrow and select the desired column(s).
- Click the Solve button to calculate the goal seek solution.

To perform a goal seek for an EBT of 1000:

❶   Click the **Model PROJECT3 window** to make this the active window.

❷   Click the **Goal Seek button** in the toolbar to display the Goal Seek dialog box. See Figure 4-20.

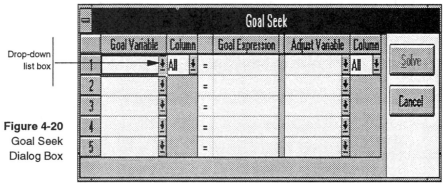

Drop-down list box

Figure 4-20
Goal Seek
Dialog Box

❸   Click the **Goal Variable** drop-down list arrow to display a list of the model's variables.

❹   Click **EBT** to select it.

TROUBLE? If you select a variable other than EBT, change it to EBT by clicking the Goal Variable drop-down list arrow again, then select EBT.

❺   Click the **Goal Expression** text box and type **1000** to enter the goal value.

TROUBLE? If you type something other than 1000, click the Goal Expression text box again and retype 1000.

❻   Click the **Adjust Variable** drop-down list arrow to display a list of the model's variables, then click **BYTES SOLD** to select it. See Figure 4-21.

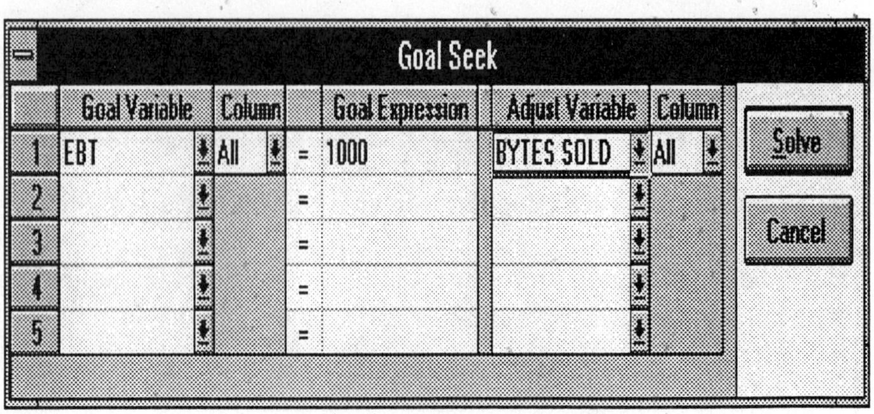

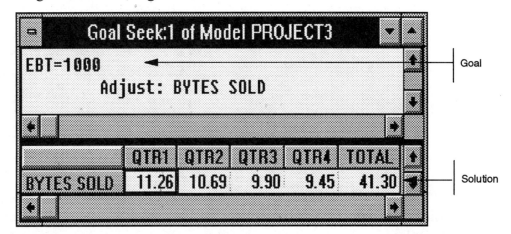

Figure 4-21
Goal Seek
Dialog Box
with Variables
Specified

TROUBLE? If you select a variable other than BYTES SOLD, change it to BYTE SOLD by clicking the Goal Variable drop-down list arrow again, then select BYTES SOLD.

❼ Click the **Solve button** to carry out the goal seeking calculation and display the goal seeking solution. See Figure 4-22.

Figure 4-22
Solution to
Goal Seek

After completing the analysis for an EBT of 1000, Herbie is ready to calculate the break-even point in units for EBT when the PRICE PER BYTE sold is the adjustment variable. The break-even alternative uses the same goal seeking command as in the last alternative, except the goal is now an EBT of zero and the adjustment variable is changed. After you complete the goal seek, then print the solution. Let's do the break-even analysis for EBT.

To use goal seek for break-even analysis:
❶ Click the **Model PROJECT3 window** to make it the active window.
❷ Click the **Goal Seek button** in the toolbar.
❸ Click the **Goal Variable** drop-down list box and select **EBT.**
❹ Click the **Goal Expression** box, delete the number in the box, then type **0** (zero) to specify the goal value.

TROUBLE? If you type another value instead of 0, click the goal expression box again and retype 0.

❺   Click the **Adjust Variable** drop-down list box and select **PRICE PER BYTE.**

❻   Click the **Solve button** to carry out the goal seeking calculation and display the goal seeking solution. See Figure 4-23.

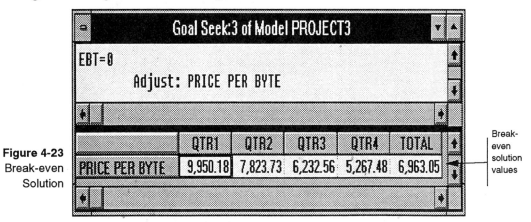

Figure 4-23
Break-even
Solution

Break-
even
solution
values

Now, let's print the solution to the goal seek.

To print the goal seek.

❶   Click the **Solution window** in the Goal Seek window to make it the active window.

❷   Click the **Solve button** in the toolbar, and then click the **OK button** to display the entire solution.

❸   Click **File**, then click **Print** to print the solution.

What If and Goal Seeking: A Great Pair

You can team up what if and goal seeking to provide a strong analytical capability. Using many what if statements and then solving these with a goal seek, you can make temporary changes to your model. Herbie first wants to see the solution with BYTES SOLD set to 14 and then determine the PRICE PER BYTE for an EBT of 10000. Let's see how a goal seek and a what if are combined.

To accomplish what if and goal seeking together:

❶   Click the **Model PROJECT3 window** to make it active.

❷   Click the **What If button** in the toolbar.

❸   Type **BYTES SOLD = 14,** then click the **Solve button** and click the **OK button** to display the solution with the what if.

❹   Click **Analysis**, then click **Goal Seek.**

❺   Click the **Goal Variable** drop-down list box and select EBT.

❻   Click the **Goal Expression** text box and type **10000.**

❼   Click the **Adjust Variable** drop-down list box and select **PRICE PER BYTE** to complete specifying the goal seek.

❽   Click the **Solve button** to display the combined what if and goal seeking results. See Figure 4-24.

Goal seek calculation

What if values

Goal Seek:2 of Case <Untitled>:1 of Model PROJECT3 Solution:2

EBT=0

Adjust: PRICE PER BYTE

	QTR1	QTR2	QTR3	QTR4	TOTAL
BYTES SOLD	14.00	14.00	14.00	14.00	56.00
PRICE PER BYTE	5,685.82	5,588.38	5,342.20	5,267.48	5,470.97
SALES	79,601.45	78,237.33	74,790.75	73,744.73	306,374.25
COST OF SALES PERCENT	0.77	0.76	0.75	0.74	0.00
COST OF SALES	61,293.12	59,460.37	56,093.06	54,571.10	231,417.64
GROSS PROFIT	18,308.33	18,776.96	18,697.69	19,173.63	74,956.61
SALARIES	12,250.00	12,250.00	12,250.00	12,250.00	49,000.00
BENEFITS	2,327.50	2,327.50	2,327.50	2,327.50	9,310.00
ADMIN EXPENSE	1,830.83	1,799.46	1,720.19	1,696.13	7,046.61
DEPRECIATION	1,500.00	2,000.00	2,000.00	2,500.00	8,000.00
INTEREST	400.00	400.00	400.00	400.00	1,600.00
TOTAL EXPENSES	18,308.33	18,776.96	18,697.69	19,173.63	74,956.61
EBT	0.00	0.00	0.00	0.00	0.00
ROS	0.00	0.00	0.00	0.00	0.00

Figure 4-24
Combined
What if and
Goal Seek
Solution

Single-Column Goal Seeking

Herbie and Pattie have been considering some additional goal-seeking alternatives for their quarterly model. They want to know the PRICE PER BYTE for the second quarter that would yield break-even with an EBT of zero for the same quarter. They want Visual IFPS to determine a PRICE PER BYTE for only the second quarter such that EBT is zero for that quarter. In Visual IFPS, this is a single-column goal seek because a goal is achieved for one column only. As Figure 4-25 illustrates, IFPS sets the EBT in the second quarter to zero and solves for only PRICE PER BYTE for that quarter.

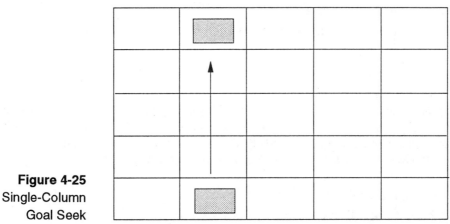

Figure 4-25
Single-Column
Goal Seek

Let's see how a single-column goal seek works for an EBT of zero and find what the PRICE PER BYTE would be.

To conduct a single-column goal seek:

❶   Click the **Model PROJECT3 window** to make it the active window.

❷   Click the **Goal Seek button** in the toolbar.

❸   Click the **Goal Variable** drop-down list arrow and select **EBT**.

❹   Click the **Column** drop-down list arrow next to the Goal Variable, and select **QTR2** to specify the desired column.

❺   Click the **Goal Expression** text box and type **0 (zero)**.

❻   Click the **Adjust Variable** drop-down list arrow and select **PRICE PER BYTE**.

❼   Click the **Column** drop-down list arrow next to the Adjust Variable, and then select **QTR2** to specify the desired column.

❽   Click the **Solve button** to calculate the goal seek. See Figure 4-26.

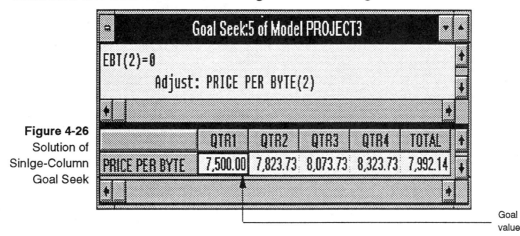

Figure 4-26
Solution of
Sinlge-Column
Goal Seek

Goal value

TROUBLE? If the message "Column 'ALL' cannot be mixed with specific columns" displays, then click OK and change the column that is ALL to QTR2.

Across-Column Goal Seeking

Herbie and Pattie wants to obtain a ROS of 10 percent for the fourth quarter. Herbie suggests they try a different type of goal seeking to find the PRICE PER BYTE in the first quarter that yields a ROS of 10 percent in the fourth quarter. Across-column goal seeking lets Herbie and Pattie specify a value in one cell of the solution matrix and solve for the value of another cell, as Figure 4-27 illustrates.

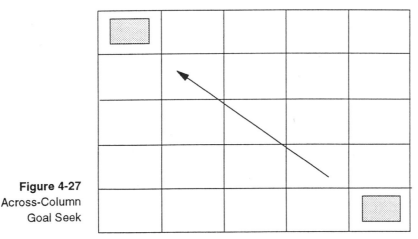

Figure 4-27
Across-Column
Goal Seek

Let's see how to do an across-column goal seek for an ROS of 10 percent and solve for the PRICE PER BYTE.

To do an across-column goal seek:

❶   Click the **Model PROJECT3 window** to make this the active window.

❷   Click the **Goal Seek button** in the toolbar to display the Goal Seek dialog box.

❸   Click the **Goal Variable** drop-down list arrow and select **ROS.**

❹   Click the **Goal Expression** box, delete the number in the box, then type **10** to specify the goal value.

> **TROUBLE?** If you type something other than 10, just click the goal expression box again and retype 10. Remember that ROS is in percent, so do not enter .10 or 10%, because this will give you one-tenth of one percent.

❺   Click the **Column** drop-down list arrow next to the Goal Variable and select **QTR4**.

❻   Click the **Adjust Variable** drop-down list arrow and select **PRICE PER BYTE**.

❼   Click the **Column** drop-down list arrow next to the Adjust Variable, and then select **QTR1**.

❽   Click the **Solve button** to display the results for the goal seek. See Figure 4-28.

Figure 4-28
Solution of
Across-Column
Goal Seek

Column number

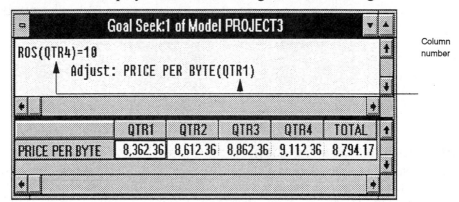

❾   Click the **Solve button**, then click the **OK button** to display the solution for the entire model with the goal seek. See Figure 4-29.

Figure 4-29
Solution of
Entrie-Model
Across-Column
Goal Seek

Goal Seek:1 of Model PROJECT3 Solution:1

ROS(QTR4)=10
     Adjust: PRICE PER BYTE(QTR1)

	QTR1	QTR2	QTR3	QTR4	TOTAL
BYTES SOLD	8.00	10.00	12.00	14.00	44.00
PRICE PER BYTE	8,362.36	8,612.36	8,862.36	9,112.36	8,794.17
SALES	66,898.85	86,123.57	106,348.28	127,572.99	386,943.69
COST OF SALES PERCENT	0.77	0.76	0.75	0.74	0.00
COST OF SALES	51,512.12	65,453.91	79,761.21	94,404.01	291,131.25
GROSS PROFIT	15,386.74	20,669.66	26,587.07	33,168.98	95,812.44
SALARIES	12,250.00	12,250.00	12,250.00	12,250.00	49,000.00
BENEFITS	2,327.50	2,327.50	2,327.50	2,327.50	9,310.00
ADMIN EXPENSE	1,538.67	1,980.84	2,446.01	2,934.18	8,899.70
DEPRECIATION	1,500.00	2,000.00	2,000.00	2,500.00	8,000.00
INTEREST	400.00	400.00	400.00	400.00	1,600.00
TOTAL EXPENSES	18,016.17	18,958.34	19,423.51	20,411.68	76,809.70
EBT	-2,629.44	1,711.31	7,163.56	12,757.30	19,002.74
ROS	-3.93	1.99	6.74	10.00	4.91

Adjust Value

Goal value

Herbie and Pattie have a much better understanding of their budget for next year. With the insight they gained in exploring their model, they are confident that Buffalo Computer Systems will be a success.

Questions

1. Advanced model interrogation encompasses the _____ system capabilities of Visual IFPS.
    a. decision
    b. transaction
    c. expert
    d. explanation

2. The _____ command describes changes in data values between adjacent columns that are calculated in a model.
    a. ANALYZE
    b. OUTLINE
    c. GOAL SEEK
    d. EXPLAIN

3. The _____ command illustrates numerically which variables are used in calculating a variable.
    a. ANALYZE
    b. OUTLINE
    c. GOAL SEEK
    d. EXPLAIN

4. The _____ command causes both direct and indirect input variables to be displayed for a selected variable.
    a. ANALYZE
    b. OUTLINE
    c. GOAL SEEK
    d. EXPLAIN

5. The _____ command lets you solve your model backwards.
    a. ANALYZE
    b. OUTLINE
    c. GOAL SEEK
    d. EXPLAIN

6. _____ equations are those in which two or more variables are defined in terms of each other.
    a. Tax
    b. Multiple
    c. Simultaneous
    d. Same

Case Problems

1. Good Morning Products

At Good Morning Products (GMP), Kim and Frosty have been reviewing the budget for the California plant. They asked Crush to interrogate their quarterly model to address several questions. (The quarterly model was created in Tutorial 2 Case Problem 1.) If you have not created this model yet, go back to Tutorial 2 and create the model before examining the questions below:

 a. Why did sales revenue go down in the third quarter?

 b. Why did EBT go up in the third quarter?

 c. Why did EBT go up so much in the fourth quarter?

2. Good Morning Products

To assist Chris and Jennifer in preparing better documentation for Good Morning Products, prepare the answers to the following questions :

 a. Analyze variable costs.

 b. Analyze fixed costs.

 c. Create an outline of ROS.

 d. Create an outline of total costs.

3. The Woodcraft Furniture Company

At Woodcraft Furniture, Ray and Talbert have been reviewing their quarterly budget by month for the main Woodcraft division. They want to interrogate their model to gain insight into several questions. (The quarterly model was created in Tutorial 2 in Case Problem 2.) If you have not created this model yet, go back to Tutorial 2 and create the model before exploring the questions below:

 a. Why did TOTAL SALES go up in September?

 b. Why did INCOME BEFORE TAXES go up in August?

 c. Why did RETURN ON SALES go up so much in September?

4. The Woodcraft Furniture Company

To assist you in preparing better documentation for Woodcraft Furniture, answer the following questions:

 a. Analyze OPERATING EXPENSES.

 b. Analyze OPERATING PROFIT.

 c. Create an outline of ROS.

 d. Create an outline of TOTAL SALES.

5. The Last National Bank

At Last National Bank, J. J. and Carrie have been reviewing the budget for the bank. They want to interrogate their quarterly model to address several questions. (The quarterly model was created in Tutorial 2 Case Problem 3.) If you have not created this model yet, go back to Tutorial 2 and create the model before examining the following questions:

 a. Why did REVENUES go up in February?

 b. Why did OTHER INVESTMENTS go up so much in March?

 c. Why did REAL ESTATE dip in February?

6. The Last National Bank

To assist Carrie and J. J. in preparing better documentation of Last National Bank, answer the following questions:

 a. Analyze NET INCOME.

 b. Analyze TOTAL EXPENSES.

 c. Create an outline of NET INCOME.

 d. Create an outline of ASSETS.

7. Harvest University

As chief financial officer, you have been reviewing Harvest's budget for next year. You want to question the quarterly model to explore several concerns. (The quarterly model was created in Tutorial 2 in Case Problem 4.) If you have not created this model yet, go back to Tutorial 2 and create the model before examining the questions below:

  a. Why did CREDIT HOURS go down so much in summer?

  b. Why did TOTAL EXPENSES peak in winter?

  c. Why did TOTAL SALARIES go down in spring?

8. Harvest University

You would like better documentation for the Harvest budget. Prepare the answers to the following questions:

  a. Analyze TUITION.

  b. Analyze TOTAL EXPENSES.

  c. Create an outline for RESERVE.

  d. Create an outline for LAB FEES.

9. Midwest Universal Gas

At Midwest Universal Gas (MUG), Mary and Sam have been reviewing MUG's budget for next year. Sam wants you to interrogate their quarterly model to explore several questions. (The quarterly model was created in Tutorial 2 in Case Problem 5.) If you have not created this model yet, go back to Tutorial 2 and create the model before examining the questions below:

  a. Why did SALES go down in the third quarter?

  b. Why did NET INCOME go up in the third quarter?

  c. Why did ROI go up so much in the fourth quarter?

10. Midwest Universal Gas

Sam Wright, at Midwest Universal Gas, would like better documentation for the company's budget. He wants you to prepare the answers to the following:

  a. Analyze TOTAL REVENUE.

  b. Analyze TOTAL EXPENSES.

  c. Produce an outline of ROI.

  d. Produce an outline of TOTAL EXPENSES.

11. General Memorial Hospital

At General Memorial Hospital (GMH), Berry and Gloria have been reviewing GMH's budget for next year. Berry wants you to examine their quarterly model to explore several questions. (The quarterly model was created in Tutorial 2 in Case Problem 6.) If you have not created this model yet, go back to Tutorial 2 and create the model before examining the questions below:

  a. Why did IN PATIENT go up in May?

  b. Why did NURSING go down in June?

  c. Why did BAD DEBTS peak in May?

12. General Memorial Hospital

Berry, at GMH, would like better documentation for their budget. He wants you to prepare the answers to the following questions:

  a. Analyze TOTAL REVENUES.

  b. Analyze BAD DEBTS.

  c. Produce an outline of NET INCOME.

  d. Produce an outline of DOCTOR STAFF.

13. River City

At River City (RC), Frank has been reviewing RC's budget for next year. Frank wants you to question their quarterly model to explore several questions. (The quarterly model was created in Tutorial 2 Case Problem 7.) If you have not create this model yet, go back to Tutorial 2 and create the model before investigating the questions below:

a. Why did BENEFITS peak in August?
b. Why did SURPLUS dip in August?
c. Why did TOTAL EXPENDITURE go down in September?

14. River City

Frank would like better documentation for the River City budget. He wants you to prepare the answers to the following:

a. Analyze CITY GOVERNMENT.
b. Analyze BENEFITS.
c. Create an outline of SURPLUS.
d. Create an outline of SALES TAX.

15. Good Morning Products

As a result of Kim's presentation to the board of directors, a number of questions have been raised concerning next year's budget for GM. Your task is to develop projections to address these questions. (The annual model was created in Tutorial 1, Case Problem 1.) If you have not created this model yet, go back to Tutorial 1 and create the model before continuing with the questions below:

a. Crush wants to know the break-even point in the number of bottles of Liquid Gold sold for the year. He defines break-even to be the case in which EBT is zero.
b. Frosty has asked Kim what the EBT and ROS would be at the production capacity of bottles of Liquid Gold for the year.
c. Chris feels that GM might be able to increase its price and still sell its entire production capacity for the year. He wants to know what price per bottle of Liquid Gold would provide GM with a 14-percent Return On Sales (ROS) at the full production capacity.
d. Although Crush feels this price will insure that GM sells its production capacity of Liquid Gold next year, he wants to know the volume in bottles sold for break-even at this price.
e. Jenny and Kim are in the process of negotiating a new labor contract with the Pressers and Squeezes Union. Frosty wants to know what labor cost per bottle would yield a 14-percent Return On Sales (ROS) at the full production capacity and the current price of $3.19 per bottle of Liquid Gold for the year.
f. Matt and Kim attended last month's international Juicers and Processors Equipment Faire in London. They became interested in a new juicing machine that would allow them to increase their production capacity by 25 percent and at the same time cut the cost of oranges per bottle by 10 percent. Chris has estimated the annual cost of owning and operating this equipment at $150,000. Although Frosty is skeptical about this newfangled machine, he would like to know the selling price per bottle of Liquid Gold to obtain the target Return On Sales of 14 percent with sales of total production capacity with the new equipment.

Quick Check Answers:

a. 659615 bottles	b. EBT = $281000	ROS = 7.341	c. $3.437	d. 447197 bottles
e. $0.6776	f. $3.346			

16. The Woodcraft Furniture Company

Woodcraft's annual budget meeting is about to start. Joe Birch and the other operating managers have gathered for your presentation of next year's anticipated financial performance. Once you conclude your presentation, the questions begin. (The annual model was created in Tutorial 1, Case Problem 1.) If you have not created this model yet, go back to Tutorial 1 and create the model before preceding with the following questions:

a. Ray Jointer is concerned that a strike is imminent unless concessions are made to union demands. Ray would like to see the financial consequences of adding three new employees and increasing all base wages to $12.50 per hour.

b. Joe then asks you how much must prices increase to achieve the same Return On Sales (ROS) if union demands in Question (a) above are met? (*Hint::* Create a new variable called PRICE ADJUSTMENT.)

c. Martha Goodguess objected to an increase in prices. She feels that unit demand can increase. What increase in unit demand must she achieve to maintain the same return on sales as that of the "base case"?

d. Martha is considering lowering the product prices. What would the return on sales be if only prices are reduced by 5 percent and no other changes are made?

e. Joe Birch would like to have a 10-percent Return On Sales (ROS). What prices are required to achieve this performance?

f. If unit demand should drop by 5 percent, what price increase is necessary to maintain the "base case" Return On Sales (ROS)?

g. What prices are necessary for Woodcraft to achieve break-even under the conditions of the union demands specified in Question (a) above?

17. The Last National Bank

J. J. and Carrie were ecstatic with the model you created for them. However, to aid in planning for next year, they have formulated a series of what ifs that they would like to have evaluated. They want you to prepare the following alternatives and be ready for a meeting tomorrow morning. (The annual model was created in Tutorial 1, Case Problem 3.) If you have not created this model yet, go back to Tutorial 1 and create the model before continuing with the questions below:

a. What will be the net interest margin and net interest margin percent if the amount of the Commercial Loans is increased to $30,000?

b. What will be the net interest margin and net interest margin percent if the amount of the Commercial Loans is set as in Question (a) above and the prime rate is increased by 2 percent more than the initial estimate?

c. Based on the original assumptions, what amount of Commercial Loans is required for a net interest margin of 5000, assuming all other loans balances remain unchanged?

d. With all assumptions set to the initial situation, what Commercial Loan amount is necessary for a break-even net interest margin? That is, a net interest margin of zero.

e. J. J. and Carrie estimate that the maximum amount of Commercial Loans is the amount in Question (a). They'd like to know what prime rate would produce a net interest margin of 35 percent at this maximum Commercial Loan amount.

f. Now, what is the break-even point in the amount of Commercial Loans at the prime rate determined in Question (e)?

g. Determine the amount of funds that should be shifted from Money Market Certificates to Regular Savings to obtain a net interest margin percent of 40? [Hint: Create a variable that is the amount of funds shifted.

18. Harvest University

As the chief financial officer, you are preparing your budget presentation for the Board of Regents of Harvest University. You have decided to create the following set of alternatives for the meeting next Friday using the annual model that was created in Tutorial 1, Case Problem 4. If you have not created this model go back to Tutorial 1 and create the model before completing the following questions:

a. What happens to the reserve if the number of credit hours per student is increased to 50?

b. What is the effect on the reserve if the credit hours are increased as in Question(a) above and the credit hour ratio is increased by 50?

c. Based on the original assumptions, how many students are required to produce a reserve of 100000 assuming all other factors remain unchanged?

d. With all assumptions set to the initial conditions, what tuition per credit hour is required for break-even? That is, a reserve of zero.

e. As the CFO, you estimate the maximum number of credit hours per student is as specified in Question (a). What tuition per credit hour would produce a reserve of 250000 at this maximum number of credit hours per student?

f. What is the break-even point in the number of students at the tuition per credit hour determined in Question (e)?

g. After considerable strategic formulation, you have developed an aggressive alternative. You feel the credit hour ratio can be increased to 450 without creating faculty unrest. The number of credit hours per student can be increased to 48. The ratio of full-time to part-time faculty can be decreased to 80 percent. Under this scenario, how many students are required to achieve a reserve of 3 percent of tuition?

19. Midwest Universal Gas

At Midwest Universal Gas, Mary Derrick has reviewed your projections for next year. She is quite pleased that your expected return on investment will be 15 percent. However, she did not get to the top by accepting everything at its face value. Therefore, she instructs you to generate the following "what if" analyses using the annual model that was created in Tutorial 1, Case Problem 5. If you have not created this model go back to Tutorial 1 and create the model before completing the questions below.

a. What will happen to the return on investment if Francis achieves a volume sold of 25 percent in retail sales?

b. If the mix of sales volumes is changed to 25 percent retail and 75 percent wholesale, how many BCF of gas must be sold to achieve a 12 percent return on investment?

c. If the mix of sales volumes is at the anticipated 22 percent retail and 78 percent wholesale, what demand in BCF is required to achieve the 12 percent return on investment?

d. Petro Newgas from production has always predicted costs of production within a percent or two of actual. If the cost of sales should go up to 65 percent of sales, what is the required demand in BCF to achieve a 12 percent return on investment?

e. Prices may swing as high as 10 percent greater than expected due to various legislation. If both retail and wholesale prices are increased by 10 percent, what demand in BCF is necessary to reach a 12 percent return on investment?

f. If demand remains at the expected rate of 720 BCF, what percent must prices be changed to achieve the 12 percent return on investment?

20. General Memorial Hospital

Berry and Gloria have reviewed your projections for Memorial Hospital. Your projection indicated a 27.9 percent return on their investment. While they both felt that this was the most probable situation, they want to explore several other possibilities using the annual model that was created in Tutorial 1, Case Problem 6. If you have not created this model go back to Tutorial 1 and create it before continuing with the questions below.

a. The-bed utilization rate was to drop from 75 percent to 65 percent?

b. Berry, being the optimist, would like to see what the return on investment would be for a 100 percent bed utilization rate. Given the hospital's current price schedule this would be the absolute maximum return for the facility.

c. Gloria wants to know, what is the absolute minimum bed utilization rate at which the hospital would break even with net income of zero?

d. Memorial Hospital strives to maintain a 25-percent (they are optimistic) Return On Investment (ROI). Berry has been considering the addition of two doctors to their staff. The new doctors would serve indigent citizens. Therefore, the bad debt rate might increase to a 10-percent level. What effect would these changes have on the ROI?

e. Given the changes made in Question (d) above, what would the bed-utilization rate need to be to achieve the return on investment?

f. Gloria believes that hospital demand has some price elasticity. First, she would like to know how the average daily charges might be adjusted to achieve the 25-percent Return On Investment (ROI), and then, what if the daily charges are reduced to $175 from $200, what utilization rate is necessary to achieve the 25-percent ROI?

21. River City

Lisa Goodnight is optimistic. She would like to reduce property taxes from their current level of $0.7141 per $100 of actual value. As mayor, the most subtle way to increase revenues is through price level increases that affect the sales tax revenue. Using the annual model created in Tutorial 1, Case Problem 7, she wants to examine several different situations. If you have not created the model in Tutorial 1 yet, then create it before completing the following questions:

   a. Lisa would like to know what would happen to the surplus if price levels in the economy rose by 8 percent.

   b. If prices rose by 8 percent, how low could she reduce property taxes to achieve no surplus?

   c. Frank Frugal does not agree with the price-level increase Lisa favors; instead he sees prices possibly decreasing to 3.5 percent. How would this affect the property tax to maintain a balanced budget?

   d. After Lisa and Frank settle their differences on price levels, they agree that 6 percent is the best compromise. Lisa wants to go to the state legislature and ask for an additional half-cent increase in city sales tax, bringing the tax rate to 1.5 cents per dollar of goods purchased. If she is successful, how low could she reduce the property tax and still maintain a balanced budget?

Notes:

Tutorial 5

Exploring Subroutines, Functions, and Datafiles

Introduction to Functions and Subroutines

In IFPS, functions and subroutines perform special purpose calculations. They provide a shorthand method of performing complex calculations. For example, functions and subroutines are available to calculate net present value, internal rate of return, depreciation, and loan payments. Functions and subroutines in IFPS operate considerably differently.. Functions are used in expressions that appear on the right-hand side of the equal sign and produce only one single-output value in a column. They can be used anywhere in an IFPS expression or equation. A formula can contain one or more functions along with other arithmetic calculations; alternatively, a function could appear alone as the entire expression or equation. On the other hand, subroutines are a complete IFPS model statement. They appear as a separate model statement on a line by themselves. Subroutines have *no* equal signs. Also, subroutines produce *more than one result in each column.* A subroutine creates values for several rows in the solution matrix.

Functions

Functions can perform several different categories of calculations, including : distribution, financial, forecasting, information, mathematical, reference, statistical, and string.

Financial functions in IFPS perform common financial calculations, such as net present value, internal rate of return, and net terminal value. **Mathematical functions** can round numbers, select minimum and maximum values, work with logarithms, and raise numbers to a power or perform exponentiation. With **forecasting functions**, IFPS can project a variable's values by a simple linear regression equation you develop in your model and other related projection techniques. **Statistical functions** allow you to calculate the mean, median, and standard deviation of a variable. Let's look at some of the financial and mathematical functions to explore how these built-in functions are used in IFPS.

Financial Functions

1. Net Present Value

There are two net present value functions in IFPS: Npvc and Npv. **Npvc** computes the net present value for a continuous investment stream where investments may occur in any or all columns of the model. **Npv**, on the other hand, allows an investment to occur in only the first year or first column of the model. The Npv function lets you specify the life of the investment, whereas Npvc does not provide this capability. Npvc is the most popular of the two functions. Let's look at Npvc first.

NET PRESENT VALUE = Npvc (INCOME, RATE, INVESTMENT)
From the Npvc function above, **INCOME** is a variable in the model that contains the stream of cash inflows; **RATE** is the interest rate or discount rate used in discounting the values back to the *first column* in the model; and **INVESTMENT** is a variable that contains the cash outflow stream. You can use whatever variable names you want for the parameters or arguments in the Npvc function. The position within the Npvc function determines the usage as inflows, rate, and outflows. You can use REVENUE instead of INCOME; INTEREST instead of RATE; and EXPENDITURE in place of INVESTMENT. Of course, you can also give the row any name you like. It does not have to be labeled NET PRESENT VALUE. Herbie sketched out a planning analysis sheet for his net present value analysis. (Figure 5-1).

Planning Analysis Sheet

My goal:
Develop a model for net present value.

What results do I want to see?
Net present value for the next five years.

What information do I need?
Columns are Year1, Year2, Year3, Year4, Year5
Income = 100
Rate = 15%
Investment [Year1 through Year3] = 100

What calculation will I perform?
COLUMNS YEAR1, YEAR2, YEAR3, YEAR4, YEAR5
INCOME = 100
RATE = .15
INVESTMENT = 100 FOR 3, 0
NET PRESENT VALUE = Npvc(INCOME,RATE,INVESTMENT)

Figure 5-1 Planning Analysis Sheet for NPVC

Let's create Herbie's model with the Npvc function.

To use the Npvc function in a model:

❶ Click **New** and select **model**.

❷ Type the model that is shown as the calculations to be performed in Figure 5-1.

❸ Click the **Solve button** in the toolbar then, then click the **OK button** to select all variables and columns. See Figure 5-2.

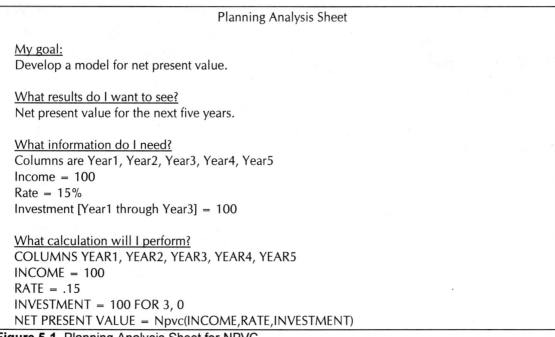

	YEAR1	YEAR2	YEAR3	YEAR4	YEAR5
RATE	0.15	0.15	0.15	0.15	0.15
INVESTMENT	100.00	100.00	100.00	0.00	0.00
NET PREVENT VALUE	-13.04	-24.39	-34.25	22.93	72.64

Model <Untitled>:1 Solution:1

Npvc

Figure 5-2
Solution from
NPVC

TROUBLE? If an undefined variable message displays, then click the Model window and edit the model.

CAUTION ALERT!

Financial functions *must* appear in column one of your model.

Suppose you did not remember the arguments in the Npvc function. Visual IFPS provides a function template. A **template** is a pattern for forming an accurate copy of a function or a subroutine. Delete the net present value formula and re-enter it, using a template to see how you can use the template for a function instead of typing the function.

To use a template for a function:

❶   Click the **Model** window to make it the active window.

❷   Move your **cursor** to the line containing the **Npvc** formula.

❸   Select the entire line by **clicking and dragging** the **cursor**.

❹   Press the **[Delete]** key to delete this line.

❺   Click the **Template button** in the toolbar to display the Templates dialog box. See Figure 5-3.

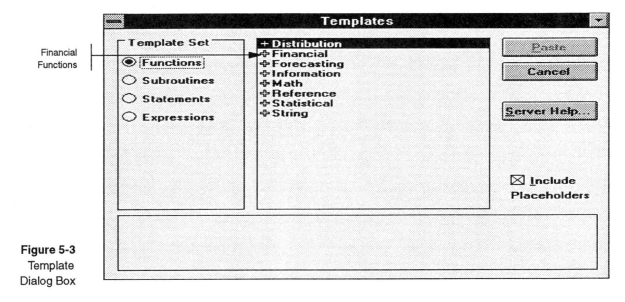

Financial Functions

Figure 5-3
Template
Dialog Box

❻   In the Templates dialog box, click **Financial**, then click **Npvc** to display the template for that function. See Figure 5-4.

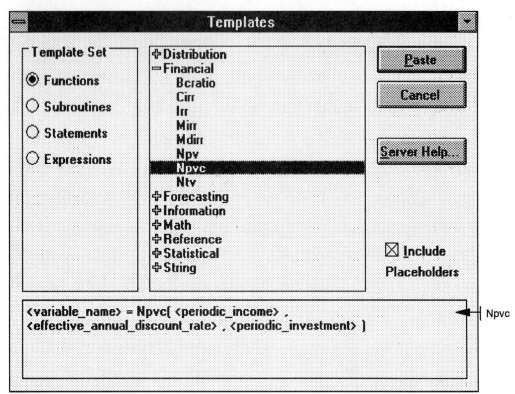

Figure 5-4
Template
for Npvc

TROUBLE? If you did not select financial, then repeat Step 6.

❼ Click the **Paste button** in the Templates dialog box to paste the template of the formula into the model. See Figure 5-5.

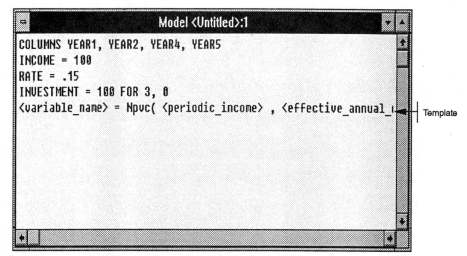

Figure 5-5
Template for Npvc
Pasted into Model

❽ In the template, change the temporary placeholders as follows:

      <variable_name> to **NET PRESENT VALUE**

      <periodic_income> to **INCOME**

      <effective_annual_discount_rate> to **RATE**

      <periodic_investment> to **INVESTMENT**

TROUBLE? If you do not change the temporary names that the template gives you for the function then, you cannot solve the model without causing errors. Remember what you named the input variables for the functions, so you can use those variable names to replace the names in the template.

❾   Click the **Solve button** in the toolbar, then click the **OK button** to select all variables and columns.

TROUBLE? If a message appears indicating undefined variables, then click the Model window and edit the model.

The second net present value function, Npv, is as follows:

NET PRESENT VALUE= Npv(INCOME, RATE, LIFE, INVESTMENT)
For this function, the LIFE is the duration of the project. It may be greater than the number of columns in the model.

2. Net Terminal Value
The Net Terminal Value (Ntv) function calculates the future value rather than a present value. Like Npvc, Ntv assumes outflows are at the beginning of each period and inflows occur at the end of the period. Ntv lets you have both a continuous outflow stream, as well as a continuous inflow stream. It is called or referenced in your model as follows :

NET TERMINAL VALUE = Ntv(INCOME, RATE, INVESTMENT)

3. Benefit Cost Ratio
The Benefit Cost Ration function (Bcratio) calculates a ratio of the total discounted inflows to the total discounted outflows. Discounting is performed similarly as in Npvc. With the Bcratio, though, a ratio is calculated, whereas with Npvc, a subtraction was performed. An example reference in a model follows:

BENEFIT COST RATIO = Bcratio(INCOME, RATE, INVESTMENT)

4. Internal Rate of Return:
IFPS calculates internal rate of return several different ways. The differences stem from the number of columns or time periods in which investments are made. The type of compounding that is to be performed and the occurrence of the inflows and outflows within a column differentiate the available internal rate of return functions. The Irr function calculates the internal rate of return for a stream of inflows and a stream of outflows. It is referenced as follows:

INTERNAL RATE OF RETURN = Irr(INCOME, INVESTMENT)

5. Modified Internal Rate of Return
The Modified Internal Rate of Return function (Mirr) calculates the internal rate of return by discounting all outflows to the first column and then computing the rate of return. This avoids the problem of multiple rates of return for outflows or investments in multiple columns because the entire investment is placed in column 1. This method is sometimes referred to as the *Robichek/Teichroew Method* or the *True Internal Rate of Return*. You decide how to perform your financial calculation of internal rate of return and the underlying assumptions. Mirr provides an alternative. The Mirr function is referenced in your model as follows:

INTERNAL RATE OF RETURN = Mirr(INCOME, RATE, INVESTMENT)

Where INCOME and INVESTMENT are the inflows and outflows (the same as in the Irr function)and the RATE is the discount rate that applied to the INVESTMENT stream to discount it back to column 1.

6. Mid-Year Rate of Return

The Mid-Year Rate of Return (Mdirr) function calculates the internal rate of return based on a single mid-year inflow. The function only allows a single outflow in column 1. Again, this is a front-end investment. If you have investment values in columns other than one, IFPS ignores them in calculating the internal rate of return. The Mdirr function is used as follows:

INTERNAL RATE OF RETURN = Mdirr(INCOME, RATE, INVESTMENT)

7. Continuous Rate of Return

The Continuous Rate of Return (Cirr) function computes the internal rate of return based upon continuous compounding, rather than discrete compounding. The outflows must all take place in column 1. Cirr only allows you to have a single front-end investment. The function is used as follows:

INTERNAL RATE OF RETURN = Cirr(INCOME, INVESTMENT)

Mathematical Functions

IFPS contains a number of mathematical functions. Several more frequently used functions are listed in Figure 5-6 for your reference.

FUNCTION	ACTION
Abs (expression)	Absolute value
Log10 (expression)	Logarithm to base 10
Roundup (expression)	Rounds up to the next-higher number
NatExp (expression)	Computes e (2.7182818...) to the power of the expression
NatLog (expression)	Natural logarithm, to base e
Maximum (expressions)	Selects the largest of two or more indicated values in the list of expressions.
Minimum (expressions)	Selects the smallest value from among the arguments the list of expressions.
Truncate (expression)	Rounds down, regardless of the size of the fractional part of the number

Figure 5-6
Function Table

Other Functions

IFPS contains a number of additional functions. Several of the more popular function are listed here for your reference. The detailed operation of each of these functions is described in the *IFPS User's Manual*.

FUNCTION	ACTION
INTERPOLATION(var-ref, x1,y1,x2,y2,...)	Value by interpolating data points of a piece-wise linear relationship
MOVAVG(ref1, wt1,wt2,...wtn)	Moving average of a variable using weights
NATEST(var-ref)	Test for Not Available condition
POLYFIT(type)	Curve fitting of a polynomial of one of three types

FUNCTION	ACTION
STDDEV(ref1,ref2)	Standard deviation of variable across a column
STEP(var-ref,x1,y1, x2,y2,...xn,yn)	Value by selection from a discontinuous, stepwise, relationship between two variables
TREND(var-ref)	Simple linear regression
VMATRIX(vor-ref,col-ref)	Matrix reference using an expression for the column-reference

Subroutines

Subroutines are available for performing depreciation and loan calculations. Depreciation can be calculated by: straight line, declining balance, sum-of-the-years digits, or accelerated capital cost recovery.

1. Straight Line Depreciation is calculated by the Stline subroutine as follows:

Stline (INVESTMENT, SALVAGE FRACTION, ASSET LIFE, '
PERIOD DEPRECIATION, BOOK VALUE, ACCUMULATED DEPRECIATION)

This subroutine has three *inputs*—INVESTMENT, SALVAGE FRACTION, and ASSET LIFE—and there are three *outputs*—PERIOD DEPRECIATION, BOOK VALUE, and ACCUMULATED DEPRECIATION. As in functions, the names you use are not important; rather, it is the position of the argument in the subroutine list of parameters that determines its use. The subroutine statement (or "call," as it is known) occupies a separate line in the IFPS model. Notice that it does *not* contain an equal sign, which is a distinguishing characteristic of a subroutine. In all subroutines, the input arguments appear first, followed by the output arguments. Herbie sketched a planning analysis sheet for straight-line depreciation analysis (Figure 5-7).

Planning Analysis Sheet

My goal:
Develop a model for straight-line depreciation.

What results do I want to see?
The straight line depreciation for five years.

What information do I need?
Columns Year1, Year2, Year3, Year4, Year5
Investment[Year1] = 1000
Salvage Fraction = 0
Asset Life = 5 years

What calculation will I perform?
COLUMNS YEAR1, YEAR2, YEAR3, YEAR4, YEAR5
INVESTMENT = 1000, 0
SALVAGE FRACTION = 0
ASSET LIFE = 5
STLINE(INVESTMENT, SALVAGE FRACTION, ASSET LIFE,'
      DEPRECIATION, BOOK VALUE, ACCUM DEPRECIATION)

Figure 5-7 *Planning Analysis Sheet for Depreciation Calculation*

Let's use the model in Herbie's planning analysis sheet to calculate straight-line depreciation.

To calculate straight-line depreciation in a model:

❶   Click **New**, select **model**, then click the **OK button**.

❷   Type the model shown as the calculations to be performed in Figure 5-7.

❸   Click the **Solve button** in the toolbar and then the **OK button** to select all variables and columns. See Figure 5-8.

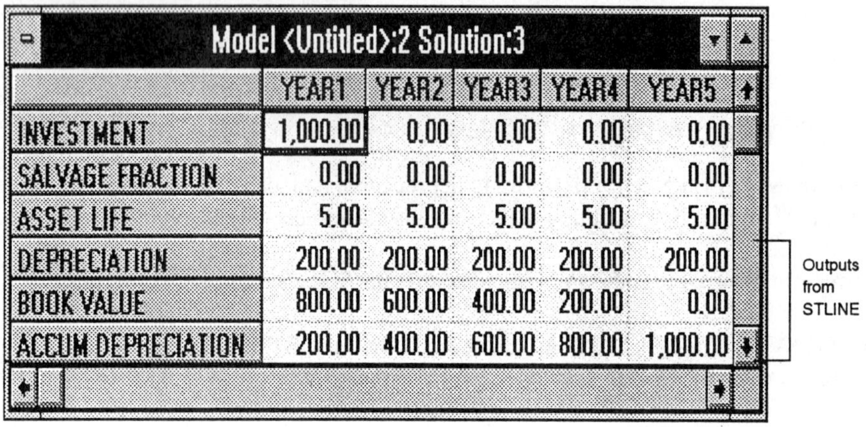

Model <Untitled>:2 Solution:3					
	YEAR1	YEAR2	YEAR3	YEAR4	YEAR5
INVESTMENT	1,000.00	0.00	0.00	0.00	0.00
SALVAGE FRACTION	0.00	0.00	0.00	0.00	0.00
ASSET LIFE	5.00	5.00	5.00	5.00	5.00
DEPRECIATION	200.00	200.00	200.00	200.00	200.00
BOOK VALUE	800.00	600.00	400.00	200.00	0.00
ACCUM DEPRECIATION	200.00	400.00	600.00	800.00	1,000.00

Outputs from STLINE

Figure 5-8
Solution for STLINE

TROUBLE? If a message appears indicating undefined variables, then click the Model window and edit the model.

Suppose you did not remember the arguments for the STLINE depreciation subroutine. Visual IFPS provides a subroutine template just like the function template. Let's delete the STLINE subroutine call and re-enter it using a template.

To use a template for the subroutine:

❶   Click the **Model window** to make it the active window.

❷   Move your **cursor** to the line where the **STLINE** subroutine is located.

❸   Select the entire line by **clicking and dragging** the **cursor**.

❹   Press the **[Delete]** key to delete this line.

❺   Click the **Template button** in the toolbar to display the Templates dialog box.

❻   Click the **Subroutines option button** to select the subroutine templates, then click **Stline** to display the template for this subroutine.

❼   Click the **Paste button** in the Templates dialog box to paste the template of the subroutine into the model.

❽   In the template, change the temporary placeholders as follows:
> **<asset_value>** to **INVESTMENT**
> **<salvage_value_fraction>** to **SALVAGE FRACTION**
> **<asset_life>** to **ASSET LIFE**
> **<period_depreciation>** to **DEPRECIATION**
> **<book_value>** to **BOOK VALUE**
> **<cumulative_depreciation>** to **ACCUM DEPRECIATION**

TROUBLE? If you do not change the temporary names that the template provides you for the function then, you cannot solve the model without encountering errors. Remember what you named the input variables for use in the function, so you can use those variable names to replace the placeholders in the template.

❾ Click the **Solve button** in the toolbar, then click the **OK button** to select all variables and columns. The same solution is displayed, as shown previously in Figure 5-8.

2. Declining Balance Depreciation

The declining balance depreciation subroutine calculates depreciation based on an acceleration constant. Double-declining balance is calculated by using an acceleration constant of 2.00. You can also switch the depreciation method from declining balance to either straight-line or sum-of-the-years digits. This occurs for the year in which the depreciation calculated by the declining balance method is less than or equal to the amount of depreciation calculated by either the straight-line or sum-of-the-years digits methods. A switchover is triggered by a switchover parameter or code (Figure 5-9).

	Code	Action
	0	No switchover
Figure 5-9	1	Straight-line switchover
Switchover Codes	2	Sum-of-years digits switchover

Declining balance depreciation is calculated by a subroutine call such as the following:

Decbal (INVESTMENT, SALVAGE FRACTION, ASSET LIFE, '
ACCELERATION CONSTANT, SWITCHOVER, PERIOD DEPRECIATION, '
BOOK VALUE, CUMULATIVE DEPRECIATION)

Here, the first five arguments through SWITCHOVER are the inputs, and the last three are the outputs. This subroutine has the same three outputs as the straight-line depreciation subroutine.

CAUTION ALERT!

> The acceleration constant is input as a decimal. Use 2.00 for double-declining balance.

3. Sum of the Years Digits Depreciation

The sum-of-the-years digits method of depreciation is implemented with an IFPS subroutine in this manner:

Sumdepr(INVESTMENT, SALVAGE FRACTION, ASSET LIFE,'
PERIOD DEPRECIATION, BOOK VALUE, CUMULATIVE DEPRECIATION)

Here, the input and output arguments or variables are the same as for straight-line depreciation, but only the method of calculation is different.

4. Accelerated Cost Recovery Depreciation

The Accelerated Cost Recovery System (ACRS) depreciation subroutine computes depreciation in conformance with the United States Economic Recovery Tax Act of 1981 as amended by the Tax Equity and Fiscal Responsibility Act of 1982. Under this Act, property placed in service from 1981 to 1986 is divided into two primary categories for depreciation: real estate and other tangible and personal property other than real estate. Real estate is depreciated differently from other property. Property other than real estate is divided into categories based on the expected life of the asset. Known as *class-life categories*, they are grouped into classes of 3-years, 5-years, 10-years, and 15-years. Real estate is divided into regular real estate and low-income real estate. The rate at which these items can be depreciated is different. The category in the depreciation subroutine is used to identify the class of the property being depreciated.

Depreciation of tangible property proceeds by applying a percentage of the asset's value each year. The percentages assume a "half-year convention" during the first year the asset is placed in service, regardless of the actual date of purchase. In cases of real estate, depreciation is based on the month of purchase. Regular real estate is depreciated at a rate that approximates that of the 175 percent declining balance method, whereas low-income real estate is depreciated at a 200 percent declining-balance rate.

Note: New tax laws enacted by the Tax Reform Act of 1986 are not reflected in the ACRS subroutine. The ACRS subroutine does not apply for any assets placed into service after December 31, 1986. The 1986 Act can be modeled with GENDECBAL subroutine. The ACRS subroutine statement is as follows:

Acrsdepr(CATEGORY, PURCHASE YEAR OR MONTH, INVESTMENT, PERIOD DEPRECIATION, BOOK VALUE, CUMULATIVE DEPRECIATION)

The CATEGORY is a variable whose value is selected from a table describing the class of the asset. (Figure 5-10).

	Category	Category of Property
	3	3-year property class
	5	5-year property class
	10	10-year property class
Figure 5-10	15	15-year property class
Category for	1	Regular real estate
ACRS Depreciation	2	Low-income real estate

PURCHASE YEAR OR MONTH is the year the asset is placed in service, except for real estate, in which case, it is the month of purchase. The other variables are the same as in the other depreciation subroutines described above.

Let's see how to create a model using the template for Accelerated Cost Recovery Depreciation.

To calculate Accelerated Cost Recovery Depreciation:

❶   Click **New**, then click **Model**.

❷   Type:
COLUMNS YEAR1, YEAR2, YEAR3, YEAR4, YEAR5
INVESTMENT = 1000, 0

❸   Click the **Template button** in the toolbar to display the Templates dialog box.

❹   Click the **Subroutines option button** to select this set of templates, then click **ARCSDepr** to display the template for this subroutine.

❺   Click the **Paste button** in the Templates dialog box to paste the template into the model.

❻   In the template, change the temporary placeholders as follows:
<category> to **5**
<start> to **1985**
<cost> to **INVESTMENT**
<period_depreciation> to **DEPRECIATION**
<book_value> highlight and press **[Delete]**
<cumulative_depreciation> to **ACCUM DEPRECIATION**

TROUBLE? If you do not change the temporary names that the template supplies you for the function then, you cannot solve the model without causing errors. Remember what you named the input variables for the functions, so you can use those variable names to replace the placeholders in the template.

❼   Click the **Solve button** in the toolbar, then click the **OK button** to select all variables and columns. See Figure 5-11.

Figure 5-11
Solution for
Accelerated
Depreciation

Model <Untitled>:1 Solution:1					
	YEAR1	YEAR2	YEAR3	YEAR4	YEAR5
INVESTMENT	1,000.00	0.00	0.00	0.00	0.00
DEPRECIATION	150.00	220.00	210.00	210.00	210.00
ACCUM DEPRECIATION	150.00	370.00	580.00	790.00	1,000.00

Outputs from ARCS

TROUBLE? If a message appears for any undefined variables, then click the Model window and edit the model.

CAUTION ALERT!

When several depreciation subroutines have the same output variable names; the results are summed for that variable name.

5. Loan Amortization Subroutine
The Loan Amortization subroutine calculates the loan payment amount, interest payment, and payment to principal for either an amortized loan or an unamortized loan. The loan amortization subroutine is accessed as follows:

**Amort (AMORTIZED LOAN, UNAMORTIZED LOAN, ANNUAL INTEREST RATE,'
LOAN LIFE, START COLUMN, PAYMENTS PER COLUMN,'
PAYMENT AMOUNT, PAYMENT TO INTEREST, PAYMENT TO PRINCIPAL,'
LOAN BALANCE)**
Either the AMORTIZED LOAN amount or the UNAMORTIZIED LOAN amount can be set to zero when only one type of loan is calculated. An UNAMORTIZED LOAN is the same as a balloon loan with all principal paid at the end of the loan. The START COLUMN can be a decimal, such as 2.5 to indicate the loan begins at the midpoint of the third column. The PAYMENT AMOUNT, PAYMENT TO INTEREST, PAYMENT TO PRINCIPAL, and LOAN BALANCE are the parameters calculated by this subroutine.

Periods

When IFPS calculates the *financial* functions and subroutines, it assumes each column represents one year in the compounding and discounting of interest rates and in the calculation of period depreciation. If the columns in your model are not years, but months, quarters, or some other interval, then you must use a PERIODS statement in the model to inform IFPS of how the compounding should be performed. The PERIODS statement does not determine whether or not your columns are months or quarters. You must logically determine the time interval for each regular column and enter all your data to correspond to the time scale selected. The PERIODS statement only makes a difference with the financial functions and subroutines. At BCS, Herbie can use this statement in his quarterly model to specify its time interval for any financial functions included in it:

PERIODS 4
Here, the four (4) indicates four time periods per year so the columns represent quarters. The location of the PERIODS statement within the model is not important as long as it is included. A good location is immediately below the COLUMNS statement so that you can easily relate the columns you have specified for your model to the time periods for the financial calculations.

CAUTION ALERT!

> Use a PERIODS statement in a model with financial functions or subroutines when the columns are not years to coordinate the interest rates and depreciation amounts for the desired time interval.

Building in Decisions

Herbie and Pattie met with the marketing representative from Gat Computer Inc. She informed them of Byte's discount structure. The structure is for total sales in any one quarter of less than $75,000 the costs are 77 percent, whereas for total sales of more than $75,000 the costs are 75 percent. As an incentive to their dealers, Gat Computer applies the discount to all sales for the quarter. Pattie sketched out a table of these discounts (Figure 5-12). (In data processing, tables such as this are known as decision tables.):

	Sales Amount	Cost of Sales Percent
Figure 5-12	Less Than $75,000	77%
Decision Table	More Than $75,000	75%

A **decision table** details various conditions that can occur and the appropriate action to take for each condition.

Using IF-THEN-ELSE Statements

Herbie then proceeds to implement the decision table in IFPS using the IF/THEN/ELSE statement. In IFPS, the IF/THEN/ELSE statement is frequently called simply an IF statement. Although shown here on three lines, it could have been entered all on one line. The IF statement consists of three parts. The IF condition appears first, followed by a THEN action and an ELSE action. IFPS evaluates the IF condition and determines whether it is *true* or *false*. If the condition is satisfied or *true*, the THEN action or expression is selected. If the condition is *not* satisfied or *false*, the ELSE action or expression is selected. Let's examine each of these lines.

COST OF SALES PERCENT = IF SALES < 75000 '
Here, SALES are compared to 75000 with a *true* indication if they are less than this amount and a *false* indication if they are greater than or equal to the amount.

THEN .77 '
The value of 77 percent is selected for the column when the condition is *true*.

ELSE .75
The value of 75 percent is selected for the column when the condition is *false*.

The general form of the IF/THEN/ELSE is:

IF relation-condition

      THEN true-expression

ELSE false-expression

Where the relation-condition is of the form: **expression-1 relational-operator expression-2**

Here, expression-1 and expression-2 may be any legal IFPS expression. The IFPS relational operators are shown in Figure 5-13.

Operator	Symbols
Equal to	= or .EQ.
Not equal to	<> or .NE.
Less than or equal to	<= or .LE.
Less than	< or .LT.
Greater than or equal to	>= or .GE.
Greater than	> or .GT.

Figure 5-13

Relational Operators

Notice how each of these relational operators with alphabetic symbols is four characters long with a period at the beginning and ending of each. The true expression may be any legal IFPS expression EXCEPT another IF/THEN/ELSE, while the false expression may be any legal IFPS expression *including* another IF/THEN/ELSE. Let's see how to implement a decision table using IF/THEN/ELSE logic.

To implement a decision table using IF-THEN-ELSE:

❶   Click the **Model PROJECT3 window** to make it the active window. Open this model, if necessary.

❷   Move your cursor to **COST OF SALES PERCENT.**

❸   Change cost of sales percent to:

    COST OF SALES PERCENT = IF SALES < 75000'

                           THEN .77'

                           ELSE .75.

The model is modified as desired. See Figure 5-14.

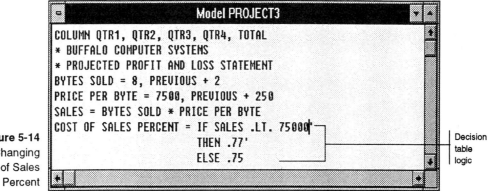

Figure 5-14

Changing

Cost of Sales

Percent

❹   Click the **Solve button** in the toolbar, then click the **OK button** to display the entire solution. See Figure 5-15.

Figure 5-15
Solution for
IF-THEN-ELSE

Model PROJECT3 Solution:4	QTR1	QTR2	QTR3	QTR4	TOT
BYTES SOLD	8.00	10.00	12.00	14.00	
PRICE PER BYTE	7,500.00	7,750.00	8,000.00	8,250.00	7,9
SALES	60,000.00	77,500.00	96,000.00	115,500.00	349,0
COST OF SALES PERCENT	0.77	0.75	0.75	0.75	
COST OF SALES	46,200.00	58,125.00	72,000.00	86,625.00	262,9
GROSS PROFIT	13,800.00	19,375.00	24,000.00	28,875.00	86,0
SALARIES	12,250.00	12,250.00	12,250.00	12,250.00	49,0
BENEFITS	2,327.50	2,327.50	2,327.50	2,327.50	9,3
ADMIN EXPENSE	1,380.00	1,782.50	2,208.00	2,656.50	8,0
DEPRECIATION	1,500.00	2,000.00	2,000.00	2,500.00	8,0
INTEREST	400.00	400.00	400.00	400.00	1,6

Logic
from
table

TROUBLE? If a message appears for any undefined variables, then click the
Model window and edit the model.

❺ Click **Save As** to display the Save As dialog box and type **PROJECT5** in the
Entity Name text box, then click the **OK button** to save the model.

Introduction to Rule Tables

The RULETABLE subsystem is an **expert system** feature of IFPS/Plus that supports integrating rule-
based decision making capabilities in IFPS models. With a **rule table**, a decision table or look-up table is
created that contains a number of different conditions or rules. A series of input variables provides values
for the evaluation of the rules contained in the table. When a match occurs between the input variables and
the values defined for a particular rule, the rule "fires" or is selected and an output value is obtained from
the rule table for use in the solution of the IFPS model that referenced or called the rule table.

The RULETABLE subsystem supports developing rule tables in a manner similar to that of
implementing rule-based decision making with an expert system shell as an inference engine. However,
the application of a rule table requires an IFPS model and any dialog management for rule-based decision
making is implemented through IFPS command files and related IFPS features. The RULETABLE
subsystem serves as the inference engine in processing rules. In general, the RULETABLE subsystem
supports an expert system capability when an IFPS application requires rule-based decision making that is
an integral part of a business model, rather than as a standalone expert system shell.

Decision Table for Rule Table Example

Gat Computer applies a discount to all sales in a quarter for its dealers such as Buffalo Computer
Systems, which serves as a sales incentive. The discount plan is based on a combination of the total dollar
sales and the total number of units sold. The discount is arranged as the following decision table describes:

	RULES		
	1	2	3
IF . . .	Condition		
SALES	<$75,000	=>$75,000 <$150,000	=>$150,000
BYTES SOLD	<10	=>10 <20	=>20
THEN . . .	Action		
COST OF SALES PERCENT	77%	73%	70%

A decision table describes the logic for processing conditional situations, as this example illustrates. Decision tables can be implemented in IFPS using either IF-THEN-ELSE statements or a RULETABLE. Each has it advantages and limitations that are illustrated and described in the sections that follow. The implementation with the IF-THEN-ELSE statement also provides you with an understanding of how a rule table operates and when a rule fires.

IF-THEN-ELSE Implementation

The decision table is implemented with IF-THEN-ELSE statements as illustrated by model PROJ_IF5 (Figure 5-16).

```
*BUFFALO COMPUTER SYSTEMS
*PROJECTED PROFIT AND LOSS STATEMENT
COLUMNS QTR1, QTR2, QTR3, QTR4, TOTAL
BYTES SOLD = 8, PREVIOUS + 2
PRICE PER BYTE  = 7500, PREVIOUS + 250
SALES = BYTES SOLD * PRICE PER BYTE
```

> **COST OF SALES PERCENT = IF SALES .LT. 75000'**
>   **.AND. BYTES SOLD .LT. 10'**
>   **THEN 77%'**
>   **ELSE IF SALES .LT. 150000'**
>   **.AND. BYTES SOLD .LT. 20'**
>   **THEN 73%'**
>   **ELSE 70%**

```
COST OF SALES = SALES * COST OF SALES PERCENT
GROSS PROFIT = SALES - COST OF SALES
SALARIES = 12250
BENEFITS = SALARIES * 19%
ADMIN EXPENSES = SALES * .023
DEPRECIATION = 1500, 2000, 2000, 2500
INTEREST = 1600 / 4
TOTAL EXPENSES = SUM(SALARIES THRU INTEREST)
EBT = GROSS PROFIT - TOTAL EXPENSES
ROS = EBT / SALES * 100
* SPECIAL COLUMN COMPUTATIONS
COLUMN TOTAL FOR BYTES SOLD, SALES, COST OF SALES, '
GROSS PROFIT THRU EBT = SUM(C1 THRU C4)
COLUMN TOTAL FOR PRICE PER BYTE = '
SALES / BYTES SOLD
COLUMN 5 FOR ROS = EBT/ SALES * 100
```

Figure 5-16
IF_THEN_ELSE
Rule Table
Implementation

When the IF-THEN-ELSE statement is solved, IFPS tests the IF-conditions beginning with the first condition and continuing until a "true" condition occurs. When a "true" occurs, the THEN expression is evaluated and testing of IF-conditions is terminated. As a result, the rest of the IF-THEN-ELSE statement is evaluated only when SALES is equal to or greater than $75,000 and BYTES SOLD is equal to or greater than 10. Since the evaluation of the IF-THEN-ELSE proceeds in this cascaded manner, you did not need to include the lower limits for rule 3 in the IF-condition.

RULE TABLE Implementation

In IFPS, rule tables are implemented with the RULETABLE Subsystem. As a result, a rule table is specified separately from your model. The model then references the rule table when the model is solved. Because a rule table exists as a separate entity, it is stored by itself in your Model and Report (M&R) file. The rule table should reside in the same M&R file as your model that references this table. This arrangement allows you to use the same rule table with several different models. The rule table for the Buffalo Computer Systems discount decision appears as Figure 5-17.

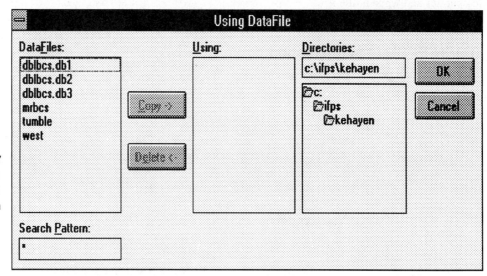

Figure 5-17
Rule Table
in RULETABLE
Subsystem

In this rule table, SALES and BYTES SOLD are the input variables or parameters. ACTION is the resulting value when the rule is evaluated as "true." That is, ACTION is the output parameter. The occurrence of a "true" condition is also known as "firing" the rule. Therefore, when a rule "fires" the output is the value for the ACTION. In this rule table, a comment statement has been included to identify the components of each rule. Each component of the rule is separated from the next component by a comma. The positions of the input parameters determines what will be evaluated, and not the variable names listed in the comment statement. The comma separates the input parameters and the output parameter for each rule and do *not* specify columns in the solution matrix of the model. Usually, the rule table is accessed for evaluation for *each regular column* of the model solution.

The RULE TABLE is referenced in the model PROJ_RT5 using the RULE function (Figure 5-18). The syntax of the RULE function is:

RULE tablename (input1, input2, ..., inputn)
Where an input can be a variable name, a constant, or an expression calculated from variables and/or constants before the value is supplied to the rule table.

```
*BUFFALO COMPUTER SYSTEMS
*PROJECTED PROFIT AND LOSS STATEMENT
COLUMNS QTR1, QTR2, QTR3, QTR4, TOTAL
BYTES SOLD = 8, PREVIOUS + 2
PRICE PER BYTE  = 7500, PREVIOUS + 250
SALES = BYTES SOLD * PRICE PER BYTE
```
COST OF SALES PERCENT = RULE DISCOUNT (SALES, BYTES SOLD)
```
COST OF SALES = SALES * COST OF SALES PERCENT
GROSS PROFIT = SALES - COST OF SALES
SALARIES = 12250
BENEFITS = SALARIES * 19%
ADMIN EXPENSES = SALES * .023
DEPRECIATION = 1500, 2000, 2000, 2500
INTEREST = 1600 / 4
TOTAL EXPENSES = SUM(SALARIES THRU INTEREST)
EBT = GROSS PROFIT - TOTAL EXPENSES
ROS = EBT / SALES * 100
* SPECIAL COLUMN COMPUTATIONS
COLUMN TOTAL FOR BYTES SOLD, SALES, COST OF SALES, '
GROSS PROFIT THRU EBT = SUM(C1 THRU C4)
COLUMN TOTAL FOR PRICE PER BYTE = '
SALES / BYTES SOLD
COLUMN 5 FOR ROS = EBT/ SALES * 100
```

Figure 5-18
Rule Table
Reference
in Model

Let's examine the implementation of the sales discount rule table for Buffalo Computer Systems. First let's create the rule table, then the model is revised to apply the rule table.

To create a rule table:

❶   Click **New**, click **Rule Table** in the **New dialog box**, type the rule table shown in Figure 5-17.

❷   Click **File**, click **Save**, Type **DISCOUNT** as the name for the rule table, click the **OK button** in the Save As Dialog box.

Next, the model is revised to include the function that calls the rule table.

To apply a rule table in a model:

❶   Click the **Model PROJECT3 window** to make it the active window. Open this model, if necessary.

❷   Move your cursor to **COST OF SALES PERCENT.**

❸   Change cost of sales percent to:
     COST OF SALES PERCENT = RULE DISCOUNT (SALES, BYTES SOLD)

❹   Click **Save As** to display the Save As dialog box and type **PROJ_RT5** in the Entity Name text box, then click the **OK button** to save the model.

❺   Click **Solve**, Click the **OK button** to display the solution using the rule table for your review.

TROUBLE? If a message appears for any undefined variables, then click the Model window and edit the model. Now repeat Steps 5 and 6 to solve the model.

In the model PROJ_RT5, the COST OF SALES PERCENT is calculated using, the rule table with the name of DISCOUNT. Input values are obtained from the variables SALES and BYTES SOLD. The rule table shown in Figure 5-17 was created to accept these variables as input parameters. The reference to a rule table uses the RULE function similar to other built-in functions in IFPS. When creating a rule table, you need to coordinate the parameters between their references in the RULE function in the model and their usage in the rule table.

Like an IF-THEN-ELSE statement, a rule table requires an ELSE action. In Figure 5-17, this action was established as UNKNOWN. So, the value "UNKNOWN" would be obtained if none of the rules "fired." The rules in the RULE TABLE are evaluated in a cascaded manner similar to the IF-THEN-ELSE statement. When a rule is "fired," the RULE TABLE processing terminated and the subsequent rules are not evaluated. For this reason, the sequencing of rules in a rule table is an important consideration.

The ELSE value for the above rule table can be modified to use a specific value rather than UNKNOWN (Figure 5-19). Either arrangement of the rule table is equally acceptable.

	* INPUT VALUES CORRESPOND TO VARIABLES:		
Figure 5-19	* SALES,	BYTES SOLD,	ACTION
Rule Table	.LT. 75000,	.LT. 10,	77%
with Specific	.LT. 150000,	.LT. 20,	73%
ELSE Value	ELSE		70%

In the RULETABLE in Figure 5-19, the output or action value was a numeric constant. IFPS/Plus also permits the use of a character text string (Figure 5-20).

Figure 5-20	* INPUT VALUES CORRESPOND TO VARIABLES:		
DISCOUNT Rule	* SALES,	BYTES SOLD,	ACTION
Table with	.LT. 75000,	.LT. 10,	"LOW"
Character String	.LT. 150000,	.LT. 20,	"MEDIUM"
Outputs	ELSE		"HIGH"

These character text strings could also be included in the IF-THEN-ELSE statement of the model. They are not limited to use in rule tables.

A limitation of rule tables, which does not exist for IF-THEN-ELSE statements, is that the output or action from the RULE TABLE must be either a numeric constant or a text string. *The output cannot be computed from an equation.* Equations can only be evaluated in the model, not in a rule table.

You should evaluate each situation in which a decision table is included in a model. Then select a RULETABLE or IF-THEN-ELSE statements to implement your decision table. Choose the method that makes it easiest for you and other end users to understand the rules of your decision tables.

Introduction to Datafiles

Datafiles provide the mechanism by which IFPS achieves model and data independence. With datafiles, you have a single model that can be used with many different datafiles. In this situation, a departmental model is used with a separate datafile for each department. When the same logic applies to each department, or other strategic business units, only one model is required. The unique data for each department resides in a departmental datafile. The datafile is linked to the model and the model is then solved to produce departmental results.

Datafiles are useful when evaluating multiple departments, plants, divisions, branches, companies, strategic business units, product lines, lines of business, alternatives, and so forth. When you are evaluating a complex alternative, such as with a real estate investment, the number of key input variables might easily exceed 25 or 30. By putting all your input assumptions into a datafile, you can review them and make any edits you like before solving your model with the datafile. Additional datafiles are readily created for evaluating other alternatives. Thus, for complex alternatives, as well as with multiple business units, datafiles provide a more convenient means of obtaining a solution.

Until now, when you obtained a solution from a model, the model contained the entire description of your problem both logic and data. Because it was all one unit, you needed to know only the name of the model. Datafiles expand the number of entities that are involved in producing an output solution or report.

Dataflow diagrams pictorially portray how all the pieces of your modeling puzzle fit together to produce the desired solution. They are a convenient software engineering technique, which readily facilitates the illustration of the interactions among models and datafiles. They are a tool of the structured analysis methodology Tom DeMarco describes in *Structured Analysis and Systems Specification*. Dataflow diagrams provide a vehicle that you can use to delineate an integrated system of IFPS models, datafiles, and report definitions. As your system of models becomes more complex, dataflow diagrams become more beneficial in describing the components of your modeling system.

Let's look at an example of some dataflow diagrams as a means of learning the components of this design tool. Figure 5-21 is a dataflow diagram (**DFD**) of a single, simple model that produces one solution. Figure 5-22 expands Figure 5-21 to show the use of a set of datafiles with a single IFPS model. The elements of a DFD are explained as follows:

1. Model (process), represented by circles
2. Reports (dataflows), represented by named vectors or arrows
3. Datafiles (files), represented by straight lines

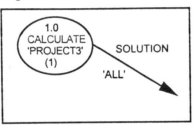

Figure 5-21
Dataflow
diagram of
simple model

Processes are numbered and named with both a long, readily recognizable and easily understood name and an IFPS model name. When a system contains several models, process numbers provide a quick reference to specific models. A long, readily understood name aids in documenting the modeling system for persons other than the individual who created the system. The IFPS model name, which is often a short mnemonic, is enclosed in apostrophes within the process symbol. Enclosed in parentheses at the bottom of the process symbol is the number of times this model is usually executed.

Dataflows also use long descriptive names. Similarly, datafiles use a long descriptive name, an IFPS datafile name enclosed in apostrophes and the number of occurrences enclosed in parentheses. In Figure 5-21, model PROJECT3, which performs the function CALCULATE, is executed once. Model execution results in the SOLUTION, which is created using the "ALL" Solve Option. In Figure 5-22, the IFPS model MASTER is solved a multiple number of times, as indicated by the "n" in parentheses. This is accomplished using a series of "n" DATA datafiles, and produces "n" SOLUTION results using the ALL Solve Option. Notice how the arrow or vector indicates the DATA is input to Process 1.0: CALCULATE. The name appears with the straight-line symbol for the datafile, and *not* on the vector itself, as in the case of the reports. Once a set of datafiles has been created, these names would be added to the diagram as datafile descriptors.

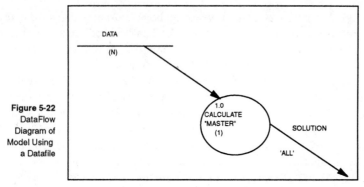

Figure 5-22
DataFlow
Diagram of
Model Using
a Datafile

You could use symbols other than the ones shown here to identify models, reports, and datafiles. The ones used here are those employed with DFDs as described by DeMarco. You can readily draw circles, straight lines, and arrows without the aid of a symbol template. Regardless of your preferences, some type of diagram of the system of models, reports, and datafiles are most useful in describing the interactions of these components of the system.

Herbie and Pattie Wattsun had such a successful year with Buffalo Computer Systems at their initial location in the Tumble Weed Shopping Mall that they decided to open a second location. After reviewing several alternatives, they selected another location in the West Roads Shopping Center. The West Roads location is larger and has more potential customer traffic than the Tumble Weed location. Herbie needs to expand his plan to include the new location. Although he could have created a second model for the West Roads location, he decided to create a single model that he uses with a datafile for each location or branch store outlet. By having only one model, he is assured that the same logic is applied to both locations. Also, if he should decide to revise any of his logic, he will have only one model with which to be concerned. This is particularly useful with larger models. Herbie's modeling system is as shown in Figure 5-23: Model MASTER, which is used with each of the datafiles, TUMBLE and WEST, to produce a SOLUTION for each location. Later, Herbie will extend his analysis to include projections for consolidated results of both locations.

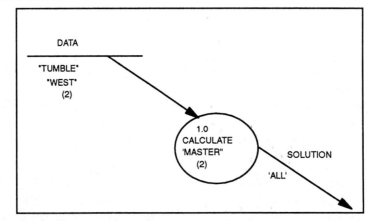

Figure 5-23
Model Master
with Datafiles

Creating a Template Model

A **template model** is an IFPS model that has been set up to receive data from a datafile. DATA is used in the template model to specify which variables obtain their values from a datafile. The data are removed from the model and placed in a datafile. Pattie prepared a planning analysis sheet for their template model and datafiles (Figure 5-24).

KEYPOINT!

A template model insures that the same formulas are used in calculating results from different entities with their unique data values.

Planning Analysis Sheet

My goal:
Develop a template model so plans can be created for several Buffalo Computer Systems outlets.

What results do I want to see?
Revenues and Expenses for each location with the appropriate subtotals.

What information do I need?
Columns are Quarter1, Quarter2, Quarter3, Quarter4
BYTES SOLD, SALARIES, DEPRECIATION, and INTEREST each quarter for each different location.

TUMBLE DATA
BYTES SOLD = 9, 11, 13, 15
SALARIES = 12250
DEPRECIATION 2000, 2000, 2000, 2500
INTEREST = 400

WEST DATA
BYTES SOLD = 15, 17, 19, 23
SALARIES = 14800
DEPRECIATION = 1800, 1800, 1800, 2200
INTEREST = 400

What calculations will I perform?
COLUMNS QTR1, QTR2, QTR3, QTR4, TOTAL
BYTES SOLD = DATA
PRICE PER BYTE = 7500, PREVIOUS + 250
SALES = BYTES SOLD * PRICE PER BYTE
COST OF SALES PERCENT = .77, PREVIOUS - .01
COST OF SALES = SALES * COST OF SALES PERCENT
GROSS PROFIT = SALES - COST OF SALES
SALARIES = DATA
BENEFITS = SALARIES * 19%
DEPRECIATION = DATA
ADMIN EXPENSE = SALES * .023
INTEREST = DATA
TOTAL EXPENSES = SUM(SALARIES THRU INTEREST)
EBT = GROSS PROFIT - TOTAL EXPENSES
ROS = EBT / SALES * 100
*SPECIAL COLUMN COMPUTATIONS
COLUMN TOTAL FOR BYTES SOLD, SALES, COST OF SALES, '
      GROSS PROFIT THRU EBT = SUM(C1 THRU C4)
COLUMN TOTAL FOR PRICE PER BYTE = SALES / BYTES SOLD
COLUMN 5 ROS = EBT /SALES * 100

Figure 5-24 Planning Analysis Sheet for Template Model

Let's create a template model for Herbie to use for BCS.

To create a template model:

❶ Click **New**, select **model**, then click the **OK button**.

❷ Click **Open**, then **PROJECT3**.

❸ Select all of the model by clicking **Edit**, then **Select All**.

❹ Click **Edit** then click **Copy** to copy the selection to the Windows clipboard.

❺ Click the new **Model window** to make it active.

❻ Click **Edit**, then click **Paste** to insert from the clipboard.

❼ Now change the formulas for these variables:

BYTES SOLD = DATA
SALARIES = DATA
DEPRECIATION = DATA
INTEREST = DATA

The model is modified as a template that will obtain these data values from a datafile. See Figure 5-25.

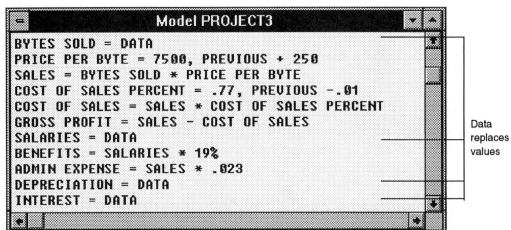

Data replaces values

Figure 5-25
Creating a
Template Model

❽ Click **File**, and click **Save As** to display the Save As dialog box, then type **MASTER** in the Entity Name text box, then click the **OK button** to save the model.

Creating a Datafile

Herbie wants to create a datafile called TUMBLE for input into model MASTER.

Reference Window

Creating a Datafile
■ Click the New button in the toolbar and click Datafile.
■ Type the data you want in the file.
■ Click File, click Save, and type the name for the file in the Entity Name text box.

Let's create a datafile for use with Herbie's template model.

To create a datafile:

❶   Click the **New button** in the toolbar.

❷   Click **Datafile** in the New dialog box, then click the **OK button**.

❸   Type this datafile:
BYTES SOLD = 9,11,13,15
SALARIES = 12250
DEPRECIATION = 1500,2000,2000,2500
INTEREST = 400

❹   Click **File**, click **Save**, type **TUMBLE** in the Entity Name text box, then click the
OK button to save this as a separate datafile.

Now, Herbie wants to create his second datafile WEST:

❶   Click the **New button** in the toolbar, click **Datafile** in the New dialog box, then
click the **OK button**.

❷   Type this datafile:
BYTES SOLD = 15,17,19,23
SALARIES = 14800
DEPRECIATION = 1800 FOR 3,2200
INTEREST = 600

❸   Click **File**, click **Save**, type **WEST** in the Entity Name text box, then click the
OK button to save this datafile.

Using Datafiles

Once Herbie has his template model (MASTER) and his datafiles (TUMBLE and WEST) created, the
next step is to combine the model and each datafile to obtain a solution.

Reference Window

Using Datafiles with Models
■   Click Open, click Model, then click the name of the model you wish to use.
■   Click the Using button, click the name of the datafile you wish to use in the Using Datafile dialog box.
■   Click Copy, then click the OK button to select that datafile.
■   Click Solve, then click the OK button to solve the model using the datafile.

Let's see how to use the template model MASTER using the data from the TUMBLE datafile.

To use a datafile with a template model:

❶   Click **Open,** click **Model** to see a listing of all the models, then click **MASTER**.

❷   Click the **Using button** in the toolbar to display the Using Datafile dialog box.
See Figure 5-26.

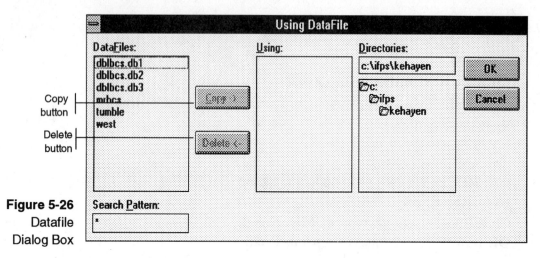

Figure 5-26
Datafile
Dialog Box

❸ Click **TUMBLE**, click the **Copy button**, then click the **OK button** to complete the using specification.

❹ Click the **Solve** button in the toolbar, then click the **OK button**.

TROUBLE? If you do not specify what datafile you will be using before solving the model MASTER, then you will get zeros where the DATA specification was used. So, make sure you specified a datafile in Step 3 before solving the **MASTER** model.

Once you have completed the solution with datafile TUMBLE, you can proceed directly to the solution of Model MASTER with datafile WEST. Let's do that now.

To use a different datafile:

❶ Click the **Model MASTER window** to make it the active window.

❷ Click the **Using button** in the toolbar to display the Using Datafile dialog box.

❸ Click **Tumble**, then click the **Delete button** to remove this datafile.

❹ Click **West** in the datafile list box, click **Copy**, then click the **OK button** to select this datafile.

❺ Click the **Solve button** in the toolbar, then click the **OK button** to see the solution with the West datafile.

Herbie likes the way the template model provides solutions for different locations with the data for each location. With this new template model, Herbie and Pattie need to sit down with their accountant to look at the solution for each location. Since you have completed exploring the alternatives of this tutorial, you may close all the Model and Solution windows and exit Visual IFPS.

Questions

1. _____ are used in expressions that appear on the right-hand side of the equal sign and produce only one single output value in a column.
   a. Functions
   b. Subroutines
   c. Statements
   d. Expressions

2. _____ are a complete IFPS model statement.
   a. Functions
   b. Subroutines
   c. Statements
   d. Expressions

3. Which of the following is *not* a category of functions?
   a. Distribution
   b. Financial
   c. Variable
   d. String

4. _____ are the mechanism by which model and data independence is achieved.
   a. Data
   b. Data stores
   c. Data templates
   d. Datafiles

5. A _____ model is a model that has been setup to receive data from a datafile.
   a. store
   b. template
   c. data
   d. datafile

Case Problems

1. Good Morning Products

Chris Frost, the treasurer of GM, wants you to improve the budget model from Tutorial 2, Case Problem 1 by including the calculation of interest expense and depreciation in the model by using the IFPS built-in subroutines. In discussions with Crush and Kim, interest expense should be calculated on debt of $400,000 at 12 percent interest for 10 years. The debt starts in column 1 and 3 payments are made each quarter (that is, the payments are monthly). Depreciation is to be calculated on assets of $360,000 using ACRS depreciation with an asset class life of 10 years and a purchase year of 1984. Revise your model with rounding to accommodate these changes. Round the values after they have been calculated by the subroutines to preserve your footing. Be sure to specify the correct periods for the interest and depreciation calculations. Save the revised model as GMP5.

2. The Woodcraft Furniture Company

Talbert Pine, the treasurer of Woodcraft Furniture, wants you to revise the quarterly model from Tutorial 2, Case Problem 2 so that interest expense is calculated using the loan amortization subroutine. Interest Expense is to be calculated on an unamortized loan with a balance of $1,836,000 at 8 percent interest rate for 5 years. Replace your previous calculation of Interest Expense with a subroutine call for this loan. Save the revised model as WCF5.

3. The Last National Bank

The loan officers at Last National Bank need to prepare loan repayment schedules. J. J. believes a good way to introduce IFPS to these individuals is by having them use IFPS to produce the schedules. Your task is to set up a model with annual columns for a loan amortization. Use the IFPS AMORT subroutine to calculate a schedule for a $100,000 loan at 12 percent interest for 10 years with monthly payments. Save the model as LNB5.

4. Harvest University

Harvest University is considering the construction to a new $20,000,000 parking facility. They believe they can float a 25-year bond issue at 10 percent tax free interest to finance the structure. Payments on the debt would be made once each quarter. Use an IFPS subroutine to determine the quarterly loan payment. Prepare a loan payment schedule. Save this model as HVS5.

5. Midwest Universal Gas

Sam Wright, comptroller of Midwest Universal Gas (MUG), wants you to create a depreciation schedule using three different methods of depreciation. For each method, the additional investment for next year will be $1,000,000 with a 25-year life and a .25-salvage fraction. Sam wants you to create a schedule of current depreciation under each of these methods ('000 omitted):

1. straight-line,
2. double-declining balance,
3. sum-of-the-years digits.

Also, Sam wants you to add this depreciation to the quarterly model from Tutorial 2 Case Problem 5. He desires to have the model select the maximum depreciation amount from among the three alternatives. In revising the model, remember the depreciation from this new investment must be added to the existing depreciation from existing assets. Save the revised model as MUG5.

6. General Memorial Hospital

Gloria Vander Balance has been instructed by the board of directors of General Memorial Hospital to establish a sinking fund to retire an outstanding debt of $2,000,000. If she can invest the fund at 8 percent interest, how much must she add to the sinking fund each month for 10 years to retire the debt. She is only concerned with the sinking fund for the principal. You then proceed to your desk and reference your dusty Intro to Finance text. You locate the formula for the sum of an annuity:

$$FVIF = \frac{(1+I^n)-1}{I}$$

Where: I = interest rate per month
n = number of months

You also recall the required monthly payment is calculated as:

$$\frac{\$2,000,000}{FVIF}$$

7. River City

River City has issued $30,000,000 in bonds to finance a new city mall and street construction. The bonds were issued at 11.5 percent interest for 20-years. Interest payments are made quarterly on the bonds. Frank Frugal has established a sinking fund for repayment of the principal. Add this interest expense to Frank's revised operating budget making use of the loan amortization subroutine. Use the model from Tutorial 2, Case Problem 7 for revising the budget. Also, determine the quarterly sinking fund payment at 9 percent interest, which is the current rate Frank can obtain on his investment portfolio. Use the formula in Problem 6 to calculate the amount of the sinking fund payment.

8. Good Morning Products

The planning and budgeting model of Good Morning (GM) Products has been functioning very well for GM's board of directors. Since Crush, Kim, and Chris have requested numerous alternatives, you have suggested the use of a template model and datafiles to facilitate the development of various scenarios. Crush has given his approval for the revision. Copy the quarterly model from Tutorial 2, Case Problem 1 and transform it into a template model. Place the data provided below into a DATAFILE. Solve the model with the DATAFILE. Print the template model, the datafile, and the solution.

	1st Quarter	2nd Quarter	3rd Quarter	4th Quarter
Bottles	330000	310000	260000	300000
Price	3.19	3.19	3.39	3.39
General and Admin	23000	23000	26000	26000
Advertising	18000	19000	21000	21000
Interest	16000	16000	16000	16000
Depreciation	25500	25500	25500	25500
Labor per Bottle	0.89	0.89	0.89	0.89
Oranges per Bottle	1.21	1.21	1.21	1.21
Packaging per Bottle	0.57	0.57	0.57	0.57

9. The Woodcraft Furniture Company

The Woodcraft Furniture Company model has performed exceptionally. Joe Birch is so pleased with the quarterly model he wants you to revise it into a template model that will receive monthly data and produce the quarterly projection with the quarterly total. To save time, you simply need to copy the quarterly model from Tutorial 2 Case, Problem 2 and edit it to accept the input variables. Then create a datafile with the input data below, which Joe has provided for you. Solve the template model with the datafile. Print the template model, the datafile, and the solution.

	July	August	September
Table Price	450	450	450
Chair Price	100	100	100
Sofa Price	300	300	300
Employees	157	160	165
Hourly Rate	9.60	9.60	9.60
Hours Worked	174	174	174
Tables Sold	850	900	950
Advertising	97760	103500	109240
Management Salaries	47250	47250	47250
General and Admin	24000	25000	26000
Interest Expense	12240	12240	12240

10. The Last National Bank

At Last National Bank, the asset and liability model has worked so well that J. J. has asked Carrie to create a template model for the monthly projection with a quarterly total. This will allow Carrie to place the assets, liabilities and interest rates in a datafile each time the model is to be solved. Carrie will have one datafile for her monthly solutions of the model. She will continue to use the average daily asset and liability balances as before, and the interest rates will still be entered as annual rates. To save yourself some effort, it is suggested that you copy the quarterly model from Tutorial 2, Case Problem 3 and edit it to change it into the template model. Then, create a datafile that contains the asset, liability, and interest data below, which Carrie has assembled for input into the model. Solve the model with the datafile and produce a solution using the Solve ALL options. Print the solution, the template model and, the datafile.

	January	February	March
Assets:			
(Amounts in Thousands)			
Real Estate Mortgages	32000	31000	29500
Installment Loans	11000	12000	14200
Commercial Loans	27000	29000	33000
Other Investments	2000	2500	3500
Liabilities:			
(Amounts in Thousands)			
Regular Savings	11000	12000	12500
Interest Plus Checking	16000	17800	18200
Money Market Certificates	40000	42000	43300
Other Borrowed Funds	3000	2500	3800
Interest Rates:			
Prime Rate Interest	14%	14.5%	14%
Real Estate Interest	10%	10.1%	10.2%
Installment Loan Interest*	1%	1.1%	1.1%
Commercial Loan Interest*	2%	1.9%	1.9%
Other Investment Interest*	1%	1.1%	1.2%
Regular Savings Interest	5.5%	5.5%	5.5%
Interest Plus Checking Interest	6%	6%	6%
Money Market Interest*	- 3%	-2.5%	-2.5%
Other Borrowed Funds Interest	- 4.5%	-4.0%	-4.0%

* Amount above or below the prime interest rate.

11. Harvest University

As chief financial officer of Harvest University, you want to run your quarterly budget model with several different sets of conditions. To accommodate this, you have decided to develop a template model with your data placed in an IFPS datafile. Copy your quarterly model from Tutorial 1, Case Problem 4 and transform it into a template model. Create a DATAFILE that contains the following data:

	Fall	Winter	Spring	Summer
Students	3200	3000	2800	1000
Credit Hours per Student	14	12	11	5
Credit Hour Ratio	150	150	150	150
Administrative Salaries	337500	337500	337500	337500
Secretarial Salaries	350000	350000	350000	200000
Full to FTE Ratio	.80	.80	.80	.95
Average Full-Time Faculty Salary	7000	7000	7000	7000
Average Part-Time Faculty Salary	1000	1000	1000	1000
TAs Salaries	60000	60000	60000	5000
Other Salaries	250000	250000	250000	100000
Utilities	550000	700000	550000	400000
Other Operating Expenses	175000	175000	175000	95000
Tuition per Credit Hour	85	85	85	85
Endowment Income	312500	312500	312500	312500
Other Income	187500	187500	187500	187500

Solve your template model using this datafile and produce a solution using the ALL solve option. Print the solution, the template model, and the datafile.

12. Midwest Universal Gas

Mary Derrick has found the quarterly model very useful in presentation to the board of directors of Midwest Universal Gas. To further facilitate the preparation of alternative plans, Mary wants you to create a template model. This will allow selected input data to be placed in a datafile for each alternative solution. Copy the quarterly model you created in Tutorial 2, Case Problem 5 and transform it into a template model. Prepare a datafile for input to the template model from the data provided below. Solve the template model with the datafile and produce a solution using the ALL solve option. Print the solution, the template model, and the datafile. Demand is the total gas sold for this division.

	1st Quarter	2nd Quarter	3rd Quarter	4th Quarter
Demand	220	210	80	210
Retail Price	3500	3500	3500	3500
Wholesale Price	2859	2859	2859	2859
Retail Volume Ratio	22%	22%	22%	22%
General Admin	40625	40625	40625	40625
Interest Expense	15250	15250	15250	15250
Tax Credits	21000	21000	21000	21000
Investments	1204000	1204000	1204000	1204000

13. General Memorial Hospital

After reviewing the quarterly planning model, Gloria Vander Balance has decided General Memorial Hospital should prepare a quarterly projection with this model on a regular basis. Berry has asked you to modify the quarterly model. By making it into a template model, the data for each quarter is more readily analyzed. Copy the model from Tutorial 2, Case Problem 6 and revise it into a template model. Berry wants your template model to use the data below. Create a datafile containing this data, solve the template model using the datafile. Print the solution, the template model, and the datafile.

	April	May	June
Bed Capacity	100	100	100
Bed Utilization Rate	.65	.80	.75
Nursing Staff	70	85	75
Doctors	4	4	5
Investment	5000000	5000000	5000000
Debt	2000000	2000000	2000000
Depreciation	41667	41667	41667
Days per Month	30	31	30

14. River City

Lisa Goodnight was delighted with the quarterly model you built. She is concerned about her operations, which consume funds at a constant rate, while revenues vary from month-to-month. Lisa wants you to create a template model from the quarterly model. This will facilitate the preparation of revised operating budgets for each quarter. Copy the quarterly model from Tutorial 2, Case Problem 7 and change it into a template model that accepts the data detailed below. Then create a datafile containing this data. Solve the model with the datafile and produce a solution using the ALL solve option. Print the solution, the template, and the datafile.

('000 omitted)	July	August	September
Property Tax	18522	0	0
Sales	245720	231266	274628
Permits	2500	100	120
City Government	375	375	375
Law	208	208	208
Public Safety	2808	2808	2808
Public Works	883	883	883
Parks	1500	1750	1000
Housing	183	183	183
Library	242	242	242
Miscellaneous	430	430	430

15. Good Morning Products

The board of directors of Good Morning (GM) Products has decided to build a branch plant in Florida in order to expand the production of Liquid Gold. The demand from their international operations has increased substantially and this location facilitates their export operations. Crush and Kim have been working on this project for several months and have assembled the following data for the Florida plant:

	1st Quarter	2nd Quarter	3rd Quarter	4th Quarter
Bottles	160000	145000	120000	140000
Price	3.19	3.19	3.39	3.39
General and Admin	12000	13000	16000	16000
Advertising	8000	9000	11000	9000
Interest	7000	7000	7000	7000
Depreciation	18500	18500	18500	18500
Labor per Bottle	0.89	0.89	0.89	0.89
Oranges per Bottle	1.21	1.21	1.21	1.21
Packaging per Bottle	0.57	0.57	0.57	0.57

Jenny suggests you make a copy of the California DATAFILE and then revise the copy of the datafile. Solve the template model with the data from the Florida branch plant and print this solution, then print the datafile.

16. The Woodcraft Furniture Company

Woodcraft has just purchased a new furniture business that specializes in oak furniture. Joe is concerned about controlling the expanded operations. He asks you to create a datafile for the Oak branch business. The branch datafile can then be solved using the template model for Woodcraft. Joe has collected the following data for the Oak branch:

	July	August	September
Table Price	450	450	450
Chair Price	100	100	100
Sofa Price	300	300	300
Employees	30	40	50
Hourly Rate	9.60	9.60	9.60
Hours Worked	174	174	174
Tables Sold	170	227	285
Advertising	2500	5000	3500
Management Salaries	9000	9000	9000
General and Admin	3500	4500	5500
Interest Expense	2750	2750	2750

Joe Birch has suggested you use a copy of the datafile and revise it for the Oak branch datafile, then print the revised datafile. Solve the template model with this datafile and print the solution.

17. The Last National Bank

Because the Last National Bank's performance has been fantastic, J. J. has purchased the bank in Weeping Water. One of his first requests was to ask Carrie to create a datafile for the Weeping Water branch bank and prepare an asset and liability projection using the template model. Carrie has gathered the following data and wants you to create the datafile and solve the model using the datafile:

Assets: (Amounts in Thousands)	January	February	March
Real Estate Mortgages	16500	15500	15000
Installment Loans	7000	7600	8200
Commercial Loans	13500	14500	16500
Other Investments	1000	1500	2500

Liabilities: (Amounts in Thousands)			
Regular Savings	6000	7000	7500
Interest Plus Checking	8000	8800	9200
Money Market Certificates	21000	21500	22400
Other Borrowed Funds	1500	2000	2400
Interest Rates:			
Prime Rate Interest	14%	14.5%	14%
Real Estate Interest	10.1%	10.2%	10.4%
Installment Loan Interest*	1.1%	1.2%	1.2%
Commercial Loan Interest*	2%	1.9%	1.9%
Other Investment Interest*	1%	1.1%	1.2%
Regular Savings Interest	5.5%	5.5%	5.5%
Interest Plus Checking Interest	6%	6%	6%
Money Market Interest*	- 3%	-2.5%	-2.5%
Other Borrowed Funds Interest	-4.5%	-4.0%	-4.0%

* Amount above or below the prime interest rate.

Carrie has suggested that you copy and revise the data values from the Broken Spoke branch for the Weeping Water branch, then print the datafile. Solve the template model with the datafile and print the solution.

18. Harvest University

In response to community demand, Harvest University has decided to open a second campus located near the business and commercial center. This campus, known as the Downtown Campus, is to have its budget prepared separately. As chief financial officer, you have prepared the following data on the Downtown Campus:

	Fall	Winter	Spring	Summer
Students	1600	1400	1400	600
Credit Hours per Student	15	14	12	6
Credit Hour Ratio	150	150	150	150
Administrative Salaries	78500	78500	78500	78500
Secretarial Salaries	150000	150000	150000	50000
Full to FTE Ratio	.80	.80	.80	.95
Average Full-Time Faculty Salary	7000	7000	7000	7000
Average Part-Time Faculty Salary	1000	1000	1000	1000
TAs Salaries	25000	25000	25000	3200
Other Salaries	95000	95000	95000	32000
Utilities	250000	300000	220000	40000
Other Operating Expenses	75000	75000	75000	35000
Tuition per Credit Hour	85	85	85	85
Endowment Income	132500	132500	132500	132500
Other Income	67500	67500	67500	67500

To save your self some time and energy, you have decided to copy your datafile from Problem 11 and revise the copy of the datafile with the data for the Downtown Campus, then print the revised datafile. Solve the template model with this datafile and print the solution.

19. Midwest Universal Gas

Under Mary Derrick's guidance, MUG has experienced a period of relatively good earnings. Francis Foresight and Petro Newgas have worked with Mary in convincing the board of directors to acquire Blue Flame Natural Gas. Blue Flame is located in the same general geographical area and serves customers similar to those of MUG. Mary wants you to prepare a projection for Blue Flame using the template model and the data that has been assembled at her request. Copy the MUG datafile and revise it to contain the data that is provided below, then print the datafile. Solve the model with the datafile and print the solution. Once again, demand is the total gas sold for this division.

	1st Quarter	2nd Quarter	3rd Quarter	4th Quarter
Demand	62	38	21	40
Retail Price	3500	3500	3500	3500
Wholesale Price	2859	2859	2859	2859
Retail Volume Ratio	57%	57%	57%	57%
General Admin	9900	9900	9900	9900
Interest Expense	600	600	600	600
Tax Credits	2400	2400	2400	2400
Investments	350000	350000	350000	350000

20. General Hospital

As a result of operating difficulties at County General Hospital, the administration of County General has been taken over by Gloria and Berry at General Memorial Hospital. Gloria and Berry were instrumental in forming the Family Health Care Corporation as the holding company for both hospitals. Both County General and General Memorial are considered as branches of Family Health Care. Berry has requested that you create a datafile for County General with the data provided below. Process this with the template model. To facilitate your creation of this datafile, copy the datafile from General Memorial Hospital, change the datafile to contain County General's data, then print the datafile. Solve the template model with this datafile and print the solution.

	April	May	June
Bed Capacity	50	50	50
Bed Utilization Rate	.75	.85	.80
Nursing Staff	35	45	40
Doctors	2	2	2
Investment	2500000	2500000	2500000
Debt	750000	750000	750000
Depreciation	20000	20000	20000
Days per Month	30	31	30

21. River City

In an attempt to broaden the tax base of River City, Lisa has annexed the neighboring suburb of Peaceful Valley. Frank Frugal has assembled data on Peaceful Valley. Lisa wants you to prepare a revenue and expense projection using the template model together with the data from Frank. Frank has suggested that you copy the datafile for River City and change the datafile for Peaceful Valley, then print the revised datafile.

('000 omitted)	July	August	September
Property Tax	3500	0	0
Sales	95000	100000	110000
Permits	400	50	10
City Government	5	5	5
Law	16	16	16
Public Safety	850	850	850
Public Works	65	65	65
Parks	2	4	6
Housing	0	0	0
Library	5	5	5
Miscellaneous	10	10	10

Solve the template model with the Peaceful Valley datafile and print the solution.

Notes:

Tutorial 6

Developing Customized Reports

Characteristics of a Management Report

Let's look at a management style report for Buffalo Computer Systems (BCS). Herbie prepared the report that appears in Figure 6-1. Several of the characteristics of the report should be pointed out. Let's start at the top and review the arrangement of the report line by line.

07/15/96

BUFFALO COMPUTER SYSTEMS
PROJECTED PROFIT AND LOSS STATEMENT

	1ST QTR	2ND QTR	3RD QTR	4TH QTR	TOTAL
BYTES SOLD	8	10	12	14	44
PRICE PER BYTE	7,500	7,750	8,000	8,250	7,932
REVENUES:					
SALES	$60,000	$77,500	$96000	$115,500	$349,000
COST OF SALES	46,200	58,900	72,000	85,470	262,570
GROSS PROFIT	$13,800	$18,600	$24,000	$30,030	$86,430
EXPENSES:					
SALARIES	12,2500	12,2500	12,2500	12,2500	49,000
BENEFITS	2,328	2,328	2,328	2,328	9,310
ADMIN EXPENSE	1,380	1,783	2,208	2,657	8,027
DEPRECIATION	1,500	2,000	2,000	2,500	8,000
INTEREST	400	400	400	400	1,600
TOTAL EXPENSES	$17,858	$18,760	$19,186	$20,134	$75,937
EBT	$(4,058)	$(160)	$4,815	$9,896	$10,493
ROS	(6.76)	(0.21)	5.02	8.57	3.01

Figure 6-1
Management Style
Report

In the upper-left-hand corner is the date of the report in the form of month, day, and year. IFPS obtained this from the computer's clock and displayed it here. The next three lines are the report heading or title, which has been centered and underlined. The underlining used here is a minus sign. It occupies a separate line in the report. In IFPS, all underlining uses a separate line. It is *not* like underlining on a typewriter or word processor.

The report skips one line; then the column titles or headings appear next, placed over each of the columns and underlined. Notice that the underlining on the next line is only under each of the columns titles.

The first variables to be reported, BYTES SOLD and PRICE PER BYTE, are displayed next. Commas appear in the numbers that represent PRICE PER BYTE. In scanning the rest of the report, notice that all figures that are in thousands are reported with commas.

Some lines are skipped and a heading, "REVENUES:," appears at the left side of the report. SALES is the first variable listed under REVENUE. Notice the appearance of the currency symbol ($) immediately to the left of each number. COST OF SALES is output and then underlined. These figures do not have a currency symbol. This section ends with the reporting of GROSS PROFIT. Notice that these figures again show the currency symbol displayed to the left of each number.

Next, the heading "EXPENSES:" is included in the report. Again, the EXPENSES heading appears left justified. The heading is immediately followed by each of the expense variables. The last expense, INTEREST, is underlined and TOTAL EXPENSES appears with the currency symbol.

The next section begins with a blank line followed by an underline. Notice that the columns of numbers are still underlined, even though the blank line occurred between the last line of numbers and the underline. EBT appears as the next variable. Here, negative numbers are enclosed in parentheses, and the currency symbol is used with each number. Following EBT, the equal sign is used to produce a double underline.

Finally, ROS is displayed after skipping one line. The numbers for the ROS appear with two places to the right of the decimal instead of with commas, negative numbers are enclosed in parentheses once again, and underlining is done with asterisks. Some of the primary characteristics of a management style report that are demonstrated by the report shown in Figure 6-1 for Buffalo Computer Systems (BCS) are as follows:

- Date
- Headings centered and underlined
- Column headings appropriately positioned and underlined
- Commas in numbers
- Decimal position selected
- Currency symbol
- Parentheses on negative numbers
- Underlining with selected character

In order to produce the report shown in Figure 6-1, Herbie creates an IFPS Report Definition. He has to enter the REPORT Subsystem to create an IFPS Report Definition, which describes how the final output report should look. An IFPS Report Definition does *not* contain the solution values that are to be displayed; rather, it contains a description of how the final output report will appear. Your model supplies the solution values that are displayed using the report definition to produce the final management style report (Figure 6-2).

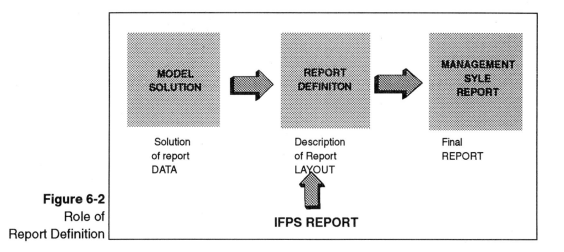

Figure 6-2
Role of
Report Definition

An IFPS report serves the same purpose as a formatting cell in a spreadsheet such as Lotus 1-2-3 or Excel does. The difference is that the entire report is described as one unit rather than attaching the format to each individual cell. When you produce a report, IFPS treats your solution like a database table. You select whatever rows and columns you want to print in whatever sequence you want them printed.

Designing a Presentation-Quality Report

Let's look at Herbie's Planning Analysis Sheet to see how he described or defined the presentation-quality report (Figure 6-3).

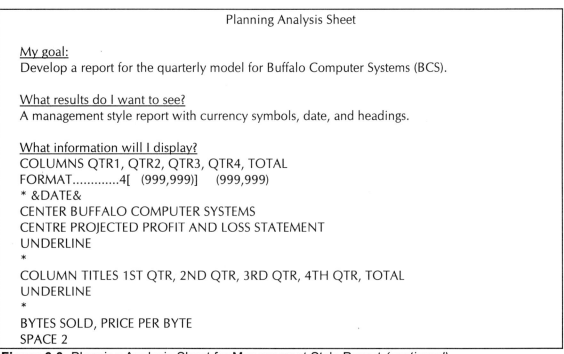

Planning Analysis Sheet

My goal:
Develop a report for the quarterly model for Buffalo Computer Systems (BCS).

What results do I want to see?
A management style report with currency symbols, date, and headings.

What information will I display?
COLUMNS QTR1, QTR2, QTR3, QTR4, TOTAL
FORMAT.............4[(999,999)]   (999,999)
* &DATE&
CENTER BUFFALO COMPUTER SYSTEMS
CENTRE PROJECTED PROFIT AND LOSS STATEMENT
UNDERLINE
*
COLUMN TITLES 1ST QTR, 2ND QTR, 3RD QTR, 4TH QTR, TOTAL
UNDERLINE
*
BYTES SOLD, PRICE PER BYTE
SPACE 2

Figure 6-3 Planning Analysis Sheet for Management Style Report *(continued)*

```
*REVENUES:
SALES $
COST OF SALES
UNDERLINE
GROSS PROFIT $
\
\EXPENSES:
SALARIES THRU INTEREST
UNDERLINE
TOTAL EXPENSES $
*
UNDERLINE
EBT $
UNDERLINE =
*
FORMAT.............4[  (9999.99)]   (9999.99)
ROS
UNDERLINE*
```

Figure 6-3 Planning Analysis Sheet for Management Style Report

Let's examine each of the statements in Herbie's report definition.

COLUMNS QTR1, QTR2, QTR3, QTR4, TOTAL

The columns statement describes which columns are to appear in the report together with the order of their appearance. The *columns can be arranged in any sequence* or you may decide to only display selected columns from the model solution.

FORMAT.............4[(999,999)]   (9,999,999)

This format statement is an image or picture of how data are displayed for a variable. It also defines the width of the report for centering headings. The "4[(999,999)]" is a shorthand method for writing the "(999,999)" four times. The number four (4) to the left of the open bracket means to repeat the specification inside the brackets four times. Notice that only four replications were specified. This is because more space was left between the fourth quarter column and the total column. In place of the nines in the FORMAT number column image, you may use either the letter D or the letter B. That is the report line could be either:

```
FORMAT.............4[  (BBB,BBB)]   (BBB,BBB)
Or:
FORMAT.............4[  (DDD,DDD)]   (DDD,DDD)
```

The difference between 9's, B's, and D's is in how the number zero is handled on output. For all other numbers, it makes no difference which specification you have used (Figure 6-4).

	Specification	Meaning
	9	When zero occurs, print 0
Figure 6-4	B	When zero occurs, print nothing (that is, print a blank)
Specification	D	When zero occurs, print a dash or minus sign in the right
for FORMAT		most position in the output field

The FORMAT statement is an image of how you would like each output line that contains numbers to appear. Here, the word FORMAT together with the 14 dots defines the width of the name field. In this case, the name field is 20 characters wide—6 for FORMAT plus 14 for the dots. The (999,999) describes a number field that will accommodate a number of up to 999,999. Since a comma appears in the image, numbers will be displayed with commas on output. Because parentheses enclose this number, any negative number will appear enclosed in parentheses. If the parentheses had not been used, then negative numbers would have appeared with a minus sign immediately to the left of the number. The spacing between each of the number field descriptions is maintained in the report that will be written from this definition. Look at the complete statement shown in Figure 6-3. Notice that two extra spaces have been placed between the fourth column and the total column. The purpose of this was to make the Total column standout from the other columns in the report by using additional white space.

The FORMAT statement also defines the entire width of the report. The report width is the entire length of this format statement line. For this reason, the FORMAT line needs to appear in the Report Definition *prior* to writing out any lines that are affected by the report width. This includes not only the variables but also any line that is to be centered. Because of this, it is strongly recommended that the second line in your report definition is either a FORMAT statement or a WIDTH statement. A WIDTH statement, described in the Selected Report Directive section, can be used in place of the FORMAT statement.

* &DATE&

This is a comment line in the Report Definition as indicated by the appearance of the asterisk as the first character. Comment lines in a Report Definition will be printed exactly as they appear. The "&DATE&" is a special feature in IFPS known as a **micro**. Here, it tells IFPS to go to the computer's clock, find the date and display it in place of &DATE&. IFPS contains several of these built-in micros. A backslash (\) may be used in place of the asterisk.

CENTER BUFFALO COMPUTER SYSTEMS

This is another comment statement. In place of the asterisk, the word CENTER is used. This means IFPS will center the text that follows the word CENTER using the FORMAT statement in determining the length of the line.

CENTRE PROJECTED PROFIT AND LOSS STATEMENT

This is another comment statement just like the one above. The only difference here is that center is spelled C-E-N-T-R-E. IFPS accepts both spellings.

UNDERLINE

This causes the last printed line to be underlined with a minus sign. Whenever the word UNDERLINE appears alone, it means to use the minus sign as the underline. The UNDERLINE character occupies a separate output line. It is not placed on the same line as usually done with a typical word processor.

*

A comment line with *no* text causes a blank line to appear in the output report.

COLUMN TITLES 1ST QTR, 2ND QTR, 3RD QTR, 4TH QTR, TOTAL

These are the column headings which are to appear above the number columns. If you want the same names as in your model, you would just enter COLUMN TITLES. To use a new name, you enter COLUMN TITLES followed by the titles you want to use.

UNDERLINE

Another directive to underline using a minus sign.

*

Another blank comment line.

BYTES SOLD, PRICE PER BYTE

This specifies that the variables BYTES SOLD and PRICE PER BYTE are to appear in the report. The order in which you specify variables is the order in which they will be obtained from the solution matrix and printed in your report. This means you may have your variables appear in a different sequence in your report than they occur in your model. In this manner, IFPS treats the model solution like a database and permits the selection of any variable in any sequence. You can use the clipboard to copy variable names for a model to your report definition. This is useful in avoiding misspelling variable names in the report definition and reduces typing.

SPACE 2
You can specify as many blank lines as you like. This report directive causes two blank lines to be printed.

*REVENUES:
Another comment that produces a heading for this section of the report.

SALES $
The variable SALES is displayed with its values. The "$" that follows the variable name causes the currency symbol to be printed immediately to the left of each value in the number columns.

COST OF SALES
The printing of COST OF SALES and its associated values is requested.

UNDERLINE
Another underline using the minus sign.

GROSS PROFIT $
GROSS PROFIT will be displayed and the solution values will be proceeded with the currency symbol.

\
Another blank line.

\EXPENSES:
Another heading provided by using a comment statement.

SALARIES THRU INTEREST
A group of variables, starting with SALARIES and going through INTEREST, is selected for reporting. The two dots (..) may be used in place of THRU.

UNDERLINE
One more underline with a minus sign.

TOTAL EXPENSES $
You know what this means.

*
Yes, another blank line.

UNDERLINE
More underlining. But, notice the underlining here is for the last line of values that appeared for TOTAL EXPENSES and is *not* for the immediately preceding blank line.

EBT $
Another variable with values to be printed using the currency symbol.

UNDERLINE=
More underlining, but this time with the equal sign.

*

One more blank line.

FORMAT..............4[(9999.99)]   (9999.99)
The FORMAT is changed so there will be two places to the right of the decimal when the ROS is displayed.

ROS
This variable is printed using the FORMAT with two places to the right of the decimal.

UNDERLINE*
Another underline, but this time with asterisks.

*

Finally, one last blank line at the end of the report.

That's it. Basically, the Report Definition is a line-by-line description of how the output report will appear. The COLUMNS statement provides for the selection of columns, and the FORMAT statements control the width of the output line, the name field width, the number field width, commas, decimals, and options for negative numbers and zeros. Variables are selected in the sequence you want them printed.

Creating a Report Definition

In the REPORT Subsystem, you enter reports as you do models, that is, one line at a time using the Visual IFPS text editor. Any time you make a mistake in entering your report, you can correct it in the same way you learned to correct errors that occur in entering models. Let's see how to create Herbie's report definition for BCS.

To create a report definition:
❶   Launch IFPS and open the **MRBCS** M&R file, as necessary.
❷   Click the **New button** in the toolbar to display the New dialog box, then click **Report**.
❸   Click the **OK button** to obtain a blank window.
❹   Type the report definition as shown in Figure 6-3.
❺   Click **File**, click **Save**, type **BUFFALO** in the Entity Name dialog box, then click the **OK button** to save the report definition in the MRBCS M&R file.

Producing a Report

Herbie has created and saved the report definition for his model. He wants to print the report using the report definition with the solution values from the model. He needs to obtain the values for his report from an active model. Let's see how to produce a report using a report definition.

To produce a report:
❶   Click the **Open button** on the toolbar, then click **PROJECT3** in the Entity Name list box to select the model whose solution is to be displayed in the report.
❷   Click the **Report button** to display the Generate Report dialog box. See Figure 6-5.

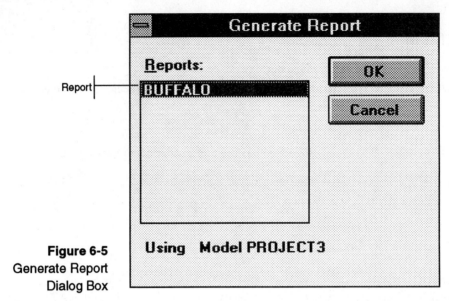

Figure 6-5
Generate Report
Dialog Box

❸ Click **BUFFALO**, then click the **OK button** to select that report definition and produce the report. See Figure 6-6.

8/18/96

BUFFALO COMPUTER SYSTEMS
PROJECTED PROFIT AND LOSS STATEMENT

	1ST QTR	2ND QTR	3RD QTR	4TH QTR	TOTAL
BYTES SOLD	8	10	12	14	44
PRICE PER BYTE	7,500	7,750	8,000	8,250	7,932
REVENUES:					
SALES	$60,000	$77,500	$96000	$115,500	$349,000
COST OF SALES	46,200	58,900	72,000	85,470	262,570
GROSS PROFIT	$13,800	$18,600	$24,000	$30,030	$86,430
EXPENSES:					
SALARIES	12,2500	12,2500	12,2500	12,2500	49,000
BENEFITS	2,328	2,328	2,328	2,328	9,310
ADMIN EXPENSE	1,380	1,783	2,208	2,657	8,027
DEPRECIATION	1,500	2,000	2,000	2,500	8,000
INTEREST	400	400	400	400	1,600
TOTAL EXPENSES	$17,858	$18,760	$19,186	$20,134	$75,937
EBT	$(4,058)	$(160)	$4,815	$9,896	$10,493
	======	======	=======	=======	=======
ROS	(6.76)	(0.21)	5.02	8.57	3.01
********	********	********	*********	********	

Figure 6-6
Managerial Style
Report from
Solution of
Model PROJECT3

TROUBLE? If your report does not look like this, then click the Report window and review the report definition by comparing it to the report definition in the planning analysis sheet. Make any corrections to the report definition and redo the Genreport by repeating Steps 2 and 3.

When you make a mistake in your report definition, you must select the Report window to correct it. Then you return to the Model window and produce the report again. As illustrated here, models and reports may have different names or they may have the same name, the choice is entirely up to you, IFPS doesn't care.

Although there is a certain amount of dependence between models and reports, it should be recognized that you may create several different Report Definitions that can be used with the same model. Or, a Report Definition can be used with several different models. The most common situation is to have several Report Definitions for a single model.

Paging Reports

Suppose Herbie wants you to create a report with 1ST and 2ND quarters on the first page and the 3RD and 4TH quarters on the second page. No TOTAL column is displayed. In preparation for producing this report, Herbie creates a Planning Analysis Sheet (Figure 6-7).

Planning Analysis Sheet

My goal:
Develop a report for the quarterly model for Buffalo Computer Systems in which 1ST QTR and 2ND QTR are on the first page and 3RD QTR and 4TH QTR are on the second page.

What results do I want to see?
A management style report with currency symbols, date, and headings.

What information will I display?
COLUMNS 1-4
FORMAT.............2[(9,999,999)]
* &DATE&
CENTER BUFFALO COMPUTER SYSTEMS
CENTRE PRO FORMA PROFIT AND LOSS STATEMENT
UNDERLINE
*
COLUMN TOTALS 1ST QTR, 2ND QTR, 3RD QTR, 4TH QTR
UNDERLINE
BYTES SOLD, PRICE PER BYTE
SPACE 2
*REVENUES
SALES $
COST OF SALES
UNDERLINE
GROSS PROFIT $
\

Figure 6-7 Planning Analysis Sheet for the PAGE report *(continued)*

```
\EXPENSES:
SALARIES THRU INTEREST
UNDERLINE
TOTAL EXPENSES $
*
UNDERLINE
EBT $
UNDERLINE =
*
FORMAT.............2[                        (99,999.99)]
ROS
UNDERLINE*
*
```

Figure 6-7 Planning Analysis Sheet for the PAGE report

Let's look at the differences between reports BUFFALO and PAGE.

COLUMNS 1-4
Only the four regular columns are selected from the model solution for printing in this example.

FORMAT.............2[(9,999,999)]
This FORMAT is the image of an output line that only contains two columns for numbers. Because there are only two number columns, but there are four columns to be displayed as requested by the Columns statement, IFPS knows to proceed throughout the report definition the first time using only columns 1 and 2; IFPS then starts over at the top of the report definition and goes through it a second time using only columns 3 and 4. You need not repeat the report definition. This feature in IFPS is known as **paging**. IFPS automatically knows how to page when the number of columns to be displayed exceeds the number of column positions available in one line of output. So, when the FORMAT describes less columns than requested by the Columns statement, IFPS does multiple passes through the report definition until all requested columns have been output.

COLUMNS TITLES 1ST QTR, 2ND QTR, 3RD QTR, 4TH QTR
Since the TOTAL columns is not requested, its name is removed from the COLUMN TITLES statement. Also, notice the COLUMNS TITLE statement contains a column tittle for *all* the columns listed in the COLUMNS statement. IFPS knows which column titles to use first and which to use second. But, you list them all in one COLUMNS TITLE statement.

To create the PAGE report definition:

❶ Click the **New button** on the toolbar, click **Report** in the New dialog box, then click the **OK button**.

❷ Click **Open**, click the **List Entities of Type drop down arrow**, click **REPORT** to specify this entity type, then select **BUFFALO** from the Entity Name list box, and click the **OK button**. See Figure 6-8.

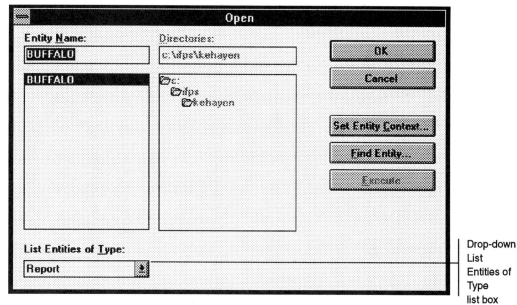

Figure 6-8

Open

Dialog Box

Drop-down
List
Entities of
Type
list box

❸   Select the entire report for copying by clicking **Edit**, then click **Select All**.

❹   Click **Edit**, then click **Copy** to copy the report definition to the Windows
clipboard.

❺   Click the **Report window** of the new report to make it active.

❻   Click **Edit**, then click **Paste** to insert the contents from the clipboard.

❼   Edit each of these lines:
COLUMNS 1-4, TOTAL
FORMAT............4[(999,999)]   (999,999)
COLUMNS TITLES 1ST QTR, 2ND QTR, 3RD QTR, 4TH QTR, TOTAL
FORMAT..............4[(9999.99)]   (9999.99)
So they appear as follows:
COLUMNS 1-4
FORMAT............2[(999,999)]
COLUMNS TITLES 1ST QTR, 2ND QTR, 3RD QTR, 4TH QTR
FORMAT............2[(9999.99)]

TROUBLE? Remember to modify both the FORMAT lines so there are only 2
number columns specified.

❽   Click **File**, click **Save As,** then type **BUFFALO2** in the Entity Name text box and
click the **OK button**.

Now that Herbie has created the report definition, he wants to see how it looks. Let's produce his
report.

To produce the Page report:

❶ Click the **Model PROJECT3 window** to make it the active window.

❷ Click the **Report button** in the toolbar to display the Generate Report dialog box, click **BUFFALO2** in the Reports list box, then click the **OK button** to produce the report. See Figure 6-9.

8/18/96

BUFFALO COMPUTER SYSTEMS
PROJECTED PROFIT AND LOSS STATEMENT

	1ST QTR	2ND QTR
	------------	------------
BYTES SOLD	8	10
PRICE PER BYTE	7,500	7,750
REVENUES:		
SALES	$60,000	$77,500
COST OF SALES	46,200	58,900
	----------	----------
GROSS PROFIT	$13,800	$18,600
EXPENSES:		
SALARIES	12,2500	12,2500
BENEFITS	2,328	2,328
ADMIN EXPENSE	1,380	1,783
DEPRECIATION	1,500	2,000
INTEREST	400	400
	----------	----------
TOTAL EXPENSES	$17,858	$18,760
	----------	----------
EBT	$(4,058)	$(160)
	======	======
ROS	(6.76)	(0.21)
	********	********

Figure 6-9
Paged Report
(continued)

8/18/96

BUFFALO COMPUTER SYSTEMS
PROJECTED PROFIT AND LOSS STATEMENT

	3RD QTR	4TH QTR
	------------	------------
BYTES SOLD	12	14
PRICE PER BYTE	8,000	8,250
REVENUES:		
SALES	$96000	$115,500
COST OF SALES	72,000	85,470
	----------	----------
GROSS PROFIT	$24,000	$30,030
EXPENSES:		
SALARIES	12,2500	12,2500
BENEFITS	2,328	2,328
ADMIN EXPENSE	2,208	2,657
DEPRECIATION	2,000	2,500
INTEREST	400	400
	----------	----------
TOTAL EXPENSES	$19,186	$20,134
	----------	----------
EBT	$4,815	$9,896
	=======	=======
ROS	5.02	8.57
	********	********

Figure 6-9
Paged Report

TROUBLE? If your report does not look like this, then click the Report window and review the report definition. Compare your report definition to the one in the Planning Analysis Sheet and make any corrections. Repeat Step 2.

Exploring Advanced Reporting

The report for Buffalo Computer Systems (BCS) is in dollar amounts. Because growth in dollar amounts can often mask the true underlying relationships, executives and managers many times prefer reports which are in percentage amounts. Percentage reports contain information in a form that is more readily usable to managers. Given a report in dollars, managers will frequently look at a few key line items such as SALES and EBT. Then, they are interested in numbers like the ROS that states EBT as a percentage of SALES. If they are not provided in this form, managers will either mentally calculate them or will perform a few side calculations with their calculators to obtain these percentage numbers. As a result, it would be nice to create the entire report as percents, rather than only providing percentage values for just one selected line item. IFPS readily accommodates the preparation of this kind of report.

Herbie decides he wants a percentage report for BCS and prepares a Planning Analysis Sheet for it (Figure 6-10).

Planning Analysis Sheet

My goal:
Develop a report for the quarterly model for Buffalo Computer Systems (BCS) in which the amounts represent the percent of sales.

What results do I want to see?
A management style report with date and headings.

What information will I display?
COLUMNS 1-4, TOTAL
FORMAT .... 4[(9999.99)]   (9999.99)
* &DATE&
CENTER BUFFALO COMPUTER SYSTEMS
CENTRE PROJECTED PROFIT AND LOSS STATEMENT
CENTER (AS PERCENT OF SALES)
UNDERLINE
*
COLUMNS TITLES 1ST QTR, 2ND QTR, 3RD QTR 4TH QTR, TOTAL
UNDERLINE
BYTES SOLD, PRICE PER BYTE
SPACE 2
*REVENUES:
FORMAT...............4[(9999.99)]   (9999.99)
SCALE .01 * SALES
SALES
COST OF SALES
UNDERLINE
GROSS PROFIT
\
\EXPENSES:
SALARIES THRU INTEREST
UNDERLINE
TOTAL EXPENSES
*
UNDERLINE
/EARN BEFORE TAX/ EBT
UNDERLINE =
*
NOSCALE
/RETURN ON SALES/ ROS
UNDERLINE*
*

Figure 6-10 Percent or Relative Report Definition Plan

Let's look at the lines that were revised.

CENTER (AS PERCENT OF SALES)
A comment statement was added to describe the content of this report.

FORMAT...............4[(9999.99)]   (9999.99)
This FORMAT, which immediately follows the REVENUES: comment line, provides for displaying the percentages with two places to the right of the decimal.

SCALE .01 * SALES

This line is the cornerstone to producing the percent report. The SCALE statement causes *each line* that follows to be *divided* by the values specified in this statement. In this case, it is SALES multiplied by the constant .01. Here, the effect of the .01 is to move the decimal place two positions to the right. Without this, SALES would have been 1.00 instead of 100.00. Most executives and managers prefer to have the decimal point moved over so the number is in this percent form.

Notice in Figure 6-10 that BYTES SOLD and PRICE PER BYTE are still reported as integer or whole numbers, while all the other variables are reported as percents. Since SALES is the basis of comparison, it is 100.00 percent for each quarter. EBT has also been renamed and is now reported as EARN BEFORE TAX. And, similarly, ROS is now referred to as RETURN ON SALES.

/EARN BEFORE TAX/ EBT

Here, Herbie used **Variable Name Replacement**. EARN BEFORE TAX replaced the variable name EBT from the model. The new variable name is enclosed in the slashes and is followed by either the variable name or the line number reference from the model. Only the name is changed, *not* the values of the variable.

NOSCALE

This turns off the SCALE directive. All variables displayed after this are *not* scaled. The FORMAT statement that was contained in Report PERCENT is no longer required since the FORMAT established is still in effect. Thus, the NOSCALE replaced the FORMAT.

/RETURN ON SALES/ ROS

Once again Variable Name Replacement is used with ROS.

One of the most interesting uses of Variable Name Replacement was with a Mexican company. In performing an investment analysis, the model was written in English. However, all the management reports were written in Spanish. Variable Name Replacement was used in the Report Definition to change the names from English to Spanish. This feature can be very beneficial to multinational companies, in which a model can be written in one language and reports prepared in several other languages to meet their reporting requirements.

The ability to perform the SCALE is the primary ingredient in producing the PERCENT Report. The SCALE directive or statement has several different forms for dividing and multiplying (Figure 6-11).

	SCALE constant
	SCALE variable
	SCALE constant * variable
	SCALE MULTIPLY constant
Figure 6-11	SCALE MULTIPLY variable
Forms of	SCALE MULTIPLY constant * variable
SCALE Directive	NOSCALE

The first three forms of the SCALE directive result in all variables that follow the directive being *divided* by the constant, variable, or constant * variable. In the SCALE, the arithmetic of IFPS is *not* commutative. That is, you may *not* use variable * constant. It *must* always be constant * variable. The last three forms of the scale directive, the SCALE MULTIPLY form, causes each variable that follows the directive to be *multiplied* by the designated value(s). NOSCALE turns off both the SCALE and SCALE MULTIPLY directives.

CAUTION ALERT!

Once the SCALE is turned on, it stays in effect until it is turned off with a NOSCALE.

Let's see how to create Herbie's percent report.

To create a percentage or relative report:

❶   Click **Open**, verify the **Report** entity type is selected, then select **BUFFALO**.

❷   Select the entire report in preparation for copying it.

❸   Click **Edit**, then click **Copy** to copy the contents of the report to the Windows clipboard.

❹   Click the **New button**, click **Report** to select this entity type, then click the **OK button**.

❺   Click **Edit**, then click **Paste** to insert the contents of the clipboard as the new report.

❻   Insert the line: **CENTER (AS PERCENT OF SALES)** immediately after CENTRE PRO FORMA PROFIT AND LOSS STATEMENT.

❼   Insert the line: **FORMAT..............4[(9999.99)]   (9999.99)** before SALES or, you may use Edit, Cut and Edit, Paste to move the line to the desired location.

❽   Insert the line: **SCALE .01 * SALES** before SALES.

❾   Change EBT to **/EARN BEFORE TAX/ EBT** and change ROS to **/RETURN ON SALES/ ROS**.

❿   Remove all of the dollar signs and make sure the report definition looks like the commands in Figure 6-10.

Now that we have the desired report definition as planned in Figure 6-10, let's save the report as PERCENT.

To save the PERCENT report:

❶   Click **File**, then click **Save As** to display the Save As dialog box.

❷   Type **PERCENT** in the Entity Name text box then click the **OK button**.

Selected Report Directives

IFPS contains a number of additional report directives. Some of the more frequently used directives, which have not been explored in this chapter, are listed here for your reference. The detailed application of each directive is described in the *IFPS/Plus User's Manual*. (The portion of the directives enclosed in the brackets, [], is optional.)

Report Directive	Action
COMMAS	Causes numbers to be printed with commas. Used with WIDTH directive.
COMDEC A COMDEC E1 COMDEC E2	Specifies how numbers are to be printed with commas and decimals used to group digits. E1 and E2 are European forms.

Report Directive	Action
COMMENT[S]	Causes Comment statements from the Model to be displayed.
CURRENCY character	Sets the currency symbol to be printed to any desired character.
DOUBLE	Double spaces all following lines.
INDENT	Causes variable names to be displayed with the same indention as in the model.
INVERT	Causes the rows and columns to be transposed when the output is displayed. This results in a 90-degree rotation of the solution matrix.
LEFTMARGIN number	Specifies the number of character spaces for the left margin.
NAMEINDENT number	Specifies the number of character spaces the variable name is to be indented. This affects only the variable name.
NEGOPT PAREN NEGOPT - NEGOPT - A NEGOPT DB NEGOPT CR	Specifies the style in which negative numbers are displayed.
NOCOMMAS	Causes numbers to be printed without commas. Turns off the COMMAS option. Used with the Width directive.
NOCOMMEMT[S]	Causes Comment statement from the model to *not* be printed.
NOINDENT	Causes the indentation of variable names in the model to be ignored.
NOPAGE	Causes all values for a variable to be printed before proceeding to the next variable regardless of the number of lines required to display all the values.
NORMAL	Turns off the INVERT option causing the solution to be displayed in the normal position.
OVERLAY [position] text	Causes "text" to be superimposed over each and every subsequent line of variable values output.
PAGE	Causes paging of the output when the number of the columns of output exceeds the number of specified columns.
PAGE	Cause pages to be numbered in sequence.
PAGELENGTH toplines, bodylines, bottomlines [[,newpage code] [RLrepeat-head-line [THRU RLrepeat-head-line]]]	Establishes the physical length of each page to be printed with margins at the top and bottom of each page, a carriage control character, and heading lines to be repeated on each page.

Report Directive	Action
POSOPT +	Specifies the style in which positive values are to printed.
RLreport-line	References a preceding Report Line for use at another location in the report.
RLreport-line1 THRU RLreport-line2	References a proceeding group of Report Lines for use at another location in the report.
SINGLE	Causes single spacing of the following lines.
SKIPNONZERO var-ref, RLreport-line	If the values of the variable in all columns are not zero, report processing continues on the specified report-line.
SKIPZERO var-ref, RLreport-line	If the values of the variable in all columns are zero, report processing continues on the specified report-line.
SORT ON col-refs (var-refs) SORT A ON col-refs(var-refs) SORT D ON col-refs(var-refs) SORT ON NAME(var-refs) SORT A ON NAME(var-refs) SORT D ON NAME(var-refs)	Specifies the sorting of variables at the time of printing in the report.
WIDTH linewidth, namewidth, colwidth, decplaces	Specifies the width of a line of printed output including the variable name width, width of each column of values, and decimal places for values.
ZEROPRINT	Causes all following variables with the value of zero in all columns to be printed.
ZEROSUP	Causes all following variables with the value of zero in all columns to not be printed.

Introduction to User-Defined Micros

In either a model or a report, a *micro* acts as a temporary placeholder in a statement. A *value* (either text or a numeric constant) is substituted for the placeholder at execution time. This greatly enhances flexibility and generality because the model or report may thus be different each time it executes. You can use a **micro** in a comment statement, a variable definition statement, or any other modeling statement. In a variable definition statement, the micro can appear as part of the variable name or as part of the expression that determines the value. The same micro can occur in as many different lines as appropriate. Furthermore, as many as fifty or more different micros can be used, including predefined IFPS/Plus system micros.

Rather than having the user define each micro at execution time, you can use a MICRO *definition* statement that contains the appropriate substitution. Such statements can occur anywhere in a model or datafile. Most often, MICRO statements are included in datafiles so that one model can be used with several datafiles. The syntax of the MICRO *definition* statement is:

> **MICRO &text&substitution&**

A number of system micros are recognized and automatically defined by IFPS/Plus, without a user prompt or a MICRO definition statement required. These micros include:

MICRO	SUBSTITUTION
&DATE&	Current date in the form MM/DD/YY
&TIME&	Time in the form HH:MM
&MONTH&	Current month as an integer
&MONTHA&	Current month as a three-letter abbreviation
&DAY&	Day of current month
&YEAR&	Current year as a four-digit number
&MNAME&	Current active model name
&DFNAME&	Datafile being used with model

In addition to the built-in micros, you may define your own micros. When users create their micros, the micro must be defined. Thus, for user-defined micros there is both a micro definition and a micro reference. Only one definition is allowed, but the micro reference may be used as many times as desired. User-defined micros may be predefined, such as those placed in a datafile, or values may be supplied interactively during execution of a model or report. See Figure 6-12 for the relation between micros and models.

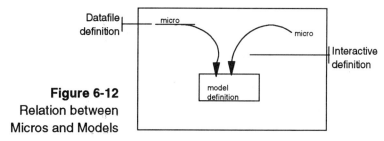

Figure 6-12
Relation between
Micros and Models

Let's look at how Herbie revised model PROJECT3 utilizing micros. He decided to use two micros: one to control the number of columns in his model and the other one to control the PRICE PER BYTE. The micro that dynamically controls the number of columns in the model is explained first.

COLUMNS 1-&NUMBER OF QUARTERS&, TOTAL
This user-defined micro &NUMBER OF QUARTERS& allows Herbie to vary the number of quarters so that he can have a projection for any number of quarters. At one time, it might be two quarters and at another time, it might be eight quarters. Herbie can still have four quarters whenever desired. To accommodate this, he also had to modify the column number specification, replacing it with the TOTAL column name. This was necessary because, with a two-column projection, column 3 (not column 5) is the TOTAL column; this is similar for all other selections except four quarters. It was also necessary to change the statement that calculates the sum in the TOTAL column as:

**COLUMN TOTAL FOR BYTES SOLD, PRICE PER BYTE, SALES, COST OF SALES,'
GROSS PROFIT THRU EBT = SUM(C1 THRU C&NUMBER OF QUARTERS&)**

Herbie made the PRICE PER BYTE into a micro similar to the following:

PRICE PER BYTE = &PRICE PER BYTE&, PREVIOUS + 250
This lets Herbie *interactively* enter a first-quarter price for each solution. Now let's revise the model with these micros.

To include user-defined micro references in model PROJECT3:

❶   Click **Open**, click **Model** in the List Entities of Type drop-down list, then click
       PROJECT3 to make this model active.

❷   Change COLUMNS 1ST QTR, 2ND QTR, 3RD QTR, 4TH QTR, TOTAL to:
       COLUMNS 1-&NUMBER OF QUARTERS&, TOTAL

❸   Change PRICE PER BYTE = 7500, PREVIOUS + 250 to:
       PRICE PER BYTE = &PRICE PER BYTE&, PREVIOUS + 250

❹   Change GROSS PROFIT THRU EBT = SUM(C1 THRU C4) to:
       GROSS PROFIT THRU EBT = SUM(C1 THRU C&NUMBER OF QUARTERS&)
       See Figure 6-13.

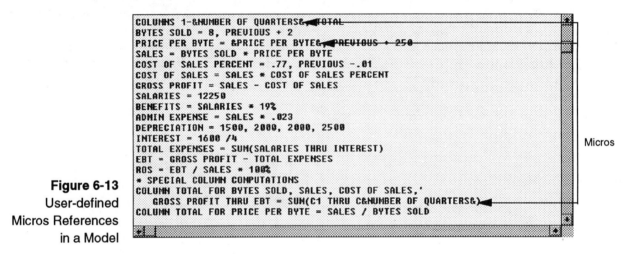

Figure 6-13
User-defined
Micros References
in a Model

Micros

Now Herbie wants to solve this model with the micros.

To solve a model with micros:

❶   Click the **Solve button** in the toolbar to display the Prompt dialog box for the
       NUMBER OF QUARTERS because this micro is defined interactively. See
       Figure 6-14.

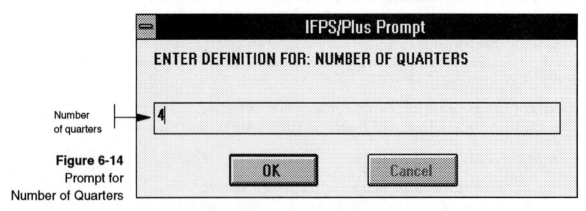

Number
of quarters

Figure 6-14
Prompt for
Number of Quarters

TROUBLE? If the Prompt dialog box does not appear, then click the model window and review the micro references added to the model. Make any corrections and repeat Step 1.

❷ Type **4** and click the **OK button** to display the next the prompt for **PRICE PER BYTE**, which is the next interactively defined micro. See Figure 6-15.

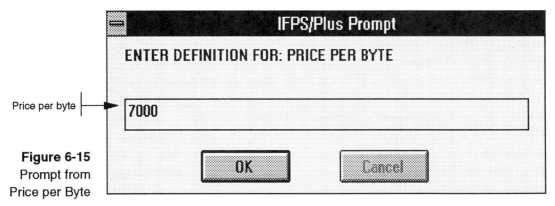

Price per byte ⟶

Figure 6-15
Prompt from
Price per Byte

❸ Type **7000**, then click the **OK button** to display the solution of the model using these micros. See Figure 6-16.

Value supplied by micro ⟶

Model PROJECT3 Solution:1	1	2	3	4	TOT
BYTES SOLD	8.00	10.00	12.00	14.00	
PRICE PER BYTE	7,000.00	7,250.00	7,500.00	7,750.00	7.4
SALES	56,000.00	72,500.00	90,000.00	108,500.00	327.0
COST OF SALES PERCENT	0.77	0.76	0.75	0.74	
COST OF SALES	43,120.00	55,100.00	67,500.00	80,290.00	246.0
GROSS PROFIT	12,880.00	17,400.00	22,500.00	28,210.00	80.9
SALARIES	12,250.00	12,250.00	12,250.00	12,250.00	49.0
BENEFITS	2,327.50	2,327.50	2,327.50	2,327.50	9.3
ADMIN EXPENSE	1,288.00	1,667.50	2,070.00	2,495.50	7.5
DEPRECIATION	1,500.00	2,000.00	2,000.00	2,500.00	8.0
INTEREST	400.00	400.00	400.00	400.00	1.6

Figure 6-16
Solution Using
Micros in Model

Herbie decides to revise his BUFFALO report definition and the TUMBLE datafile so that the name of the outlet location would appear as the heading. He wants to do this with a micro. See Figure 6-17, which shows the relationship between the micros and the models, reports, and datafiles.

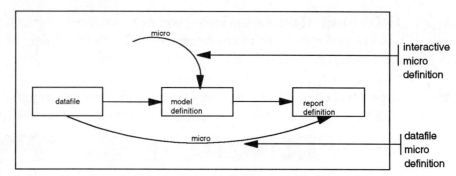

Figure 6-17
Relation between
Micros and Models,
Reports, and Datafiles

The report definition BUFFALO3 that is used to produce the report is shown in Figure 6-18. The &BRANCH NAME& is a micro reference used to display the name of the location on the report.

```
COLUMNS QTR1, QTR2 ,QTR3, QTR4 TOTAL
FORMAT..............4[ (999,999)]  (999,999)
*&DATE&
CENTER BUFFALO COMPUTER SYSTEMS
CENTER PROJECTED PROFIT AND LOSS STATEMENT
*
CENTER &BRANCH NAME&
UNDERLINE
*
COLUMN TITLES 1ST QTR, 2ND QTR, 3RD QTR, 4TH QTR, TOTAL
UNDERLINE
BYTES SOLD, PRICE PER BYTE
SPACE 2
*REVENUES:
SALES $
COST OF SALES
UNDERLINE
GROSS PROFIT $
\
\EXPENSES:
SALARIES THRU INTEREST
UNDERLINE
TOTAL EXPENSES $
*
UNDERLINE
EBT $
UNDERLINE=
*
FORMAT............4[ (999.99)]  (999.99)
ROS
UNDERLINE*
```

Micro
reference ——▶

Figure 6-18
Report Definition
from BUFFALO3

Let's see how you can change the report and the datafile to use a micro for the location name.

To add a user-defined micro to a report definition:

❶   Click the **Open button** on the toolbar, select **Report** in the List Entities of Type drop-down list arrow, then select **BUFFALO** from the Entity Name list**.**

❷   Click the **New button** on the toolbar, and select **Report** in the New dialog box.

❸   Click the **Report BUFFALO window** to make this the active window.

❹   Click **Edit**, then click **Select All** to select the entire report definition.

❺   Click **Edit**, then click **Copy** to copy the selection to the Windows clipboard.

❻   Click the **new Report window**, click **Edit**, then click **Paste** to paste the contents of the Windows clipboard into the new report.

❼   Enter * as the line below CENTRE PROJECTED PROFIT AND LOSS STATEMENT to insert a blank line in the report.

❽   Enter **CENTER &BRANCH NAME&** on the next line for the location name in the report.

❾   Click **File**, click **Save As**, type **BUFFALO3** in the Entity Name text box, then click the **OK button** to save the new report definition.

With the placement of the micro reference in the report description, Herbie wants to put the micro definition in his datafiles for the outlets. Let's see how a user-defined micro is included in a datafile.

To add a user-defined micro definition to a datafile:

❶   Click the **Open button** on the toolbar, select **Datafile** in the List Entities of Type drop-down list, then select **TUMBLE** from the Entity Name list.

❷   Move the I-beam cursor to the beginning of the datafile and press the **[Enter]** key to insert a blank line.

❸   Type:
MICRO&BRANCH NAME&TUMBLE WEED SHOPPING MALL&
where BRANCH NAME is the micro's name and TUMBLE WEED SHOPPING MALL is the definition or replacement value for this micro.

❹   Click **File**, click **Save** to resave the datafile with the micro.

Herbie is now ready to use the datafile with his template model MASTER and the report BUFFALO3. Let's see how to produce the report for this outlet.

To produce a report using a micro:

❶   Click the **Open button**, select **Model** from the List Entities of Type drop-down list, select **MASTER** from the Entity Name list.

❷   Click the **Using button** in the toolbar, double-click **TUMBLE** from the datafile list to select it, then click the **OK button**.

❸   Click the **Report button** in the toolbar, then select **BUFFALO3** from the Genreport dialog box to produce the report. See Figure 6-19.

8/18/96

BUFFALO COMPUTER SYSTEMS

PROJECTED PROFIT AND LOSS STATEMENT
TUMBLE WEED SHOPPING MALL

	1ST QTR	2ND QTR	3RD QTR	4TH QTR	TOTAL
BYTES SOLD	9	11	13	15	48
PRICE PER BYTE	7,500	7,750	8,000	8,250	7,927
REVENUES:					
SALES	$67,500	$85,250	$104,000	$123,750	$380,500
COST OF SALES	51,975	64,790	78,000	91,575	286,340
GROSS PROFIT	$15,525	$20,460	$26,000	$32,175	$94,160
EXPENSES:					
SALARIES	12,2500	12,2500	12,2500	12,2500	49,000
BENEFITS	2,328	2,328	2,328	2,328	9,310
ADMIN EXPENSE	1,553	1,961	2,392	2,846	8,752
DEPRECIATION	1,500	2,000	2,000	2,500	8,000
INTEREST	400	400	400	400	1,600
TOTAL EXPENSES	$18,030	$18,938	$19,370	$20,324	$76,662
EBT	$(2,505)	$1,552	$6,631	$11,851	$17,499
	======	======	======	======	======
ROS	(3.71)	1.79	6.38	9.58	4.60
	********	********	********	*********	********

Figure 6-19
Report with
MICRO

TROUBLE? If your report doesn't look like this, then click the Report window and review the report definition. Compare it to the report definition in Figure 6-18. Make any corrections, and then repeat Step 3.

Similarly, a micro definition is added to the WEST datafile, and a report is generated. Herbie has the reports he wants. He is ready to meet with Gat Computer Inc. (GCI) to arrange a line of credit for more computers.

Questions

1. The _____ statement describes which columns are to appear in the report.
    a. format
    b. column
    c. underline
    d. width

2.   The _____ statement controls the width of the output line, the name field
      width, the number field width, commas, decimals, and options for negative values
      and zeros.
      a. format
      b. column
      c. underline
      d. scale

3.   IFPS will ____ the text that follows the word CENTER.
      a. left-justify
      b. right-justify
      c. indent
      d. center

4.   Executives and managers many times prefer reports that are in _____ amounts.
      a. dollar
      b. peso
      c. percent
      d. cash

5.   The ability to perform the _____ is the primary ingredient in producing the
      Percent report.
      a. NOSCALE
      b. SCALE
      c. DIVIDE
      d. MULTIPLY

6.   In either a model or a report, a _____ acts as a temporary placeholder in a
      statement.
      a. macro
      b. comment
      c. micro
      d. record

Case Problems

1. Good Morning Products

Kim and Crush have careful reviewed the quarterly projection in preparing for their presentation to the
board of directors. Jenny has suggested that it would help if they had a management style report for the
meeting. She wants you to create a Report Definition that will produce a report arranged similar to this
design. Jenny wants you to check on the number of places to the left of the decimal since she isn't sure she
has allowed a sufficient number of places. Use the quarterly model from Tutorial 2 to produce this report.
Print a copy of your report definition.

MM/DD/YY <---(e.g., date report created in form MM/DD/YY)
GOOD MORNING PRODUCTS CORPORATION
NEXT YEAR'S BUDGET

	1st Quarter	2nd Quarter	3rd Quarter	4th Quarter	Total
Bottles	XXX,XXX	XXX,XXX	XXX,XXX	XXX,XXX	X,XXX,XXX
Price	X.XX	X.XX	X.XX	X.XX	X.XX
Sales Revenue	$XXX,XXX	$XXX,XXX	$XXX,XXX	$XXX,XXX	$X,XXX,XXX
Expenses					
Fixed	XXX,XXX	XXX,XXX	XXX,XXX	XXX,XXX	X,XXX,XXX
Variable	XXX,XXX	XXX,XXX	XXX,XXX	XXX,XXX	X,XXX,XXX
	------------	------------	------------	-----------	----------------
Total Expenses	XXX,XXX	XXX,XXX	XXX,XXX	XXX,XXX	X,XXX,XXX
Earnings					
Before Tax	$XXX,XXX	$XXX,XXX	$XXX,XXX	$XXX,XXX	$X,XXX,XXX
	=========	=========	=========	=========	===========
Return On Sales	XX.XX	XX.XX	XX.XX	XX.XX	XX.XX
	******	******	******	******	******

2. The Woodcraft Furniture Company

Joe Birch wants you to create a management style report for the quarterly plan. Create an IFPS report definition that has the company name centered and column titles underlined. Place a double underline after Income Before Taxes. Include the date on the report since several plans will be created. Use the model from Tutorial 2 for this report and print a copy of the report definition.

3. The Last National Bank

J. J. wants a management style formatted report created of the quarterly plan so he can present it to the board of directors. Create a report that has the bank name centered and column titles that are underlined. Place other underlining in the report for the breaks between revenues and expenses. Use double underlining on the net interest margin. Since several plans may be produced, be sure to include the report date. Use the model from Tutorial 2 for the solution values displayed in this report. Print a copy of your report definition.

4. Harvest University

As chief financial officer, you need a quality management report created to present your plan to the chancellor at Harvest University. Your report should have a heading that is centered and column titles that are underlined. The report should only contain key assumption such as students and tuition per credit hour. The revenues and expenses in dollar amounts should be included in the report. Other assumption should not appear in the report. Apply appropriate underlining within the report and use the currency symbol as you feel necessary. Make sure your plan includes a report date. Use the model from Tutorial 2 for this report. After you print the report, print the report definition.

5. Midwest Universal Gas

Prepare a management style report for Mary Derrick at Midwest Universal Gas (MUG). Mary wants the annual report by quarter to have a heading with the company name centered, column titles, and the date the report was created. Place underlining in the report for breaks between revenues and expenses. Use double underline and the currency symbol to enhance the appearance of the report. Obtain the solution from the model from Tutorial 2 for report, then also print the report definition.

6. General Memorial Hospital

Berry Wellman wants you to prepare a management style report for his presentation of his quarterly plan to the hospital's board. The report should contain the hospital's name centered, column titles underlined, and the date the report was produced. Use underlining and currency symbols as appropriate to improve the appearance of the report. Any negative numbers are to be enclosed in parentheses. Use the model from Tutorial 2 for obtaining the solution displayed in this report. Print this report definition.

7. River City

Create a management style report for River City's quarterly operating budget. The report is to have the city's name centered, column titles and the date of the report. Use underline as appropriate. Commas should appear in the data together with parentheses on any negative numbers. Use the currency symbol as desired. Obtain the solution for this report from the model created in Tutorial 2. After you print the report, also print the report definition.

8. Good Morning Products

Jenny and Frosty have been discussing the report you developed in Problem 1 above. Jenny has explained to Frosty the benefits of a relative or percentage report. They want you to create one. You should do this by making a copy of the Report Definition and then using Sales as the base for the scale. Display the solution from the model created in Tutorial 2 and print this report; then print the report definition.

9. The Woodcraft Furniture Company

Joe Birch wants you to create a percentage report for Woodcraft. Copy the management report definition from Problem 2 above and perform the percentage scaling based on Total Sales. Use the model solution from Tutorial 2 to produce this report. Print the report and your report definition.

10. The Last National Bank

Now that the management report has been set up for the Last National Bank, J. J. wants a percentage report created to accompany the management report. Copy your management report definition from Problem 3 above and alter it with appropriate scaling to produce a percentage report (scale assets as a percentage of total assets and liabilities as a percentage of total liabilities). Interest income and interest expense are to be scaled by total interest income. If you did not include these totals in your model, go back and modify your model so they are available for scaling. Use the model from Tutorial 2 for producing this report. Print this report, and then print your report definition.

11. Harvest University

The chancellor has requested that you prepare a percentage report. (The chancellor attended an executive overview on IFPS and knows you can readily produce this report.) All dollar planning items are to be scaled by tuition. The solution is to come from the model created in Tutorial 2. Print the percent report and your report definition.

12. Midwest Universal Gas

Mary Derrick wants to create a percentage report for MUG. Copy the report definition you have already developed and produce the percentage report with all planning items scaled by Total Revenue, except the ROS. Get the solution values from the model created in Tutorial 2. Print this percent report, and then print the report definition.

13. General Memorial Hospital

Gloria Vander Balance wants you to create a percentage report for General Memorial Hospital. Copy your previous report definition and use it to produce a percentage report. All dollar amount planning items are to be scaled by Total Revenue. Use the same model from Tutorial 2 for this report. Print your percent report, and then print the report definition.

14. River City

Prepare a percentage report of River City's revised operating budget for Lisa Goodnight. Copy your previous report definition and modify it to produce this report. You are to SCALE by Total Revenue. The solution is obtained from the model prepared in Tutorial 2 for printing this report. Also print your report definition.

15. Good Morning Products

After reviewing the reports to be presented to the board of directors of Good Morning Products (GM), Jenny has decided it is desirable to include the branch name on each of the reports. She suggests this is implemented with user-defined micros. The micro definitions are to be placed in each of the branch datafiles. Use the template model from Tutorial 5. Copy each datafile and place appropriate micros in them from the report heading. Copy the report definition and modify it as needed for use with the micros. Print a report using each datafile. Print the report definition and the datafiles.

16. The Woodcraft Furniture Company

To improve on the appearance of the reports from Woodcraft's financial planning model, Talbert wants to have the name of each of the strategic business units printed on the report and the date the report was produced. You decide to accomplish this with user-defined micros . Place a micro definition in each of the business unit datafiles. Use the solution from the template model created in Tutorial 5. Copy each datafile and place appropriate micros in them for the report heading, then copy the report definition and modify it as needed for use with the micros. Print a report using each datafile. Print the report definition and the datafiles.

17. The Last National Bank

To improve upon the Last National Bank's asset and liability planning system, J. J. asked Carrie to include the bank name on each of the reports together with the processing date. Carrie wants you to implement this using micros. Place the micro definition for each bank in that bank's datafile. Get the solution values from the template model created in Tutorial 5. Reproduce each datafile and place appropriate micros in them form the report heading. Duplicate the report definition and modify it as needed for use with the micros. Print a report using each datafile. Print the report definition and the datafiles.

18. Harvest University

In preparing your financial reports for Harvest University's president, you have decided to include the campus name and processing date on report. Implement this with user-defined micros. Place the micro definition for each campus in the datafile for that campus. Use the template model from Tutorial 5. Copy each datafile and place appropriate micros in them from the report heading. Copy the report definition and modify it as needed for use with the micros. Print a report using each datafile. Print the report definition and the datafiles.

19. Midwest Universal Gas

Mary Derrick wants you to improve the appearance of the report from MUG's financial planning model. The name of each business unit is to be displayed in the heading of each report along with the date the report was produced. Implement this by using user-defined micros in the datafile for Midwest Universal and for Blue Flame. Revise the report definition to accept these micros. Use the template model from Tutorial 5. Copy each datafile and place appropriate micros in them for the report heading, then copy the report definition and modify it as needed for use with the micros. Print a report using each datafile. Print the report definition and the datafiles.

20. General Memorial Hospital

To enhance the appearance of the hospital reports for the board of directors, Gloria wants you to revise the datafiles and report definitions.. The hospital name is to be supplied by a micro defined in the datafile for each hospital and referenced in the report definition. The date the report is produced is to be obtained through a built-in micro. Get the solution values from the template model created in Tutorial 5. Replace each datafile and place appropriate micros in them for the report heading. Copy the report definition and modify it as needed for use with the micros. Print a report using each datafile. Print the report definition and the datafiles.

21. River City

Before Lisa presents the financial reports to the city council of River Valley, she wants you to make some cosmetic revisions to them. She wants you to have the name of each governmental area, River City and Peaceful Valley, to appear in the report heading together with the date on which the reports are prepared. You are to implement this by using micros. Place the micro definition containing the name of the governmental area in that area's datafile. Use a built-in micro for the date. Use the template model from Tutorial 5. Copy each datafile and place appropriate micros in them for the report heading. Copy the report definition and modify it as needed for use with the micros. Print a report using each datafile. Print the report definition and the datafiles.

Notes:

Tutorial 7

Creating and Using a Database

Introduction to IFPS Databases

Herbie and Pattie want to add two more outlets to their company. Herbie prefers to keep data from all four outlets in a database. A **database** is a collection of information organized into related groups that support IFPS modeling activities for several entities and is a convenient method of storing data in one place. It provides for activities that include:

- Using database relations that contain both textual and numeric fields. The textual data are frequently used to uniquely identify the numeric data.

- Storing and accessing data using multiple fields to identify rows or variables containing data. This facilitates a multidimensional arrangement of data used with IFPS models.

- Forming IFPS model and datafile variable names by using a single text field or concatenated text fields from a database relation.

- Generating reports directly from a database relation.

- Consolidating data in a relation directly from the relation when solving an IFPS model.

- Operating directly on data in a relation without using a model.

- Using data stored in a relation to provide lists of entities, such as departments or products, that can be used to control processing with IFPS command files.

With IFPS, a database is organized in a collection of one or more relations with all data stored in a relation as Figure 7-1 illustrates.

IFPS/Plus Database

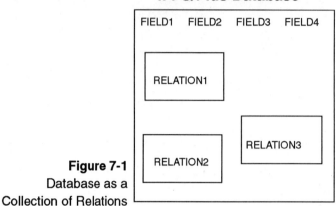

Figure 7-1
Database as a
Collection of Relations

Fields are defined to apply to the entire database. Relations reside in the database and contain a subset of database fields. An example of an IFPS/Plus database **relation** for Buffalo Computer Services (BCS) is shown in Figure 7-2. The **append row** is a blank row at the bottom of the relation that is used when placing additional data in a relation.

Text fields
ACCOUNT and
LOC uniquely
identify row

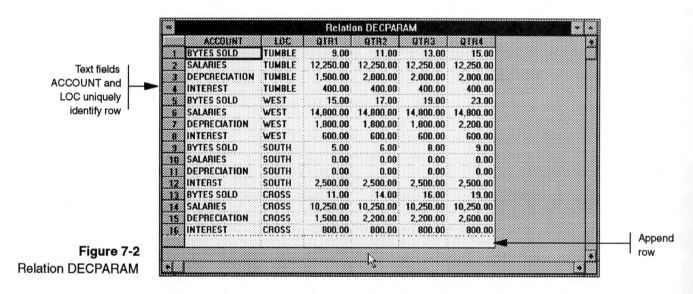

Append
row

Figure 7-2
Relation DECPARAM

In this example, text fields uniquely identify each row in the relation. Numeric fields contain the appropriate data values for each of these columns. This particular arrangement was selected for this example because it closely resembles the manner in which variables of an IFPS model are defined. This arrangement is a matter of choice and not a database requirement.

Creating an IFPS Database

The information provided by the database helps a business organize data more efficiently. A **data definition** describes the information included in the database. From this data definition, Pattie can produce several reports from the same model using different data. When she plans a database, she needs to determine what information BCS will include in the database (Figure 7-3).

Planning Analysis Sheet

My goal:
Develop a database for the Buffalo Computer Services (BCS) for the quarterly model.

What results do I want to see?
Data in one place so it can be changed easily.
Report of each outlet.

What information do I need?
Database with data for each outlet for selected variables.

What calculations will I perform?
Solution of template model with revenues and expenses.

Figure 7-3 Planning Analysis for Database

Planning the Database

Herbie wants the database to contain information about each outlet. Pattie's database definition for the database appears in Figure 7-4.

Field Name	Description
ACCOUNT	Planning item name. (These match the variable names used in the MASTER model.)
LOC	Outlet location identifier.
QTR1	Data value for the 1st quarter.
QTR2	Data value for the 2nd quarter.
QTR3	Data value for the 3rd quarter.
QTR4	Data value for the 4th quarter.

Figure 7-4
Database
Definition

Creating the Database

Now that Herbie has a plan for his database, let's see how to create the database using the database definition from Figure 7-3.

To create a database:

❶   Click the **Context button** in the toolbar.

❷   Click the **IFPS Database option button**. See Figure 7-5.

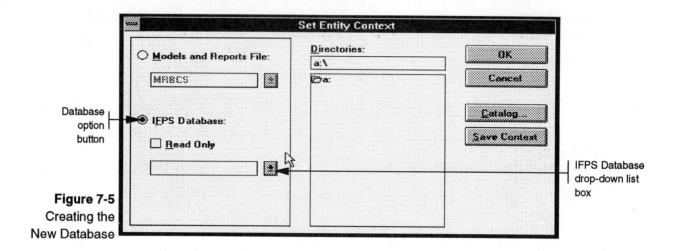

Figure 7-5
Creating the
New Database

❸   Type **DBBCS** in the IFPS database drop-down list box, click the **OK button**, then click the **OK button** in the message box. See Figure 7-6.

Figure 7-6
Creating a New
Database Message
Box

❹   Click the **New button**, click **Relation** in the New dialog box, then click the **OK button** in the message box. See Figure 7-7.

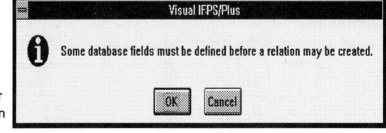

Figure 7-7
Message Box for
Creating Fields in
New Database

❺   Type **ACCOUNT** in the Field drop-down list box, click the **Text option button**, type **24** in the Length text box, then click the **Apply button** to save this field. See Figure 7-8.

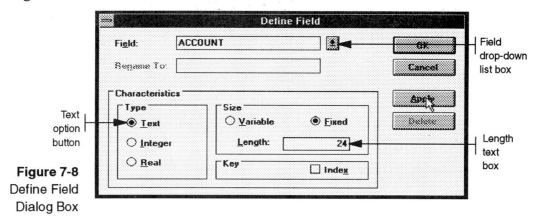

Text option button

Length text box

Field drop-down list box

Figure 7-8
Define Field
Dialog Box

TROUBLE? If the number 8 is in the Length text box, then delete the number and type your number. If you forget to do this, then click the field drop-down list arrow, select ACCOUNT, and change the length of the field.

❻   Type **LOC** in the Field drop-down list box, click the **Text option button**, type **6** in the Length text box, then click the **Apply button** to save this field.

TROUBLE? If the number 8 is in the Length text box, delete the number and type your number. If you forget to do this, then click the field drop-down list arrow, select LOC, and change the length of the field.

❼   Type **QTR1** in the Field drop-down list box, click the **Real option button**, then click the **Apply button** to save this field.

❽   Repeat Step 7 for **QTR2**, **QTR3**, and **QRT4**.

❾   Click the **OK button** to save the fields for the database, then click the **Cancel button** in the Define Relation box.

Now that Herbie and Pattie have created the database, let's see where the data will be stored.

Creating Relations

Two relations are established for the database. A **relation** is where the data are stored in the database. These relations usually separate the data on how they are used with models. Herbie wants to create two relations as described in Figure 7-9.

Relation	Description
BUDGET	Contains selected budget data that is calculated using the MASTER2 model and the DECPARAM relation. These data are expected to be used for subsequent summary reports and consolidation.
DECPARAM	Contains decision parameter data that are entered directly by end users for use in the MASTER2 model to calculate the results for each outlet.

Figure 7-9
Contents of
Data Relations

Herbie thinks the DECPARAM relation should be constructed first. A relation needs to be created before data are placed in it. Let's see how the DECPARAM relation is created.

To create the relation DECPARAM:

❶   Click the **New button** in the toolbar, click **Relation**, then click the **OK button** to display the Define Relation dialog box. See Figure 7-10.

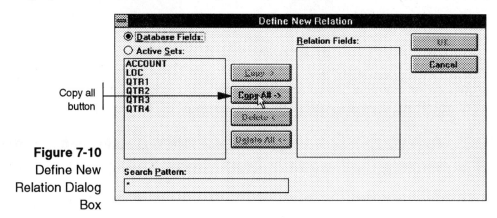

Copy all
button

Figure 7-10
Define New
Relation Dialog
Box

❷   Click the **Copy All button** in the Define New Relation dialog box, then click the **OK button** to accept those fields from the database.

❸   Type **DECPARAM** in the New Relation text box, then click the **OK button** to accept that name. See Figure 7-11. Be sure to remove any unwanted text before you click the **OK button**.

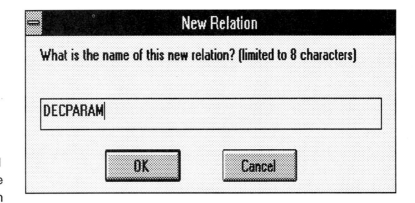

Figure 7-11
Naming the
Relation

❹   Click the **control box**, then click **Close** to close the window. You will put data in this relation in a subsequent step.

Once the DECPARAM relation was defined, Herbie wanted to create the other relation BUDGET. This relation will have only the information from the solution. Let's create the second database relation BUDGET.

To create the relation BUDGET:

❶   Click the **New button**, click **Relation**, then click the **OK button** to display the Define New Relation dialog box.

❷   Click the **Copy All button** in the New Relation dialog box, then click **OK button** to accept those fields from the database.

❸   Type **BUDGET** in the New Relation text box, then click the **OK button** to accept that name.

❹   Click the **control box**, then click **Close** to close the window.

Entering Data in Relations

Herbie has defined both relations. Now he wants to put the data into the relations so he can reference the data. Data may be placed in a relation by one of several methods, as described in Figure 7-12.

METHOD	DESCRIPTION
DIRECT	Data are typed directly into a relation.
DATAFILE	A data file is solved, and the solution values are placed in the relation.
MODEL	A model is solved (which may include using a datafile), and the solution values are placed in the relation.
QUERY	Selected rows and fields from one relation may be placed in another relation.

Figure 7-12
Methods of
Placing Data
into Relations

Herbie decides the data for the DECPARAM relation should be entered by the direct method. The data for this relation are shown in Figure 7-13.

ACCOUNT	LOC	QTR1	QTR2	QTR3	QTR4
BYTES SOLD	TUMBLE	9	11	13	15
SALARIES	TUMBLE	12250	12250	12250	12250
DEPRECIATION	TUMBLE	1500	2000	2000	2500
INTEREST	TUMBLE	400	400	400	400
BYTES SOLD	WEST	15	17	19	23
SALARIES	WEST	14800	14800	14800	14800
DEPRECIATION	WEST	1800	1800	1800	2200
INTEREST	WEST	600	600	600	600
BYTES SOLD	SOUTH	5	6	8	9
SALARIES	SOUTH	2500	2500	2500	2500
DEPRECIATION	SOUTH	0	0	0	0
INTEREST	SOUTH	0	0	0	0
BYTES SOLD	CROSS	11	14	16	19
SALARIES	CROSS	10250	10250	10250	10250
DEPRECIATION	CROSS	1500	2200	2200	2600
INTEREST	CROSS	800	800	800	800

Figure 7-13
Data for
DECPARAM

Let's see how to enter the data from Figure 7-13 into the DECPARAM relation using the direct method.

Reference Window

Entering Data into a Relation Using the Direct Method
■ Click Open, click Relation in the List Entities of Type drop-down list, then click the relation that you want to use from the Entity Name list box.
■ Click the OK button in the Define Select dialog box to open the relation.
■ Move the cursor to the ACCOUNT field or the first field in the relation.
■ Start entering the data in the relation by typing it.
■ After all the data are entered, click the control box, then click Close to save the data in that relation.

To enter data into the DECPARAM relation using the direct method:

❶   Click the **Open button** in the toolbar, select **Relation** from the List Entities of Type drop-down list, click **DECPARAM** from the Entity Name list box, then click the **OK button** to open the Define Select dialog box. See Figure 7-14.

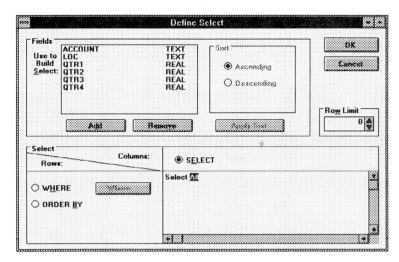

Figure 7-14
Define Select
Dialog Box

❷   Click the **OK button** in the Define Select dialog box to open the relation.

❸   Verify that your cursor is located in the first field of the relation. This field should be the ACCOUNT field.

❹   Type **BYTES SOLD**, press **[Tab]** to move to the next field, type **TUMBLE**, then press **[Tab]**. See Figure 7-15. Do not be concerned with the fact that the names are truncated in the field. You can fix it later after the data are entered.

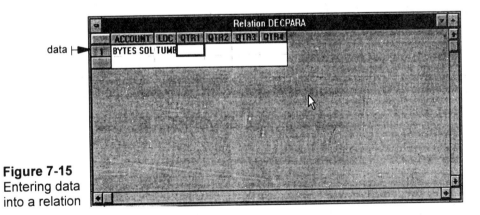

Figure 7-15
Entering data
into a relation

❺   Type **9**, press **[Tab]**. Type **11**, and continue by repeating this step for the rest of the data values for BYTES SOLD for TUMBLE.

❻   Enter **SALARIES** and **TUMBLE** in the second row of the relation, then **[Tab]** to the QTR1 field.

❼   Type **12250** as the data value for QTR1. A beep sounds because this field is too narrow for the number displayed with two places to the right of the decimal, which is the IFPS default.

⑧   Select all four column names by highlighting them. This selects each of the QTR1 through QTR4 columns.

⑨   Move the mouse pointer to the line at the right side of the QTR4 column title until its shape appears as <-|-> for changing the column width. Drag the edge of the column to the right to indicate the desired width for QTR4. When you release the mouse button, the width of all four columns is increased. Now click the cell in row 2 for QTR1 and type **12250**, which is the desired value.

⑩   Follow Steps 3, 4, and 5 until all the names and numbers from Figure 7-13 are input. When you finish, the relation should look like Figure 7-16.

Figure 7-16
All the Data
Entered into
the Relation

	ACCOUNT	LOC	QTR1	QTR2	QTR3	QTR4
1	BYTES SOLD	TUMBLE	9.00	11.00	13.00	15.00
2	SALARIES	TUMBLE	12,250.00	12,250.00	12,250.00	12,250.00
3	DEPRECIATION	TUMBLE	1,500.00	2,000.00	2,000.00	2,000.00
4	INTEREST	TUMBLE	400.00	400.00	400.00	400.00
5	BYTES SOLD	WEST	15.00	17.00	19.00	23.00
6	SALARIES	WEST	14,800.00	14,800.00	14,800.00	14,800.00
7	DEPRECIATION	WEST	1,800.00	1,800.00	1,800.00	2,200.00
8	INTEREST	WEST	600.00	600.00	600.00	600.00
9	BYTES SOLD	SOUTH	5.00	6.00	8.00	9.00
10	SALARIES	SOUTH	2,500.00	2,500.00	2,500.00	2,500.00
11	DEPRECIATION	SOUTH	0.00	0.00	0.00	0.00
12	INTEREST	SOUTH	0.00	0.00	0.00	0.00
13	BYTES SOLD	CROSS	11.00	14.00	16.00	19.00
14	SALARIES	CROSS	10,250.00	10,250.00	10,250.00	10,250.00
15	DEPRECIATION	CROSS	1,500.00	2,200.00	2,200.00	2,600.00
16	INTEREST	CROSS	800.00	800.00	800.00	800.00

Relation DECPARAM

TROUBLE? If the computer still beeps when you are entering a number, go to the top of that column until the pointer changes. Then move the mouse pointer to the right to increase the size of the column. Now re-enter the number again.

Selecting Data

When Herbie initially entered the data in the relation, the data are listed in the order in which he entered them. He wants to look at the SALARIES for all four outlets. He can do this by selecting rows from relation DECPARAM. Let's select data from the relation DECPARAM.

To select data from a relation:

❶   Click **Open**, click **Relation** in the List Entities of Type drop-down list, click **DECPARAM**, then click the **OK button** to display the Define Select box.

❷   Click the **WHERE option button**, then type **ACCOUNT = "SALARIES"** in the Select Box. See Figure 7-17.

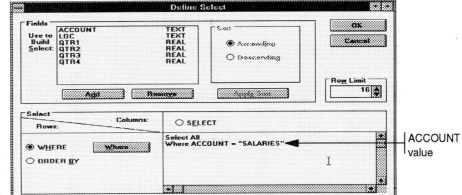

Figure 7-17
Setting ACCOUNT
to SALARIES

❸   Click the **OK button** to perform the select. See Figure 7-18.

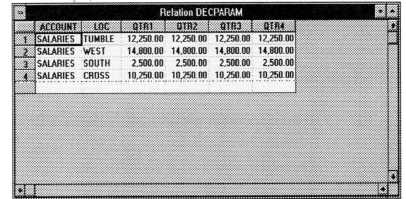

Figure 7-18
Selected
Data

❹   Click **File**, then click **Print** to print a copy of the selected data.

Querying a Database

The **QUERY** Subsystem facilitates the direct reporting of selected rows from a database relation. No model is used with a QUERY. Report-writing capabilities exist in QUERY that permit calculating totals and subtotals. New fields can be computed from existing fields. Reports can include these new fields.

Creating a Query

After reviewing the selected data, Herbie thinks that a query will provide a better display of data from all the outlets. He wants to create a query from their DECPARAM relation using the two query commands: Break on and Subtotal.

Break on serves several purposes:

• It specifies fields and optional field-values to be used for sorting.

• It sequences the left-to-right order in which those fields are displayed when you list the relation.

- The actual field values provide a classification scheme of headings and subheadings, much like a branching tree structure.

Subtotal provides summary values for each variable. You need to identify one or more fields that are assigned to Break on as well as any break field value changes. IFPS calculates subtotals for the preceding category (field value) before the query continues.

Reference Window

Creating a Query
■ Click New and Click Query to display the Query dialog box.
■ Click the Break On option button and type the desired field.
■ Click the Subtotal option button and type the desired subtotal field.
■ Click the OK button to display the query.

Let's create a query with a Break on ACCOUNT and a Subtotal for QTR1 through QTR4 of ACCOUNT and LOC.

To create a query:

❶   Click **New**, click **Query**, and click the **OK button** to display the Define Query dialog box. In the Relations drop-down list box, select **DECPARAM**.

❷   Click the **BREAK ON option button** in the Query area of the dialog box, then type **ACCOUNT** as the desired field. See Figure 7-19.

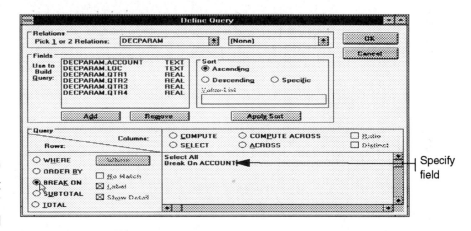

Figure 7-19
Select
BREAK ON ACCOUNT
Field

❸   Click the **SUBTOTAL option button**, then type **QTR1 .. QTR4 FOR ACCOUNT, LOC**. See Figure 7-20.

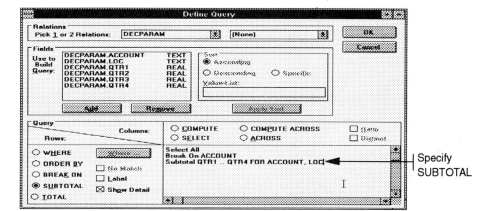

Figure 7-20
Specify the
SUBTOTAL

❹   Click the **OK button** to process the query. See Figure 7-21.

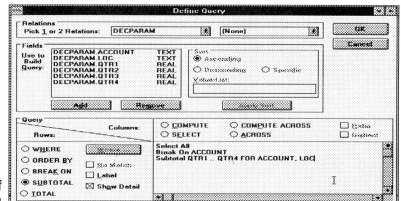

Figure 7-21
Results of
Query with BREAK ON

Changing an Existing Query

After looking at the last query, Herbie decides a query that has the totals for all the data from the outlets would be useful. To accomplish this, you need to use a new command: Compute. **Compute** allows you to calculate a new field based on data in the existing fields. Let's create a query with a compute option that calculates a total of all four quarters. The subtotal is revised to QTR1 through QTR4, YRTOT FOR ACCOUNT and LOC, so the computed field is included with the subtotal.

To change an existing query:
❶   Click the **Query button** in the toolbar to display its dialog box.
❷   Click the **Compute option button** so you can enter a formula.
❸   Type **YRTOT = SUM(QTR1 .. QTR4)** as the desired calculation.
❹   Verify that **Break On ACCOUNT** is still specified. If not, enter this command**.**
❺   Edit the **Subtotal** command so it now includes the YRTOT field and appears like this: **QTR1 .. QTR4, YRTOT FOR ACCOUNT, LOC**
❻   Click the **OK button** to display the query. See Figure 7-22.

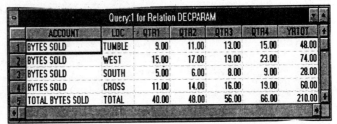

Figure 7-22
Result of Query

❼ Click **File,** click **Print** to obtain a printed copy of this Query, then close the query window.

Using Relations with Models

When data values are obtained from a database relation for *input* into a model, the specification of the data obtained from the relation may be either external to the model or internal to the model. With the **external method**, the values to be extracted are specified with the statements *outside* the model. For the **internal method**, the *model is modified* to contain a description of the data values to be extracted from the relation. Special model statements specify the linkage between the model and the desired relation. As a result, a model must be set up for use with database relations. Often, a special customized model is specifically designed for use with database relation. Herbie wants to use his DECPARAM relation with his model using the internal method because this keeps all the data references within the model and eases coordination between the linkage between the model and relation. Figure 7-23 shows a DFD of relations used with a model.

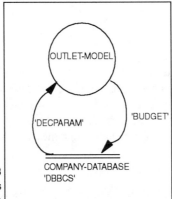

Figure 7-23
DFD for Relations
Used with Models

Model MASTER2 is a customized version of model MASTER from Tutorial 5 that accesses the DECPARAM relation. The model only contains the specification for data that are input to the model. Data values that are stored to a relation from a model solution are always specified external to the model with the **STOREDB** command. An *internal* definition forces the use of the model with the internally defined database relations. For Buffalo Computer Services (BCS), the revised model with the internal method is shown in Figure 7-24.

Planning Analysis Sheet

<u>My goal:</u>
Develop a model with the internal method of using the data from the database.

<u>What results do I want to see?</u>
Revenues and expenses for the next four quarters with an annual total.

<u>What information do I need?</u>
Selected data from the relation for a specified outlet.

<u>What calculations will I perform?</u>
*BUFFALO COMPUTER SERVICES
*PROJECTED PROFIT AND LOSS STATEMENT
COLUMNS 1-4, TOTAL
DBDEFINE ACCTDATA FROM DECPARAM
VARIABLE IS ACCOUNT
COLUMNS ARE QTR1 QTR2 QTR3 QTR4
WHERE LOC = "&LOC IDENTIFIER&"
BYTES SOLD = **DBDATA FROM ACCTDATA**
PRICE PER BYTE = 7500, PREVIOUS + 250
SALES = BYTES SOLD * PRICE PER BYTE
COST OF SALES PERCENT = .77, PREVIOUS - .01
COST OF SALES = SALES * COST OF SALES PERCENT
GROSS PROFIT = SALES - COST OF SALES
SALARIES = **DBDATA FROM ACCTDATA**
BENEFITS = SALARIES * .19
ADMIN EXPENSE = SALES * .023
DEPRECIATION = **DBDATA FROM ACCTDATA**
INTEREST = **DBDATA FROM ACCTDATA**
TOTAL EXPENSES = SUM (SALARIES THRU INTEREST)
EBT = GROSS PROFIT - TOTAL EXPENSES
ROS = EBT / SALES * 100
*SPECIAL COLUMNS COMPUTATIONS
COLUMN TOTAL FOR BYTES SOLD, SALES, COST OF SALES'
       GROSS PROFIT THRU EBT = SUM(C1 THRU C4)
COLUMN TOTAL FOR PRICE PER BYTE = SALES / BYTES SOLD
COLUMN TOTAL FOR ROS = EBT /SALES * 100

Figure 7-24 Planning Analysis Sheet

In the MASTER2 model, the primary statements that link the model and database relation DECPARAM are described as follows:

DBDEFINE ACCTDATA FROM DECPARAM

This DBDEFINE statement specifies ACCTDATA as an *internal model reference name* for the rows and/or fields selected from the DECPARAM database relation. This statement links the model to the relation specified after FROM. An internal model reference name is required because under certain conditions several model references to the same database relation may occur within the same model. If you wish, you can make the internal reference name the same as the database relation name for one reference to the relation.

VARIABLE IS ACCOUNT
COLUMNS ARE QTR1 QTR2 QTR3 QTR4

The **VARIABLE IS** and **COLUMNS ARE** statements specify how fields from the relation are to be associated with the model. Here, the variable name in the model is associated with the ACCOUNT field in the relation. The field QTR1 through QTR4 are identified as those from which the columns of the model receive data from the relation.

WHERE LOC = "&LOC IDENTIFIER&"

This **WHERE** clause specifies the row set to be obtained from the database relation. Since the model is designed to be used with several different locations, the LOC IDENTIFIER micro is used to obtain the value for each solution of this model. In general, the WHERE clause should provide values for all TEXT fields other than those designated from the model variable name field. Although a specific text value such as "WEST" could be used in this WHERE clause, you would need to revise the model for use with a different retail outlet. For this reason, the micro provides the flexibility for accessing data from different outlets without making any edit changes to the model. The WHERE clause performs the same action in the model as it does in a query.

BYTES SOLD = *DBDATA FROM ACCTDATA*

In the definition of the variable BYTES SOLD and the other variables in the model that receive data from the DECPARAM relation, the DBDATA FROM ACCTDATA specifies that database values are to be obtained from the relation defined by the internal model reference name of ACCTDATA. Because ACCTDATA was defined as coming from the DECPARAM relation, these data will be placed in the model when it is solved. With these statements, the relation and the model are linked. Figure 7-25 shows how the model and relation are linked.

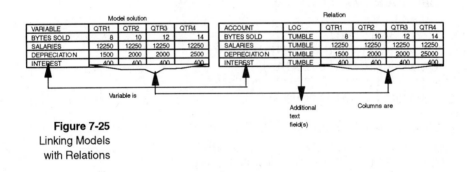

Figure 7-25
Linking Models
with Relations

Let's see how to create the model using the internal database definition.

To create a model with the internal definition:

❶   Click the **New button**, select model in the New dialog box.

❷   Type the model from Figure 7-24 or copy the entire Model MASTER and paste it into this new window. Then modify it with the changes for the database relation references.

❸   Click **File**, click **Save**, then type **MASTER2** in the Entity Name list box, then click the **OK button** to save this model.

Now that we have created the model containing the internal reference for a relation, let's try to solve the model.

Reference Window

Solving a Model with an Internal Database Reference
■   Click Solve, then type the definition for any interactive micros in your model.
■   Click OK to accept the predefined solution variables and columns.

Now let's solve the model.

To solve a model with an internal database reference:

❶   Click the **Solve button** to display the IFPS/Plus Prompt dialog box for entering the LOC IDENTIFIER micro value. See Figure 7-26.

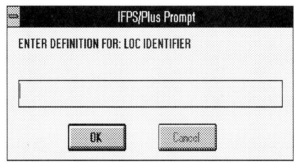

Figure 7-26
Location Identifier
Dialog Box

❷   Type **TUMBLE** in the text box to select only the data for this entity.

❸   Click the **OK button** to select the data from the database and use it in the model solution. See Figure 7-27.

Model MASTER2 Solution:1					
	1	2	3	4	TOTAL
BYTES SOLD	9.00	11.00	13.00	15.00	48.00
PRICE PER BYTE	7,500.00	7,750.00	8,000.00	8,250.00	7,927.08
SALES	67,500.00	85,250.00	104,000.00	123,750.00	380,500.00
COST OF SALES PERCENT	0.77	0.76	0.75	0.74	0.00
COST OF SALES	51,975.00	64,790.00	78,000.00	91,575.00	286,340.00
GROSS PROFIT	15,525.00	20,460.00	26,000.00	32,175.00	94,160.00
SALARIES	12,250.00	12,250.00	12,250.00	12,250.00	49,000.00
BENEFITS	2,327.50	2,327.50	2,327.50	2,327.50	9,310.00
ADMIN EXPENSE	1,552.50	1,960.75	2,392.00	2,846.25	8,751.50
DEPRECIATION	1,500.00	2,000.00	2,000.00	2,500.00	8,000.00
INTEREST	400.00	400.00	400.00	400.00	1,600.00
TOTAL EXPENSES	18,030.00	18,938.25	19,369.50	20,323.75	76,661.50
EBT	-2,505.00	1,521.75	6,630.50	11,851.25	17,498.50
ROS	-3.71	1.79	6.38	9.58	4.60

Figure 7-27
Solution for Model
MASTER2 Selecting TUMBLE

Storing a Model Solution to a Relation

Now that the model solution for TUMBLE is calculated, Herbie wants to store this solution in the relation BUDGET. Figure 7-28 shows the DFD for this process.

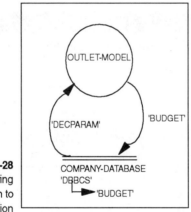

Figure 7-28
DFD for Storing
a Model Solution to
a Relation

Let's examine the procedure for storing the model solution in a relation.

To store a model solution in the relation BUDGET:

❶ Click the **Open button** in the toolbar, select **Model** from the List Entities of Type drop-down list box, click **MASTER2** from the Entity Name list box.

❷ Click the **Solve button** in the toolbar, type **TUMBLE**, then click the **OK button**.

❸ Click **File**, click **Save**, then click **Relation** in the Save As Entity Type drop-down list. See Figure 7-29.

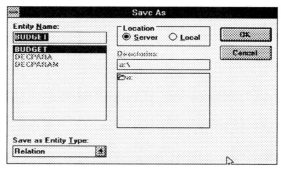

Figure 7-29
Selecting a Relation
for Storing a
Model Solution

❹   Click **BUDGET** in the Entity Name list box, click the **OK button** to accept the relation, click **YES** to store information in the relation.

❺   Click the **VARIABLE IS** button in the Save As Relation dialog box. See Figure 7-30.

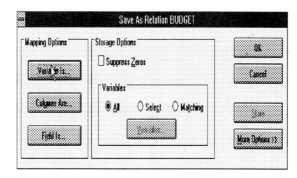

Figure 7-30
Selecting VARIABLE IS in
the Save As Relation
Dialog Box

❻   Select **ACCOUNT** as the field for VARIABLE IS, click the **Copy button** to accept this field, then click the **OK button** to save the VARIABLE IS field as ACCOUNT. This means the variable name in the solution is stored in the ACCOUNT field in the relation. See Figure 7-31.

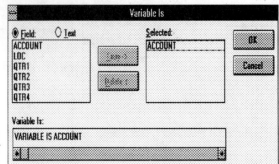

Figure 7-31
Selecting ACCOUNT
for Variable Is

❼   Click the **COLUMNS ARE button** in the Save As Relation dialog box.

❽   Under the **Columns** drop-down list box, select **QTR1, QTR2, QTR3, QTR4** and
       click the **Copy Column button** to complete this selection.

❾   Under the **Fields** list box, select **QTR1, QTR2, QTR3, QTR4** and click the
       Copy Field button, then look at the Columns Are text box and see if it says:
       COLUMNS QTR1, QTR2, QTR3, QTR4 ARE QTR1 QTR2 QTR3 QTR4
       Click the **OK button** to complete the Columns Are specification that links the
       model columns to the appropriate field on the relation. See Figure 7-32.

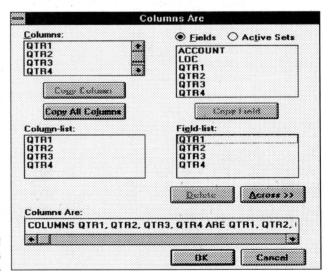

Figure 7-32
Selecting the Columns
for Columns Are

Now that the ACCOUNT and COLUMNS ARE is set for the relation, all we need is the FIELD IS for the identification of the location and what variables will be stored from the model. Let's see how to do this.

To set the FIELD IS and the VARIABLES for the Relation:

❶ Make sure that the Save As Relation dialog box shown previously in Figure 7-30 is still displayed.

TROUBLE? If the Save As Relation dialog box is not displayed, then go back and redo the first nine steps for storing a relation from a model.

❷ Click the **FIELD IS button** to specify the remaining text field in the relation that identifies the retail outlet.

❸ Click the **Field** box drop-down list and click **LOC**, to select this field. Type "**TUMBLE**" under the value box, click the **OK button** to accept this value for the LOC field. This means that every variable that is stored in the relation will have a LOC field value of TUMBLE. See Figure 7-33.

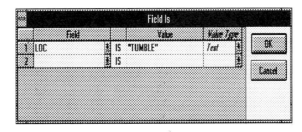

Figure 7-33
Setting LOC
to "TUMBLE"

TROUBLE? If you typed TUMBLE without quotations, repeat Step 3.

❹ Click the **Select option button** in the Variable box of the Save As Relation dialog box to display the dialog box for specifying selected variables. See Figure 7-34.

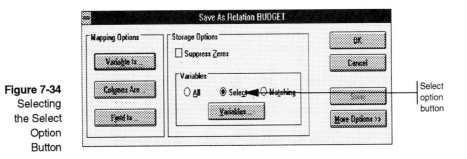

Figure 7-34
Selecting
the Select
Option
Button

Select
option
button

❺   Click the **Variables option button** to select the variables to store in the relation.

❻   Click **BYTES SOLD** then click the **COPY button** to copy that variable.

❼   Click **SALES** then click the **COPY button** to copy that variable.

❽   Click **COST OF SALES**, hold down the **[Shift]**, click **ADMIN EXPENSE**, then click the **Copy button** to copy those variables.

❾   Click the **INTEREST**, hold down the **[Shift]**, click **ROS**, then click the **Copy button** to copy those variables. See Figure 7-35.

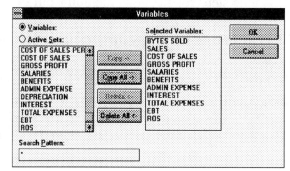

Figure 7-35
Selecting
the Variables

❿   Click the **OK button** to accept the variables, type TUMBLE into the entity box to save the relation with this information. Place the other data in the BUDGET relation by repeating these data storage steps and replacing TUMBLE by WEST, SOUTH, and CROSS.

Extracting Variables from a Relation

A model can be set up to extract data for a particular row in the database by using a micro to specify the value for a particular field at the moment the model is solved. Pattie wants to set up a model to extract variables from a relation. She thinks it would be a good idea to have a model that extracts data values for a particular variable for all the outlets. The model to extract variables from a relation is shown in Figure 7-36.

```
COLUMNS 1-4, TOTAL
DBDEFINE ACCTDATA FROM BUDGET
VARIABLE IS LOC
COLUMNS ARE QTR1 QTR2 QTR3 QTR4
WHERE ACCOUNT EQ "&ACCT NAME&"
TUMBLE = DBDATA FROM ACCTDATA
WEST = DBDATA FROM ACCTDATA
SOUTH = DBDATA FROM ACCTDATA
CROSS = DBDATA FROM ACCTDATA
TOTAL = SUM(TUMBLE THRU CROSS)
COLUMN TOTAL = SUM(C1 THRU C4)
```

Figure 7-36
Variable
Extraction Model

VARIABLE IS LOC
The **VARIABLE IS** clause specifies a template pattern that variable names in the model follow when their values come from the relation.

COLUMNS ARE QTR1 QTR2 QTR3 QTR4
The **COLUMNS ARE** specification indicates which fields will be used for column values. Let's see how to create a model using extracted variables from a relation.

To create a model that extracts variables from a relation:
❶   Click the **New button** in the toolbar, click **Model** in the New dialog box.
❷   Type the model from Figure 7-36.

Now, let's solve the model for the account SALES.

To solve the model with a selected variable:
❶   Click the **Solve button**.
❷   Type **SALES**, click the **OK button**, click the **OK button** to accept the default variables for the solution.

> **TROUBLE?** If you do not enter SALES, but enter another variable name you will get the values for that variable. If you enter a misspelled or nonexistent variable name nothing is displayed.

The extract model from above can be simplified by using the **GETDB** statement as a template line in the model to create variables in the model based on entries in the relation. With the GETDB statement you don't need to list the values for the LOC field in the model. These model variable names are *dynamically created* from the relation at the moment the model is solved. The model with the GETDB statement is shown in Figure 7-37.

	100 COLUMNS 1-4
	110 DBDEFINE ACCTDATA FROM BUDGET
	120 VARIABLE IS LOC
	130 COLUMNS ARE QTR1 QTR2 QTR3 QTR4
	140 WHERE ACCOUNT EQ "&ACCT NAME&"
	150 PROTECT
Figure 7-37	160 **GETDB LOC BY 10 FROM ACCTDATA**
Model with	170 LOC = DATA
GETDB	500 &ACCT NAME& = SUM(L180 THRU L&LASTLINE&)

The model uses the **GETDB** statement in association with the template line causing a series of temporary model lines to be created from the values in the database relation. The &LASTLINE& micro is a system generated micro produced by the GETDB statement the specifies the "last line" of the series of temporary lines created when the GETDB is performed. This model produces the same results as the last model. However, because the variables names are generated from the database relation, you do not need to create and maintain a model that contains the specific variable names. But you do need to include line numbers as shown in Figure 7-37 because line numbers are used to dynamically generate variable names in the model. Now, let's create the model that uses the GETDB statement.

To create a model with the GETDB statement:

❶   Click the **New button** in the toolbar and select Model from the New dialog box.

❷   Type the model from Figure 7-37.

Now let's solve the model with the GETDB statement in it for the account COST OF SALES.

To solve the model with the GETDB statement:

❶   Click the **Solve button** to get a request of ENTER DEFINITION FOR: ACCT NAME.

❷   Type **COST OF SALES**, then click the **OK button** to complete specifying this variable.

❸   Click the **OK button** to display the solution.

Consolidating Data from a Relation

IFPS readily facilities creating a model that permits data values from a relation to be consolidated. Besides consolidating data from relations, IFPS supports consolidating datafiles and model solutions. Because data from multiple entities are more readily managed when stored in a database relation, that method is described. When consolidating data from a relation, the rows in the model are created at the moment the model is solved using entries in the database. Therefore, it is not necessary to determine which rows are summed before the model is solved. Any growth rates and ratios that do not make business sense to sum can be calculated after the consolidation with additional variables in the model.

CAUTION ALERT!

> A *model* is the principal method of consolidating data in database relations!

The following is a fundamental model for performing the consolidation of values stored in a database relation. This model does not contain any variable names since they are *all generated from the relation* when the model is solved and the consolidation is actually performed. A CONSOLDB statement is used in the model similarly to the GETDB to generate the model variable names. Let's see how to create a consolidation model.

To create a consolidation model:

❶   Click the **New button** in the toolbar, select **Model** in the new dialog box.

❷   Type:
        100 COLUMNS 1-4, TOTAL
        110 *DBDEFINE* ACCTDATA FROM BUDGET
        120 COLUMNS ARE QTR1 QTR2 QTR3 QTR4
        130 *CONSOLDB* L140 AT L150 BY *10* FROM ACCTDATA LIMIT 100
        140 ACCOUNT = DBDATA

Once the database relation has been specified in the model with the **DBDEFINE** and associated statements, the **CONSOLDB** and template line (**ACCOUNT = DBDATA**) are the main components in performing a consolidation on a database relation. The template line specifies the field(s) that are to be matched in carrying out the consolidation. Whenever the designated field contains the same values, they are consolidated.

The **CONSOLDB** actually causes the consolidation to be performed when the model is solved. The template line should immediately follow the line containing the **CONSOLDB** statement. *Line numbers are included with the model statement* to facilitate creating variable names from the solution at the moment the model is solved. The L150 (that is, Line 150) indicates the beginning line number of the temporary model lines that are generated as the consolidation is carried out. The **BY 10** indicates the line numbering increment of the temporary lines. The **LIMIT 100** specifies the maximum number of lines that are generated when the model is solved and the consolidation is performed. The default value is 25, so often this value needs to be set to a larger value, such as 100 or 1000. Now, let's solve the model and consolidate the data from the BUDGET Relation.

To solve a consolidation model:

❶   Click the **Solve button**, then click the **OK button**.

❷   Click **File**, then click **Print**, to print the consolidated results. See Figure 7-38.

Figure 7-38
Solution for
CONSOLDB

	1	2	3	4	TOTAL
BYTES SOLD	35.00	42.00	48.00	57.00	57.00
SALES	300,000.00	372,000.00	448,000.00	544,500.00	544,500.00
COST OF SALES	231,000.00	282,720.00	336,000.00	402,930.00	402,930.00
GROSS PROFIT	69,000.00	89,280.00	112,000.00	141,570.00	141,570.00
SALARIES	37,300.00	37,300.00	37,300.00	37,300.00	37,300.00
BENEFITS	7,087.00	7,087.00	7,087.00	7,087.00	7,087.00
ADMIN EXPENSE	6,900.00	8,556.00	10,304.00	12,523.50	12,523.50
INTEREST	1,800.00	1,800.00	1,800.00	1,800.00	1,800.00
TOTAL EXPENSES	56,387.00	58,743.00	60,491.00	63,510.50	63,510.50
EBI	12,613.00	30,537.00	51,509.00	78,059.50	78,059.50
ROS	0.25	0.40	0.51	0.62	0.62

The consolidation gives Herbie and Pattie an overall summary of the expected performance of BCS for all four outlets.

Database Commands, Statements, and References

IFPS/Plus contains a number of database commands, directives, statements, and references. Some of the more frequently used commands are listed here with a brief description for your reference. The detail operation of each command is described in the *IFPS/Plus User's Manual*.

Database Command	Action
BREAK ON field list	Specifies fields used for sorting in Query.
COLUMNS [col-list] ARE field-list	Identifies fields in database and optionally specifies columns from model/datafile solution.
COMPUTE fieldname = expression	Compute new field in database relation as part of Query.
CONSOLDB Ltemp-num At Lline-num BY incr FROM subname [LIMIT n]	Model statement that generates variables which are consolidated results from a relation named by DBDEFINE statement.

Database Command	Action
DATA [[FOR n], [expression]]	Keyword used in model variable definition that permits values to be supplied by either datafile or relation specified by the USING command.
DATABASE dbname [password] [READONLY]	Specify which database to access with optional password and read status.
varname = DBDATA [FROM subname] [FOR ncols], [expression]	Specify data values that are supplied for a relation subname provided by DBDEFINE statement.
DBDEFINE subname FROM relname	Used in a model to specify a subset of rows in the model that receive data from the specified relation.
FIELD fieldname [type] [length] [KEY]	Set up fields in database, separate FIELD commands are required for each database FIELD.
FIELDS [ARE] field-list	Specify subset of database field for relation.
GETDB Ltemp-num AT Lline-num BY incr FROM subname [LIMIT n]	Model statement that generates separate variable for each matching row in relation named by DBDEFINE statement.
LIST [[APPEND] [ONLY] [ONTO filename]]	Produces listing of all rows/fields in active relation.
LISTFLD[S]	List fields in active database and in each relation.
LISTREL [relname]	List relation names of relations in active database and optionally list structure of specified relation.
ORDER BY field-list	Query command which sorts rows for display with LIST command.
QUERY relname , [relname2]	Activates Query Subsystem and specifies relation(s).
RELATION relname WITH field-list	Set up relation in active database and specify fields in relation.
SAVE AS relname	Create new relation from specified Query options.
SELECT field-list	Specify fields to be displayed with a LIST command.

Database Command	Action
SELECT DISTINCT field-list	Specify relation into which current model/datafile solution will be stored.
STOREDB relname	Specify relation into which current model/datafile solution will be stored.
STOREDF filename	Specify datafile into which values from current relation will be stored.

USING datalist
  where datalist is a
  combination of:
    filename
    RELATION relname [WHERE clause]
    RELATION [rel-list] [WHERE clause]
	Specify datafiles and/or relations that provide data values to model subject to WHERE definition.

VARIABLE IS field-list	Specify template of fields for relation from which data is obtained or to which data is stored.
WHERE condition 1 [logic-oper condition 2]	Specify conditions that restrict eligible rows that will be processed.

Questions

1. An IFPS/Plus _____ is a data management capability that supports IFPS modeling activities.
   a. data
   b. database
   c. datafile
   d. model

2. A _____ is where data are stored through the database structure.
   a. relation
   b. database
   c. query
   d. micro

3. What method has the data values to be extracted specified with the statements outside the model?
   a. internal
   b. external
   c. COLUMNS ARE
   d. LOC IS

4.   What method has the model modified to contain a description of the data values to be extracted from the relation?
        a. internal
        b. external
        c. COLUMNS ARE
        d. LOC IS

5.   The _____ statement specifies ACCTDATA as an internal model reference name for the rows and fields selected from a database relation.
        a.   DBDEFINE
        b.   VARIABLE IS
        c.   COLUMNS ARE
        d.   LOC IS

Case Problems

1. Good Morning Products

Good Morning Products (GM) has continued to expand as an international bottler and distributor of the Liquid Gold brand of fresh orange juice by acquiring two additional plants. To better manage their data, Kim designed a database that contains fields described by this data dictionary definition:

Field Name	Length	Description
ACCOUNT	20	Planning item name (variable name used in model).
LOC	8	Plant location identifier.
QTR1	Real	Data value for 1st quarter.
QTR2	Real	Data value for 2nd quarter.
QTR3	Real	Data value for 3rd quarter.
QTR4	Real	Data value for 4th quarter.

Under the guidance of Frosty and Good Morning Products' board of directors, operations have expanded at these two new plants. Frosty has received the data that are needed from the new plants:

ACCOUNT	LOC	QTR1	QTR2	QTR3	QTR4
BOTTLES	CALIF	330000	310000	260000	300000
PRICE PER BOTTLE	CALIF	3.19	3.19	3.39	3.39
GENERAL AND ADMIN	CALIF	23000	23000	26000	26000
ADVERTISING	CALIF	18000	19000	21000	21500
INTEREST	CALIF	16000	16000	16000	16000
DEPRECIATION	CALIF	25500	25500	25500	25500
LABOR	CALIF	.89	.89	.89	.89
ORANGES	CALIF	1.21	1.21	1.21	1.21
PACKAGING	CALIF	.57	.57	.57	.57
BOTTLES	FLORIDA	160000	145000	120000	140000
PRICE PER BOTTLE	FLORIDA	3.19	3.19	3.39	3.39
GENERAL AND ADMIN	FLORIDA	12000	13000	16000	16000
ADVERTISING	FLORIDA	8000	9000	11000	9000
INTEREST	FLORIDA	7000	7000	7000	7000
DEPRECIATION	FLORIDA	18500	18500	18500	18500
LABOR	FLORIDA	.89	.89	.89	.89

ORANGES	FLORIDA	1.21	1.21	1.21	1.21
PACKAGING	FLORIDA	.57	.57	.57	.57
BOTTLES	TEXAS	120000	95000	115000	105000
PRICE PER BOTTLE	TEXAS	3.19	3.19	3.39	3.39
GENERAL AND ADMIN	TEXAS	12000	13000	16000	16000
ADVERTISING	TEXAS	4000	7000	6000	5500
INTEREST	TEXAS	3500	3500	3500	3500
DEPRECIATION	TEXAS	12500	12500	12500	12500
LABOR	TEXAS	.83	.83	.83	.83
ORANGES	TEXAS	1.23	1.23	1.23	1.23
PACKAGING	TEXAS	.54	.54	.54	.54
BOTTLES	GOLDEN	80000	65000	85000	75000
PRICE PER BOTTLE	GOLDEN	3.19	3.19	3.39	3.39
GENERAL AND ADMIN	GOLDEN	10000	11000	12000	12000
ADVERTISING	GOLDEN	0	0	0	0
INTEREST	GOLDEN	0	0	0	0
DEPRECIATION	GOLDEN	8500	8500	8500	8500
LABOR	GOLDEN	.89	.89	.89	.89
ORANGES	GOLDEN	1.21	1.21	1.21	1.21
PACKAGING	GOLDEN	.57	.57	.57	.57

Task 1:   Create a database named DBGMP.

Task 2:   Create two relations: one named BUDGET and the other named DECPARAM, which contain all the database fields.

Task 3:   Using the direct method for entering data into the relation, enter all the data into the DECPARAM relation from the above table.

Task 4:   Create a model like that shown in Figure 7-24, save and solve the model. Use the model from Tutorial 5 Case Problem 15 as a starting place for this model.

Task 5:   Store the entire model solution from each plant into the BUDGET relation.

Task 6:   Print the DECPARAM and BUDGET relations and the revised model.

2. The Woodcraft Furniture Company

Under the guidance of Joe Birch, Woodcraft Furniture Company has continued to expand its operations by acquiring two additional regional furniture manufacturing companies with similar product lines: Custom Interior Designs (CID) and Scandia Interior Creations (SIC). Talber "Tall" Pine and Ray Jointer designed the database that contains fields described by this data dictionary definition:

Field Name	Length	Description
ACCOUNT	24	Planning item name (variable name used in model).
CO	8	Company identifier.
M1	Real	Data value from the 1st month.
M2	Real	Data value from the 2nd month.
M3	Real	Data value from the 3rd month.

Ray has collected input data for their operations:

ACCOUNT	CO	M1	M2	M3
TABLES SOLD	WOOD	850	900	950
SOFAS SOLD	WOOD	561	694	627
TABLE PRICE	WOOD	450	450	450
CHAIR PRICE	WOOD	100	100	100

SOFA PRICE	WOOD	300	300	300
EMPLOYEES	WOOD	157	160	165
HOURLY RATE	WOOD	9.60	9.60	9.60
HOURS WORKED	WOOD	174	174	174
ADVERTISING	WOOD	97760	103500	109240
MANAGEMENT SALARIES	WOOD	47250	47250	47250
GENERAL AND ADMIN	WOOD	24000	25000	26000
INTEREST EXPENSE	WOOD	12240	12240	12240
TABLES SOLD	OAK	170	227	285
SOFAS SOLD	OAK	170	227	285
TABLE PRICE	OAK	450	450	450
CHAIR PRICE	OAK	100	100	100
SOFA PRICE	OAK	300	300	300
EMPLOYEES	OAK	30	40	50
HOURLY RATE	OAK	9.60	9.60	9.60
HOURS WORKED	OAK	174	174	174
ADVERTISING	OAK	2500	5000	3500
MANAGEMENT SALARIES	OAK	9000	9000	9000
GENERAL AND ADMIN	OAK	3500	4500	5500
INTEREST EXPENSE	OAK	2750	2750	2750
TABLES SOLD	CID	270	258	168
SOFAS SOLD	CID	164	220	210
TABLE PRICE	CID	375	375	375
CHAIR PRICE	CID	90	90	90
SOFA PRICE	CID	350	350	350
EMPLOYEES	CID	35	43	53
HOURLY RATE	CID	9.90	9.90	9.90
HOURS WORKED	CID	168	168	168
ADVERTISING	CID	3800	4200	4000
MANAGEMENT SALARIES	CID	12000	12000	12000
GENERAL AND ADMIN	CID	4300	4800	5500
INTEREST EXPENSE	CID	2250	2250	2250
TABLES SOLD	SIC	560	720	680
SOFAS SOLD	SIC	190	250	340
TABLE PRICE	SIC	360	360	360
CHAIR PRICE	SIC	75	75	75
SOFA PRICE	SIC	400	400	400
EMPLOYEES	SIC	86	90	98
HOURLY RATE	SIC	9.40	9.40	9.40
HOURS WORKED	SIC	174	174	174
ADVERTISING	SIC	14600	15800	16300
MANAGEMENT SALARIES	SIC	22000	22000	22000
GENERAL AND ADMIN	SIC	9300	9800	10500
INTEREST EXPENSE	SIC	3200	3200	3200

Task 1:   Create a database named DBWOOD.

Task 2:   Create two relations named INPUT and BUDGET that contain all the database fields.

Task 3:   Using the direct method of entering data into a relation, enter the data from the above table into the INPUT relation.

Task 4:   Create a model like that shown in Figure 7-24 by copying and modifying your model from Tutorial 5 Case Problem 16. Save the model with a new name.

Task 5:   Store the model solutions from all the companies (CO field) in the BUDGET relation. The variables to be stored are:
EMPLOYEES, OVERHEAD, HOURS WORKED, COST OF SALES, TABLES SOLD, GROSS PROFIT, CHAIRS SOLD, ADVERTISING, SOFAS SOLD, INSURANCE, TABLES SALES, MANAGEMENT SALARIES, CHAIR SALES, GENERAL AND ADMIN, SOFA SALES, OPERATING EXPENSES, TOTAL SALES, INTEREST EXPENSE, RAW MATERIAL , INCOME BEFORE TAXES, and LABOR

Task 6:   Print the INPUT and BUDGET relations and your modified model.

3. The Last National Bank

Last National Bank has continued its expansion with acquisition of two additional banks in the same area: Broken Wheel (BROKEN) and Passage West (PASS).

Carrie designed the database fields described by this data dictionary definition:

Field Name	Length	Description
ACCOUNT	36	Planning item name (variable name used in model).
LOC	8	Location identifier.
JAN	Real	Data value for January.
FEB	Real	Data value for February.
MAR	Real	Data value for March.

Data for all locations are as follows:

ACCOUNT	LOC	JAN	FEB	MAR
REAL ESTATE MORTGAGES	SPOKEN	32000	31000	29500
INSTALLMENT LOANS	SPOKEN	1100	12000	14200
COMMERCIAL LOANS	SPOKEN	27000	29000	33000
OTHER INVESTMENTS	SPOKEN	2000	2500	3500
REGULAR SAVINGS	SPOKEN	11000	15000	12500
INTEREST PLUS CHECKING	SPOKEN	16000	17800	18200
MONEY MARKET CERTIFICATES	SPOKEN	40000	42000	43300
OTHER BORROWED FUNDS	SPOKEN	3000	2500	3800
REAL ESTATE MORTGAGES	WEEP	16500	15500	15000
INSTALLMENT LOANS	WEEP	7000	7900	8200
COMMERCIAL LOANS	WEEP	13500	14500	16500
OTHER INVESTMENTS	WEEP	1000	1500	2500
REGULAR SAVINGS	WEEP	6000	7000	7500
INTEREST PLUS CHECKING	WEEP	8000	8800	9200
MONEY MARKET CERTIFICATES	WEEP	21000	21500	22400
OTHER BORROWED FUNDS	WEEP	1500	2000	2400
REAL ESTATE MORTGAGES	BROKEN	15500	14500	13500
INSTALLMENT LOANS	BROKEN	4000	4400	6000
COMMERCIAL LOANS	BROKEN	13500	14500	16500
OTHER INVESTMENTS	BROKEN	500	1000	1500
REGULAR SAVINGS	BROKEN	5000	6000	6500
INTEREST PLUS CHECKING	BROKEN	6000	6800	6500
MONEY MARKET CERTIFICATES	BROKEN	19000	20500	20900
OTHER BORROWED FUNDS	BROKEN	1500	1900	2300
REAL ESTATE MORTGAGES	PASS	20000	21000	19500
INSTALLMENT LOANS	PASS	9000	10000	12200
COMMERCIAL LOANS	PASS	20000	22000	26000
OTHER INVESTMENTS	PASS	1500	2000	3000

REGULAR SAVINGS	PASS	9000	10000	10500
INTEREST PLUS CHECKING	PASS	12000	13800	14200
MONEY MARKET CERTIFICATES	PASS	25000	27000	28300
OTHER BORROWED FUNDS	PASS	2000	1500	2800

Task 1:   Create a database named DBLNB.

Task 2:   Create two relations named INPUT and BUDGET that contain all the database fields.

Task 3:   Using the direct method of entering data into a relation, enter the data from the table into the INPUT relation.

Task 4:   Create a model like the one in Figure 7-24. Give the model a new name when you save it.

Task 5:   Store the model solutions for all the divisions in the BUDGET relation. The variables to be stored are:
REAL ESTATE MORTGAGES EARNINGS, INSTALLMENT LOANS EARNINGS, COMMERCIAL LOANS EARNINGS, OTHER INVESTMENTS EARNINGS, TOTAL INTEREST EARNINGS ON ASSETS, REGULAR SAVINGS EARNINGS, INTEREST PLUS CHECKING EARNINGS, MONEY MARKET EARNINGS, OTHER BORROWED FUNDS EARNINGS, TOTAL INTEREST EXPENSE, and INTEREST MARGIN

Task 6:   Print the INPUT and BUDGET relations and the model used with each division.

4. Harvest University

Harvest University, under the chief financial officer's guidance, has continued to expand its operations by acquiring two additional campuses: Southwest State (SSHU) and Metropolitan (MHU). The chief financial officer designed the database that contains fields specified by this data dictionary definition:

Field Name	Length	Description
ACCOUNT	24	Planning item name (variable name used in model).
CAMP	8	Campus identifier.
FALL	Real	Data value for fall.
WINT	Real	Data value for winter.
SPR	Real	Data value for spring.
SUMM	Real	Data value for summer.

The chief financial officer has collected input data for the INPUT relation:

ACCOUNT	CAMP	FALL	WINT	SPR	SUMM
STUDENTS	MAIN	32000	3000	2800	1000
CREDIT HOURS PER STUDENT	MAIN	14	12	11	5
ENDOWMENT INCOME	MAIN	312500	312500	312500	312500
OTHER INCOME	MAIN	187500	187500	187500	187500
ADMINISTRATIVE SALARIES	MAIN	337500	337500	337500	337500
SECRETARIAL SALARIES	MAIN	350000	350000	350000	350000
TAS SALARIES	MAIN	60000	60000	60000	5000
OTHER SALARIES	MAIN	250000	250000	250000	100000
UTILITIES	MAIN	550000	700000	550000	400000
OTHER OPERATING EXPENSES	MAIN	1750000	1750000	1750000	1750000
STUDENTS	DOWN	1600	1466	1466	600
CREDIT HOURS PER STUDENT	DOWN	15	14	12	6
ENDOWMENT INCOME	DOWN	132500	132500	132500	132500
OTHER INCOME	DOWN	67500	67500	67500	67500
ADMINISTRATIVE SALARIES	DOWN	78500	78500	78500	78500
SECRETARIAL SALARIES	DOWN	150000	150000	150000	150000

TAS SALARIES	DOWN	25000	25000	25000	3200
OTHER SALARIES	DOWN	95000	95000	95000	32000
UTILITIES	DOWN	250000	300000	220000	40000
OTHER OPERATING EXPENSES	DOWN	175000	175000	175000	175000
STUDENTS	SSHU	2000	1800	1700	1000
CREDIT HOURS PER STUDENT	SSHU	16	15	11	5
ENDOWMENT INCOME	SSHU	200500	200500	200500	200500
OTHER INCOME	SSHU	90000	90000	90000	90000
ADMINISTRATIVE SALARIES	SSHU	250000	250000	250000	250000
SECRETARIAL SALARIES	SSHU	200000	200000	200000	200000
TAS SALARIES	SSHU	40000	40000	40000	4000
OTHER SALARIES	SSHU	100000	100000	10000	50000
UTILITIES	SSHU	350000	450000	350000	250000
OTHER OPERATING EXPENSES	SSHU	175000	175000	175000	175000
STUDENTS	MHU	3600	3400	3200	1400
CREDIT HOURS PER STUDENT	MHU	13	9	8	3
ENDOWMENT INCOME	MHU	400000	400000	400000	400000
OTHER INCOME	MHU	200000	200000	200000	200000
ADMINISTRATIVE SALARIES	MHU	30000	30000	30000	30000
SECRETARIAL SALARIES	MHU	200000	200000	200000	200000
TAS SALARIES	MHU	70000	70000	70000	10000
OTHER SALARIES	MHU	150000	150000	150000	90000
UTILITIES	MHU	50000	70000	50000	40000
OTHER OPERATING EXPENSES	MHU	150000	150000	150000	150000

Task 1:   Create a database named DBHU.

Task 2:   Create two relations named INPUT and BUDGET that contain all the database fields.

Task 3:   Using the direct method of entering data into a relation, enter the data from the table into the INPUT relation.

Task 4:   Create a model like the one shown in Figure 7-24.

Task 5:   Store the model solutions for all the campuses in the BUDGET relation. The variables to be stored are:
STUDENTS, CREDIT HOURS PER STUDENT, AVERAGE FULL TIME FACULTY SALARY, AVERAGE PART TIME FACULTY SALARY, TUITION PER CREDIT HOUR, CREDIT HOURS, TUITION, LAB FEES, ENDOWMENT INCOME, OTHER INCOME, TOTAL REVENUES, ADMINISTRATIVE SALARIES, SECRETARIAL SALARIES, FTE FACULTY, FULL TIME FACULTY SALARIES, PART TIME FACULTY SALARIES, TAS SALARIES, OTHER SALARIES, TOTAL SALARIES, FRINGE BENEFITS, UTILITIES, OTHER OPERATING EXPENSE, TOTAL EXPENSES, and RESERVE.

Task 6:   Print the INPUT and BUDGET relations and the model used with each campus.

5. Midwest Universal Gas

Midwest Universal Gas (MUG) has continued it expansion with acquisition of two additional gas distribution companies in the same general geographical area: Consumers Overland Gas (COG) and Northern Lite Natural Gas (NLNG).

Sam designed the database that contains fields described by this data dictionary definition:

Field Name	Length	Description
ACCOUNT	24	Planning item name (variable name used in model).
DIV	8	Division identifier.
QTR1	Real	Data value for 1st quarter.
QTR2	Real	Data value for 2nd quarter.
QTR3	Real	Data value for 3rd quarter.
QTR4	Real	Data value for 4th quarter.

Data for all divisions are as follows:

ACCOUNT	DIV	QTR1	QTR2	QTR3	QTR4
TOTAL GAS SOLD	MUG	220	210	80	210
RETAIL PRICE	MUG	3500	3500	3500	3500
WHOLESALE PRICE	MUG	2859	2859	2859	2859
RETAIL VOLUME RATIO	MUG	.22	.22	.22	.22
GENERAL ADMIN	MUG	40625	40625	40625	40625
INTEREST EXPENSE	MUG	15250	15250	15250	15250
TAX CREDITS	MUG	21000	21000	21000	21000
INVESTMENTS	MUG	1204000	1204000	1204000	1204000
TOTAL GAS SOLD	BLUE	62	38	21	40
RETAIL PRICE	BLUE	3500	3500	3500	3500
WHOLESALE PRICE	BLUE	2859	2859	2859	2859
RETAIL VOLUME RATIO	BLUE	.57	.57	.57	.57
GENERAL ADMIN	BLUE	9900	9900	9900	9900
INTEREST EXPENSE	BLUE	600	600	600	600
TAX CREDITS	BLUE	2400	2400	2400	2400
INVESTMENTS	BLUE	350000	350000	350000	350000
TOTAL GAS SOLD	COG	110	95	35	98
RETAIL PRICE	COG	3300	3300	3300	3300
WHOLESALE PRICE	COG	2741	2741	2741	2741
RETAIL VOLUME RATIO	COG	.43	.43	.43	.43
GENERAL ADMIN	COG	10980	10980	10980	10980
INTEREST EXPENSE	COG	730	730	730	730
TAX CREDITS	COG	0	0	0	0
INVESTMENTS	COG	450000	450000	450000	450000
TOTAL GAS SOLD	LITE	160	125	75	137
RETAIL PRICE	LITE	3400	3400	3400	3400
WHOLESALE PRICE	LITE	2793	2793	2793	2793
RETAIL VOLUME RATIO	LITE	.36	.36	.36	.36
GENERAL ADMIN	LITE	12760	12760	12760	12760
INTEREST EXPENSE	LITE	970	970	970	970
TAX CREDITS	LITE	8700	8700	8700	8700
INVESTMENTS	LITE	630000	630000	630000	630000

Task 1:   Create a database named DBMUG.

Task 2:   Create two relations named INPUT and BUDGET that contain all the database fields.

Task 3:   Using the direct method of entering data into a relation, enter the data from the table into the INPUT relation.

Task 4:   Create a model like the one shown in Figure 7-24, by copying and editing your model from Tutorial 5, Case Problem 19. Give the model a new name when you save it.

Task 5:   Store the model solutions for all the divisions in the BUDGET relation. The variables to be stored are:

TOTAL GAS SOLD, DEPRECIATION, RETAIL SALES, TOTAL EXPENSES, WHOLESALES SALES, OPERATING INCOME, TOTAL REVENUE, INTEREST EXPENSE, COST OF SALES, INCOME BEFORE TAXES, TAX CREDITS, SELLING EXPENSE, INCOME TAXES, GENERAL ADMIN, and NET INCOME

Task 6:   Print the INPUT and BUDGET relations and your modified model used with each division.

6. General Memorial Hospital

Gloria decided to take over the remaining hospitals in Family Health Care. The hospitals are St. Joseph Hospital (SJH) and Family Health Care Hospital (FHCH). Berry has designed the database that contains fields described by this data dictionary definition:

Field Name	Length	Description
ACCOUNT	24	Planning item name (variable name used in model).
HOP	8	Hospital identifier.
APR	Real	Data value for April.
MAY	Real	Data value for May.
JUN	Real	Data value for June.

Data for all hospitals are as follows:

ACCOUNT	HOP	APR	MAY	JUN
BED CAPACITY	GMH	100	100	100
BED UTILIZATION RATE	GMH	.65	.80	.75
GERONTOLOGY SERVICE	GMH	70	85	78
STAFF DOCTORS	GMH	4	4	5
DEPRECIABLE ASSETS	GMH	41667	41667	41667
INTEREST	GMH	5000	5000	5000
BAD DEBITS	GMH	2000	2000	2000
BED CAPACITY	CGH	50	50	50
BED UTILIZATION RATE	CGH	.75	.85	.80
GERONTOLOGY SERVICE	CGH	35	45	40
STAFF DOCTORS	CGH	2	2	2
DEPRECIABLE ASSETS	CGH	20000	20000	20000
INTEREST	CGH	2500	2500	2500
BAD DEBITS	CGH	750	750	750
BED CAPACITY	SJH	75	75	75
BED UTILIZATION RATE	SJH	.60	.70	.65
GERONTOLOGY SERVICE	SJH	50	60	55
STAFF DOCTORS	SJH	3	4	5
DEPRECIABLE ASSETS	SJH	30000	30000	30000
INTEREST	SJH	4000	4000	4000
BAD DEBITS	SJH	1000	1000	1000
BED CAPACITY	FHCH	25	25	25
BED UTILIZATION RATE	FHCH	.85	.95	.90
GERONTOLOGY SERVICE	FHCH	45	60	50
STAFF DOCTORS	FHCH	5	5	5
DEPRECIABLE ASSETS	FHCH	35000	35000	35000
INTEREST	FHCH	4500	4500	4500
BAD DEBITS	FHCH	1500	1500	1500

Task 1:   Create a database named DBGMH.

Task 2:   Create two relations named INPUT and BUDGET that contain all the database fields.

Task 3:   Using the direct method of entering data into a relation, enter the data from the table into the INPUT relation.

Task 4:   Create a model like the one in Figure 7-23. Give the model a new name when you save it.

Task 5:   Store the model solutions for all the hospitals in the BUDGET relation. The variables to be stored are: IN PATIENT through NET INCOME

Task 6:   Print the INPUT and BUDGET relations and the model.

7. River City

River City is a metropolis that includes three suburbs and a downtown. Two additional suburbs are Cass City (CASS) and Happyville (HAPPY). Frank designed the database that contains field described by this data dictionary definition:

Field Name	Length	Description
ACCOUNT	24	Planning item name (variable name used in model).
SUB	8	Suburb identifier.
JUL	Real	Data value for July.
AUG	Real	Data value for August.
SEPT	Real	Data value for September.

Data for all the suburbs and downtown are as follows:

ACCOUNT	SUB	JUL	AUG	SEPT
RETAIL SALES	MAIN	245720	231266	274628
PROPERTY TAXES	MAIN	18522	0	0
PERMITS	MAIN	2500	100	120
CITY GOVERNMENT	MAIN	375	375	375
LAW ENFORCEMENT	MAIN	208	208	208
PUBLIC SAFETY	MAIN	2808	2808	2808
PUBLIC WORKS	MAIN	883	883	883
PARKS	MAIN	1500	1750	1000
HOUSING	MAIN	183	183	183
LIBRARIES	MAIN	242	242	242
MISCELLANEOUS	MAIN	430	430	430
RETAIL SALES	PEACE	95000	100000	110000
PROPERTY TAXES	PEACE	3500	0	0
PERMITS	PEACE	400	50	10
CITY GOVERNMENT	PEACE	5	5	5
LAW ENFORCEMENT	PEACE	16	16	16
PUBLIC SAFETY	PEACE	850	850	850
PUBLIC WORKS	PEACE	65	65	65
PARKS	PEACE	2	4	6
HOUSING	PEACE	0	0	0
LIBRARIES	PEACE	5	5	5
MISCELLANEOUS	PEACE	10	10	10
RETAIL SALES	CASS	100000	105000	115000
PROPERTY TAXES	CASS	4500	0	0
PERMITS	CASS	300	40	0
CITY GOVERNMENT	CASS	10	10	10
LAW ENFORCEMENT	CASS	6	6	6
PUBLIC SAFETY	CASS	950	950	950
PUBLIC WORKS	CASS	85	85	85

PARKS	CASS	10	12	14
HOUSING	CASS	10	10	10
LIBRARIES	CASS	0	0	0
MISCELLANEOUS	CASS	5	5	5
RETAIL SALES	HAPPY	85000	90000	100000
PROPERTY TAXES	HAPPY	2500	0	0
PERMITS	HAPPY	500	60	20
CITY GOVERNMENT	HAPPY	0	0	0
LAW ENFORCEMENT	HAPPY	26	26	26
PUBLIC SAFETY	HAPPY	750	750	750
PUBLIC WORKS	HAPPY	45	45	45
PARKS	HAPPY	0	2	4
HOUSING	HAPPY	5	5	5
LIBRARIES	HAPPY	10	10	10
MISCELLANEOUS	HAPPY	15	15	15

Task 1:   Create a database named DBRC.

Task 2:   Create two relations named INPUT and BUDGET that contain all the database fields.

Task 3:   Using the direct method of entering data into a relation, enter the data from the table into the INPUT relation.

Task 4:   Create a model like the one shown in Figure 7-23 by copying and editing your model from Tutorial 5 Case Problem 21. Give the model a new name when you save it..

Task 5:   Store the entire model solution from each suburb into the BUDGET relation.

Task 6:   Print the INPUT and BUDGET relations and your modified model that uses these data.

8. Good Morning Products

At Good Morning Products (GM), Kim wants you to perform a query on the BUDGET relation that contains the data stored there from Case Problem 1. The query is to compute a total column. Results are to be displayed with a BREAK ON ACCOUNT and SUBTOTAL by ACCOUNT.

9. Good Morning Products

Chris wants you to perform a Select on Good Morning Products' BUDGET relation from Case Problem 1 to display selected data.

(a) Display the EBT for all plants.

(b) Display the data for the SALES in the fourth quarter for all plants.

(c) Create a list of plants that are stored in the database.

10. Good Morning Products

Crush wants a consolidated report of the Good Morning Products' company results. He wants you to create a model that will consolidate the accounts in the BUDGET relation from Case Problem 1 using the CONSOLDB statement in a model. Print the consolidated solution and your model used for this processing.

11. The Woodcraft Furniture Company

At Woodcraft Furniture Company, Joe Birch wants you to perform a query on the BUDGET relation from Case Problem 2. The query is to compute a TOTAL column. Results are to be displayed with a BREAK ON ACCOUNT and SUBTOTAL by ACCOUNT.

12. The Woodcraft Furniture Company

"Tall" Pine want you to perform a select on Woodcraft Furniture's BUDGET relation from Case Problem 2 to display selected data.

(a) Display the TOTAL SALES for all the companies.

(b) Display the data for INCOME BEFORE TAXES in the fourth quarter for all companies.

(c) Create a list of companies that are stored in the database.

13. The Woodcraft Furniture Company

"Tall" Pine wants to produce a consolidated report of Woodcraft Furniture's quarterly results. He wants you to create a model that will consolidate the accounts in the BUDGET relation from Case Problem 2 using the CONSOLDB statement. Print your model for this consolidation and its solution.

14. The Last National Bank

At Last National Bank, Carrie wants you to perform a query on the BUDGET relation form Case Problem 3. The query is to compute a TOTAL column. Results are to be displayed with a BREAK ON ACCOUNT and SUBTOTAL by ACCOUNT.

15. The Last National Bank

J. J. wants you to perform a select on the BUDGET relation from Case Problem 3 to display selected data.
   (a) Display the data for TOTAL INTEREST EXPENSE for all locations.
   (b) Display the data for TOTAL INTEREST EARNINGS ON ASSETS in MARCH for all locations.
   (c) Create a list of locations.

16. The Last National Bank

Carrie wants a consolidated report of the Last National Bank Company results. She wants you to create a model that will consolidate the accounts in the BUDGET relation from Case Problem 3 using the CONSOLDB statement to implement the database consolidation. Print your consolidation model together with its solution.

17. Harvest University

At Harvest University, the chief financial officer wants a query on the BUDGET relation that contains the data stored from Case Problem 4. The query is to compute a TOTAL column. Results are to be displayed with a BREAK ON ACCOUNT and SUBTOTAL BY ACCOUNT.

18. Harvest University

The chief financial officer wants you to perform a select on the BUDGET relation from Case Problem 4 to display selected data.
   (a) Display the RESERVE for all campuses.
   (b) Display the TUITION in SUMMER for all campuses.
   (c) Create a list of all campuses stored in the database.

19. Harvest University

The chief financial officer wants a consolidated report of the Harvest University results. You are to create a model that will consolidate the accounts in BUDGET relation from Case Problem 4 using the CONSOLDB statement to implement the database consolidation. Print your model for this consolidation and its solution.

20. Midwest Universal Gas

At Midwest Universal Gas, Mary wants you to perform a query on the BUDGET relation from Case Problem 5. The query is to compute a TOTAL column. Results are to be displayed with a BREAK ON ACCOUNT and SUBTOTAL by ACCOUNT.

21. Midwest Universal Gas

Sam wants you to perform a select on the Midwest Universal Gas BUDGET relation from Case Problem 5 to display selected data.
   (a) Display the TOTAL REVENUE and NET INCOME for all divisions.
   (b) Display the data for the RETAIL SALES in the third quarter for all divisions.
   (c) Create a list of division that are stored in the database.

22. Midwest Universal Gas

Sam is thinking about consolidating the Midwest Universal Gas company results. He wants you to create a model that will consolidate the accounts in the BUDGET relation from Case Problem 5 using the CONSOLDB statement to implement the database consolidation. Print your model for this consolidation and its solution.

23. General Memorial Hospital

At General Memorial Hospital, Berry wants you to perform a query on the BUDGET relation from Case Problem 6. The query is to compute a TOTAL column. Results are to be displayed with a BREAK ON ACCOUNT and SUBTOTAL by ACCOUNT.

24. General Memorial Hospital

Berry wants you to perform a select on the General Memorial Hospital BUDGET relation from Case Problem 6 to display selected data.
    (a) Display the TOTAL EXPENSES and INCOME FROM OPERATIONS for all hospitals.
    (b) Display the data for the IN PATIENT in June for all hospitals.
    (c) Create a list of hospitals that are stored in the database.

25. General Memorial Hospital

Gloria is thinking about consolidating the General Memorial Hospital results. She wants you to create a model that will consolidate the accounts in the BUDGET relation from Case Problem 6 using the CONSOLDB statement to implement the database consolidation. Print the model used for this consolidation and its solution.

26. River City

At River City, Frank wants you to perform a query on the BUDGET relation that contains the data stored there from Case Problem 7. The query is to compute a total column. Results are to be displayed with a BREAK ON ACCOUNT and SUBTOTAL BY ACCOUNT.

27. River City

Lisa wants you to perform a Select on River City's BUDGET relation from Case Problem 7 to display selected data.
    (a) Display the SURPLUS for all suburbs.
    (b) Display the data for the PROPERTY TAXES for July.
    (c) Create a list of suburbs that are stored in the database.

28. River City

Frank is considering consolidation of River City's results. He wants you to create a model that will consolidate the accounts in the BUDGET relation from Case Problem 7 using the CONSOLDB statement in the model. Print the model you created for doing the consolidation together with its solution.

Notes:

PART II: USING IFPS/PLUS

Tutorial 8

Creating and Using Command Files

Introduction to the IFPS/Plus Server

The IFPS/Plus Server functions as the processing engine for Visual IFPS. It solves all the applications for Visual IFPS. The same processing that you request in the Visual Client may be performed directly by the Server. The Server includes a number of advanced modeling capabilities that are not available from the Visual IFPS Client. In the Server mode, you open a window that appears as a computer terminal screen, which allows you to type each IFPS command directly and display your output. That is, both your input and your output appear together on the same screen.

Accessing Models and Reports

Accessing models and reports in the IFPS/Plus Server is similar to accessing them in Visual IFPS. The only difference is that you type all the commands to open a model or a report instead of just clicking a button or menu. In the Server mode, only one model or report is active at a time, similar to an active window in the Visual mode. Because models and reports are not displayed in separate windows, you need to individually request the entity you are working on. In the Server mode, IFPS/Plus has an on-line editor that lets you readily revise your models and report definitions. If you created models or reports in Visual IFPS, it is easiest for you to edit them in Visual IFPS, rather than in the Server mode. However, you can create and edit them in either mode. Let's access the Models and Reports file and open a model.

To open an M&R file and access the model in the Server mode:

❶   Launch Visual IFPS. This automatically sets the Models and Reports file for you.

        TROUBLE? If you want a different M&R file than the one indicated in the status bar, click the Context button, then in the M&R file drop-down list choose the M&R file you wish to use.

❷   Click the **Server button** in the toolbar to open the Server mode.

❸   Enter **MODEL PROJECT3** to activate that model. The "Ready for edit" message appears indicating IFPS is waiting for your next command. See Figure 8-1.

Figure 8-1   ? Model PROJECT3
Accessing Model PROJECT3   Model PROJECT3 ready for edit last line is 22

Now let's open and list a report definition for the report BUFFALO.

To open a report definition in the Server mode:

❶   Enter **Report BUFFALO** to activate the report definition. See Figure 8-2.

Figure 8-2   ?Report BUFFALO
Accessing Report BUFFALO   Report BUFFALO is read for edit last line is 29

❷   Enter **LIST** to display the report definition. The LIST command displays your
       currently active entity.

❸   Enter **EDITNUMBERS YES**, then enter **LIST**. The report definition should
       have numbers on the left side attached to it.

❹   Enter **EDITNUMBERS NO**, then enter **LIST**. The report definition should *not*
       have numbers on the left side.

With the **EDITNUMBERS** command, you can add temporary line numbers to an entity for editing
purposes. The command has these forms:

EDITNUMBERS NO
EDITNUMBERS YES

EDITNUMBERS NO is the default. As indicated, EDITNUMBERS YES causes temporary edit line
numbers to be assigned beginning with the number 1, whereas EDITNUMBERS NO causes the temporary
edit line number to *not* be assigned. When using the Server's editor it is usually desirable to have edit
numbers. If you created a model in the Visual model *without* the numbers, then EDITNUMBERS YES
provides these temporary numbers. If you created the model in Visual *with* line numbers and two sets of
line numbers appear with your model or report accessed in the Server mode, the EDITNUMBERS NO
gives you one set of line numbers for editing in the Server mode. When you revise a model or report in the
Server mode, you use the IFPS Server's editor. To change a line, you retype the line beginning with its
line number. Other IFPS Server edit commands are summarized in Figure 8-3.

Example	Explanation
15 statement	*Insert* new line *or* *Replace* existing line
15D 15, 21D 123, $D	*Delete* existing line *or* range of lines
22C/la/al/ 22C"la"al" 11,31C/la/al/ 11,31CS/la/al/	*Change* the *first* occurrence of the first text string with the second, in the line or specified range of lines. The optional use of S suppresses the echo printing.
22G/la/al/ 22G"la"al" 11,31G/la/al/ 11,31GS/la/al/	*Global* change of *each* occurrence of the first text string with the second, in the line or specified range of lines. The optional use of S suppresses the echo printing.
23COPY90 14,17COPY70 93, 42COPY 80 3	Copy the specified line or range of lines to the specified line number and optionally specify the line number increment.

Figure 8-3
Selected Editing
Commands
(continued)

Example	Explanation
24 42, 83 60, $	*Print* the specified line or range of lines.
"text" "	*Find* or locate the first or next occurrence or the characters between the delimiters.

Figure 8-3
Selected Editing
Commands

CAUTION ALERT!

- There must *not* be any spaces between the line number and the edit command letter!
- If you leave a space here, your original line is wiped out and replaced by the edit command!
- No editing takes place because you performed a line replacement rather that a Change or Global edit.

Solving Models

Now that you know how to access a model or report, let's make model PROJECT3 the currently active entity and solve it.

To solve a model in the Server mode:

❶   Enter **MODEL PROJECT3**.

❷   Enter **SOLVE** to calculate the solution. The IFPS/Plus compilation message appears to indicate the solution can be calculated. See Figure 8-4.

Figure 8-4

Compilation Message

from Solve

?Solve

Model PROJECT3 Version of 06/06/96

Enter Solve Options

❸   Enter **ALL** to calculate and display the solution with all variables and all columns. See Figure 8-5.

	QTR1	QTR2	QTR3	QTR4	TOTAL
BUFFALO COMPUTER SYSTEMS					
PROJECTED PROFIT AND LOSS STATEMENT					
BYTES SOLD	8	10	12	14	44
PRICE PER BYTE	7500	7750	8000	8250	7932
SALES	60000	77500	96000	115500	349000
COST OF SALES PERCENT	.7700	.7600	.7500	.7400	
COST OF SALES	46200	58900	72000	85470	262570
GROSS PROFIT	13800	18600	24000	30030	86430
SALARIES	12250	12250	12250	12250	49000
BENEFITS	2328	2328	2328	2328	9310
ADMIN EXPENSE	1380	1783	2208	2657	8027
DEPRECIATION	1500	2000	2000	2500	8000
INTEREST	400	400	400	400	1600

Figure 8-5
Solution for
Model
PROJECT3
(continued)

Figure 8-5	TOTAL EXPENSES	17858	18760	19186	20134	75937
Solution for	EBT	-4058	-160	4815	9896	10493
Model	ROS	-6.76	-0.21	5.02	8.57	3.01
PROJECT3	SPECIAL COLUMN COMPUTATIONS					

TROUBLE? If you get the message "undefined variables," then type LIST to obtain a listing of the model, correct any errors by editing the model, then repeat Steps 2 and 3. The model is edited by retyping the line beginning with its line number or by using one of the other edit commands.

Generating Reports

Now that you know how to solve the model, let's see how you could display the model's solution using the report definition BUFFALO. In order to produce a report in the Server mode, you need a model solution from which the data values are obtained that are displayed using the report definition.

Reference Window

Generating Reports in the Server mode
■   Activate the desired model.
■   Enter SOLVE to produce a model solution.
■   Enter GENREPORT with the name of report you want to use.

To generate a report in the Server mode:

❶   Enter **MODEL PROJECT3** to activate this model.

❷   Enter **SOLVE** to solve the current model.

❸   Enter **GENREPORT BUFFALO** to produce the report. See Figure 8-6.

BUFFALO COMPUTER SYSTEMS
PROJECTED PROFIT AND LOSS STATEMENT

		1ST QTR	2ND QTR	3RD QTR	4TH QTR	TOTAL
	PRICE PER BYTE	7,500	7,750	8,000	8,250	7,932
	REVENUES:					
	SALES	$60,000	$77,500	$96,000	$115,500	$349,000
	COST OF SALES	46,200	58,900	72,000	85,470	262,570
	GROSS PROFIT	$13,800	$18,600	$24,000	$30,030	$86,430
	SALARIES	12,250	12,250	12,250	12,250	49,000
	BENEFITS	2,328	2,328	2,328	2,328	9,310
	ADMIN EXPENSE	1,380	1,783	2,208	2,657	8,027
Figure 8-6	DEPRECIATION	1,500	2,000	2,000	2,500	8,000
Generated Report	INTEREST	400	400	400	400	1,600
(continued)	TOTAL EXPENSES	$17,858	$18,760	$19,186	$20,134	$75,937

EBT	$(4,058)	$(160)	$4,815	$9,896	$10,493

Figure 8-6   ROS   -6.76   -0.21   5.02   8.57   3.01
Generated Report   *******   *******   *******   *******   *******

TROUBLE? If you do not get a report, check to see if you typed the correct commands. If not, repeat Steps 1 through 3. Check to see if your model is correct. To do this, type MODEL PROJECT3, then type LIST to obtain a listing of your model. Fix any errors, then repeat Steps 2 and 3.

Using Datafiles and Relations with Models

Datafiles or relations are used with models in the situation where the model is the template and the datafiles or relations contain the data. The **USING** command specifies the datafile(s) used when solving the model. Let's use the model MASTER with the TUMBLE datafile.

To use a datafile with a model in the Server mode:

❶   Enter **MODEL MASTER USING TUMBLE** to activate the model and make the connection with the datafile.

❷   Enter **SOLVE** to prepare for the solution.

❸   Enter **ALL** to solve the model with the datafile. See Figure 8-7.

	QTR1	QTR2	QTR3	QTR4	TOTAL
BUFFALO COMPUTER SYSTEMS					
PROJECTED PROFIT AND LOSS STATEMENT					
BYTES SOLD	9	11	13	15	48
PRICE PER BYTE	7500	7750	8000	8250	7932
SALES	67500	85250	104000	123750	380500
COST OF SALES PERCENT	.7700	.7600	.7500	.7400	
COST OF SALES	51975	64790	78000	91575	286340
GROSS PROFIT	15525	20460	26000	32175	94160
SALARIES	12250	12250	12250	12250	49000
BENEFITS	2328	2328	2328	2328	9310
ADMIN EXPENSE	11553	1961	2392	2846	8752
DEPRECIATION	1500	2000	2000	2500	8000
INTEREST	400	400	400	400	1600
TOTAL EXPENSES	18030	18938	19370	20324	76662
EBT	-2505	1522	6631	11851	17499
ROS	-3.71	1.79	6.38	9.58	4.60
SPECIAL COLUMN COMPUTATIONS					

Figure 8-7
Solution of
Model MASTER
Using TUMBLE

TROUBLE? If you did not get a solution, your model could have undefined variables or you could have typed an incorrect command. For the undefined variable, go back to your model by typing MODEL MASTER, then type LIST to get a listing and correct any errors. Repeat Steps 1 through 3. For an incorrect command, just type the line again.

Now let's open and solve the model MASTER 2, this model uses a relation of retrieving data.

To open a database and use a relation with a model in the Server mode:

❶   Enter **DATABASE DBBCS** to open the database for the relation.

❷   Enter **MODEL MASTER2** to activate this model with the internal database definition.

❸   Enter **SOLVE** to solve the model and request the micro definition.

❹   Enter **CROSS** when prompted for the location to access the appropriate data in the BUDGET relation, then enter **ALL** to produce the solution for the model using the relation. See Figure 8-8.

	QTR1	QTR2	QTR3	QTR4	TOTAL
BUFFALO COMPUTER SYSTEMS					
PROJECTED PROFIT AND LOSS STATEMENT					
BYTES SOLD	11	14	16	19	60
PRICE PER BYTE	7500	7750	8000	8250	7929
SALES	82500	108500	128000	156750	475750
COST OF SALES PERCENT	.7700	.7600	.7500	.7400	
COST OF SALES	63525	82460	96000	115995	375980
GROSS PROFIT	18975	26040	32000	40755	117770
SALARIES	10250	10250	10250	10250	41000
BENEFITS	1948	1948	1948	1948	7790
ADMIN EXPENSE	1898	2496	2944	3605	10942
DEPRECIATION	1500	2200	2200	2600	8500
INTEREST	0	0	0	0	0
TOTAL EXPENSES	15595	16893	17342	18403	68232
EBT	3380	9147	14659	22352	49538
ROS	4.097	8.430	11.45	14.26	10.41
SPECIAL COLUMN COMPUTATIONS					

Figure 8-8
Model MASTER2
Using CROSS

Consolidating with Datafiles

Herbie wants to obtain a single solution which has the results for all outlets added together or consolidated. IFPS lets Herbie do this in two ways. Each model can be solved and the solutions added together using the solution matrix of the Model Subsystem, or the datafiles can be consolidated and then input into the model. With the datafile method, only the variables in the datafile are summed, while summing the solution matrices adds all variables in the model' solution matrix. Since Herbie has a choice, let' perform the datafile method. Let's see how to consolidate the TUMBLE and WEST datafiles into a new datafile called COMPANY. Then let's use the COMPANY datafile to solve the MASTER model.

To consolidate the TUMBLE and WEST datafiles into a COMPANY datafile and solve the MASTER model using the COMPANY datafile:

❶   Enter **CONSOLDF TUMBLE WEST NONE** to consolidate the two datafiles, where NONE indicates you have entered all the datafile names for the CONSOLDF.

❷   Enter **COMPANY** to specify the name of the datafile where the consolidated results are stored.

❸   Enter **MODEL MASTER USING COMPANY** to activate the model and link it to the datafile.

❹   Enter **SOLVE**, then enter **ALL** to display the solution. See Figure 8-9.

	QTR1	QTR2	QTR3	QTR4	TOTAL
BUFFALO COMPUTER SYSTEMS					
PROJECTED PROFIT AND LOSS STATEMENT					
BYTES SOLD	24	28	32	38	122
PRICE PER BYTE	7500	7750	8000	8250	7922
SALES	180000	217000	256000	313500	966500
COST OF SALES PERCENT	.7700	.7600	.7500	.7400	
COST OF SALES	138600	164920	192000	231990	727510
GROSS PROFIT	41400	52080	64000	81510	238990
SALARIES	27050	27050	27050	27050	108200
BENEFITS	5140	5140	5140	5140	20558
ADMIN EXPENSE	4140	4991	5888	7211	22230
DEPRECIATION	3300	38000	3800	4700	15600
INTEREST	1000	1000	1000	1000	4000
TOTAL EXPENSES	40630	41981	42818	45100	170588
EBT	770.5	10100	21123	36410	68403
ROS	4.28	4.65	8.25	11.61	7.08
SPECIAL COLUMN COMPUTATIONS					

Figure 8-9
Solution of MASTER
with Consolidated
Datafiles

Is anything wrong with this consolidation? The answer is no, because TUMBLE and WEST contain units sold and total dollar amounts that make business sense to add together. With any consolidation, even CONSOLDB as well, you need to make sure that it makes business sense to add the results. IFPS adds the data values for variable names that match, regardless of whether it makes sense to sum them. The best situation is to make sure your datafiles or relations contain only those variables that make sense to add such as total dollar amounts and total units. Unit prices and growth rates usually do not make sense to add together and should *not* be consolidated. When using CONSOLDF or CONSOLDB, you need to carefully arrange your variables in the datafiles or relation to insure the desired variables are summed. You may need to separately store those variables from a model solution that you want to subsequently consolidate, as was done for the CONSOLDB in Tutorial 7.

Querying a Database

Querying a database in the Server mode is similar to that in the Visual mode. The commands are typed rather than selected in a dialog box. Let's query the relation BUDGET using BREAK ON ACCOUNT and SUBTOTAL QTR1 THRU QTR4 FOR ACCOUNT, LOC. These were used previously in the Visual mode in Tutorial 7.

To query a database in the Server mode:

❶   Enter **DATABASE DBBCS** to open the database.

❷   Enter **QUERY BUDGET** to open the relation.

❸   Enter **BREAK ON ACCOUNT** to set the field to break on.

❹   Enter **SUBTOTAL QTR1 THRU QTR4 FOR ACCOUNT, LOC** to set the subtotal fields.

❺   Enter **LIST** to display the query. See Figure 8-10.

SALARIES	TUMBLE	12250	12250	12250	12250
	WEST	14800	14800	14800	14800
	SOUTH	2500	2500	2500	2500
	CROSS	10250	10250	10250	10250
		---------	---------	---------	---------
*SALARIES		39800	39800	39800	39800
SALES	TUMBLE	67500	85250	10400	123750
	WEST	112500	121750	152000	189750
	SOUTH	37500	46500	64000	74250
	CROSS	82500	108500	128000	156750
		---------	---------	---------	---------
*SALES		300000	372000	448000	544500
TOTAL EXPENSES	TUMBLE	18030	18938	19370	20384
	WEST	22600	23042	23508	24776
	SOUTH	3838	4045	4447	4683
	CROSS	15595	16893	17342	18403
		---------	---------	---------	---------
*TOTAL EXPENSES		60062	62918	64666	68186

Figure 8-10
Creating a Query
with Subtotals

Using a SPOOL File

The SPOOL command lets you "open" a file into which you can write several reports. In this manner, Herbie can get all of his PROJECTED-REPORTs written into one file. Once he' finished his processing, he can then exit the IFPS/Plus Server and have all his reports printed at one time. This is convenient when you have long reports to print. Once opened, a SPOOL file remains open to receive additional output until it is closed. Let's examine the use of the SPOOL command to place a model listing and solution in the same output file.

To use the spool command in the Server mode:

❶   Enter **SPOOL PRNTFILE** to open a file and give this file the name PRNFILE. Any file name is acceptable as long as it is not your M&R file or any other file you have created.

❷   Enter **MODEL PROJECT3** to make it the active model.

❸   Enter **LIST** to produce a listing of the model.

❹   Enter **GENREPORT BUFFALO ONLY ONTO SPOOL** to produce a report of the model solution. ONLY causes the report to be written to the file but *not* displayed on the screen.

❺   Enter **CLOSE SPOOL** to close the spool file.

Now that we have the report in a spool file, let's see how we can print this spool file.

To print a spool file:

❶   Click **File**, then **Close** to close the session with the Server mode and return to the Visual mode.

❷   Click the **Open button**, click the **List of Entities of Types drop-down arrow**, click **Command file**, then click **PRNTFILE** to open the spool file.

❸   Click **File**, then click **Print** to print the spool file.

Introduction to Command Files

Command files are computer files in which IFPS instructions and command file directives are stored. Command files execute like computer programs, allowing you to automate certain IFPS/Plus processes which one otherwise can be performed manually during an interactive session; they reduce repetitive typing and potential errors.

Command files are useful in several application tasks, including:

- **Production tasks** - These command files process the same models and generate the same reports each time they run. These can be simple and are useful when models and reports are run on a regular basis.

- **Application tasks** - Command files of this type assist in setting up IFPS/Plus applications by initializing datafiles, combining models, performing consolidations, and so forth.

- **Familiarization tasks** - These command files are built by sophisticated users for the benefit of less knowledgeable users. They require little or no experience to execute and lead users through prescribed tasks by employing menus, prompting, and similar interactive techniques.

Planning a Command File

Various IFPS commands are used to associate a model with a datafile and solve it, to consolidate datafiles, to generate reports, and to perform the selection of data. If each of these activities were only to be carried out one time, Herbie could manually enter these commands for their execution. However, if the commands are to be executed several times, it is considerably more convenient for Herbie to place these commands into a file. IFPS lets Herbie do this with **COMMAND files**. He can place all his IFPS/Plus commands into a file and edit them for any typing errors. Then, when desired, Herbie executes the commands in the command file. He doesn't have to re-enter each command for every execution or be concerned with typing errors.

Once Herbie has created a command file, whenever he wants to run a new "what if" alternative, he can revise each of the outlet datafiles and then have the command file executed. The command file will direct the production of the PROJECTED-REPORTs for both the outlets and the company and have the BUDGET-DATA stored.

In IFPS, command files are specified as CMDFILEs in the Server mode. Let's look at the CMDFILE CFBCS01 which conducts the processing through the storing of the BUDGET-DATA. In the file name **CFBCS01**, the "BCS" indicates this is for Buffalo Computer Systems, "CF" identifies this as a Command File, and the "01" numbers this as the first command file. This method of file identification is useful in keeping the files of an IFPS modeling system organized and easily recognized.

The **!COMMENT** command is used to place comments into CMDFILEs. The ! or exclamation point or escape character in front of the word "comment" identifies this as a special command file command. That is, you would use this and other commands preceded by an exclamation point ONLY in a CMDFILE. In IFPS/Plus, these special commands are known as **command file control statements**. They control the action of the other IFPS/Plus commands that you have put in your CMDFILE but do *not* cause models to be solved or reports to be generated. A variety of command file control statements are available for your use in providing control over your command file. Command file CFBCS01 is shown as Figure 8-11.

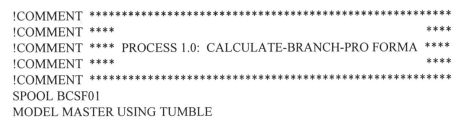

```
!COMMENT  ******************************************************
!COMMENT  ****                                            ****
!COMMENT  ****  PROCESS 1.0:  CALCULATE-BRANCH-PRO FORMA  ****
!COMMENT  ****                                            ****
!COMMENT  ******************************************************
SPOOL BCSF01
MODEL MASTER USING TUMBLE
```

```
                    SOLVE
                    GENREPORT BUFFALO3 ONLY ONTO SPOOL
                    USING WEST
                    SOLVE
                    GENREPORT BUFFALO3 ONLY ONTO SPOOL
                    CONSOLDF
                    TUMBLE
                    WEST
                    NONE
                    COMPANY
                    !COMMENT  ********************************************************
                    !COMMENT  ****                                              ****
                    !COMMENT  ****  PROCESS 2.0:  CALCULATE-COMPANY-PRO FORMA ****
                    !COMMENT  ****                                              ****
                    !COMMENT  ********************************************************
                    MODEL MASTER USING COMPANY
```

Figure 8-11   GENREPORT BUFFALO3 ONLY ONTO SPOOL
Command File   PERFORMANCE CONSOLIDATED COMPANY
CFBCS01   SPOOL CLOSE

Creating a Command File

A command file is created by typing each of the IFPS commands. This can be done using the Server line editor or by using a window in the Visual mode.

Reference Window

Creating a Command File in the Server
■ Enter CMDFILE and its file name.
■ Enter the commands you want included in your command file.
■ Enter END to terminate entering commands.
■ Enter SAVE, then enter YES to save the command file.

Let's see how to create the command file CFBCS01 in Figure 8-11 using the Server editor.

To create a command file in the Server mode:

❶   Access the Server mode, if necessary.

❷   Enter **CMDFILE CFBCS01**.

❸   Enter the commands shown in Figure 8-11.

❹   Enter **END** to terminate the command file entry.

❺   Enter **SAVE**, then **YES** to save the command file.

Executing a Command File

Once a command file is created, it can be executed. You can initiate the execution of a command file from either the Server mode or the Visual model. Now that the command file is entered and saved, you are ready to run or execute the command file.

Executing a Command File
■   Enter COMMANDS and the name of the command file.

Let's execute the command file that you just created and saved from the Server mode.

To cause IFPS to execute a command file from the Server:

❶   Enter **COMMANDS CFBCS01**.

❷   Wait while the command file is executed until the message "End of Command file(s)" is displayed. The results are written to the SPOOL file and may be printed as described previously.

Debugging Command Files

When a command file doesn't perform the processing you expect, you need to debug the command file. You could have typed a wrong command in the command file. Debugging a command file is like debugging a program in COBOL or BASIC. Let's examine the IFPS/Plus commands for debugging command files.

Using Record

The **RECORD command** makes an exact copy of terminal entries and responses. It enables you to obtain a copy of a session in the Server mode. The RECORD command creates a file that can be directed to a printer so you can get a hard copy of it. The RECORD command has several options:

- •RECORD [filename]
- •NORECORD
- •CLOSE RECORD

Each of these options does something different. The **RECORD [filename]** opens a file that stores all information after that command is entered. The **NORECORD** temporarily halts the recording session. The **CLOSE RECORD** closes the file from storing any more information. Let's see how the RECORD command works.

CAUTION ALERT!

If you give your Record file the SAME name as your Model and Report file, you have just *destroyed* your Model and Report file. Your Record file *must* have a *different* name than your M&R. So, be careful and *do not* give the Record file the same name as the M&R file or any other file!

To use RECORD in the Server mode:

❶   Enter **RECORD RCBUF** to open the Record file with all input and output following that command placed in the file, even misspelled commands and mistakes.

❷   Enter **MODEL PROJECT3** to access the desired model.

❸   Enter **SOLVE**, then enter **ALL** to display the solution.

Now let's leave the Record mode.

To leave the Record mode:

❶   Enter **CLOSE RECORD** to close the file, which is now ready for printing.

The RECORD file can be printed by accessing it as a command file entity in a Visual IFPS window and then printing it.

Using Suppress

The !SUPPRESS command or directive suppresses subsequent output to the terminal while the command file processes, except reports or file listings. The basic command takes these forms:
!SUPPRESS
!SUPPRESS OFF

Each of these command options does something different. The **!SUPPRESS** command suppresses subsequent output of the command execution during the Server session. The **!SUPPRESS OFF** command resumes displaying the commands to the Server screen.

Using Trace

The !TRACE command processes all subsequent lines of the command file with the corresponding output displayed to the terminal and/or is sent to a file. The command takes these forms:
!TRACE
!TRACE ONTO filename
!TRACE OFF

Each of these command options does something different. The **!TRACE** command causes each line of the command file to be displayed to the screen as the command file executes, even if the command file contains !SUPPRESS directives. The **!TRACE ONTO filename** command does the same thing as !TRACE but, it captures command processing to a file and does not send it to the screen. The **!TRACE OFF** command causes the screen display to show normal command file operations. Let's see how the !TRACE command works.

To use the !TRACE command in a command file:

❶   Enter **CMDFILE CFBCS01** to make this your active entity.

❷   Enter **LIST** to list the contents of the command file.

❸   Before the **SPOOL** command, enter an appropriate line number and !**TRACE** to
         add !TRACE to the command file. You may use a fractional line number, such as
         30.1, if necessary, to insert a line in your command file.

❹   Enter **SAVE**, then enter **YES** to save the command file.

❺   Enter **COMMAND CFBCS01** to execute the command file using !TRACE.

Did you see each command in the command file as it was executed? This is what !TRACE does. !TRACE is the best way to examine commands in the command file to isolate a problem with them.

Using DATAEDIT

The IFPS/Plus Data Editor greatly increases the ease with which you can edit IFPS/Plus datafiles and relations. The Data Editor puts a file or relation into a grid of regular rows and columns, similar to the spreadsheet arrangement for editing data in relations in Visual IFPS. As your data are entered, it looks like a report, making it easy to read and understand. In the Data Editor, you can move the screen cursor around the spreadsheet freely, adding or editing data as you wish.

The DATAEDIT command activates the Data Editor from the Server mode. The command takes these forms:

DATAEDIT DATAFILE filename
DATAEDIT RELATION relationname

The DATAFILE form is used to edit a new or existing datafile. The RELATION form is used to edit an existing relation. Let's examine the Dataedit screen.

To use DATAEDIT in the Server mode:

❶   Enter **DATABASE DBBCS.**

❷   Enter **DATAEDIT RELATION DECPARAM** to access the relation for editing and to cause the DATAEDIT screen to appear. See Figure 8-12.

	1	2	3	4	5	6
ACCOUNT	LOC	QTR1	QTR2	QTR3	QTR4	
BYTES SOLD	TUMBLE	9	11	13	15	
SALARIES	TUMBLE	12250	12250	12250	12250	
DEPRECIATION	TUMBLE	1500	2000	2000	2500	
INTEREST	TUMBLE	400	400	400	400	
BYTES SOLD	WEST	15	17	19	23	
SALARIES	WEST	14800	14800	14800	14800	
DEPRECIATION	WEST	1800	1800	1800	2200	
INTEREST	WEST	600	600	600	600	
BYTES SOLD	SOUTH	5	6	8	9	
SALARIES	SOUTH	2500	2500	2500	2500	
DEPRECIATION	SOUTH	0	0	0	0	
INTEREST	SOUTH	0	0	0	0	
BYTES SOLD	CROSS	11	14	16	19	
SALARIES	CROSS	10250	10250	10250	10250	
DEPRECIATION	CROSS	1500	2200	2200	2600	
INTEREST	CROSS	800	800	800	800	

Figure 8-12
Dataedit screen

The DATAEDIT command causes the Data Editor screen to appear. If you are editing a relation, your screen should look like Figure 8-12. Command-line data entry allows you to use IFPS DATAEDIT commands to change data values in the spreadsheet/data area. These commands are entered at the command line which is indicated by the "==" symbol in the lower-left corner of the screen. Two commands, **FIND** and **CHANGE** are the most useful in entering data using DATAEDIT. The general syntax of these DATAEDIT commands is as follows:

FIND command:
FIND row-number, col-number

Relations and Datafiles:
Relations: FIND row-number, field
Datafiles: FIND variable-name, column
            FIND row-number, column

CHANGE command:
Relations: CHANGE row-number FOR field-ref = data-values
(one data value is entered for each field)
Datafiles: CHANGE row-name FOR col-ref = data-value
        CHANGE row-number FOR col-ref = data-value

Examples of these commands are:
FIND 3
CHANGE 3 FOR QTR2 .. QTR4 = 2250 FOR 3

After your changes are made, you need to leave the DATAEDIT mode and return to the Ready mode. Let's see how to leave the Dataedit screen.

To leave the Dataedit screen:
❶   Type **EXIT** at the command line.
❷   Press **[Enter]** to leave the screen and return to the ready mode, or you may just press [F3] to leave the DATAEDIT mode.

Herbie is now ready to try implementing these command files and the Dataedit screen so he can have someone else run their system of IFPS planning models.

Questions

1.   The IFPS/Plus _____ does the processing for Visual IFPS.
       a. client
       b. processor
       c. server
       d. connector

2.   The IFPS/Plus full-screen data _____ is used for presenting an entire screen of data in a row and column arrangement for ease in data entry and updating by an end user.
       a. screen
       b. editor
       c. row
       d. column

3.   _____ lets you "open" a file into which several reports can be written.
       a. Spool
       b. Record
       c. !Trace
       d. !Suppress

4.   The !COMMENT command is used to _____ in a cmdfile.
      a. define a command
      b. show a character
      c. locate a comment
      d. place comments

5.   By entering _____, you turn ON what is known in IFPS as the record file.
      a. Spool
      b. Record
      c. !Trace
      d. !Suppress

6.   The _____ command suppresses subsequent output to the terminal while the
      command file processes, except reports or file listings.
      a. Spool
      b. Record
      c. !Trace
      d. !Suppress

Case Problems

1. Good Morning Products

Frosty, Crush, and Kim of Good Morning Products have been satisfied with their planning and
budgeting model. Each quarter, Chris compiles the data for both the California and the Florida operations.
Jenny then places these data in datafiles for each branch location and uses the template model to produce a
report for each business unit and a consolidated report for the company. Your task is to create this
COMMAND file like the one shown in Figure 8-11. Print your command file and the spool file containing
your reports.

2. The Woodcraft Furniture Company

The planning and budgeting model for Woodcraft continues to perform very well. Each month, Talbert
assembles data for the main company and the Oak branch. The datafile for each of these business units is
updated with this data. The template model is solved for each business unit and than a consolidated report
is produced for the company. Talbert wants you to create an IFPS COMMAND file like the one in Figure
8-11 to do this processing. Print your command file and the spool file that contains the reports generated
by executing the command file.

3. The Last National Bank

The asset and liability planning model at the Last National Bank has been working quite well. Each
month, Carrie obtains data from both the Broken Spoke and Weeping Water banks. Their datafiles are
updated with this data. The template model is solved for each bank and then a consolidated report is
produced of the bank's overall operations. Carrie wants you to create an IFPS COMMAND file like the
one in Figure 8-11 to perform this processing. After executing the command file, print your spool file and
print the command file.

4. Harvest University

As the chief financial officer of Harvest University, you have decided to improve the operation of your financial planning model by creating a COMMAND file to perform the processing for each campus. You then prepare a consolidated report. Harvest University wants you to create an IFPS COMMAND file like the one shown in Figure 8-11 to do this. After executing the command file, print your spool file and the command file.

5. Midwest Universal Gas

Mary Derrick of Midwest Universal Gas has been pleased with the performance of your financial planning model. Monthly data are collected and used to update the datafiles for both of the strategic business units. Mary has found the end of the month processing sequence is routine. First, each business unit is solved using the template model, then the consolidation is performed and the reports printed. Mary wants you to create a COMMAND file like the one in Figure 8-11 to carry out this processing. Print the spool file containing the reports and your command file.

6. General Memorial Hospital

Gloria and Berry of Family Health Care are so pleased with the financial planning model that they want you to improve processing by employing additional IFPS capabilities. Each month, the datafiles are updated for General Memorial and County General Hospitals. Gloria wants you to develop a COMMAND file like the one in Figure 8-11 that does this repetitive processing. Print the command file and the spool file containing the output reports.

7. River City

Frank Frugal has detected a repetitive pattern in the end of the month processing of River City's financial plan. The template model is solved with each of the datafiles for River City and for Peaceful Valley. Then, these two files are consolidated using the template model and the report is written using a report definition. Frank wants you to create an IFPS COMMAND file like the one illustrated in Figure 8-11 for this processing. Print the command file and the spool file containing the reports.

8. Good Morning Products

At Good Morning Products, Crush has reviewed the methods for entering the data for each plant in a datafile or a database relation. Since these data may be changed frequently as different alternatives are explored, he wants you to access the DECPARAM relation using Dataedit and change BOTTLES in the first quarter to 250000 for the CALIF location. Then solve the quarterly model from Tutorial 7 using this data and print the solution. Print the Dataedit screen displayed in the Server mode with the data change.

9. The Woodcraft Furniture Company

Talbert "Tall" Pine, at Woodcraft Furniture, has reviewed the methods for entering the data for each company in either a datafile or a database relation. Because these data may change frequently as different budget alternatives are explored, he wants you to access the INPUT relation using Dataedit and change TABLES SOLD in the second quarter to 1300 for OAK. Then solve the quarterly model from Tutorial 7 using this data and print the solution. Print the Dataedit screen in the Server mode to show your data change.

10. The Last National Bank

At Last National Bank, J. J. has reviewed the methods of entering the data from each location in either a datafile or database relation. Since these data may be changed frequently as different alternatives are explored, he wants you to access the INPUT relation using Dataedit and change the INSTALLMENT LOANS in FEB to 13000 for WEEP. Then solve the model from Tutorial 7 using this data and print the solution. Print the Dataedit screen in the Server mode that shows you data change.

11. Harvest University

At Harvest University, you reviewed the methods for entering data for each campus in either a datafile or a database relation. Since these data may be changed frequently as different alternatives are explored, access the INPUT relation with Dataedit and change STUDENTS in winter (WINT) to 4000 for MAIN. Then solve the quarterly model from Tutorial 7 using this data and print the solution. Print the Dataedit screen in the Server mode to show your new data entry.

12. Midwest Universal Gas

At Midwest Universal Gas, Sam has reviewed the methods for entering the data for each division in either a datafile or a database relation. Since these data may be changed frequently as different alternatives are explored, he wants you to access the INPUT relation using Dataedit and change demand in the third quarter to 90 for COG. Then solve the quarterly model from Tutorial 7 using this data and print the solution. Print the Dataedit screen in the Server mode that shows this change and print the entire INPUT relation from the Visual mode.

13. General Memorial Hospital

At General Memorial Hospital, Berry has reviewed the methods for entering the data from each hospital in either a datafile or a database relation. Since these data may change frequently as different alternatives are explored, he wants you to access the INPUT relation using Dataedit and change STAFF DOCTOR in JUNE to 6 for FHCH. Then solve the quarterly model from Tutorial 7 using this data and print the solution. Print the Dataedit screen in the Server mode showing this revision, then print the entire INPUT relation from the Visual mode.

14. River City

At River City, Frank has reviewed the methods for entering the data from each suburb in either a datafile or a database relation. Since these data may be changed frequently as different alternatives are explored, he wants you to access the INPUT relation using Dataedit and change CITY GOVERNMENT in JULY to 35 for HAPPY. Then solve the quarterly model from Tutorial 7 using this data and print the solution. Print the Dataedit screen in the Server mode to show this change, then print the entire INPUT relation.

Notes:

Tutorial 9

Developing Advanced Command Files

Introduction to Structured Systems

Structured systems are systems in which everything is organized so an end user with little knowledge about IFPS can run the system. IFPS command files provide the ability to build complex modeling systems that end users can readily operate. This application of command files is known as **system building**. In this tutorial, you will learn how Herbie set up a system for his retail outlets so that a manager from each outlet can run the system.

Calling Command Files

A command file is an object in which commands such as SOLVE and GENREPORT are placed so they are reusable and need not be typed each time they are used. To begin executing another command file from a command file that is already running, all you need to do is use the **!CALL command** (Figure 9-1).

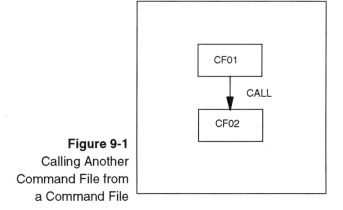

Figure 9-1
Calling Another
Command File from
a Command File

As Figure 9-1 illustrates, command file **CF01** "calls" file **CF02**. The commands in CF02 are executed and execution returns to command file CF01. Usually, each command file is organized as a module or object that performs a desired task. When a command file is called, its task is performed.

Using Parameters

Parameters are similar to micros in IFPS except they are used in command files to create modules that are dynamically changed as the command file is executed. Parameters are unique to a command file, whereas micros are used across all command files. As a result, the same parameter number in two different command files can have values that are used differently. For Buffalo Computer Systems (BCS), Herbie can use parameters to set up a command file for a single location and then use that command file for each of the locations much like a template model. Parameters are designated in the directives of a command file by integers, as follows:

&n

Command file directives are entered with the "&n" acting as a placeholder for any desired item that may vary during different executions. The same "&n" may appear in one or more directives—anywhere the same substitution is appropriate. During command file execution, "&n" is defined and the corresponding value substituted each time the "&n" appears. IFPS/Plus provides three methods for defining parameters:

- The default method of having IFPS/Plus prompt for them.
- Using a command file directive to define them.
- Defining them on the COMMAND line or the !CALL directive line.

Building Systems with Command Files

There are two things you can use to plan the system: a planning analysis sheet and a data flow diagram. Before you start creating the system, let's take a look at how the !CALL directive and &n are used in two command files. The two command files are used to solve the model with relation DECPARAM for each outlet and store the solution into the relation BUDGET (Figure 9-2). The first command file contains a list of the outlets to be processed and calls the second command file to do the actual processing for each outlet. In this manner, the processing steps only need to be entered once for the processing of an outlet. The first command file provides the parameters that are passed to the second command file designating which outlet is to be processed.

Planning Analysis Sheet

My goal:
Develop a set of command files to solve all the outlets and put the solved data into a relation.

What results do I want to see?
The solution of each outlet in a report to be placed in a print file.

What information do I need?
The commands to create the command files to accomplish the goal.

Figure 9-2 Planning Analysis Sheet for Command Files *(continued)*

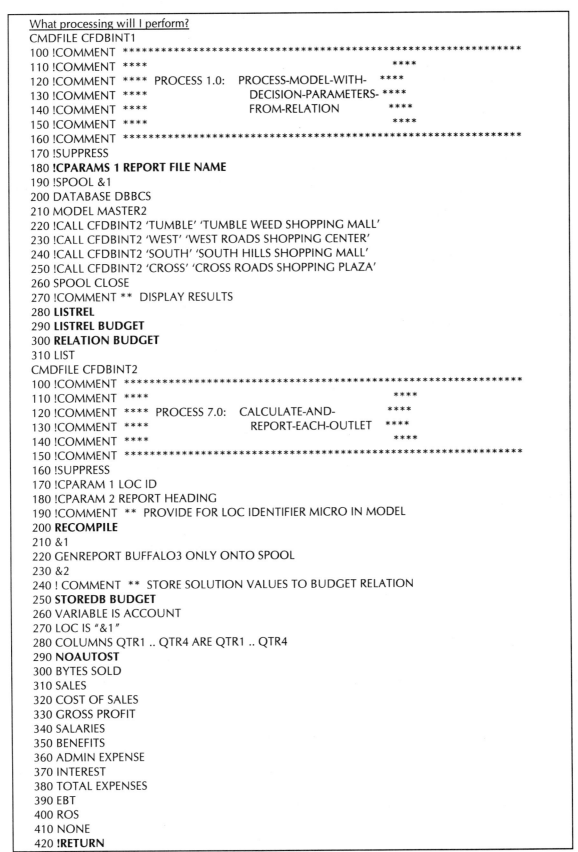

```
What processing will I perform?
CMDFILE CFDBINT1
100 !COMMENT  ***********************************************************
110 !COMMENT  ****                                      ****
120 !COMMENT  ****  PROCESS 1.0:   PROCESS-MODEL-WITH-   ****
130 !COMMENT  ****                 DECISION-PARAMETERS-  ****
140 !COMMENT  ****                 FROM-RELATION         ****
150 !COMMENT  ****                                      ****
160 !COMMENT  ***********************************************************
170 !SUPPRESS
180 !CPARAMS 1 REPORT FILE NAME
190 !SPOOL &1
200 DATABASE DBBCS
210 MODEL MASTER2
220 !CALL CFDBINT2 'TUMBLE' 'TUMBLE WEED SHOPPING MALL'
230 !CALL CFDBINT2 'WEST' 'WEST ROADS SHOPPING CENTER'
240 !CALL CFDBINT2 'SOUTH' 'SOUTH HILLS SHOPPING MALL'
250 !CALL CFDBINT2 'CROSS' 'CROSS ROADS SHOPPING PLAZA'
260 SPOOL CLOSE
270 !COMMENT **  DISPLAY RESULTS
280 LISTREL
290 LISTREL BUDGET
300 RELATION BUDGET
310 LIST
CMDFILE CFDBINT2
100 !COMMENT  ***********************************************************
110 !COMMENT  ****                                      ****
120 !COMMENT  ****  PROCESS 7.0:   CALCULATE-AND-        ****
130 !COMMENT  ****                 REPORT-EACH-OUTLET    ****
140 !COMMENT  ****                                      ****
150 !COMMENT  ***********************************************************
160 !SUPPRESS
170 !CPARAM 1 LOC ID
180 !CPARAM 2 REPORT HEADING
190 !COMMENT **  PROVIDE FOR LOC IDENTIFIER MICRO IN MODEL
200 RECOMPILE
210 &1
220 GENREPORT BUFFALO3 ONLY ONTO SPOOL
230 &2
240 ! COMMENT **  STORE SOLUTION VALUES TO BUDGET RELATION
250 STOREDB BUDGET
260 VARIABLE IS ACCOUNT
270 LOC IS "&1"
280 COLUMNS QTR1 .. QTR4 ARE QTR1 .. QTR4
290 NOAUTOST
300 BYTES SOLD
310 SALES
320 COST OF SALES
330 GROSS PROFIT
340 SALARIES
350 BENEFITS
360 ADMIN EXPENSE
370 INTEREST
380 TOTAL EXPENSES
390 EBT
400 ROS
410 NONE
420 !RETURN
```

Figure 9-2 Planning Analysis Sheet for Command Files

Let's take a look at selected commands in these command files that you have not used previously.

!CPARAMS 1 REPORT FILE NAME

This command is used to prompt the user for parameters or micro definitions during command file processing or execution. The !CPARAM directive line is conditional; prompting occurs only if the indicated parameter or micro is not defined currently. The REPORT FILE NAME is the text displayed when prompting the user for a value for parameter 1.

LISTREL
LISTREL BUDGET

These two commands are used to determine the names and structure of the relations in the current database. The first one lists the names (only) of all relations in the database. The second one displays the structure for the indicated relation.

RELATION BUDGET

This command accesses the specified BUDGET relation.

RECOMPILE

This command completely recompiles the currently active model and causes new values to be substituted for any micro references that appear in the model. A recompile is necessary when a different micro value is used for each solution of the model.

STOREDB BUDGET

This command specifies the relation into which the current model or datafile solution will be stored.

NOAUTOST

This command ensures that no existing variables will be updated unless you include them in the list of variable names. The default in IFPS is to automatically update all data in a database unless this command is used.

!RETURN

This command returns execution control to the command file that called it.

When you enter commands in a command file, you can type each command from your memory, or you can use a template line to provide the correct command name and syntax. Let's enter the command files by typing them using a window in Visual IFPS.

To create a command file by typing it in the Visual mode:

❶   Make sure Visual IFPS is running. If it is not running, then start Visual IFPS.

❷   Click **New** in the toolbar to display the New dialog box.

❸   Double click **Command File** in the New list box to specify the entity type.

❹   Enter the !COMMENT statements in lines 100 through 160 for the CFDBINT1 command file as shown in Figure 9-2.

A template line is used by selecting it from the Template dialog box and pasting it into your active window. Each of the placeholders is then selected and replaced with the desired text. A template is available for entering the !CPARAM directive on line 180. Let's enter this directive using a template.

To enter a command file directive using a template:

❶   Click **Templates** in the toolbar to display the Template dialog box. See Figure 9-3.

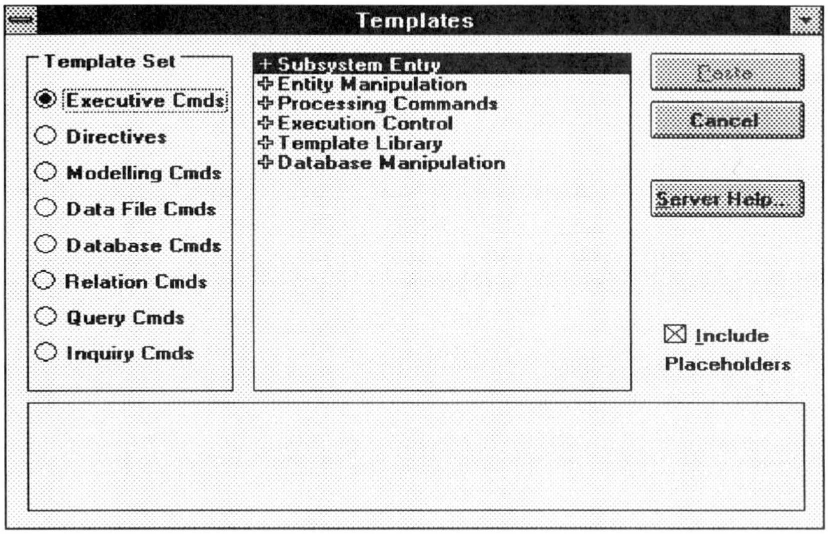

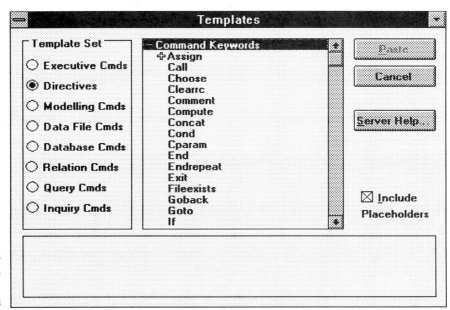

Figure 9-3
Template
Dialog Box

❷   Click the **Directives option button**, then click the **Command keywords** to
display a list of the available directives. See Figure 9-4.

Figure 9-4
Available
Command
Keywords

❸   Click **Cparam**, the desired command, then click the **Paste button**, to place the template in the Window clipboard.

❹   Select **[S]** and press **[Delete]** to remove this unneeded argument from the template. The "S" causes the message "ENTER DEFINITION FOR:" to be suppressed when the command file is executed. If you want the "S," then you need to delete the brackets from the template.

❺   Select **<arg>** and type **1** to specify the parameter number. The <arg> may be either a parameter number or a micro name, as desired.

❻   Select **<prompt>** and type REPORT FILE NAME as the desired text for the prompt.

❼   Type **180** as the line number for this command at the beginning of the inserted template line.

The remainder of the command file can be entered by either typing or using templates as desired. Let's enter the rest of the command file.

To enter the rest of the command file:

❶   Enter the commands in lines 190 through 300 for the CFDBINT1 command file shown in Figure 9-2.

❷   Click **File**, click **Save**, type **CFDBINT1** as the command file name in the Entity Name box, then click the **OK button** to save the file.

The second command file CFDBINT2, listed in Figure 9-2, is entered in the same manner. Let's enter the second command file.

To enter the second command file:

❶   Click **New** in the toolbar, then double-click **Command File** to display a new window.

❷   Enter the commands for command file CFDBINT2 from Figure 9-2.

❸   Click **File**, click **Save**, type **CFDBINT2** as the command file name in the Entity Name box, then click the **OK button** to save the file.

The command files are executed beginning either from the Visual mode or the Server mode. When a command file is executed from the Visual mode, you are placed in the Server mode. Upon completion of the command file execution, the Server mode remains the active mode. If you want to continue working in the Visual mode, you need to close the Sever.

To execute a command file from the Visual mode:

❶   Click the **CFBINT1 command file window** to make this the active window.

❷   Click **Execute** in the toolbar to begin running this command file and wait for it to run.

❸   Doubleclick the **Control-menu box** of the commands Session window to return to the Visual model from the Server mode.

The next section expands the application of command files by showing different methods of creating a menu-driven IFPS system. You may create these command files in either the Visual or Server mode. However, the steps are described for the Server mode.

Using Full-Screen Processing

Full-screen processing is a component of command files in IFPS/Plus. A full screen is defined as a series of commands in a command file. Each full-screen definition consists of two parts: the screen to be displayed and the data values to be displayed or obtained from the screen as micros or parameters. The screen display is created using a form of **screen painting**. That is, an image of the screen is created as it is to appear when the command file is executed.

A design consideration in using full-screen processing involves either integrating the full-screen commands with other command file processing or creating a separate command file as an object that contains the full-screen commands. A separate command file increases processing time slightly as an object, because of the CALL to the command file. As a command file object for each full screen, the screen can be displayed as needed at any point in an application. If the screen is used at several different points in processing, this avoids duplicating the screen description. The testing and maintenance of the screen are usually easier when each screen is organized as a separate command file or object. Considering experience, the additional processing time, which occurs with separate command file objects, is usually not noticed by the system's operator. For these reasons, the organization of each full screen as a separate command file is recommended. This object-oriented design strategy is used in this tutorial.

The screens illustrated contain a "header" or "banner" at the top of each screen. This feature has been demonstrated as a means of identifying the system being executed. The desirability of including this information at the top or bottom of each screen should be evaluated as part of the system design. It is *not* required in implementing full-screen processing.

Several different types of full screens are considered in this tutorial. They are:

- a message screen
- a fill-in-the-blank screen
- a menu selection
- a fill-in-the-blank from a system generated list of choices
- a selection from a system generated list of choices

Each of these screens is created by using different features of the commands that are available for developing full screens. These screen types have been selected for exploration because they are representative of the kind of processing that is often implemented using full screens.

Fill-In-The-Blank Screen

A fill-in-the-blank screen presents one or more blanks that receive an input value. These values are stored as micros or parameters for use in controlling processing or providing values for use in models, reports, datafiles, and database relations. Messages are displayed on the screen indicating the required user input. Command file processing is suspended until the [Enter] key is pressed. In IFPS/Plus, a **SET** is a feature that is used to communicate external lists of text items to IFPS entities. A set must first be activated before IFPS can use it. Then, during execution, IFPS will successively substitute the elements of a set for the set name that is used as a placeholder in an entity, command, or option, essentially anywhere that IFPS expects a list of items. The following command file uses the **SETLOAD** command to specify the entities used in processing. The **SETLOAD** command interactively defines and activates a set in one step (Figure 9-5).

Figure 9-5
Command File
with SETLOAD
(continued)

```
100 !COMMENT ***** FILE: CFSCRN10
110 !COMMENT ***** LAST CHANGED BY:   HRW
120 !COMMENT ***** LAST CHANGED DATE: 10/10/..
130 !COMMENT  ****************************************************
```

```
140 !COMMENT  *****                                          *****
150 !COMMENT  *****  PROCESS 3.0:   SELECT-INDIVIDUAL-OUTLET- *****
160 !COMMENT  *****                 FOR-PROCESSING            *****
170 !COMMENT  *****                                          *****
180 !COMMENT  **************************************************
190 !COMMENT
200 !COMMENT  **  INITIALIZE MICROS AND PARAMETERS FOR USE
210 !COMMENT  **  WITH FULL-SCREEN PROCESSING
220 !SUPPRESS
230 !SETLOAD OUTLET  = TUMBLE, WEST, SOUTH, CROSS
240 !ASSIGN SELECT = " "
250 !COMPUTE SYSNUM = 2.3
260 !ASSIGN MSG = " "
270 !COMMENT  **  BEGIN FULL-SCREEN DISPLAY
280 !SCREEN
290 **************************************************************
300 *****      FINANCIAL PLANNING AND FORECASTING SYSTEM   *****
310 *****                 OUTLET PROCESSING                *****
320 *****                   RELEASE: 9.9                   *****
330 **************************************************************
340
350         -------------- SELECT OUTLET FOR UPDATING ----------------
360
370
380                  OUTLET: TTTTTTT
390
400
410
420
430
440
450
460
470
480                  ENTER DESIRED OUTLET
490
500   M: TTTTTTTTTTTTTTTTTTTTTTTTTTTTTTTTTTTTTTTTTTTTTTT
510
520  SCRN 10          USE PF1 FOR HELP
530 !ENDSCREEN LABEL YES, COLON NO, MSGAREA M, MESSAGE MSG
540 !AREA RELEASE, VALUE MICRO SYSNUM, PROTECT
550 !AREA M, BOLD
560 !AREA OUTLET, VALUE MICRO SELECT, UNDERLINE, '
570    !VERIFY = OUTLET OR = "CANCEL", '
580    !UPPER, HELPMSG "     ENTER NAME OF DESIRED OUTLET."
590 !CURSOR IN OUTLET
600 !SHOWSCREEN
610 !COMMENT  **  PERFORM UPDATE PROCESSING
620 !IF "&SELECT&" <> "CANCEL" THEN !CALL CFDEREL &SELECT&
630 !COMMENT ** !SHOWMICRO SELECT
640 !COMMENT  **  DROP MICROS
650 !DROPMICRO MSG
660 !RETURN
```

Figure 9-5
Command File
with SETLOAD

A fill-in-the-blank screen lets Herbie request the processing for a particular outlet by prompting him to input the outlet's name. Let's take a look at the new commands used for this full-screen processing.

!SETLOAD OUTLET = TUMBLE, WEST, SOUTH, CROSS
This command defines and activates a set in one step. OUTLET is the set name, whereas TUMBLE, WEST, SOUTH, and CROSS are the set's elements.

!ASSIGN SELECT = " "
This command assigns a text value of blank, to the user-defined micro SELECT. The blank is used to initialize the micro's value.

!SCREEN
This command marks the beginning of the display screen.

RELEASE: 9.9
This line is an output area that displays a numeric value. "RELEASE:" is the label for this screen area. The 9's specify a numeric format used in displaying the number in the same manner as they are used in the FORMAT directive of a Report Definition.

OUTLET: TTTTTTT
This line is used as an input area for collecting the user's response. "OUTLET:" is the label for this screen area. The T's specify a field for a text value with a maximum size defined by the string of T's.

M: TTTTTTTTTTTTTTTTTTTTTTTTTTTTTTTTTTTTTTTTTTTTTTTTTTTTTTTTTTTTTTTTTTTTT
This line defines a text field for displaying user-defined help commands.

!ENDSCREEN LABEL YES, COLON NO, MSGAREA M, MESSAGE MSG
The **ENDSCREEN** command has several options. The option **LABEL YES** displays the text and trailing colon of all screen-area labels. The option **COLON NO** controls the display of every label's trailing colon. The option **MSGAREA M** enables you to specify where messages will be displayed, where **M** is the name of an area label. The last option **MESSAGE MSG** specifies an initial message that will appear in the message area with the initial screen display, where MSG is the name of a micro containing the desired message.

!AREA RELEASE, VALUE MICRO SYSNUM, PROTECT
The **AREA** command has several options. The option **RELEASE** is the name of the area where a data value is displayed. The option **VALUE MICRO SYSNUM** specifies that a global micro will supply a value for the area described by the "9.9" format. The option **PROTECT** protects the line from being altered by the user during execution. That is, the micro value is displayed but may not be changed.

!AREA M, BOLD
In this **AREA** command, the option **M** is the name of the area label and the option **BOLD** highlights that area's value.

!AREA OUTLET, VALUE MICRO SELECT, UNDERLINE, '
!VERIFY = OUTLET OR = "CANCEL", '
!UPPER, HELPMSG "   ENTER NAME OF DESIRED OUTLET."
In this **AREA** command, the option **OUTLET** is the name of the area label. The option **VALUE MICRO SELECT** specifies a global micro that will supply an initial value for the area. The option **UNDERLINE** underlines the area. The option **VERIFY** insures a correct location name has been entered. The value **CANCEL** will let the user abandon the processing that takes place. The option **UPPER** converts text values entered by the user to all uppercase before storing them into the designated parameter or micro.

!CURSOR IN OUTLET
This command specifies the area where the cursor appears when the screen is first displayed.

!SHOWSCREEN
This command displays the currently defined display screen by executing the screen-formatting directives and options. Note that the **!AREA**, **!LABEL**, and **!CURSOR** commands must *precede* the !SHOWSCREEN directive that they affect.

!IF "&SELECT&" <> "CANCEL" THEN !CALL CFDEREL &SELECT&
This command is used to execute a desired statement that follows the THEN and is conditional upon the user-defined IF test.

!DROPMICRO MSG
This command deletes any existing micro(s) and corresponding definition(s) from the current IFPS/Plus internal table.

Now, that you have an understanding of these commands, let's create the command file and do a unit test. The command file is both created and executed in the Server model. You could create it in the Visual mode as well

To create a fill-in-the-blank full screen with a SETLOAD that obtains a user define set of values:

❶   Click the **Server button** in the toolbar to switch to the Server model, if necessary.

❷   Enter **CMDFILE CFSCRN10** to name the command file.

❸   Enter the commands in Figure 9-5 for the desired processing. However, to do the unit test on this command file, enter line 620 as:
620 !SHOWMICRO SELECT
This will display the value for the SELECT micro rather than perform the CALL to another command file. After the unit test, this line is then revised as shown in Figure 9-5.

❹   Enter **END**, then enter **SAVE** to save the command file.

❺   Enter **COMMANDS CFSCRN10** to do a unit test and display the full-screen form. See Figure 9-6.

TROUBLE? If your screen does not appear like that in Figure 9-6, then do a RECORD and take a look at the recorded output.

```
****************************************************************
*****        FINANCIAL PLANNING AND FORECASTING SYSTEM   *****
*****                    OUTLET PROCESSING               *****
*****                    RELEASE: 2.3                    *****
****************************************************************


            -------------- SELECT OUTLET FOR UPDATING ----------------



                        OUTLET:_____






                            ENTER DESIRED OUTLET

SCRN 10            USE PF1 FOR HELP
```

Figure 9-6 Screen Prompts for Outlet Name

In the IF statement the *false* condition results in a call to another command file that facilitates entering data in a relation for the select outlet. Let's take a look at that command file the false condition calls. This command file is shown in Figure 9-7.

```
100 !COMMENT **** FILE CFDEREL
110 !COMMENT **** LAST CHANGED BY: HRW
120 !COMMENT **** LAST CHANGE DATE: 10/21/..
130 !COMMENT  *************************************************
140 !COMMENT *****                                        *****
150 !COMMENT *****   PROCESS 4.0: PERFORM-DATAEDIT-        *****
160 !COMMENT *****             FOR-SELECTED-OUTLETS        *****
170 !COMMENT *****                                        *****
180! COMMENT  *************************************************
190 !CPARAMS 1 LOC IDENTIFIER
200 !COMMENT  **  ACCESS DESIRED RELATION
210 RELATION DECPARAM
220 WHERE LOC  = "&1"
230 DATAEDIT
240 !COMMENT  ** ACCOUNT NAMES CANNOT BE CHANGED
250 PROTECT ACCOUNT
260 !INPUTC
270 !COMMENT  **  SAVE REVISED RELATION
280 SAVE
290 !RETURN
```

Figure 9-7
Command File
for Dataedit

Let's look at the new commands in this command file that implement the Dataedit processing.

DATAEDIT

This command displays the selected relation in a row and column arrangement in the Server's window. This is similar to the spreadsheet arrangement displayed in Visual. However, you *cannot* use the mouse pointer to move to a cell to enter a new data value. Instead, you press [F4] to move the cursor to the spreadsheet area. Then the [Tab] is used to move from field to field going across a row, while the [Up] and [Down] arrow keys are used to change rows. New data values are typed with the [spacebar] used to remove unwanted characters. The [F3] is used to exit from Dataedit processing once the changes are complete. In this manner, Dataedit lets you look at and revise data during command file execution.

PROTECT ACCOUNT

This command enables you to specify column(s) in a datafile or field(s) in a relation that cannot be edited or deleted when using a Dataedit screen.

!INPUTC

This command temporarily suspends command file execution while a user provides inputs to IFPS. When these inputs are completed, the command file execution continues. Input is completed by pressing [F3] from within the Dataedit screen. The INPUTC allows multiple user inputs.

Let's prepare this command file and test its operation.

To create and test a command file for doing data entry:

❶   Enter **CMDFILE CFDEREL** to name the command file from the Server mode.

❷   Enter the commands in Figure 9-7.

❸   Enter **END**, then enter **SAVE** to save the command file.

❹   Enter **COMMANDS CFDEREL** to do a unit test on the command file.

❺   Enter **WEST** when prompted for the micro value for LOC IDENTIFIER.

❻   Press [**F3**] to exit from the Dataedit screen.

Now let's revise command file CFSRN10 that requested the outlet name and re-run these two command files:

To revise the CFSCRN10 command file:

❶   Enter **CMDFILE CFSCRN10** form the Server mode.

❷   Enter **620 !IF "&SELECT&" <> "CANCEL" THEN !CALL CFDEREL &SELECT&**

❸   Enter **SAVE** to save this command file.

Next, the command files are executed.

To execute the command files to select an outlet and carry out the Dataedit processing:

❶   Enter **COMMANDS CFSCRN10** in the Server mode.

❷   Enter **CROSS** as the desired outlet.

❸   Press [**F3**] to exit from the Dataedit subsystem.

Menu-Selection Screen

A menu-selection screen contains a list of menu choices. A user moves the cursor to the desired selection and presses enter to cause the selection to be processed. The [Tab] key is used to move the menu cursor from one menu selection to the next.

Once the selection has been made in this example, the micro **CHOICE** is given the number of the menu item selected. This micro can then be used to control subsequent processing based on the selected menu choice (Figure 9-8). By using a menu screen, Herbie is prompted for the selection of his desired processing activity. His choice is then processed.

```
100 !COMMENT ***** FILE: CFSCRN05
110 !COMMENT ***** LAST CHANGED BY:   PAW
120 !COMMENT ***** LAST CHANGED DATE: 11/11/..
130 !COMMENT ********************************************************
140 !COMMENT *****                                              *****
150 !COMMENT ***** PROCESS 2.0:  SELECT-OUTLET-MODEL-           *****
160 !COMMENT *****                 PROCESSING-TO-BE-PERFORMED   *****
170 !COMMENT *****                                              *****
180 !COMMENT ********************************************************
190 !COMMENT
200 !COMMENT ** INITIALIZE MICROS AND PARAMETERS FOR USE WITH
210 !COMMENT ** FULL-SCREEN PROCESSING
220 !SUPPRESS
230 !COMPUTE CHOICE = 0
240 !ASSIGN SELECT = " "
250 !ASSIGN MSG = " "
260 !REPEAT WHILE PARAM 1 IS 1..4
270    !COMPUTE PICK&1 = &1
280 !NEXT
290 !CLEARSCREEN NOPAUSE
300 !COMMENT ** BEGIN FULL-SCREEN DISPLAY
310 !SCREEN
320 **************************************************************
330 *****    FINANCIAL PLANNING AND FORECASTING SYSTEM    *****
340 *****                  OUTLET PROCESSING              *****
250 *****                    RELEASE: 9.9                 *****
360 **************************************************************
370
380               ----------------- MAIN MENU -----------------
390
400
410 T1: <"PROCESSING OPTIONS:">
420
430     A1: 9  INPUT DECISION PARAMETERS ONLY
440     A2: 9  SOLVE MODEL ONLY
450     A3: 9  INPUT PARAMETERS AND SOLVE MODEL
460
470
480     A4: 9  TERMINATE PROCESSING
490
500
510
520               SELECT DESIRED OPTION
530   M: TTTTTTTTTTTTTTTTTTTTTTTTTTTTTTTTTTTTTTTTTTTTTTTTTTTTTTTT
540
550 SCRN05             USE PF1 FOR HELP
560 !ENDSCREEN LABEL NO, COLON NO, MSGAREA M, MESSAGE MSG
570 !AREA RELEASE, LABEL, VALUE MICRO SYSNUM, PROTECT
```

Figure 9-8
Command File
for Screen
Menu
(continued)

```
580 !AREA M, BOLD
590 !AREA T1, PROTECT, BOLD
600 !REPEAT WHILE PARAM 1 IS 1..4
610   !AREA A&1, VALUE MICRO PICK&1, UNDERLINE, '
620   !HELPMSG "MOVE CURSOR WITH <TAB>, THEN PRESS <ENTER>."
630 !NEXT
640 !CURSOR IN A1, LASTAREA SELECT
650 !SHOWSCREEN
660 !IF "&SELECT&" = " " THEN !GOBACK 310
670 !COMMENT  **  DETERMINE VALUE FOR CHOICE AND DROP MICROS
680 !REPEAT WHILE  PARAM 1 IS 1..4
690   !IF "&SELECT&" = "A&1" THEN !SETPARAM CHOICE &1
700   !DROPMICRO PICK&1
710 !NEXT
720 !DROPMICRO MSG
730 !RETURN
```

Figure 9-8
Command File
for Screen
Menu

Let's examine the new commands used for this command file.

!COMPUTE CHOICE = 0

This command allows a command file to compute values for it parameters and micros during execution. Numbers specify a parameter, while text characters designate a micro. Here, "**CHOICE**" is text so a micro is created and set to a numeric value of zero. Remember, the !ASSIGN directive is used to give a micro a text value.

!REPEAT WHILE PARAM 1 IS 1..4
!COMPUTE PICK&1 = &1
!NEXT

These three lines form a loop that is processed repetitively to initialize global micros for menu item numbers. The **REPEAT WHILE** command implements a loop that is used to repeat a block of lines in a command file a specified number of times. The **COMPUTE** command assigns user-defined micro values from parameter values incremented by the REPEAT. The **NEXT** command specifies the end of the loop.

A1: 9 INPUT DECISION PARAMETERS ONLY
A2: 9 SOLVE MODEL ONLY
A3: 9 INPUT PARAMETERS AND SOLVE MODEL
A4: 9 TERMINATE PROCESSING

These four lines are used to set up a menu that allows a user to select one of the four choices. The A1, A2, A3, and A4 are each labels for the menu choices. When the command file is executed, you use the [Tab] key to move the cursor from one menu item to the next. Then, press [Enter] to select the menu choice at the location of the cursor.

!REPEAT WHILE PARAM 1 IS 1..4
!AREA A&1, VALUE MICRO PICK&1, UNDERLINE,'
!HELPMSG "MOVE CURSOR WITH <TAB>, THEN PRESS <ENTER>."

These three lines form a loop that is processed repetitively. The **REPEAT** command begins the loop. The **AREA** command specifies each A area with the &1 parameter designating the specific area label in this loop. The **HELPMSG** command establishes the help line. This loop simplifies the definition of each of the four areas for the menu choices. Otherwise, the AREA command would need to be repeated four times. The importance of using loops increases as the number of times similar command file directives are required in a command file.

!IF "&SELECT&" = " " THEN !GOBACK 310
This command says that if the SELECT micro is blank, then the entire screen is redisplayed because the command file is re-executed beginning at line 310. This would occur if the user places the cursor at some location on the screen other than for one of the menu choices.

!REPEAT WHILE PARAM 1 IS 1..4
  !IF "&SELECT&" = "A&1" THEN !SETPARAM CHOICE &1
  !DROPMICRO PICK&1

These three lines form a loop that is processed repetitively. The **REPEAT** command begins this loop. The **IF** statement specifies what will happen if you choose any of the selections from the menu. In this manner, the screen selection is placed in the **CHOICE** micro for use in subsequent processing. The **DROPMICRO** command deletes the PICK&1 micro. The **!SETPARAM** command places the value of parameter &1 in the CHOICE micro. Let's create the command file and test it.

To create a full-screen menu screen:

❶   Enter **CMDFILE CFSCRN05** to name the command file from the Server mode.

❷   Enter the commands shown in Figure 9-8.

❸   Enter **END**, then enter **SAVE** to save the command file.

❹   Enter **COMMANDS CFSCRN05** to initiate testing of the command file. See Figure 9-9.

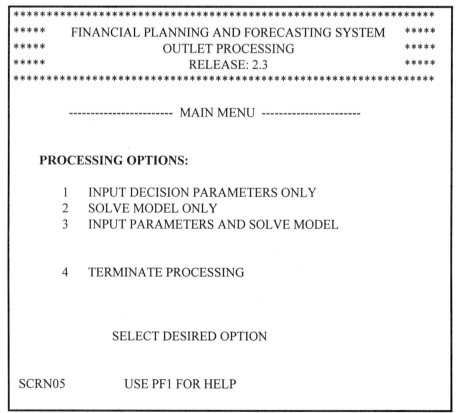

```
****************************************************************
*****       FINANCIAL PLANNING AND FORECASTING SYSTEM     *****
*****                   OUTLET PROCESSING                 *****
*****                    RELEASE: 2.3                     *****
****************************************************************


                 ----------------- MAIN MENU ----------------------


        PROCESSING OPTIONS:

            1     INPUT DECISION PARAMETERS ONLY
            2     SOLVE MODEL ONLY
            3     INPUT PARAMETERS AND SOLVE MODEL


            4     TERMINATE PROCESSING



                  SELECT DESIRED OPTION


     SCRN05            USE PF1 FOR HELP
```

Figure 9-9 Screen Prompts from Menu Selection

TROUBLE? If your screen does not appear like that shown in Figure 9-9, then do a RECORD and take a look at the record file to help locate your error.

❺   Press **[Tab]** to move to the second menu item for solving the model.

❻   Press **[Enter]** to select the menu item and continue the command file processing.

❼   Enter **SHOWMICRO CHOICE** to display the value stored in the micro CHOICE.

In this manner, a user-define menu is created that runs in the Server mode.

Remember, if you do *not* want to see all the commands as they are executed, then include the !SUPPRESS command at the beginning of your command file. You may want to use this with any of the command files in this tutorial.

Generated List of Choices Screen

Full-screen processing can be used to present a list of system generated choices with the selection performed by moving the cursor to the desired choice and pressing the [Enter] key. In this processing, the list of system generated choices are provide by an IFPS/Plus **SET**. As a result, the choices are *not* entered in the command file logic, which is the situation with the previous menu selection screen. It is possible to have a different SET of choices displayed on this screen each time it is processed. The CANCEL alternative is displayed on the screen to allow users to abandon the processing, if desired.

Command file CFSCRN15 implements the selection of a choice from a SET of choices displayed for the user (Figure 9-10). The location of the cursor in the SET of choices is determined in the full-screen processing by using the **LASTAREA** and **LASTITEM** options of the **CURSOR** command. This allows the desired value to be determined from the selection and stored in a micro or parameter for use in guiding subsequent processing.

```
100 !COMMENT ***** FILE: CFSCRN15
110 !COMMENT ***** LAST CHANGED BY:   HRW
120 !COMMENT ***** LAST CHANGED DATE:  10/21/..
130 !COMMENT *********************************************************
140 !COMMENT *****                                              *****
150 !COMMENT ***** PROCESS 6.0:  SELECT-INDIVIDUAL-OUTLET       *****
160 !COMMENT *****                    -FOR-PROCESSING            *****
170 !COMMENT *****                                              *****
180 !COMMENT *********************************************************
190 !COMMENT
200 !COMMENT **  INITIALIZE MICROS AND PARAMETERS FOR USE
210 !COMMENT **  WITH FULL-SCREEN PROCESSING
220 !SUPPRESS
230 !QUERY DECPARAM
240 !SELECT DISTINCT LOC
250 !SAVE AS BRANCH
260 !SETLOAD RELATION BRANCH.LOC
270 !ASSIGN SELECT = " "
280 !ASSIGN MSG = " "
290 !ASSIGN CANCEL = "CANCEL"
300 !COMMENT **  BEGIN FULL-SCREEN DISPLAY
310 !SCREEN
```

Figure 9-10
Listing of
Choices Screen
(continued)

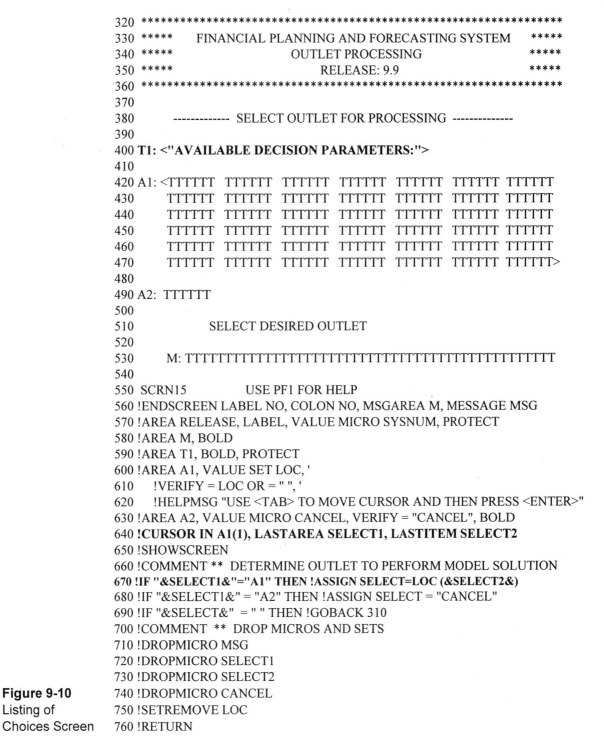

```
320 ********************************************************************
330 *****       FINANCIAL PLANNING AND FORECASTING SYSTEM       *****
340 *****                   OUTLET PROCESSING                   *****
350 *****                     RELEASE: 9.9                      *****
360 ********************************************************************
370
380        ------------- SELECT OUTLET FOR PROCESSING --------------
390
400 T1: <"AVAILABLE DECISION PARAMETERS:">
410
420 A1: <TTTTTT  TTTTTT  TTTTTT  TTTTTT  TTTTTT  TTTTTT  TTTTTT
430      TTTTTT  TTTTTT  TTTTTT  TTTTTT  TTTTTT  TTTTTT  TTTTTT
440      TTTTTT  TTTTTT  TTTTTT  TTTTTT  TTTTTT  TTTTTT  TTTTTT
450      TTTTTT  TTTTTT  TTTTTT  TTTTTT  TTTTTT  TTTTTT  TTTTTT
460      TTTTTT  TTTTTT  TTTTTT  TTTTTT  TTTTTT  TTTTTT  TTTTTT
470      TTTTTT  TTTTTT  TTTTTT  TTTTTT  TTTTTT  TTTTTT  TTTTTT>
480
490 A2:  TTTTTT
500
510            SELECT DESIRED OUTLET
520
530       M: TTTTTTTTTTTTTTTTTTTTTTTTTTTTTTTTTTTTTTTTTTTTTTTTTTTTT
540
550 SCRN15           USE PF1 FOR HELP
560 !ENDSCREEN LABEL NO, COLON NO, MSGAREA M, MESSAGE MSG
570 !AREA RELEASE, LABEL, VALUE MICRO SYSNUM, PROTECT
580 !AREA M, BOLD
590 !AREA T1, BOLD, PROTECT
600 !AREA A1, VALUE SET LOC, '
610    !VERIFY = LOC OR = " ", '
620    !HELPMSG "USE <TAB> TO MOVE CURSOR AND THEN PRESS <ENTER>"
630 !AREA A2, VALUE MICRO CANCEL, VERIFY = "CANCEL", BOLD
640 !CURSOR IN A1(1), LASTAREA SELECT1, LASTITEM SELECT2
650 !SHOWSCREEN
660 !COMMENT ** DETERMINE OUTLET TO PERFORM MODEL SOLUTION
670 !IF "&SELECT1&"="A1" THEN !ASSIGN SELECT=LOC (&SELECT2&)
680 !IF "&SELECT1&" = "A2" THEN !ASSIGN SELECT = "CANCEL"
690 !IF "&SELECT&" = " " THEN !GOBACK 310
700 !COMMENT ** DROP MICROS AND SETS
710 !DROPMICRO MSG
720 !DROPMICRO SELECT1
730 !DROPMICRO SELECT2
740 !DROPMICRO CANCEL
750 !SETREMOVE LOC
760 !RETURN
```

Figure 9-10
Listing of
Choices Screen

Let's review the new commands for this command file.

!SELECT DISTINCT LOC

This command is used to specify that only unique values or combinations of values for the designed field(s) are determined from the database relation.

!SAVE AS BRANCH

This command is used to copy data from the currently active relation entity into permanent storage using the specified name. A new relation is created containing only the selected fields. For this example, this is the LOC field.

!SETLOAD RELATION BRANCH.LOC

This command is used to obtain the SET values from the relation. BRANCH is the name of the relation and LOC is the field in that relation.

T1: <"AVAILABLE DECISION PARAMETERS:">.

This line is used as a title for the menu.

!CURSOR IN A1(1), LASTAREA SELECT1, LASTITEM SELECT2

This command line has several components. **!CURSOR** is used to control the cursor position on the screen display. **A1(1)** specifies the first element in A1, which is an array or vector area with multiple elements. **LASTAREA** is used to record the last screen area where the cursor resided before the user exits from the display screen. **LASTITEM** is used to record the last subscript of the cursor in a vector area before the user exits from the display screen.

!IF "&SELECT1&" = "A1" THEN !ASSIGN SELECT = LOC (&SELECT2&)

The end of this command line **LOC (&SELECT2&)** is used to place the value from the LOC set that is selected in the menu.

Let's prepare the command file and do a test run.

To create a user-defined menu screen with a list of choices:

❶ Enter **CMDFILE CFSCRN15** to name the command file from the Server mode.

❷ Enter the commands in Figure 9-10.

❸ Enter **END**, then enter **SAVE** to save the command file.

❹ Enter **COMMANDS CFSCRN15** to test the command file. See Figure 9-11.

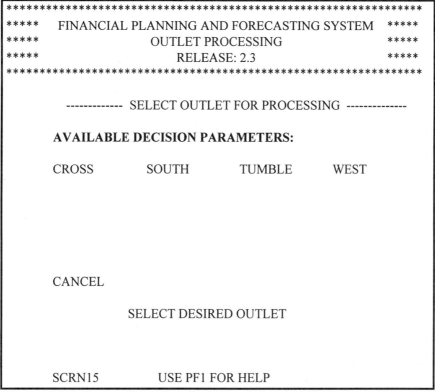

Figure 9-11 Screen Prompts with Generated List of Choices

TROUBLE? If your screen does not appear as shown in Figure 9-11, then use TRACE and RECORD to a look your processing in detail. Locate and correct your error, then re-execute the command file. Carefully review your use of the "<" and ">" to define the A1 area as a vector.

❺ Press **[Tab]** twice to move to TUMBLE, then press **[Enter]** to complete the selection of this choice.

❻ Enter **SHOWMICRO SELECT** to display the value you picked.

System Building with Full-Screen Forms

Many of the elements of full-screen processing can be combined into a system that guides the processing for the outlets at Buffalo Computer Systems (BCS). The purpose of this example is to provide ideas on integrating full-screen processing with other command file processing activities. The overall processing proceeds as illustrated in the structure chart shown in Figure 9-12. This system makes use of many of the command files developed earlier in this tutorial. Other arrangement of command files can be used to further enhance this processing.

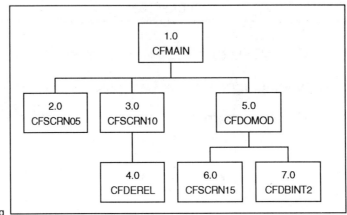

Figure 9-12
Structure Chart
for System Building

CFMAIN is the main command file that is executed by the user. This command file opens a database and calls the next level command file to direct processing. Command file CFDOMOD is a command file which processes the model solution for an individual retail outlet. The "CFSCRN" command files are those described previously in this tutorial. The CFDEREL and CFDBINT2 command files are those presented in this tutorial. CFDBINT2 makes use of the internal method of defining the database relation input to the model. The command file CFMAIN is shown in Figure 9-13.

```
100 !COMMENT ***** FILE:  CFMAIN
110 !COMMENT ***** LAST CHANGED BY:   HRW
120 !COMMENT ***** LAST CHANGED DATE: 10/21/..
130 !COMMENT ****************************************************
140 !COMMENT *****                                         *****
150 !COMMENT ***** PROCESS 1.0:  CONTROL-OUTLET-PROCESSING *****
160 !COMMENT *****                                         *****
170 !COMMENT ****************************************************
180 !COMMENT
190 !SUPPRESS
200 !COMMENT ** INITIALIZE SELECT MICROS
210 !COMPUTE SYSNUM = 2.3
220 !COMPUTE OPTION = 0
230 !ASSIGN SELECT = " "
240 !COMMENT ** OPEN THE DATABASE
250 DATABASE DBBCS
260 SPOOL RFSPOOL
270 !CLEARSCREEN NOPAUSE
280 !CALL CFSCRN05
290 !COMMENT ** PROCESS SELECTED MENU CHOICE
```

Figure 9-13
CFMAIN
Command File
(continued)

```
300 !IF &CHOICE& .EQ. 1 .OR. &CHOICE& .EQ. 3 THEN !CALL CFSCRN10
310 !IF &CHOICE& .EQ. 2 .OR. &CHOICE& .EQ. 3 THEN !CALL CFDOMOD
320 !IF &CHOICE& .EQ. 4 THEN !GOTO 340
330 !GOBACK 280
340 !CLEARSCREEN
350 CLOSE DATABASE
360 CLOSE SPOOL
370 !COMMENT ** REMOVE MICROS
380 !DROPMICRO CHOICE
390 !DROPMICRO OPTION
400 !DROPMICRO SELECT
410 !RETURN
```

Figure 9-13
CFMAIN
Command File

Let's take a look at lines 300 through 340 that are highlighted in Figure 9-13. These lines are linked to the choice the users makes in the menu CFSCRN05. If the user selects choice one, this command file calls the screen command file CFSCRN10. If the user selects choice two, this command file calls the command file CFDOMOD. If the user selects choice three, it calls CFSCRN10, then calls CFDOMOD. Last, if the user selects choice four, then the screen is cleared, and the system ends. Let's create this command file and test it.

To create the main processing command file and test it:

❶   Enter **CMDFILE CFMAIN** to name the command file.

❷   Enter the commands in Figure 9-13.

❸   Enter **END**, then enter **SAVE** to save the command file.

❹   Enter **COMMANDS CFMAIN** to test the command file.

With this command file developed and tested you are ready to create the last command file CFDOMOD for the system (Figure 9-14). This command file processes Herbie's template model for an individual outlet that he selects.

```
100 !COMMENT ***** FILE: CFDOMOD
110 !COMMENT ***** LAST CHANGED BY:   HRW
120 !COMMENT ***** LAST CHANGED DATE: 10/21/..
130 !COMMENT ************************************************
140 !COMMENT *****                                    *****
150 !COMMENT ***** PROCESS 5.0: PROCESS-MODEL-WITH-   *****
160 !COMMENT *****            DECISION-PARAMETERS      *****
170 !COMMENT *****                                    *****
180 !COMMENT ************************************************
190 !COMMENT
200 !SUPPRESS
210 !CALL CFSCRN15
220 !IF "&SELECT&" = "CANCEL" THEN !GOTO 250
230 MODEL MASTER2
240 !CALL CFDBINT2 &SELECT& '&SELECT& SHOPPING MALL'
250 !RETURN
```

Figure 9-14
CFDOMOD
Command File

In Figure 9-14, the parameter value included in the command on line 240 creates a report title for each outlet that is the outlet name combined with "Shopping Mall." This method is readily implemented with the previous command files. In IFPS/Plus, this may be provided by several other means, including obtaining the report name from a database relation. The method selected is easy to implement without revising the previous command files. Let's create and test this command file.

To create and test command file CFDOMOD in the Server mode:

❶   Enter **CMDFILE CFDOMOD** to name the command file.

❷   Enter the commands in Figure 9-14.

❸   Enter **END**, then enter **SAVE** to save the command file.

❹   Enter **COMMANDS CFDOMOD** to test the command file.

Let's run the entire system to do a system test of all the command files.

To run the entire system:

❶   Enter **COMMANDS CFMAIN**, which gets you to the first screen.

❷   Enter your desired selection to test each option.

❸   Enter **LIST FILE RFSPOOL** to display the contents of your spool file. If you wish, return to the Visual mode, then open and print your spool file.

The command files explored in this tutorial provide a system for entering data and generating reports that will let someone other than Herbie and Pattie run the system and do data entry with the Dataedit subsystem.

Full-Screen Commands

Full-screen processing makes use of several commands that assist in creating full-screen panels. Some of the more frequently used commands are listed here for your reference. Detailed operation of each command is described in the *IFPS/Plus User's Manual.*

Full-Screen Command	Action
!AREA areaname [(subscript)] optionlist	Associates values of parameters, micros, or sets with an area for the screen
!CURSOR optionlist	Controls and monitors cursor position on the screen
!ENDSCREEN [optionlist]	Marks end of lines defining template screen image
!LABEL arealabel [optionlist]	Specifies characteristics of text labels which appear in screen from template image
!SCREEN	Marks beginning of lines defining template screen image
!SHOWSCREEN [optionlist]	Causes the defined template screen to be displayed

The options for each of these commands are decried below. Several options are used with more than one command. Those options used with the AREA command apply only to the single area defined by the command. When the same options are used with the other full-screen commands, they apply to all AREA commands unless the option is specifically repeated in the AREA command. ENDSCREEN and

SHOWSCREEN are used to establish those characteristics that are desired for all AREAs, unless otherwise specified.

Full-Screen Command Options	Action
!AREA OptionList	
BOLD [YES] BOLD NO	Causes area to appear in bold type, may be a different color, BOLD is used with PROTECT to produce different colors
CENTER CENTRE	Causes text to be centered within defined text area
COLON [YES] COLON NO	Specifies display of colon with label
COMDEC A COMDEC E1 COMDEC E2	Specifies numeric formats for commas in display
HELPMSG "text" HELPMSG arg	Specifies help message to be displayed on request
HIDE [YES] HIDE NO	Specifies whether values entered are to be visible or not
IFCHANGE arg	Records indication of a change to parameters or micros
LABEL [YES] LABEL NO	Specifies display of area label text and colon
LEFT	Causes text to be left justified within text area
PROTECT [YES] PROTECT [ON] PROTECT OFF PROTECT NO	Specifies protection of area from editing, may be used to control color of text, used with BOLD for color control
RIGHT	Causes text to be right justified within text area
UNDERLINE [YES] UNDERLINE NO	Specifies underlining of text or numeric format in area
UPPER [YES] UPPER NO	Specifies upper- or lowercase conversion of text values entered
VALUE MICRO name VALUE PARAM name VALUE SET name [(subscript)]	Specifies value to be displayed or obtained from area

Full-Screen Command Options	Action
!AREA OptionList (continued)	
VERIFY [subscripts] NOT NULL VERIFY [subscripts] clause VERIFY [sub] clause AND clause VERIFY [sub] clause OR clause	Specifies data validation rules for input values
!CURSOR Optionlist	
IN labelarea[(subscript)]	Specifies where cursor is initially located onscreen
LASTAREA arg	Records name of screen area where cursor was last located
LASTITEM arg	Records subscript of last location of cursor in a vector area
!ENDSCREEN Optionlist	
BEEP [YES] BEEP NO	Causes a "beep" sound when a screen is displayed
CENTER CENTRE	Causes text to be centered within defined text area
COLON [YES] COLON NO	Specifies display of colon with label
COMDEC A COMDEC E1 COMDEC E2	Specifies numeric formats for commas in display
HELPMSG "text" HELPMSG arg	Specifies help message to be displayed on request
LABEL [YES] LABEL NO	Specifies display of area label text and colon
LEFT	Causes text to be left justified within text area
MESSAGE "text" MESSAGE arg	Specifies the message to be displayed in the message area
MSGAREA msglabel MSGAREA LINE[S] range MSGAREA	Specifies the area where messages will be displayed
MSGWAIT [n]	Specifies the length of time a message is displayed

Full-Screen Command Options	Action
!ENDSCREEN Optionlist *(continued)*	
PROTECT [YES] PROTECT [ON] PROTECT NO PROTECT OFF	Specifies protection of area from editing, may be used to control color of text, used with BOLD for color control
RIGHT	Causes text to be right justified within text area
UNDERLINE [YES] UNDERLINE NO	Specifies underlining of text or numeric format in area
UPPER [YES] UPPER NO	Specifies upper- or lowercase conversion of text values entered
!LABEL Optionlist	
BOLD [YES] BOLD NO	Causes area to appear in bold type, may be a different color, BOLD is used with PROTECT to produce different colors
COLON [YES] COLON NO	Specifies display of colon with label
HIDE [YES] HIDE NO	Specifies whether values entered are to be visible or not
!SHOWSCREEN Optionlist	
BEEP [YES] BEEP NO	Causes a "beep" sound when a screen is displayed
PROTECT [YES] PROTECT [ON]	Specifies protection of entire screen from editing, this overrides PROTECT in the ENDSCREEN command
VALIDATE [YES] VALIDATE INPUT VALIDATE NO	Controls validation checks on screen AREAs which use VERIFY

Questions

1.   A _____ file is an object in which commands such as SOLVE and GENREPORT are placed so that the commands can be re-used as desired.
    a. model
    b. report
    c. command
    d. template

2.   A _____ screen presents one or more blanks that are to receive an input value.
   a. fill-in-the-blank
   b. message
   c. menu selection
   d. selection-from-a-list

3.   A _____ screen contains a list of menu choices.
   a. fill-in-the-blank
   b. message
   c. menu selection
   d. selection-from-a-list

4.   The _____ command determines the name and the structure of the relations in the current database.
   a. LIST
   b. LIST REAL
   c. LISTREL
   d. RELATION

5.   The _____ directive is used to select certain fields from the active relation and assign their corresponding text values to a micro or parameter.
   a. !ASSIGN
   b. !AREA
   c. !ENDSCREEN
   d. !SCREEN

Case Problems

1. Good Morning Products

Kim wants to improve the front end to the data entry processing for Good Morning Products. She wants you to create a full-screen command file that requests the name of the plant for which data are to be entered. The plant location names to be used are the same as those used previously: CALIF, FLORIDA, TEXAS, and GOLDEN. To insure a valid plant name is used, Kim wants you to use a SET that contains the valid plant names. The full screen is to validate the input plant name using this SET. The desired plant name is to be stored in the micro PLANT. This command file should include the capability to abandon processing, if desired.

Also, Kim needs a command file like CMDFILE CFDBINT2 from Figure 9-2. To unit test the command file, Kim wants you to execute the file and then display the value of the PLANT micro using the SHOWMICRO ALL command. Document this command file by producing a hardcopy listing of the commands, of the screen during execution, and of the micro value for PLANT.

2. Good Morning Products

Chris wants you to create a full-screen menu that provides Good Morning Products with the ability to select processing activities. This screen should facilitate:
   • input of decision parameters
   • solution of the plant model
   • both input of data and solution of the model

- the termination of processing

Chris wants the menu to be operated by moving the cursor to the desired activity and pressing [Enter]. The menu selection is to be a number of one through four which is stored in the micro CHOICE. To test the command file, execute it and then display the value of the CHOICE micro using the SHOWMICRO ALL command.

3. Good Morning Products

Jennifer usually runs Good Morning Products' model with the input data for each plant, after the data have been entered in their database. She wants you to create a full-screen panel that presents a list of the plants. She can then selected the desired plant from the list of available plants that have data in the database relation. As part of the full-screen processing, QUERY the database relation containing the decision parameters to obtain a SET of available plants. Present this SET on the screen for selection. Once Jennifer has entered her selection, verify the selection as an existing selection in the SET. Store Jennifer's selection in the micro PLANT for use in controlling the model solution. She wants to include the capability of entering CANCEL to abandon processing. To unit test the command file, activate the database for Good Morning Products, then execute the command file. The database must be active in order to obtain the SET of available plants. After the command file has been executed, use the SHOWMICRO ALL command to check the value of the PLANT micro. Document this command file and its execution.

4. Good Morning Products

Good Morning Products wants you to create an integrated system for entering data and producing model solutions similar to that presented for Buffalo Computer Systems (BCS). Write the other command files as needed to complete this system. You may use portions of command files that you developed in the preceding case problems of this tutorial to assist you in this effort. Test your integrated system on at least two plants. As part of the system testing, be sure to check the operation of each menu choice. Draw a structure chart that documents the calling arrangement among your command files. Document the system with listings and executions of your command files.

5. The Woodcraft Furniture Company

Joe Birch believes the front-end processing can be improved for entering data into the quarterly budget system at Woodcraft Furniture. He wants you to create a full-screen command file that requests the name of the company for entering or updating data. The company names to be used are the same as those used previously: WOOD, OAK, CID, and SIC. To validate the company name entered, Joe wants you to create a SET that contains the valid company names. The full screen is to validate the requested company name using the values from this SET. The desired company name for processing is to be stored in the micro COMPANY. This command file should include the capability to terminate processing, if desired. Also, Joe needs a command file like CMDFILE CFDBINT2 from Figure 9-2. To test the command file, Joe wants you to execute the file and then display the value of the COMPANY micro using the SHOWMICRO ALL command. Document this command file by producing a hardcopy listing of the commands, of the screen during execution, and of the micro value for COMPANY.

6. The Woodcraft Furniture Company

"Tall" Pine wants you to develop a full-screen menu that provides Woodcraft Furniture with the ability to select processing activities. This screen should facilitate:

- input of values for decision variables
- solution of the quarterly company budget model
- both input of data and solution of the model
- the termination of processing

"Tall" wants the menu to be operated by moving the cursor to the desired activity and pressing [Enter]. The menu selection is to be a number of one through four which is stored in the micro CHOICE. To test the command file, run it and then display the value of the CHOICE micro using the SHOWMICRO ALL command. Produce hardcopy listings of both the command file and the screen displayed during the command file's execution.

7. The Woodcraft Furniture Company

Joe Birch usually runs Woodcraft's quarterly budget model after all the input data for each company have been entered. He wants you to create a full-screen menu that presents a list of the companies. He can then select the desired company from the list of available companies that have data in the database relation. As part of the full-screen processing, QUERY the database relation containing the decision parameters to obtain a SET of available companies. Present this SET on the screen for selection. Once Joe has entered his selection, verify the selection as an existing selection in the SET. Store Joe's selection in the micro COMPANY for use in controlling the model solution. He wants to include the capability of entering CANCEL to abandon processing. To test the command file, activate the database for Woodcraft Furniture, then execute the command file. The database must be active in order to obtain the SET of available divisions. After the command file has been executed, use the SHOWMICRO ALL command to check the value of the COMPANY micro. Document this command file by producing a hardcopy listing of the file and of the screen obtained when the command file is executed.

8. The Woodcraft Furniture Company

For Woodcraft Furniture, Joe wants you to create an integrated system for entering data and producing model solutions similar to that presented for Buffalo Computer Systems (BCS). Write any other command files as needed to complete this system. You may use portions of command files that you developed in the prior case problems of this tutorial to assist you in this effort. Test your integrated system on at least two companies. As part of the system testing, be sure to check the operation of each menu choice. Produce a hardcopy listing of the command file and of the screens displayed during command file execution. Draw a structure chart that documents the calling arrangement among your command files.

9. The Last National Bank

Carrie believes the front-end processing can be improved for entering data into the budget system at Last National Bank. She wants you to create a full-screen command file that requests the name of the branch bank for entering data. The location names to be used are the same as those used previously: SPOKEN, WEEP, BROKEN, and PASS. To insure a valid bank name is used, Carrie wants you to create a SET that contains the valid location names. The full screen is to validate the requested bank name using this SET. The desired location name is to be stored in the micro LOCATION. This command file should include the capability to terminate processing, if desired. Also, Carrie needs a command file like CMDFILE CFDBINT2 from Figure 9-2. To unit test the command file, Carrie wants you to execute the file and then display the value of the LOCATION micro using the SHOWMICRO ALL command. Document this command file by producing a hardcopy listing of the command, of the screen during execution, and of the micro value for LOCATION.

10. The Last National Bank

J. J. wants you to create a full-screen menu that provides Last National Bank the ability to select processing activities. This screen should facilitate:
- input of values for decision variables
- solution of the bank budget model
- both input of data and solution of the model
- the termination of processing

J. J. wants the menu to be operated by moving the cursor to the desired activity and pressing [Enter]. The menu selection is to be a number of one through four which is stored in the micro CHOICE. To unit test the command file, execute it and then display the value of the CHOICE micro using the SHOWMICRO ALL command. Produce hardcopy listings of both the command file and the screen displayed during the command file's execution.

11. The Last National Bank

Carrie usually runs the model for Last National Bank with the input data for each location, once the data have been entered. She wants you to create a full-screen panel that presents a list of the locations. She can then select the desired location from the list of available banks that have data in the database relation. As part of the full-screen processing, QUERY the database relation containing the decision parameters to obtain a SET of available banks. Present this SET on the screen for selection. Once Carrie entered her selection, verify the selection as an existing selection in the SET. Store Carrie's selection in the micro LOCATION for use in controlling the model solution. She wants to include the capability of entering CANCEL to abandon processing. To test the command file, activate the database for Last National Bank, then execute the command file. The database must be active in order to obtain the SET of available banks. After the command file has been executed, use the SHOWMICRO ALL command to check the value of the LOCATION micro. Document this command file by generating a hardcopy listing of the file and of the screen obtained when the command file is executed.

12. The Last National Bank
For Last National Bank, J. J. wants you to create an integrated system for entering data and producing model solutions similar to that presented for Buffalo Computer Systems (BCS). Write the other command files as needed to complete this system. You can use portions of command files that you developed in the preceding case problems in this tutorial to assist you in this effort. Test your integrated system on at least two banks. As part of the system testing, be sure to check the operation of each menu choice. Produce hardcopy listings of all the command files and of the screens displayed during command file execution. Draw a structure chart that documents the calling arrangement among your command files.

13. Harvest University
The chief financial officer believes the front-end processing can be improved for entering data into the budget system at Harvest University. Create a full-screen command file that requests the name of the campus for entering data. The campus names to be used are the same as those used previously: MAIN, DOWN, SSHU, and MHU. To insure a valid campus name is used, you are to create a SET that contains the valid campus names. The full screen is to validate the requested campus name using this SET. The desired campus name is to be stored in the micro CAMPUS. This command file should include the capability to terminate processing, if desired. Also, you need a command file like CMDFILE CFDBINT2 from Figure 9-2. To unit test the command file, you are to execute the file and then display the value of the CAMPUS micro using the SHOWMICRO ALL command. Document this command file by producing a hardcopy listing of the command, of the screen during execution, and of the micro value for CAMPUS.

14. Harvest University
The chief financial officer wants you to create a full-screen menu that provides Harvest University the ability to select processing activities. This screen should facilitate:
- input of values for decision variables
- solution of the campus budget model
- both input of data and solution of the model
- the termination of processing

Your menu is to be operated by moving the cursor to the desired activity and pressing [Enter]. The menu selection is to be a number of one through four which is stored in the micro CHOICE. To unit test the command file, execute it and then display the value of the CHOICE micro using the SHOWMICRO ALL command. Produce hardcopy listings of both the command file and the screen displayed during the command file's execution.

15. Harvest University
The CFO usually runs the model for Harvest University with the data for each campus, once it is entered. Create a full-screen panel that presents a list of the campuses. You can then select the desired campus from the list of available campuses that have data in the database relation. As part of the full-screen processing, QUERY the database relation containing the decision parameters to obtain a SET of available campuses. Present this SET on the screen for selection. Once the CFO has entered her selection, verify the selection as an existing selection in the SET. Store the CFO's selection in the micro CAMPUS for use in controlling the model solution. Include the capability of entering CANCEL to abandon processing. To test the command file, activate the database for Harvest University, then execute the command file. The database must be active in order to obtain the SET of available campuses. After the command file has been executed, use the

SHOWMICRO ALL command to check the value of the CAMPUS micro. Document this command file by generating a listing of the command file and of the screen obtained when the command file is executed.

16. Harvest University

For Harvest University, the chief financial officer wants you to create an integrated system for entering data and producing model solutions similar to that presented for Buffalo Computer Systems (BCS). Write the other command files as needed to complete this system. You may use portions of command files that you developed in preceding case problems in this tutorial to assist you in this effort. Test your integrated system on at least two campuses. As part of the system testing, be sure to check the operation of each menu choice. Produce hardcopy listings of all the command files and of the screens displayed during command file execution. Draw a structure chart that documents the calling arrangement among your command files.

17. Midwest Universal Gas

Mary believes the front-end processing can be improved for entering data into the budget system at Midwest Universal Gas. She wants you to create a full-screen command file that requests the name of the division for entering data. The division names to be used are the same as those used previously: MUG, BLUE, COG, and LITE. To insure a valid division name is used, Mary wants you to create a SET that contains the valid division names. The full screen is to validate the requested division name using this SET. The desired division name is to be stored in the micro DIVISION. This command file should include the capability to terminate processing, if desired. Also, Mary needs a command file like CMDFILE CFDBINT2 from Figure 9-2. To unit test the command file, Mary wants you to execute the file and then display the value of the DIVISION micro using the SHOWMICRO ALL command. Document this command file by producing a hardcopy listing of the command file, of the screen during execution, and of the micro value for DIVISION.

18. Midwest Universal Gas

Sam wants you to create a full-screen menu that provides Midwest Universal Gas the ability to select processing activities. This screen should facilitate:
- input of values for decision variables
- solution of the division budget model
- both input of data and solution of the model
- the termination of processing

Sam wants the menu to be operated by moving the cursor to the desired activity and pressing [Enter]. The menu selection is to be a number of one through four which is stored in the micro CHOICE. To unit test the command file, execute it and then display the value of the CHOICE micro using the SHOWMICRO ALL command. Produce hardcopy listings of both the command file and the screen displayed during the command file's execution.

19. Midwest Universal Gas

Mary usually runs the model for Midwest Universal Gas (MUG) with the input data for each division, once the data have been entered. She wants you to create a full-screen panel that presents a list of the divisions. She can then select the desired division from the list of available divisions that have data in the database relation. As part of the full-screen processing, QUERY the database relation containing the decision parameters to obtain a SET of available divisions. Present this SET on the screen for selection. Once Mary has entered her selection, verify the selection as an existing selection in the SET. Store Mary's selection in the micro DIVISION for use in controlling the model solution. She wants to include the capability of entering CANCEL to abandon processing. To test the command file, activate the database for MUG, then execute the command file. The database must be active in order to obtain the SET of available divisions. After the command file has been executed, use the SHOWMICRO ALL command to check the value of the DIVISION micro. Document this command file by generating a hardcopy listing of the file and of the screen obtained when the command file is executed.

20. Midwest Universal Gas

For Midwest Universal Gas, Sam wants you to create an integrated system for entering data and producing model solutions similar to that presented for Buffalo Computer Systems (BCS). Write the other command files as needed to complete this system. You may use portions of command files that you developed in preceding case problems in this tutorial to assist you in this effort. Test your integrated system on at least two divisions. As part of the system testing, be sure to check the operation of each menu choice. Produce hardcopy listings of all the command files and of the screens displayed during command file execution. Draw a structure chart that documents the calling arrangement among your command files.

21. General Memorial Hospital

Berry believes the front-end processing can be improved for entering data into the budget system at General Memorial Hospital. He wants you to create a full-screen command file that requests the name of the hospitals for entering data. The hospital names to be used are the same as those used previously: GMH, CGH, SJH, and FHCH. To insure a valid hospital name is used, Berry wants you to create a SET that contains the valid hospital names. The full screen is to validate the requested hospital name using this SET. The desired hospital name is to be stored in the micro HOSPITAL. This command file should include the capability to terminate processing, if desired. Also, Berry needs a command file like CMDFILE CFDBINT2 from Figure 9-2. To unit test the command file, Berry wants you to execute the file and then display the value of the HOSPITAL micro using the SHOWMICRO ALL command. Document this command file by producing a listing of the file, of the screen during execution, and of the micro value for HOSPITAL.

22. General Memorial Hospital

Gloria wants you to create a full-screen menu that provides General Memorial Hospital the ability to select processing activities. This screen should facilitate:
- input of data values for decision variables
- solution of the hospital budget model
- both input of data and solution of the model
- the termination of processing

Gloria wants the menu to be operated by moving the cursor to the desired activity and pressing [Enter]. The menu selection is to be a number of one through four, which is stored in the micro CHOICE. To unit test the command file, execute it and then display the value of the CHOICE micro using the SHOWMICRO ALL command. Produce hardcopy listings of both the command file and the screen displayed during the command file's execution.

23. General Memorial Hospital

Berry usually runs the model for General Memorial Hospital with the input data for each hospital, once the data have been entered. He wants you to create a full-screen panel that presents a list of the hospitals. He can then select the desired hospital from the list of available hospitals that have data in the database relation. As part of the full-screen processing, QUERY the database relation containing the decision parameters to obtain a SET of available hospitals. Present this SET on the screen for selection. Once Berry has entered his selection, verify the selection as an existing selection in the SET. Store Berry's selection in the micro HOSPITAL for use in controlling the model solution. He wants to include the capability of entering CANCEL to abandon processing. To test the command file, activate the database for General Memorial Hospital, then execute the command file. The database must be active in order to obtain the SET of available hospitals. After the command file has been executed, use the SHOWMICRO ALL command to check the value of the HOSPITAL micro. Document this command file by generating a hardcopy listing of the file and of the screen obtained when the command file is executed.

24. General Memorial Hospital

For General Memorial Hospital, Gloria wants you to create an integrated system for entering data and producing model solutions similar to that presented for Buffalo Computer Systems. Write the other command files as needed to complete this system. You may use portions of command files that you developed in preceding case problems in this tutorial to assist you in this effort. Test your integrated system on at least two hospitals. As part of the system testing, be sure to check the operation of each menu choice.

Produce hardcopy listings of all the command files and of the screens displayed during command file execution. Draw a structure chart that documents the calling arrangement among your command files.

25. River City

Lisa believes the front-end processing can be improved for entering data into the budget system at River City. She wants you to create a full-screen command file that requests the name of the suburbs for entering data. The suburb names to be used are the same as those used previously: MAIN, PEACE, CASS, and HAPPY. To insure a valid suburb name is used, Lisa wants you to create a SET that contains the valid suburb names. The full screen is to validate the requested name using this SET. The desired suburb name is to be stored in the micro SUBURB. This command file should include the capability to terminate processing, if desired. Also, Lisa needs a command file like CMDFILE CFDBINT2 from Figure 9-2. To unit test the command file, Lisa wants you to execute the file and then display the value of the SUBURB micro using the SHOWMICRO ALL command. Document this command file by producing a hardcopy listing of the command file, of the screen during execution, and of the micro value for SUBURB.

26. River City

Frank wants you to create a full-screen menu that provides River City the ability to select processing activities. This screen should facilitate:
- input of data values for decision variables
- solution of the suburb budget model
- both input of data and solution of the model
- the termination of processing

Frank wants the menu to be operated by moving the cursor to the desired activity and pressing [Enter]. The menu selection is to be a number of one through four which is stored in the micro CHOICE. To unit test the command file, execute it and then display the value of the CHOICE micro using the SHOWMICRO ALL command. Produce hardcopy listings of both the command file and the screen displayed during the command file' execution.

27. River City

Lisa usually runs the model for River City with the input data for each suburb, once the data have been entered. She wants you to create a full-screen panel that presents a list of the suburbs. She can then selected the desired suburb from the list of available suburbs that have data in the database relation. As part of the full-screen processing, QUERY the database relation containing the decision parameters to obtain a SET of available suburbs. Present this SET on the screen for selection. Once Lisa has entered her selection, verify the selection as an existing selection in the SET. Store Lisa's selection in the micro SUBURB for use in controlling the model solution. She wants to include the capability of entering CANCEL to abandon processing. To test the command file, activate the database for River City, then execute the command file. The database must be active in order to obtain the SET of available suburbs. After the command file has been executed, use the SHOWMICRO ALL command to check the value of the SUBURB micro. Document this command file by generating a hardcopy listing of the file and of the screen obtained when the command file is executed.

28. River City

For River City, Frank wants you to create an integrated system for entering data and producing model solutions similar to that presented for Buffalo Computer Systems (BCS). Write the other command files as needed to complete this system. You may use portions of command files that you developed in the preceding case problems in this tutorial to assist you in this effort. Test your integrated system on at least two suburbs. As part of the system testing, be sure to check the operation of each menu choice. Produce hardcopy listings of all the command files and of the screens displayed during command file execution. Draw a structure chart that documents the calling arrangement among your command files.

Tutorial 10

Using Risk Analysis

Introduction to Risk Analysis

All of Herbie's projections for Buffalo Computer Services (BCS) have been single estimates for each variable or line item. This type of analysis is known as a **point estimate**; it is also frequently called the "most likely" or "best" estimate. Herbie explored different cases where his estimates might vary using what if and goal seeking, but each of these was a single-point estimate or case study. This type of modeling is also known as **deterministic**, since all the values are determined by a single set of equations which have only one solution for a given set of input values.

There are two categories of models: deterministic and stochastic. **Deterministic** modeling results in a single "most likely estimate" whereas **stochastic** modeling provides an estimate of risk through the use of probability distributions in evaluating alternatives. By using probability distributions on input or assumption variables, a range or probability distribution is obtained for the output or calculated variables.

Chances are that results can vary from the "best" or "most likely" estimate. This variability is what is known as **risk**. One way of thinking about risk is to think in terms of three possible situations: a "worst" or low case, a "most likely" case, and a "best" or high case. If the difference between the "worst" case and the "best" case (also known as the **range**) is large, then the variability is high. On the other hand, if the range is small, the variability is low. A low variability indicates a good chance of obtaining an outcome, which is close to the "most likely" case.

Risk analysis provides a method for directly and quantitatively stating the variability of input parameters so that the variability in output parameters can be evaluated. Herbie could state the variability in the number of BYTES SOLD and determine its affect on the EBT and ROS. Variability is specified by what is known as a *probability distribution*. (If you are not familiar with these from statistics, a visit with a local statistical expert is strongly recommended.)

So, then, risk, which is also known as uncertainty (no distinction is made here between risk and uncertainty, although it is recognized that some disciplines carefully distinguish between them), is expressed by a probability distribution. Probability distributions come in two types: objective and subjective. An **objective** probability distribution is one that is determined by statistical techniques. For example, a large oil company may estimate a probability distribution on recoveries from data on past experience in a given oil field. When statistical data are not available (such as in Herbie's situation, in which he has never operated this type of retail outlet before) the probabilities may be determined subjectively. **Subjective** probability distributions are the best "guess" an individual can make concerning the level of risk. Subjective probabilities are often used in investment analysis where no statistical data are available. They are also applied in budgeting to provide an indication of the risk or variability.

Consider how Herbie might subjectively state the risk for the Tumble Weed Shopping Mall outlet. BYTES SOLD for the first quarter might be estimated to range from 6 units to 12 units with 9 units being most likely. So, knowing the range or variability provides an indication of the risk. It is this type of situation for which risk analysis provides a means of evaluation.

Let's look at how Herbie implemented risk analysis for his quarterly projected profit and loss statement. He revised model PROJECT3, creating model PROJECT6, which contains the probability distribution generating functions for his estimates of risk. Model PROJECT6, in Figure 10-1, uses probability functions for four input variables—BYTES SOLD, PRICE PER BYTE, COST OF SALES PERCENT, and SALARIES. These probability functions are just another type of built-in IFPS function. Their application and usage is similar to the other IFPS functions.

Planning Analysis Sheet

<u>My goal:</u>
Develop a model with probability distribution for key variables for Buffalo Computer Systems (BCS).

<u>What results do I want to see?</u>
The range of values for the probability distributions for EBT and ROS.

<u>What information do I need?</u>
The estimated probability distributions.

<u>What calculations will I perform</u>
*BUFFALO COMPUTER SERVICES
*PROJECTED PROFIT AND LOSS STATEMENT
COLUMNS 1-4, TOTAL
BYTES SOLD = **ROUND(NORRAND(9,1)), PREVIOUS + 2**
PRICE PER BYTE = **UNIRAND (6500,9000)**
SALES = BYTES SOLD * PRICE PER BYTE
COST OF SALES PERCENT = **UNIRAND(.70,.80)**
COST OF SALES = SALES * COST OF SALES PERCENT
GROSS PROFIT = SALES - COST OF SALES
SALARIES = **TRIRAND(9000,9800,10200)**
BENEFITS = SALARIES * .19
ADMIN EXPENSE = SALES * .23
DEPRECIATION = 1500, 2000, 2000, 2500
INTEREST = 400
TOTAL EXPENSES = SUM(SALARIES THRU INTEREST)
EBT = GROSS PROFIT - TOTAL EXPENSES
ROS = EBT / SALES *100
*SPECIAL COLUMN COMPUTATIONS
COLUMN TOTAL FOR BYTES SOLD, SALES, COST OF SALES, '
            GROSS PROFIT THRU INTEREST
COLUMN TOTAL FOR PRICE PER BYTE = SALES / BYTES SOLD
COLUMN TOTAL FOR ROS = EBT / SALES * 100

Figure 10-1 Planning Analysis Sheet for Risk Analysis

Let's look at the new functions in the model. Herbie used the NORRAND function for the normal probability distribution or the "bell shaped" curve for BYTES SOLD in this manner:

BYTES SOLD = ROUND(NORRAND(9,1)), PREVIOUS + 2

In NORRAND, the first parameter is the mean of the normal distribution, and the second parameter is the standard deviation of the normal distribution, where variability or risk is specified by the standard distribution. Since the number of units sold are a whole number, the value from NORRAND is rounded to yield a whole number of units sold. This is the use of a function within a function. Herbie only used NORRAND in the first quarter. After that, he assumed the same point estimate growth of two units per quarter. Of course, this growth could be a probability distribution if Herbie so desires. Graphically, Herbie's normal probability distribution is as shown in Figure 10-2. The general form of the normal probability function in IFPS is:

NORRAND(mean, standard deviation)

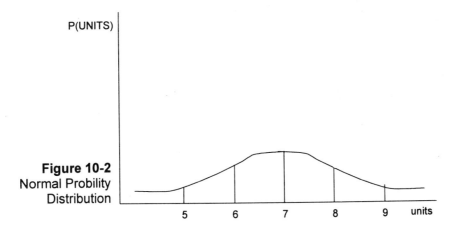

Figure 10-2
Normal Probility
Distribution

To arrive at the PRICE PER BYTE, Herbie used the UNIRAND probability distribution in this manner:

PRICE PER BYTE = UNIRAND(6500,9000)

UNIRAND provides a uniform random distribution as shown in Figure 10-3. This probability distribution provides values uniformly distributed over its range (in this case, from 6500 to 9000). The chance of any value occurring in this range is equal to the chance of any other value occurring. It is similar to rolling a fair die where each side has an equal likelihood of appearing on any one roll. The general form of the uniform random distribution in IFPS is:

UNIRAND(lower limit, upper limit)

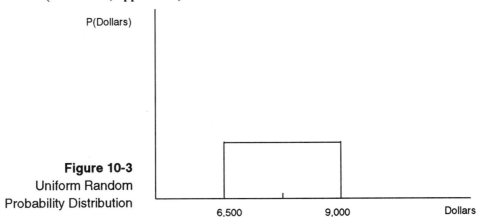

Figure 10-3
Uniform Random
Probability Distribution

The calculation of SALARIES makes use of the TRIRAND or triangular probability distribution like this:

SALARIES = TRIRAND(9000,9800,10200)

In IFPS, the general form of the triangular distribution is:

TRIRAND(lower limit, most probable (peak) value, upper limit)

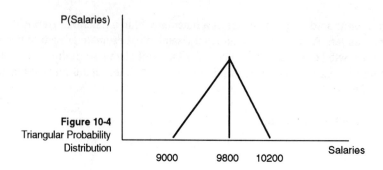

Figure 10-4
Triangular Probability
Distribution

P(Salaries)

9000   9800   10200   Salaries

Let's create Herbie's model with the probability functions.

To create a model with probability functions:

❶   If you are in the Server mode, click **File**, then **Close** to switch to the Visual mode for creating the model.

❷   Click the **New button** in the toolbar and select **Model** in the New dialog box.

❸   Click the **Open button** in the toolbar, select **Model** from the List Entities of Type drop-down list, then select **PROJECT3** from the Entity Name list.

❹   Click **Edit**, click **Select All** to select the entire model, click **Edit**, then click **Copy** to copy the contents of the model into the Windows clipboard.

❺   Click the **new Model window**, click **Edit**, then click **Paste** to paste the contents from the clipboard to the new Model window.

❻   Edit the new Model to contain the probability functions as shown in Figure 10-1.

❼   Click **File**, click **Save**, type **PROJECT6** in the Entity Name text box, then click the **OK button** to save the model.

Since Herbie has explicitly stated his subjective risks with these probability functions, it is possible to have his model solved deterministically. Solving the model with these changes produces the results shown in Figure 10-5. Which values did IFPS select from each probability distribution? To answer this, several case studies are reviewed that produce a series of "what if" evaluations.

	QTR1	QTR2	QTR3	QTR4	TOTAL
BYTES SOLD	9	11	13	15	48
PRICE PER BYTE	7750	7750	7750	7750	7750
SALES	69750	85250	100750	116250	372000
COST OF SALES PERCENT	.75	.75	.75	.75	
COST OF SALES	52313	63928	75563	87188	279000
GROSS PROFIT	17748	21313	25188	29063	93000
SALARIES	9667	9667	9667	9667	38667
BENEFITS	1837	1837	1837	1837	7347
ADMIN EXPENSE	1604	1961	2317	2674	8556
DEPRECIATION	1500	2000	2000	2500	8000
INTEREST	400	400	400	400	1600
TOTAL EXPENSES	15007	15864	8966	11985	28830
EBT	2429	5448	8966	11985	28830
ROS	3.48	6.39	8.90	10.31	7.75

Figure 10-5
Results of Model
Soltion Containing
Probability Distribution

Let's consider case studies where the probability distributions have values selected as follows:

1.   All variables set to the most probable values
2.   All variables set to the "expected" or mean values
3.   A worst-case solution with revenues set to their lowest values and expenses set to the highest values
4.   A best-case solution with revenues set to their highest values and expenses set to the lowest values
5.   A mixed case with one variable set to its high value, one set to its mean value, one set to its low value, and one set to its most probable value
6.   The same mixed case as in (5), but with the high-value variable switched to its low value

The IFPS commands for performing risk analysis are commands that are used in the Server mode. Although a model can be created and edited in the Visual model, you need to switch to the Server mode to do the risk analysis calculation. Let's examine each of these cases.

To obtain the most probable case.

❶   Click the **Server button** in the toolbar, to access this mode.

❷   Enter **MODEL PROJECT6**, then enter **SOLVE** to prepare for entering solve options.

❸   Enter **MOSTP ALL** to request the most probable case.

❹   Enter **ALL** to display the solution. See Figure 10-6.

		QTR1	QTR2	QTR3	QTR4	TOTAL
	BYTES SOLD	9	11	13	15	48
	PRICE PER BYTE	7750	7750	7750	7750	7750
	SALES	69750	85250	100750	116250	372000
	COST OF SALES PERCENT	.75	.75	.75	.75	
	COST OF SALES	52313	63928	75563	87188	279000
	GROSS PROFIT	17748	21313	25188	29063	93000
	SALARIES	9800	9800	9800	9800	39200
	BENEFITS	1862	1862	1862	1862	7448
	ADMIN EXPENSE	1604	1961	2137	2674	8556
Figure 10-6	DEPRECIATION	1500	2000	2000	2500	8000
Solution of	INTEREST	400	400	400	400	1600
Most Probable	TOTAL EXPENSES	15166	16023	16379	17236	64804
Case for	EBT	2271	5290	8808	11837	28196
Model PROJECT6	ROS	3.25	6.20	8.74	10.17	7.58

The most probable value for the normal distribution is its mean. For the uniform distribution, it's the midpoint; and for the triangular distribution, it's the peak value. Let's examine the case where the mean values are desired.

To obtain the mean case from a previously solved model:

❶   Enter **MEAN ALL**.

❷   Enter **ALL** to display the solution. See Figure 10-7.

	QTR1	QTR2	QTR3	QTR4	TOTAL
BYTES SOLD	9	11	13	15	48
PRICE PER BYTE	7750	7750	7750	7750	7750
SALES	69750	85250	100750	116250	372000
COST OF SALES PERCENT	.75	.75	.75	.75	
COST OF SALES	52313	63928	75563	87188	279000
GROSS PROFIT	17748	21313	25188	29063	93000
SALARIES	9667	9667	9667	9667	38667
BENEFITS	1837	1837	1837	1837	7347
ADMIN EXPENSE	1604	1961	2317	2674	8556
DEPRECIATION	1500	2000	2000	2500	8000
INTEREST	400	400	400	400	1600
TOTAL EXPENSES	15007	15864	8966	11985	28830
EBT	2429	5448	8966	11985	28830
ROS	3.48	6.39	8.90	10.31	7.75

Figure 10-7
Solution of
Mean Case for
Model PROJECT6

Here, the MEAN ALL causes IFPS to select the mean value for all variables. The mean and most probable are the same for the normal and uniform distributions, but it's different for the triangular distribution. The results of MEAN ALL are the same as those in Figure 10-5. So, if you just enter SOLVE, the IFPS default is to choose the mean values. This is the result you would get when you solve a model with probability function in the Visual mode. Let's examine the worst case with revenues set to their lowest and expenses set to the highest values.

To obtain the "worst" case:

❶   Enter **LOW BYTES SOLD, PRICE PER BYTE**

❷   Enter **HIGH COST OF SALES PERCENT, SALARIES**

❸   Enter **ALL** to display the solution. See Figure 10-8.

	QTR1	QTR2	QTR3	QTR4	TOTAL
BYTES SOLD	7	9	11	13	40
PRICE PER BYTE	6500	6500	6500	6500	6500
SALES	45500	58500	71500	84500	260000
COST OF SALES PERCENT	.80	.80	.80	.80	
COST OF SALES	36400	46800	57200	67600	208000
GROSS PROFIT	9100	11700	14300	16900	52000
SALARIES	10200	10200	10200	10200	40800
BENEFITS	1938	1938	1938	1938	7752
ADMIN EXPENSE	1047	1346	1645	1994	5980
DEPRECIATION	1500	2000	2000	2500	8000
INTEREST	400	400	400	400	1600
TOTAL EXPENSES	15085	15884	16183	16982	64132
EBT	-5985	-4184	-1883	-81.50	-12132
ROS	-13.15	-7.151	-2.633	-.0964	-4.666

Fgiure 10-8
Solution of
Worst Case for
Model PROJECT6

The LOW values are selected for BYTES SOLD and PRICE PER BYTE, whereas the HIGH values are picked for COST OF SALES PERCENT and SALARIES. For the normal distribution, IFPS identifies the value that is 2.5 standard deviations less than the mean as the LOW value, and the one at 2.5 standard deviations more than the mean as the HIGH value. Let's examine the best case, where revenues are set to their highest values and expenses are set to the lowest values.

To obtain the "best" case:

❶ Enter **HIGH BYTES SOLD, PRICE PER BYTE**.

❷ Enter **LOW COST OF SALES PERCENT, SALARIES**.

❸ Enter **ALL** to display the solution. See Figure 10-9.

	QTR1	QTR2	QTR3	QTR4	TOTAL
BYTES SOLD	12	14	16	18	60
PRICE PER BYTE	9000	9000	9000	9000	9000
SALES	108000	126000	144000	162000	540000
COST OF SALES PERCENT	.70	.70	.70	.70	
COST OF SALES	75600	88200	100800	113400	378000
GROSS PROFIT	32400	37800	43200	48600	162000
SALARIES	9000	9000	9000	9000	36000
BENEFITS	1710	1710	1710	1710	6840
ADMIN EXPENSE	2484	2898	3312	3726	12420
DEPRECIATION	1500	2000	2000	2500	8000
INTEREST	400	400	400	400	1600
TOTAL EXPENSES	15094	16008	16422	17336	64860
EBT	17306	21792	26778	31264	97140
ROS	16.02	17.30	18.60	19.30	17.99

Figure 10-9
Solution of
Best Case for
Model PROJECT6

Let's examine the mixed case where one variable is set to its high value, one is set to its mean value, one is set to its low values, and one is set to its most probable value.

To obtain a mixed-case situation:

❶ Enter **HIGH BYTES SOLD**.

❷ Enter **MEAN PRICE PER BYTE**.

❸ Enter **LOW COST OF SALES PERCENT**.

❹ Enter **MOSTP SALARIES**.

❺ Enter **ALL** to display the solution. See Figure 10-10.

	QTR1	QTR2	QTR3	QTR4	TOTAL
BYTES SOLD	12	14	16	18	60
PRICE PER BYTE	7750	7750	7750	7750	7750
SALES	93000	108500	124000	139500	465000
COST OF SALES PERCENT	.70	.70	.70	.70	
COST OF SALES	65100	75950	86800	97650	325500
GROSS PROFIT	27900	32550	37200	41850	139500
SALARIES	9800	9800	9800	9800	39200
BENEFITS	1862	1862	1862	1862	7448
ADMIN EXPENSE	2139	2496	2852	3209	10695
DEPRECIATION	1500	2000	2000	2500	8000
INTEREST	400	400	400	400	1600
TOTAL EXPENSES	15701	16558	169214	17771	66943
EBT	12199	15993	20286	24080	72557
ROS	13.12	14.74	16.36	17.26	15.60

Figure 10-10
Solution of
Mixed Case for
Model PROJECT6

So, one use of IFPS risk analysis is to use probability distributions to provide a selected range of values for creating several deterministic solutions. This is an enhanced form of the what if since you specify risk through the probability distributions. The other use of risk analysis is to perform what is known as **Monte Carlo** simulation. This type of analysis produces stochastic results that are described by probabilities. The values of the derived or output variables take on a range of values with certain probabilities associated with those values.

Selected Probability Distribution Functions

The following table shows the probability functions available in IFPS and the action each function takes.

FUNCTION	ACTION
NORRAND (mean, std-dev)	Generates a normal distribution
UNIRAND (lower, upper)	Generates uniform distribution
TRIRAND (lower, most-prob, upper)	Generates triangularly shaped distribution
TR1090RAND(ten-pct, most-prob, ninety-pct)	This is a variation of the TRIRAND function with the ten percentile and ninety percentile values supplied as inputs
GENRAND(x1,y1, x2,y2, ..., xn,yn)	Generates a linear approximation from input coordinates of a piecewise linear function
CUMRAND(X0, X1, X2, ... X10)	Generates a cumulative distribution with points specified for each one-tenth probability increment

Monte Carlo Simulation

Monte Carlo analysis or Monte Carlo simulation requires the solution of a model multiple times. During each solution, values are selected randomly from the probability distribution of each variable. For each solution, the results are tabulated. For example, a model might be solved 200 times. The results would be tabulated and summarized so probability distributions of the *calculated variables* could be obtained. Herbie wants to see the results for EBT and ROS using his model with the probability functions. Let's observe the use of Monte Carlo simulation.

To do a Monte Carlo simulation:

❶   Enter **MONTE CARLO 200** to specify Monte Carlo simulation and the number of iterations.

❷   Enter **DEFAULT HIST** to request a histogram plot of the results.

❸   Enter **EBT, ROS** to specify the output variables to be displayed.

❹   Enter **NONE** to indicate the end of the Monte Carlo options and cause the calculations to be performed. See Figure 10-11.

FREQUENCY TABLE

PROBABILITY OF VALUE BEING GREATER THAN INDICATED

	90	80	70	60	50	40	30	20	10
EBT									
TOTAL	-132870	-126196	-121972	-117898	-113018	-107429	-103328	-97018	-90361
ROS									
TOTAL	-.424	-.385	-.357	-.321	-.300	-.282	-.264	-.231	-.212

SAMPLE STATISTICS

	MEAN	STD DEV	SKEWNESS	KURTOSIS	10PC	CONF MEAN 90PC
EBT						
TOTAL	-111979	15952	.2	2.3	-113423	-110536
ROS						
TOTAL	-.3110	.0806	-.4	2.5	-.3183	-.3037

```
     HISTOGRAM FOR COLUMN            TOTAL OF EBT
  25- 26        *
  23- 24        *
  21- 22      * * *  *
  19- 20      * * *  *
  17- 18    *  * * * * *
  15- 16    *  * * * * *
  13- 14    * * * * * * * * *
  11- 12    * * * * * * * * *
   9- 10    * * * * * * * * *
   7-  8    * * * * * * * * * *
   5-  6    * * * * * * * * * * *
   3-  4  * * * * * * * * * * * * * *
   1-  2  * * * * * * * * * * * * * *
         ----------------------------
          -   -   -
          1   1   1   -   -
          4   2   1   9   8
          3   8   3   9   4
          5   7   9   1   3
          3   3   3   3   3
          3   3   3   3   3
```

START -146000.0 STOP -72000.0 SIZE OF INTERVAL 4933.33

```
     HISTOGRAM FOR COLUMN          TOTAL OF ROS
  27- 28          * *  *
  25- 26          * *  *
  23- 24          * *  *
  21- 22          * *  *
  19- 20          * *  *
  17- 18      *   * *  *
  15- 16      * * * * *  *
  13- 14      * * * * *  *
  11- 12      * * * * * * *
   9- 10      * * * * * * * * *
   7-  8    * * * * * * * * * *
   5-  6    * * * * * * * * * * *
   3-  4  * * * * * * * * * * * *
   1-  2  * * * * * * * * * * * * *
         ----------------------------
          -   -   -   -   -
          .   .   .   .   .
          5   4   3   2   2
          2   4   7   9   2
          4   9   3   7   1
```

START   -.5 STOP   -.2 SIZE OF INTERVAL   .03

Figure 10-11
Monte Carol
Solution

Note: Your results will differ because different random numbers are selected for each solution. However, the values should be about the same.

The MONTE CARLO 200 specifies that a Monte Carlo analysis will be performed with the model being solved 200 times. The DEFAULT HIST indicates a histogram will be printed for each requested output variable unless it is specified to not print one. IFPS also provides the ability to choose the variables for which a histogram or other Monte Carlo output is obtained. The EBT, ROS input is the specification of the variables for which results are to be displayed. This follows the IFPS conventions for variable referencing. When you have entered the final MONTE CARLO OPTION, the keyword NONE provides this indication. In response to the NONE, IFPS then proceeds with the Monte Carlo analysis. Herbie's results are shown in Figure 10-11. These results are for the TOTAL column, which is the IFPS default unless you specify some other column by using the COLUMNS statement, such as COLUMNS 1..4, TOTAL, before the NONE is entered. In the frequency table, the value of 10220 for EBT is interpreted to mean there is a 60-percent chance EBT would be greater than this value, or conversely, there is a 40-percent chance the EBT would be less than this value. This is similar for the other values of EBT and for ROS. In the same statistics, the skewness is a measure of whether the distribution is a mountain that leans to the left or the right. Kurtosis is not a rare disease, but is a measure of whether the mountain is peaked or is more like a pancake. (You might want to review this with your local statistical expert.) The histograms that were produced let you visually assess the skewness and kurtosis.

When a random value is generated by a probability function if IFPS, that one value is used in *all regular columns* of the model, as illustrated by SALARIES in Figure 10-10. If you want *a different value in each column,* then you need to request the regeneration of the probability functions. You can accomplish this by adding the 'R' suffix to the probability function so a new value is used in all regular columns. For example, TRIRANDR produces a difference value for each regular column because the R suffix causes a new value to be selected. The R suffix is used for both the what if and Monte Carlo solutions calculated using probability functions.

To sum up, Monte Carlo analysis allows you to explicitly state the risk associated with your input variables so that you can explore the chances of achieving your derived output parameters. You may evaluate your model by either *deterministic case solutions,* which are a special type of what if, or by *stochastic simulation* with a number of solutions calculated, and the results are summarized and reported as the probabilities associated with obtaining a range of possible outcomes. Thus, Monte Carlo analysis allows you to include risk or uncertainty directly as part of your IFPS planning model.

Questions

1.   This type of modeling produces a single "most likely estimate."
    a. Deterministic
    b. Stochastic
    c. Most
    d. Least

2.   _____ modeling provides an estimate through the use of probability distributions in evaluating alternatives.
    a. Deterministic
    b. Stochastic
    c. Most
    d. Least

3.   _____ analysis provides a method for directly and quantitatively stating the variability of input parameters so that the variability in output parameters can be evaluated.
   a. Change
   b. Case
   c. Risk
   d. Power

4.   A(n) _____ probability distribution is one that is determined by statistical techniques.
   a. subjective
   b. objective
   c. subtractive
   d. observe

5.   A(n) _____ probability distribution is one with no statistical data.
   a. subjective
   b. objective
   c. subtractive
   d. observe

6.   The _____ function provides a uniform random distribution.
   a. NORRAND
   b. TRIRAND
   c. UNIRAND
   d. IFPSRAND

Case Problems

1. Good Morning Products

Frosty, chairman of the board of Good Morning Products (GM), knows the demand and cost of Liquid Gold orange juice can vary because of factors such as the weather and economic activity, which are beyond GM's control. The price of oranges can fluctuate significantly as a result of growing conditions. At the last meeting of the board of directors, it was decided to incorporate this risk or uncertainty directly into the planning model for each branch location. Since Frosty has some difficulty conceptualizing means and standard deviations, Crush and Kim believe it would be best to use the triangular probability distribution. With the triangular distribution they can specify a low value, a most likely value, and a high value. After considerable discussion, these key variables have been selected together with their associated values as follows:

	LOW	MOST LIKELY	HIGH
Oranges per bottle	0.98	1.21	1.39
Labor per bottle	0.76	0.89	1.03
Packaging per bottle	0.54	0.57	0.61

	LOW	MOST LIKELY	HIGH
For California:			
Bottles	250,000	310,000	350,000
Price per bottle	2.89	3.29	3.59
For Florida:			
Bottles	110,000	140,000	180,000
Price per bottle	2.79	3.29	3.49

Revise a copy of the template model from Tutorial 5 Case Problem 15 to use in this risk analysis. Since this is the first time for using risk analysis probability distributions, create two models: one for California and one for Florida. Enter the data for the probability distributions directly into the model. Then perform several "what ifs" on each model: for example, what if all the LOW values occur, what if the MOST LIKELY values occur, what if the HIGH values occur and what if some combination of LOW, MOST LIKELY, and HIGH values occur. For this last combination, choose the LOW costs and the HIGH revenues, and then reverse this situation and use HIGH costs and LOW revenues. This last situation is the "worst" case. Use the ALL Solve Option to obtain an output report of every variable for each of these cases. Next, try a MONTE CARLO 100 and have a histogram output for each quarter and for the annual total for the variables BOTTLES, SALES, EBT, and ROS. Remember that the RECORD command can be used to capture your screen output to a file for printing.

2. Good Morning Products

Now change the TRIRAND probability function to TRIRANDR. (Notice the 'R' suffix.) Repeat the LOW, MOST LIKELY, and HIGH solutions and the Monte Carlo solution. What do you notice that is different about the probability values supplied by IFPS in the "what ifs"? You should see that the R, causes a new value to be selected in each regular column. Without the R you should notice the same value is used in all regular columns of the model.

3. The Woodcraft Furniture Company

Joe Birch is uncertain of the price that can be obtained in the market for Woodcraft's furniture. To quantify the effect of various prices which may be received, Joe wants you to use the triangular probability distribution on the pricing input variables. This will allow him to specify a low, most likely and high value for each of his product prices. The price ranges are as follows:

	LOW	MOST LIKELY	HIGH
Table Price	400	450	500
Chair Price	75	100	125
Sofa Price	250	300	350

Joe wants you to revise a copy of the template model from Tutorial 5, Case Problem 16 to include these pricing distributions. Solve the revised model with the datafile from Tutorial 5 for each business unit. Joe wants you to perform a what if analysis on the consolidated plan making use of these probability distributions: what if all LOW values occur, what if all MOST LIKELY values occur, and what if all HIGH values occur. Explore "what if" combinations of some LOW, MOST LIKELY, and HIGH values for variables you select. Produce a report of each alternative with the ALL Solve Option so you can observe the prices selected. To produce a range of output values, use a MONTE CARLO 100 and have a histogram displayed for Income Before Taxes for each month and for the quarter. Use the RECORD command to capture and print your outputs.

4. The Woodcraft Furniture Company

Revise the TRIRAND function changing it to TRIRANDR. Create solutions for LOW, MOST LIKELY, and HIGH values and for MONTE CARLO 100. What do you notice that is different about your probability values in these what ifs? You should observe that the R, causes a new value to be selected in each regular column, whereas without the R, one value is selected and used in all regular columns.

5. The Last National Bank

J. J. Green of the Last National Bank realizes that the prime rate is *not* known with certainty. He wants to introduce this risk into their model. Although all the input variables could take on a range of possible values, J. J. wants to focus on a few key variables that he has selected. J. J. has decided to use the triangular probability distribution since it lets him specify a low value, a most likely value, and a high value. He doesn't think very well in means and standard deviations, and the triangular distribution is easiest for him to comprehend. Maybe after he becomes more familiar with these probability concepts, then he will take the plunge into the normal distribution. To help himself, J. J. has enrolled in a night course in probability and statistics at Harvest University. His selected key variables and their associated values for all three months of the first quarter are as follows:

	LOW	MOST LIKELY	HIGH
Prime rate	13.5%	14.0%	15.0%
Installment Loan Rate	10.0%	11.0%	12.5%
Money Market Rate	-4.5%	-3.0%	-1.5%
For Broken Spoke:			
Installment Loans	10000	12000	15000
Commercial Loans	23000	29000	35000
Regular Savings	9000	12000	14000
Interest Plus Checking	12000	17000	20000
For Weeping Water:			
Installment Loans	6000	7600	9000
Commercial Loans	12500	15000	17000
Regular Savings	5500	7000	8000
Interest Plus Checking	7400	8600	9800

He has assigned you the task of revising a copy of the template bank model from Tutorial 5, Case Problem 17 to accommodate these changes. Since this is your first time using risk analysis, you decide to create two models one for Broken Spoke and the other for Weeping Water so you can enter the data for the probability distributions directly into the model. Then perform several "what ifs" on each model. What if all the LOW values occur, what if the MOST LIKELY values occur, what if the HIGH values occur, and what if some combination of LOW, MOST LIKELY, and HIGH values occur. For the combination choose the LOW interest expense accounts, and for the HIGH interest income accounts try a reverse of these HIGH and LOW options. Use ALL to obtain an output report of every variable. Next, try a MONTE CARLO 100 and have a histogram output for the NET INTEREST MARGIN and the NET INTEREST MARGIN PERCENT for each month and for the quarter. Use the RECORD command to capture and print your results.

6. The Last National Bank

Change your TRIRAND function to TRIRANDR. (Notice the 'R' suffix, which has been appended.) Repeat the LOW, MOST LIKELY, and HIGH solutions and the Monte Carlo solution. What do you notice that is different about your probability value in the what ifs? You should see that the R causes a new value to be selected in each regular column, whereas without the R, one value is used in all regular columns.

7. Harvest University

As the chief financial officer of Harvest University, you know several of your key input variables have a range of values that might occur. You want to introduce this risk into your model. The key variables you have selected and their range of values are as follows:

	LOW	MOST LIKELY	HIGH
Students *	-12%	0%	+10%
Credit Hours per Student *	-6	0	+3
Credit Hour Ratio	120	150	175
Average Full-Time Faculty Salary	6400	7000	7300
Average Part-Time Faculty Salary	900	1000	1100

Note: These values represent changes from the values given for each semester.

Use the triangular probability distribution which accepts the low, most likely, and high value for each variable. Copy the template model from Tutorial 5, Case Problem 18 and insert these changes. Solve the template model with the consolidated datafiles. Be sure to remove these probability variables from the datafiles. Explore several what-if alternatives by selecting all the LOW values, all the MOST LIKELY values, and all the HIGH values. Then try another what if by selecting the LOW enrollment and HIGH salary values. Reverse this and select the HIGH enrollment and LOW salary values. Use the ALL Solve Option to obtain a printout of every variable. Next try a MONTE CARLO 100 and have a histogram printed out for the Reserve for each quarter and the total for the year. Change the TRIRAND function to TRIRANDR. Notice the R suffix. Repeat the Monte Carlo solution. Inspect the output. What do you notice about the probability values? You should observe that the R causes a new value to be selected for each regular column, while without the R, one value is used in all regular columns. Use the RECORD command to capture your output for printing.

8. Midwest Universal Gas

At Midwest Universal Gas (MUG), Mary Derrick knows the demand for gas can vary because factors such as the weather and economic activity are beyond the control of MUG. As a result, she knows there is a range of possible values for the demand for retail and wholesale gas. Mary wants you to use a triangular probability distribution on the demand for gas and on general administration costs which can also vary considerably. Mary provides the following data:

('000 omitted)	LOW	MOST LIKELY	HIGH
Midwest Universal Gas			
Retail Sales	55000	60000	65000
Wholesale Sales	160000	165000	170000
General Admin	13000	13500	14000
Blue Flame Natural Gas			
Retail Sales	14000	18000	20000
Wholesale Sales	40000	55000	65000
General Admin	3000	3300	3600

Mary wants you to revise a copy of the template model from Tutorial 5, Case Problem 19 to accommodate these probability distributions. Place these values in copies of your datafiles from Tutorial 5 and solve each business unit using the datafiles. Using the Midwest Universal Gas data, perform a what if analysis by obtaining solutions with all the variables set to LOW, all set to MOST LIKELY, and all of them set to HIGH. Using the Blue Flame data, explore a combination what if by setting Sales LOW and General Admin HIGH, then reverse these and set Sales HIGH and General Admin LOW. Use the ALL Solve Option to obtain your results so you can see the effect of the probability distribution. Using the Midwest Universal Gas data, run a MONTE CARLO 100 and have a histogram displayed for Net Income and Return on Investment for each quarter and the total for the year. Change your TRIRAND function to TRIRANDR. Produce another solution for the MONTE CARLO 100. What is the effect of the R suffix on the TRIRANDR function? Use the RECORD command to capture and print your output.

9. General Memorial Hospital

Berry and Gloria of Family Health Care know that several key input variables might have a significant impact on their plan. From experience, they have estimated the following ranges for the key variables:

	LOW	MOST LIKELY	HIGH
General Memorial Hospital			
Bed Utilization Rate	65%	75%	80%
Nursing Staff	70	75	85
Medicines	200000	240000	265000
County General Hospital			
Bed Utilization Rate	75%	80%	85%
Nursing Staff	35	40	45
Medicines	120000	130000	140000

Berry wants you to revise a copy of the template model from Tutorial 5, Case Problem 20 to accommodate these probability distributions using the TRIRAND function. Revise copies of your datafiles from Tutorial 5 to include these probability functions. Solve the model using the datafile for each hospital. Select all LOW values, all MOST LIKELY values, all HIGH values, all LOW values for revenues and HIGH values for expenses, and all HIGH values for revenues and LOW values for expenses. Use the ALL Solve Option to obtain an output of every variable. Using MONTE CARLO 100, have a histogram output for Net Income and Return on Investment for each month and for the quarterly total. Change the TRIRAND function to TRIRANDR, notice the R suffix. Repeat the Monte Carlo solution and compare the results. What are the differences? You should observe that the R which stands for Random, causes a new probability value to be selected for each regular column. Without the R, the same value is used in all regular columns. Capture and print your output by using the RECORD command.

10. River City

Lisa and Frank realize they cannot be certain of their estimates of revenues and expenditures for the revised River Valley operating budget. Because of this, they have decided to use risk analysis in preparing the budget. They have selected the triangular probability distribution since it is the easiest for them to explain to the city council. Frank has suggested that probabilities be applied to several key input variables for their analysis. They have developed these estimates:

('000 omitted)	LOW	MOST LIKELY	HIGH
River City			
Sales	220000	250000	275000
Public Safety	2000	2500	3000
Public Works	300	350	400
Law	200	250	300

('000 omitted)	LOW	MOST LIKELY	HIGH
	------	---------	--------
Peaceful Valley			
Sales	900000	1000000	1100000
Public Safety	700	850	900
Public Works	60	65	75
Law	15	20	30

Frank suggests you revise a copy of the template model from Tutorial 5, Case Problem 21 and of your datafiles to accommodate these changes. Use the TRIRAND function to implement the triangular probability distributions that you put in the datafiles. Conduct a what-if analysis by using the LOW, MOST LIKELY, and HIGH selection of values from the probability distributions. Prepare one alternative with all values set LOW, one with all set MOST LIKELY, one with all set HIGH, one with revenues set HIGH and expenditures set LOW, and one with revenues set LOW and expenditures set HIGH. Use the ALL Solve Option to obtain the value of every variable so you can see the effect of the TRIRAND function. Now, Frank wants you to prepare a solution of MONTE CARLO 100 and display a histogram of the Surplus or Deficit for each month and for the quarter. Change the TRIRAND function to TRIRANDR, watch the R suffix. Run another MONTE CARLO 100 with this change and compare the results with the first Monte Carlo solution. What are the differences in the values of the variables produced by the probability distribution? What is the effect of the R suffix on TRIRANDR? Use the RECORD command to capture your output for printing.

PART III: MODELING FINANCIAL STATEMENTS

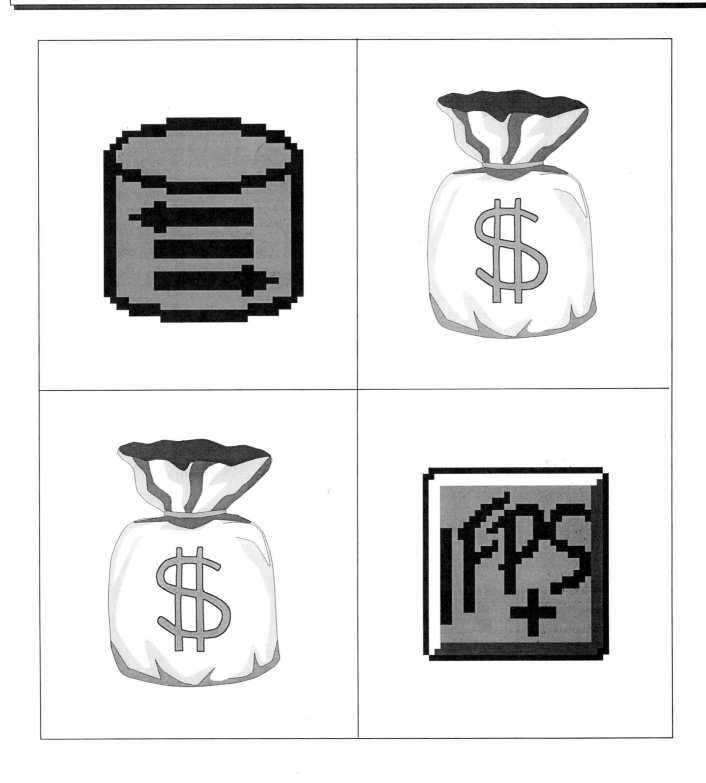

Tutorial 11

Integrating Financial Statements

Introduction to Integrated Financial Statements

Business planning models frequently consist of integrated pro forma income statements, statements of financial position, and cash flow statements. A **business planning model** is a vehicle for quantitatively expressing the goals and objectives of a business that allows managers to gain a better understanding of the impact of potential future decisions on the well-being of their organization. This quantitative expression of goals and objectives is achieved through pro forma or projected financial statements. Projected financial statements are a mechanism for bringing together marketing plans, production plans, personnel plans, expense control objectives, and capital financing requirements (Figure 11-1). The combined effect of these factors are evaluated against desired business goals and objectives. Overall, a business planning model yields a financially stated plan describing the "bottom line" where the future direction of an organization is evaluated in dollars.

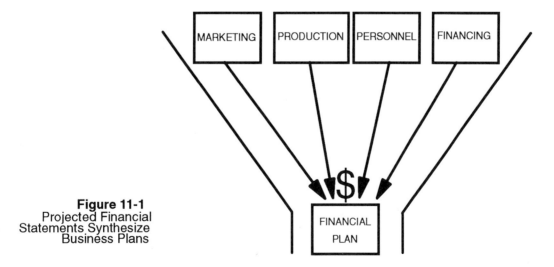

Figure 11-1
Projected Financial
Statements Synthesize
Business Plans

How is a valid business planning model used? Managers engage in what-if planning, whereby changes are made in the plans for attaining the goals and objectives of the business. They observe the potential results of these changes in the recalculated pro forma statements, gaining insight and a better understanding of the potential impacts, which is precisely the goal of modeling. From this information, better decisions are made.

Pro Forma Statements

Pro forma financial statements that are produced to reflect business plans usually include several characteristics: (1) income or profit and loss statements; (2) balance sheets or statements of financial position; and (3) cash flow statements, cash budgets, or statements of change in financial position (Figure 11-2).

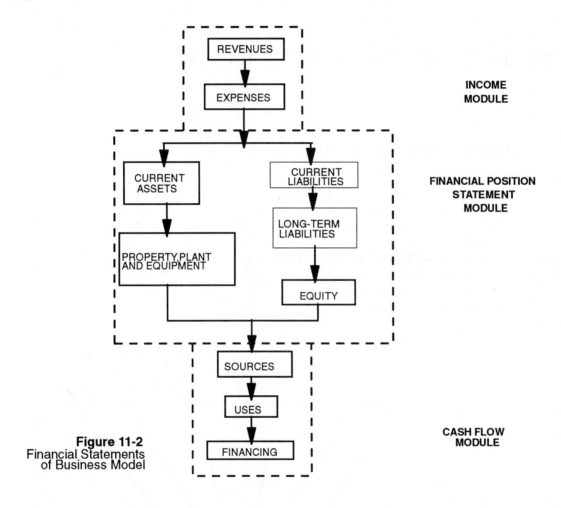

Figure 11-2
Financial Statements
of Business Model

A business planning model consists of the logic or set of equations that embody the planning assumptions for projecting each planning item, line item, or account into the future over a predetermined planning horizon. Integrated financial plans occur when two or more of these pro forma statements are combined in a *single* planning model. Because of the manner in which financial statements are interrelated, a planning model that integrates all three financial statements is the preferred method for creating these pro forma statements.

While an income or profit and loss statement may be satisfactory for plant or division-level planning, it is inadequate for a comprehensive business plan. Businesses have an existing configuration of assets, liabilities, and equities that are affected by future activities. In an integrated financial plan, the income statement and statement of financial position are linked, stressing accounting relationships that dictate a concurrent, rather than individual solution. These statements are linked through such accounts as net income and retained earnings; accounts receivable and sales; inventory and cost of sales; material purchased and accounts payable; depreciation and fixed assets; and interest expenses and debt. Therefore, a comprehensive planning analysis requires minimally a business model that includes both of these statements.

Business planning models often require hundreds of calculations to generate one what-if alternative future or scenario. Modeling software such as IFPS removes the arithmetic barrier that allows what if policy assumptions to be quickly and accurately calculated for management evaluation. With model logic developed using IFPS, the assumptions are readily entered, reviewed, and understood. Without question, effective business modeling requires the benefits of a planning language such as IFPS. IFPS is *not,* however, a pre-specified program; rather, it is a planning language. All the "knowledge" about accounting, forecasting, and financial statements that comprise the business model must come from you. The logic is *not* already known by IFPS. This is the price that you must pay for the flexibility to deal with the unique characteristics of individual businesses. Examples of this logic are explored in this tutorial.

Planning Model Organization

How should you organize your solution matrix for an integrated financial planning model? Figures 11-3 and 11-4 portray the usual relationships among the financial statements. Starting with the statement of financial position or balance sheet amounts for last year, income statement values are calculated for this year. These values are applied to the time *t-1* financial position amounts to arrive at this year's time *t* financial position values.

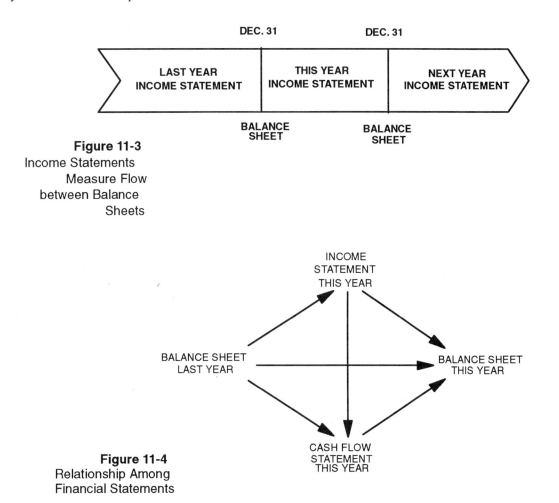

Figure 11-3
Income Statements
Measure Flow
between Balance
Sheets

Figure 11-4
Relationship Among
Financial Statements

An effective solution matrix arrangement is illustrated in Figure 11-5. Suppose that planning periods 2 through 6 are those calculated for your plan with the first column used for last year's history. How is each column or planning period defined? For the income statement, the planning period values indicate the revenue or expense that occurs and represents flows during the period. For the statement of financial position or balance sheet, the planning period value is the balance at the *end* of the period. In the cash flow statement, beginning and ending cash represent balances at the *beginning* and *ending* of the planning period. All other accounts represent changes or flows that occur *during* the planning period.

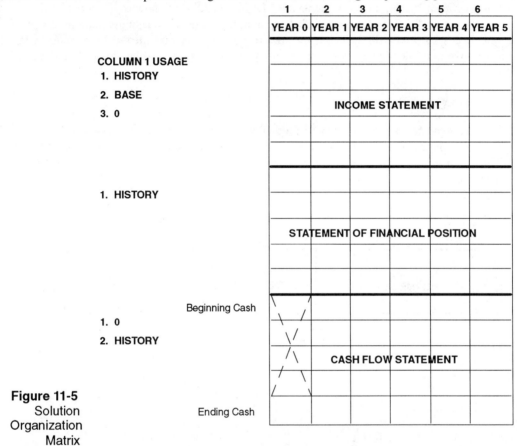

Figure 11-5
Solution
Organization
Matrix

With this solution matrix arrangement, it is essential to have an initial or opening balance amount for each account in the statement of financial position. These values are placed in the initial planning period or column one. Even a new business has an opening balance sheet, although the only accounts containing nonzero values may be cash and owner's equity. The values placed in column one of the income statement may be either actual or historical values, or they could be any desired base value. A **base value** is any convenient amount from which values in future columns are calculated. A third option for column one of the income statement is to use zeros when either history or a base value is not used. This is often the situation encountered with a new business that has no prior income. The use of a base value usually does not cause any reporting difficulties because with IFPS you can choose not to print this column.

For the cash flow statement, a cash balance is obtained from the balance in the cash account at the *end* of the accounting period. In effect, this is equivalent to looking at your checkbook to see the current balance. The prior period's transactions that created this cash balance are not of sufficient importance to include in your pro forma statements. Usually, because of various accounting adjustments, it is beyond the scope of a financial statement model to reconcile all the *historical* cash transactions. After all, if you really want to know the details, then you could review your checkbook. As a result, only one account is of importance in the initial planning period or column one of the cash flow statement and that is the *ending cash*. All other initial or base values are readily set to zero without any loss in the quality of the information generated by the financial statement model. On the other hand, because the checkbook transactions are not known for the future planning periods, a primary purpose of the pro forma cash flow statement is to produce these anticipated cash flows.

Techniques for Expressing Model Logic

Several techniques are available for developing the logic of a business planning model that specify how each planning item is calculated. Some of the more common calculation techniques include the use of growth rates, constant changes, zero based budgeting, percent of sales, complementary logic, and financial ratios. One method is not necessarily better than another. Each of these methods is described for your consideration in selecting the most appropriate technique for a particular planning item.

Planning Psychology

How do business people think about the future? In general, they often consider changes in revenues, expenses, and so forth into the future in one of three ways.

The most frequently observed method is the **growth rate**: that is, a percent increase or decrease over what existed the previous planning period (year, quarter, month, or week). Two of the most common growth rates are the annual salary increase and compound interest, such as a 5 percent salary increase or a 7- percent interest rate. Both of these are usually expressed as a percent of an existing prior period's amount. This method reflects how people frequently think and articulate changes.

The second most frequently observed method is the fixed amount or **linear change**. That is, given a current value, the amount in the next time period increases or decreases by some specified amount, such as $291, rather than a percent.

In recent years, a third method has emerged: **zero-based budgeting.** With zero-based budgeting , the entire amount is justified each planning period. Specifically, the amount does not depend on what occurred in prior periods. Since individual values are determined for each period independently from any existing amounts, little analysis of past history is useful. Also, forecasting techniques are not applicable. Therefore, as it relates to analytical procedures, zero-based budgeting is uninteresting.

Let's examine growth rates and fixed amount changes in more depth because analytical procedures are available for discovering historical changes and equations can be included in a planning model. Figure 11-6 is a comparative illustration between growth rates and fixed amount or linear changes. Beginning with a base or existing value of $100, the two curves compare a 10 percent compounded growth rate to a $10 fixed annual increase. For the first year, the amount of the increase ($10) is equal under both methods, because $10 is 10 percent of $100. However, after that time period, you can see the effect of compounding from the growth rate.

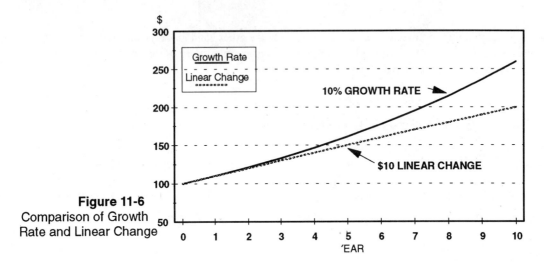

Figure 11-6
Comparison of Growth
Rate and Linear Change

Since both the growth rate and fixed amount change produce identical results the first year, there is little difference between the methods if a one period or one year plan is created. In fact, you probably translated the $10 increase into a 10-percent growth rate automatically. This further substantiates that people think in terms of percent or relative increases (decreases).

Constant growth rates and linear changes can be discovered from historical data using statistical regression analysis or curve fitting. The linear change is determined directly with linear regression analysis as the slope of the straight line. For the growth rate, a logarithmic transformation is required in using linear regression analysis to discover this historical relationship. Linear regression analysis is beyond the scope of this book, but you should consider applying this statistical procedure if adequate historical data are available. Once historical values are discovered, they can be used directly in a planning model or adjusted, based on managerial judgment and insight. Because managers frequently have new ideas for the future, merely projecting the past is inadequate. You must make these judgments in developing your planning model. This is part of the art of building business planning models.

The world does not operate on constant growth rates or linear changes for all future periods. That is, a 10 percent growth rate is not necessarily applied in all future periods of a business plan. The growth rate or linear change of an item in a business plan is likely to vary from one period to another. In one period, a 9 percent growth rate may be expected, while it's 11 percent the following period, and similarly for linear changes. Planning model logic is readily adapted to fit both constant and variable methods of projection.

Figures 11-7 and 11-8 are examples of the model logic and results of the growth rate and linear change methods of projections. Using a constant growth rate or linear change for SALES, the change can be placed directly in the equation. However, with the variable growth rate or linear change for SALES illustrated in Figures 11-9 and 11-10, two planning items or accounts are used. One contains the growth rate or linear change for each period, whereas the other contains the formula for calculating the results with that growth rate or linear change. Two planning items are necessary so the desired variable growth rates or linear changes can be readily input for use in the calculation of the projected values. Although other IFPS model logic can be used to implement variable growth rates and linear changes, this arrangement using two planning items is usually the best because of its flexibility.

	YEAR1	YEAR2	YEAR3	YEAR4	YEAR5
CONSTANT GROWTH RATE					
SALES	100	110	121	133	146
CONTSTANT GROWTH RATE					
SALES = 100, PREVIOUS SALES * (1 + .10)					

Figure 11-7
Constant
Growth
Rate

	YEAR1	YEAR2	YEAR3	YEAR4	YEAR5
CONSTANT AMOUNT (LINEAR) CHANGE					
SALES	100	110	120	130	140
CONTSTANT AMOUNT (LINEAR) CHANGE					
SALES = 100, PREVIOUS SALES + 10					

Figure 11-8
Constant
Linear
Change

	YEAR1	YEAR2	YEAR3	YEAR4	YEAR5
VARIABLE GROWTH RATE					
GROWTH RATE	0	0.12	0.10	0.08	0.12
SALES	100	112	123	133	146
VARIABLE GROWTH RATE					
GROWTH RATE = 0, .12, .10, .08, .10					
SALES = 100, PREVIOUS SALES * (1 + GROWTH RATE)					

Figure 11-9
Variable
Growth Rate

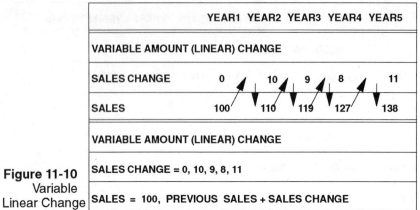

Figure 11-10
Variable
Linear Change

If you wish, you can use the variable growth rate and linear change logic for constant growth rate and linear change calculations. All you need to do is input the same value for each period. With the automatic column replication feature of IFPS, the data value entered in the first column is automatically used in the remaining columns when no other values are entered. Therefore, with the constant growth rate or linear change situation, you have a choice of logic. Because the use of a separate IFPS model variable for the growth rate or linear change allows these values to be obtained more readily from a datafile or database relation and because these assumption values are easily included in any output reports, the use of two planning items in an IFPS model is the preferred method of implementing this logic.

The choice of projection method is yours. In making this decision, you need to focus on the causal conditions and replicate how people think about and articulate values changing into the future. This is especially important because planning projections represent an extension of human thought processes.

Percent-of-Sales Method

The **percent-of-sales method** is a simple but often practical method of forecasting financial statement variables. The procedure is based on three assumptions: (1) that many income statement accounts are tied directly to sales, (2) that many balance sheet accounts are related directly to sales, and (3) that the current levels of assets are optimal for the current sales level.

The first step in the percent of sales forecast is to isolate those income statement and balance sheet items that vary directly with sales. With increased sales, the cost of sales, wages, other expenses, account receivables, inventory, and new plant may increase proportionately. If some assets are not being fully utilized, then sales can increase without increasing those assets, in which case the percent of sale method may not be appropriate. Likewise, liabilities and equities such as accounts payable rise proportionately with sales. On the other hand, retained earnings, notes payable, long term debt, and common stock usually do not rise spontaneously with sales. A causal relationship between sales and other planning items needs to be established in using the percent of sales method.

Figures 11-11 and 11-12 illustrate the percent of sales method used to determine ratios that can be applied in creating a financial statement forecast. Those items that are usually not appropriate for the percent of sales method are indicated as not applicable (NA). For each forecasting situation, you need to determine the appropriate method. Figure 11-13 summarizes financial items frequently tied directly to sales. Some items, such as plant and equipment, may include a component that is tied directly to sales, while increased sales may result without an increase in these assets.

SAMPLE COMPANY, INC.

INCOME STATEMENT

January 1 to December 31

Sales	$500,000
Cost of Goods Sold	275,000
Gross Profit	$225,000
Wages & Salaries	100,000
Benefits	20,000
Other Expenses	80,000
Total Expenses	200,000
Income Before Tax	25,000
Income Tax	5,000
Net Income	$20,000

SAMPLE COMPANY, INC.

BALANCE SHEET

December 31

Figure 11-11
Income Satement
and Balance Sheet
for Percent of
Sales Method

Cash	$10,000		Accounts payable	$50,000
Receviables	85,000		Accured taxes & wages	25,000
Inventories	100,000		Mortgage bonds	70,000
Fixed assets(net)	150,000		Common Stocks	100,000
			Retained earnings	100,000
Total Assets	$345,000		Total Liabilites & net worth	$345,000

SAMPLE COMPANY, INC.

INCOME STATEMENT

January 1 to December 31

(PERCENT OF SALES)

Sales	100.0%
Cost of Goods Sold	55.0%
Gross Profit	45.0%
Wages & Salaries	20.0%
Benefits	4.0%
Other Expenses	na
Total Expenses	na
Income Before Tax	na
Income Tax	na
Net Income	na

SAMPLE COMPANY, INC.

BALANCE SHEET

December 31

(PRECENT OF SALES)

Figure 11-12
Income Satement
and Balance Sheet
Expressed as
Precent of Sales

Cash	2.0%	Accounts payable	10.0%
Receviables	17.0%	Accured taxes & wages	5.0%
Inventories	20.0%	Mortgage bonds	na
Fixed assets(net)	30.0%	Common Stocks	na
Total Assets	69.0%	Total Liabilites & net worth	15.0%

Figure 11-13
Financial Statement
Items Relationship
to Sales

BALANCE SHEET ITEMS DIRECTLY TIED TO INCREASE IN SALES		BALANCE SHEET ITEMS NOT DIRECTLY TIED TO INCREASE IN SALES	
Assets	Liabilities	Assets	Liabilities
Cash	Accounts	Investments	Notes payable
Receivables	payable	Property, Plant,	Long-term debt
Inventories	Provision for	and Equipment	Preferred stock
Property, Plant,	income tax		Common stock
and Equipment	Accruals		Retained earnings

The percent-of-sale method can be generalized as just the **percent of method**. For example, employee benefits may be stated as a percent of wages and salaries, where wages and salaries are not directly tied to sales. Here, the same concept applies as that of the percent of sales method. The difference is the causal variable. When appropriate, the percent of method is a convenient means for forecasting planning items.

Complementary Logic

Complementary logic can be used when planning item amounts are allocated among the income statement, balance sheet, and cash flow statement. **Complementary logic** is the calculation of a planning item in one of the financial statements when the related planning items are known for the other two financial statements. For example, consider the repayment of an amortized loan using the logic illustrated in Figure 11-14. The annual payment is known and specified in the cash flow statement because this is a use of cash. The interest expense is calculated and appears in the income statement. The principle reduction (annual payment less interest expense) is calculated from the values in the cash flow statement and the income statement; it is used in the formula for the loan balance in the balance sheet. In this manner, the two known planning items are used to calculate the third planning item. When a complementary logic situation exists, calculating the planning item in the third financial statement from values in the other two statements is the *preferred method* because this often helps avoid apparent errors caused by rounding.

Figure 11-14
Complementary Logic
for Amortized Loan
Payment

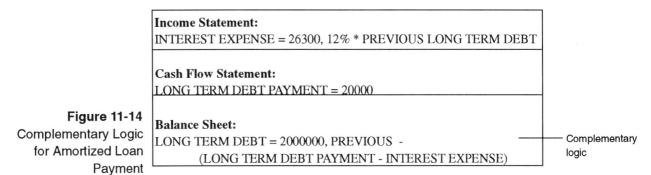

Income Statement:
INTEREST EXPENSE = 26300, 12% * PREVIOUS LONG TERM DEBT

Cash Flow Statement:
LONG TERM DEBT PAYMENT = 20000

Balance Sheet:
LONG TERM DEBT = 2000000, PREVIOUS -
       (LONG TERM DEBT PAYMENT - INTEREST EXPENSE)

— Complementary logic

Financial Ratio Analysis

Financial ratio analysis is used in two ways with pro forma financial statements: (1) to analyze the expected financial results in the same manner as ratios are used to evaluate past performance and (2) to provide a source for potential methods of forecasting selected planning items. For example, if the average collection period is used to evaluate the accounts receivables turnover, then a goal average collection period may be used in the planning model. The formula AVERAGE COLLECTION PERIOD = RECEIVABLES / SALES PER DAY, that is used for ratio analysis and comparison to an industry average, is restated as RECEIVABLES = AVERAGE COLLECTION PERIOD * SALES PER DAY to calculate the forecasted balance for receivables. If managers think about and articulate receivables as an average collection period, rather than as a percent of sales, then the average collection period should be used to input this decision in the planning model. Common financial ratios used for evaluating financial results and their formulas appear as Figure 11-15.

	FORMULA FOR CALCULATION	CALCULATION	INDUSTRY AVERAGE	EVALUATION
I. Liquidy				
1. Current	current assets / current liabilities	$700,000 / $300,000 = 2.3 times	2.5 times	Satisfactory
2. Quick, or acid test	current assets - inventory / current liabilities	$400,000 / $300, 000 = 1.3 times	1.0 times	Good
II. Leverage				
3. Debt to total assets	total debt / total assets	$1,000,000 / $2,000,000 = 50%	33%	High
4. Timed interest earned	profit before taxes + interest charges / interest charges	$245,000 / $45,000 = 54. times	8.0 times	Fair
5. Fixed charge coverage	income available for meeting fixed charges / fixed charges	273,000 / $106,333 = 2.6 times	4.0 times	Low
III. Activity				
6. Inventory turnover	sales / inventory	$3,000,000 / $30,000 = 10 times	9 times	Satisfactory
7. Average collection period	receivables / sales per day	$200,000 / $8,333 = 24 times	20 times	Satisfactory
8. Fixed assets turnover	sales / fixed assets	$3,000,000 / $1,300,000 = 2.3 times	5 times	Poor
9. Total assets turnover	sales / total assets	$3,000,000 / $2,000,000 = 1.5 times	2 times	Low
IV. Profitability				
10. Profit margin on sales	net profit after taxes / sales	$120,000 / $3,000,000 = 4%	5%	Low
11. Return on total assets	net profit after taxes / total assets	$120,000 / $2,000,000 = 6.0%	10%	low
12. Return on net worth	net profit after taxes / net worth	$120,000 / $1,000,000 = 12.0%	15%	Fair

Figure 11-15
Selected Financial Ratios

Approaches to Modeling Accounting Equations

While the components of pro forma income statements and statements of financial position are well established in business planning, the purpose and form of the cash flow statement is more nebulous. An integrated financial plan may consist of (1) only an income statement and statement of financial position or (2) an income statement, statement of financial position, and cash flow statement. For integrated financial plans, the first alternative represents the practice of using a **funds needed-to-balance approach**, whereas the second alternative represents using a **cash-flow-reconciliation approach**. While the two approaches are not mutually exclusive, the cash-flow-reconciliation approach provides an extremely strong test for the *validation* of a business planning model's accounting logic and is the method emphasized in these tutorials. However, both methods of model construction are presented and contrasted so you are familiar with the differences and can make an informed choice in selecting an appropriate approach for your modeling requirements.

Funds-Needed-to-Balance Approach

The funds-needed-to-balance, or traditional, approach is primarily a balance sheet and income statement model. Under this approach, starting with sales, projections are made for each income statement account. Assets are revised in the statement of financial position with cash being a specified minimum balance. All liabilities and equities are revised *except* for short term debt. Net income is added to retained earnings. At this juncture, assets are totaled, liabilities and equities are totaled, and the two totals compared. With projected financial statements (except in rare situations, when total assets are compared to total liabilities plus equity), they are *not* equal, a totally unacceptable accounting relationship.

In a similar manner, a trial balance procedure may be used in which the total assets are added yielding "trial assets" while total liabilities plus equities other than short term debt are summed as "trial liabilities." These trial accounts are then compared rather than merely using total assets and total liabilities plus equities.

This fundamental accounting identity must be satisfied:

assets = liabilities + equity

To achieve this, total assets are compared to total liabilities plus equity other than short term debt. Then, the balance sheet is balanced with the short term debt account. The debt balance is *assumed* to be total assets less the sum of all liabilities and equity other than short term debt. If total assets are less than total liabilities plus equity, a "funds surplus" exists. The difference is added to investments or marketable securities and a balance achieved. If total assets are greater than total liabilities plus equities, a "funds shortfall" exists. The difference is added to short term debt and a balance achieved. In both cases, an account is identified into which an "amount needed to balance" is plugged or added to achieve a balance as illustrated in Figures 11-16 and 11-17. Accounts used in this manner are sometimes known as "plug accounts." The approach is reasonably simple and straightforward. However, it *assumes* a value for the short term debt or investments account that *forces* the balance sheet to balance in a manner that *defeats* the common application of the total assets equal total liabilities plus equities accounting identity.

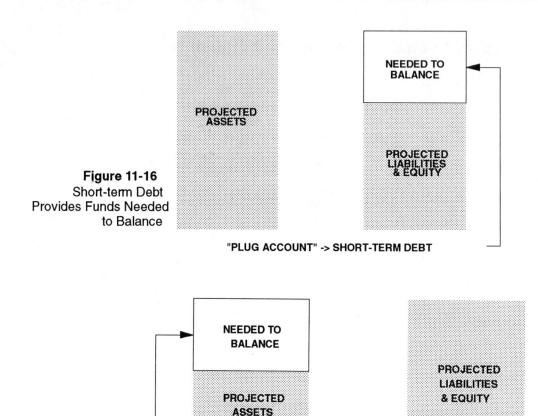

Figure 11-16
Short-term Debt
Provides Funds Needed
to Balance

Figure 11-17
Investments Provide Funds
Needed to Balance

With a debt plug account used to achieve balance, a focus of the business planning model is to determine how much money a company needs to borrow or how much money is available to invest in marketable securities with no short term borrowing or repayment taking place. In either case, the pro forma statement of financial position is *forced* to balance by either changing short term debt or investments. When pro forma calculations are approached sequentially with manual methods, this is often an acceptable procedure because of the calculation effort required for other methods. However, when a planning language such as IFPS is used, a business plan evolves as a series of solutions in which changes may be made to any of the accounts or planning items in the model. Other accounts such as bonuses or dividends can alternatively be identified as "plug accounts," depending on the particular focus of the business plan.

A "funds surplus" may occur over a portion of the planning horizon and a "funds shortfall" in other periods. When this results, the planning model selects between short term debt or investments as the balancing account. The complexity of this is compounded when investments are first reduced and then short term debt makes up the residual shortfall. The validation of model logic under these conditions becomes, to say the least, extremely difficult.

Once the pro forma income statement and statement of financial position have been completed, a funds flow sources and use of funds statement or statement of change in financial position can be backed into by calculating financial position changes. That is, each statement of financial position account for the previous period is subtracted from the corresponding account for the current period. With this traditional approach, a funds flow statement appears to be an afterthought rather than an integral part of the planning model.

The underlying difficulty with the traditional approach is the fact that it is an open model of a closed system of accounting relationships. If not, there would be no requirement for using needed-to-balance plug accounts. For other than the simplest planning model, the validation of a needed-to-balance model is extremely difficult. It is possible to have a host of errors covered up by the needed-to-balance calculation. For example, an amortized loan payment, consisting of interest expense and loan principle reduction, could have the interest charged correctly as an expense and the *entire* loan payment, including interest, deducted as principle. If total assets were greater than total liabilities plus equity, then the needed-to-balance short term debt would be greater than it should be. Of course, a careful review of the logic in a walkthrough may detect this problem. On the other hand, values produced by the model could be compared to historical values for the first period. This historical comparison, however, could be correct while projections into the future are incorrect because different logic is used for future periods. When a planning model consists of hundreds of planning items and their methods of calculation, the complete detection of possible logic errors by walkthroughs and comparisons with historical data becomes extremely difficult.

Therefore, it is desirable to build the logic of a business planning model in such a manner that conditions of imbalance are readily apparent. Error signals are generated that cannot be ignored until the *logic* is correct. The funds needed to balance approach does *not* create these signals because it presumes a perfect world where *no* errors ever occur in model logic. That is, builders of business planning models never make logic errors, they only occur when processing historical accounting transactions. A solution to the dilemma of errors in model logic is to build a closed model with the characteristics of a double entry account system. Although individual accounting transactions are *not* processed with the model, aggregate planning account amounts for each period are handled in a manner similar to a double-entry system.

Cash-Flow-Reconciliation Approach

The cash-flow-reconciliation approach represents a closed system in which income statement, statement of financial position and cash flow statement logic are interconnected eliminating the balance sheet needed-to-balance plug account logic. Like double-entry accounting, this approach is founded on an *imperfect* world in which errors may occur in model logic. The three pro forma statements—income statement, statement of financial position, and cash flow statement—are essential for the "cash flow reconciliation approach" and *must* be calculated concurrently in a *single* planning model. The cash balance, which drives the need for short term debt or investments, is such a complex balance sheet asset account that it cannot adequately be dealt with after the other two financial statements are calculated. Eventually, sales generate cash whereas expenses consume it. But some sales result in cash generated during the income statement period while others become accounts receivable collected in a future period. Similarly, expenses may be paid or become accounts payable. Further, some expenses are the result of cash flows in prior periods. These transactions must be reconciled; the cash flow statement is the necessary linkage vehicle between the income statement and the balance sheet or statement of financial position for this reconciliation so that the system can be closed.

The primary purpose of the cash flow statement is to *directly* calculate the balance in the cash account at the end of a period with changes affecting the cash balance detailed and summarized. Then, from this cash balance, changes in short term debt and/or investments are calculated separately from total assets and total liabilities plus equity. A cash balance is determined directly from the cash flow statement accounting relationships and is *not assumed* to be the amount needed to balance the statement of financial position. With pro forma financial statements that are projected into the future, determination of a cash balance is considerably more difficult than evaluating historical transactions. However, the direct determination of short term debt from a cash balance and reporting the components separately with the planning model is superior to the assumed cash balance with the funds-needed-to-balance approach.

The cash flow statement used in the cash flow reconciliation approach can take one of several forms including a statement of change in financial position or a statement of cash receipts and cash disbursements. With a statement of cash receipts and cash disbursements, each account that manipulates cash is treated as a receipt, disbursements, or financing change. Ending cash in this cash flow statement and its counterpart cash in the statement of financial position may be allowed to take on a negative value during validation of the planning model. Although this may seem undesirable, it reflects the manner in which historical financial statements are prepared. Negative cash balances have been observed on the balance sheets of small companies and in effect reflect short term debt or float. Although this may appear as a plug account, the cash balance obtained directly through the accounting identities of the model is *not* an assumed, after-the-fact amount needed merely to balance.

Complementary logic is frequently used throughout the cash flow statement with input ratios and percentages being applied in the income statement and the statement of financial position, since most people have a greater familiarly with decision making for those financial statements. Furthermore, complementary logic underscores the role of a cash flow statement in developing a closed set of accounting relationships—no new decisions are input—rather, the income statement and statement of financial position are reconciled.

Following model validation, managers can make decisions that modify their plan and correct a cash deficiency or cash surplus situation. As each decision is made, it is incorporated into the planning model to determine its effect. This is readily implemented through several planning iterations with IFPS. Also, the cash flow reconciliation approach allows managers to determine how cash problems will be handled: short term debt, long term debt, stock issuance, or expense reduction. Until the magnitude of the problem is known, the best method or combinations of methods cannot be readily addressed. And this is done by exploring various what-if alternatives with IFPS.

With the cash-flow-reconciliation approach, model validation is conducted by independently calculating total assets, and total liabilities plus equity. If they are not equal, then an error occurred in the *logic*. To assess this model validity, a "check" account may be used for error detection that is merely total assets minus total liabilities plus equities. If this account is *not* zero, one or more *errors* have occurred, similar to using this test with historical data.

It must be underscored that the "funds needed to balance" approach does *not* allow for the use of the accounting identity of total assets equal to total liabilities plus equities in validating the logic of a business planning model. Although the cash flow reconciliation approach may appear as an elaborate plug account, its purpose it the same as that of a double-entry accounting. Model logic requires built-in checks that help to insure errors do not exist in an imperfect world and is the approach used in these tutorials.

Example Integrated Financial Statements

The logic of a business planning model must come from you and is *not* pre-specified by IFPS. Your model should include whatever planning items are appropriate along with their formulas for your particular planning situation. As a result, it is appropriate to examine example logic to illustrate the contents of a pro forma financial statement model. The model includes sufficient planning items for a complete income statement, statement of financial position, and cash flow statement. Each financial statement is examined individually, although they form components of a *single* planning model. You should consider these examples as ideas for building your own model with appropriate changes for different planning items and their formulas.

Income Statement

An example income statement for a business planning model appears as Figure 11-18. In this example, the SALES are input. However, they could be calculated using a growth rate or other formula. Several line items are calculated using the percent of sales method. These include COST OF SALES, SELLING EXPENSES, and ADMINISTRATIVE EXPENSES. INTEREST EXPENSES is calculated from the loan balances, while a ratio is used for DEPRECIATION EXPENSES.

```
\ INCOME STATEMENT
COLUMNS YEAR0, YEAR1, YEAR2, YEAR3, YEAR4, YEAR5
\
SALES = 270000, 285000, 290000, 310000, 320000, 340000
        COS PERCENT = 0, 40%
COST OF SALES = 109500, COS PERCENT * SALES
GROSS PROFIT = SALES - COST OF SALES
        SELLING EXP RATIO = 0, 10%
SELLING EXPENSES = 24300, SELLING EXP RATIO * SALES
        ADVERTISING EXP RATIO = 0, 5%
ADVERTISING EXPENSES = 13700, ADVERTISING EXP RATIO * SALES
        ADMIN EXP RATIO = 0, 8%
ADMINISTRATIVE EXPENSES = 21300, ADMIN EXP RATIO * SALES
INTEREST EXPENSES = 26300, 10% * PREVIOUS SHORT TERM DEBT + '
        12% * PREVIOUS LONG TERM DEBT
        DEPREC EXP RATIO = 0, 9%
DEPRECIATION EXPENSES = 32000, DEPREC EXP RATIO * '
        (PLANT AND EQUIPMENT)
OPERATING EXPENSES = SELLING EXPENSES + '
        ADVERTISING EXPENSES + ADMINISTRATIVE EXPENSES + '
        INTEREST EXPENSES + DEPRECIATION EXPENSES
INCOME BEFORE TAXES = GROSS PROFIT - OPERATING EXPENSES
        INCOME TAX RATE = 0, 40%
INCOME TAX = 17600, INCOME TAX RATE * INCOME BEFORE TAX
NET INCOME = INCOME BEFORE TAXES - INCOME TAX
```

Figure 11-18 Income Statement Logic

A depreciation ratio is used here rather than an IFPS depreciation subroutine because this represents an overall depreciation rate for all plant and equipment. This is a common practice for an aggregate class or category of assets and represents a weighted value for assets depreciated over different time periods. If a new asset is acquired in a particular year of the plan, such as the purchase of a specific piece of equipment, then the IFPS depreciation subroutines are most appropriate. However, with classes of assets with mixed lives, a depreciation ratio similar to that shown in Figure 11-18 is most appropriate.

The OPERATING EXPENSES are calculated by specifying the individual line items that are added. The IFPS SUM function is *not* used because the ratios would be included in the summation. So, for this organization of the model with the planning assumptions adjacent to where they are used in calculating a planning item, the SUM function is inappropriate.

The INCOME TAX is calculated using a single, overall average tax rate. This is the simplest tax calculation. More complex logic can be used to obtain the rate from a table of tax rates, to avoid negative income tax, and to implement tax loss carryforward or carryback. With IFPS, its English-like syntax readily supports creating logic for these more complex tax calculations.

Let's begin creating model FINPLAN, which is an integrated financial statement model, by entering the income statement.

To enter the income statement:

❶   Select **MRBCS** as your Models and Reports File using the Set Entity Context dialog box.

❷   Click **File**, click **New** to display the New dialog box, then doubleclick **Model** to open a new window for entering model FINPLAN.

❸   Type the income statement that appears as Figure 11-18, then review it and make any edit corrections, as necessary.

❹   Click **File**, click **Save** to display the Save As dialog box, then type **FINPLAN** in the Entity Name text box and click the **OK button** to complete naming and saving the model.

Now that the income statement is entered, you are ready to examine the statement of financial position.

Statement of Financial Position

An example statement of financial position or balance sheet for a business plan is examined by considering the assets separately from the liabilities and equities. An example of the logic for the asset section of the balance sheet appears in Figure 11-19. In this example, SHORT TERM DEBT is calculated directly from the cash flow statement and is used in reconciling the income statement and balance sheet. The short term debt BORROWING is determined from the cash deficiency or excess in the cash flow statement. As a result, CASH AND INVESTMENTS are inputs that represent zero-based amounts specified for each year of the plan in this example. These values could also be calculated by using a percent of sales, a growth rate, or any other appropriate equation. The ACCOUNTS RECEIVABLE are calculated using a financial ratio based on the number of days of receivables. DAYS RECEIVABLE is used in this example to demonstrate the use of a ratio and the application of calculating a planning item based on the manner in which assumptions are input to the model. That is, this illustrates a preferred method of specifying the input as days rather than as a percent of sales.

```
\ STATEMENT OF FINANCIAL POSITION
COLUMNS YEAR0, YEAR1, YEAR2, YEAR3, YEAR4, YEAR5
\
\ ASSETS:
CASH AND INVESTMENTS = 53000, 65000, 95000, 97000, 107000, 108000
        AVERAGE DAILY REVENUE = 0, ROUND(SALES / 360)
        DAYS RECEIVABLE = 0, 30
ACCOUNTS RECEIVABLE = 20900, AVERAGE DAILY REVENUE * '
        DAYS RECEIVABLE
        INVENTORY RATIO = 0, 22%
INVENTORY = 21000, INVENTORY RATIO * COST OF SALES
TOTAL CURRENT ASSETS = CASH AND INVESTMENTS + '
        ACCOUNTS RECEIVABLE + INVENTORY
PROPERTY = 100000, PREVIOUS + PROPERTY PURCHASES
PLANT AND EQUIPMENT = 350000, PREVIOUS + EQUIPMENT PURCHASES
ACCUMULATED DEPRECIATION = -60000, PREVIOUS - DEPRECIATION EXPENSES
NET PP AND E = PROPERTY + PLANT AND EQUIPMENT + '
        ACCUMULATED DEPRECIATION
TOTAL ASSETS = TOTAL CURRENT ASSETS + NET PP AND E
```

Figure 11-19 Balance Sheet Logic for Assets

The INVENTORY calculation uses the percent of method with COST OF SALES as the causal variable. Of course, this also could be stated as a percent of sales. Again, the choice becomes one of picking the arrangement that best matches the manner in which managers think about and articulate these assumptions.

The TOTAL CURRENT ASSETS are not added using the SUM function for the same reason it was not used in the income statement. If the AVERAGE DAILY REVENUE is included in the TOTAL CURRENT ASSETS by using a SUM function, a significant error results in the TOTAL ASSETS.

PROPERTY, PLANT AND EQUIPMENT, and ACCUMULATED DEPRECIATION are all calculated using complementary logic. The values obtained from either the income statement or the cash flow statement are used to calculated these balances. As a result, no decision variables or planning assumptions are input for calculating these variables in this statement.

Because ACCUMULATED DEPRECIATION is a contra asset, it appears as a negative value in the balance sheet. This reinforces the accounting equation for calculating the NET PP AND E by subtracting the amount of ACCUMULATED DEPRECIATION from the PLANT AND EQUIPMENT. Also, when negative numbers are displayed using a format with parentheses, these amounts appear enclosed in parentheses to reinforce the reduction in assets.

Let's enter the asset section to the statement of financial position by adding it onto model FINPLAN that is the income statement you entered previously:

To enter the assets portion of the statement of financial position:

❶   Verify that model FINPLAN is displayed in your currently active window. If it's not displayed, then access this model.

❷   Type the assets section of the statement of financial position that appears as Figure 11-19. Do not enter the COLUMNS statement because the model already includes this statement that is provided in the figure for your reference. Review the logic and make any necessary edits.

❸   Click **File**, click **Save** to save model FINPLAN that now includes the logic for the assets.

You are now ready to review the logic for the liabilities and equity section of the statement of financial position. An example of this logic appears as Figure 11-20. Here, the percent of method is applied in calculating the ACCOUNTS PAYABLE, ACCRUED WAGES, and ACCRUED TAXES. For each of these planning items, an appropriate causal variable is selected for determining and inputting these percent assumptions.

```
\ STATEMENT OF FINANCIAL POSITION
COLUMNS YEAR0, YEAR1, YEAR2, YEAR3, YEAR4, YEAR5
\
\ LIABILITIES AND EQUITY:
        ACCTS PAY RATIO = 0, 12%
ACCOUNTS PAYABLE = 12400, ACCTS PAY RATIO * COST OF SALES
        ACCRUED WAGES RATIO = 0, 5%
ACCRUED WAGES = 1000, ACCRUED WAGES RATIO * '
        ADMINISTRATIVE EXPENSES
        ACCRUED TAXES RATIO = 0, 25%
ACCRUED TAXES = 3900, ACCRUED TAXES RATIO * INCOME TAX
SHORT TERM DEBT = 19000, PREVIOUS + BORROWING - REPAYMENT
TOTAL CURRENT LIABILITIES = ACCOUNTS PAYABLE + ACCRUED WAGES + '
        ACCRUED TAXES + SHORT TERM DEBT
LONG TERM DEBT = 200000, PREVIOUS - LONG TERM DEBT PAYMENT
COMMON STOCK = SHARES * 50
RETAINED EARNINGS = 148600, PREVIOUS + NET INCOME
TOTAL EQUITY = COMMON STOCK + RETAINED EARNINGS
TOTAL LIABILITIES PLUS EQUITY = TOTAL CURRENT LIABILITIES + '
        LONG TERM DEBT + TOTAL EQUITY
\
SHARES = 2000
```

Figure 11-20 Balance Sheet Logic for Liabilities and Equity

The balances for SHORT TERM DEBT and LONG TERM DEBT are calculated using complementary logic with values for the variables in these equations obtained from the cash flow statement. Similarly, the

RETAINED EARNINGS is calculated using the NET INCOME from the income statement. Let's add the liabilities and equities section to model FINPLAN.

To enter the liabilities and equity portion of the statement of financial position:

❶ Verify that model FINPLAN is displayed in your currently active window. If it's not displayed, then access this model.

❷ Type the liabilities and equity section of the statement of financial position that appears as Figure 11-20. Do not enter the COLUMNS statement because the model already contains this statement. Include the number of shares of common stock with this logic, then review it and make any edit corrections, as necessary.

❸ Click **File**, click **Save** to save model FINPLAN that now includes the logic for the liabilities and equities.

This completes the logic for the statement of financial position. You are ready to examine the cash flow statement.

Cash Flow Statement

The cash flow statement may follow one of several different arrangements. An example of the model logic for a sources and uses of funds cash flow statement appears as Figure 11-21. Samples of alternative cash flow statements are presented in the next tutorial. For this example, nearly all the planning items are calculated using values determined from other formulas in the planning model. The exceptions are PROPERTY PURCHASES, EQUIPMENT PURCHASES, and LONG TERM DEBT PAYMENT. This emphasizes the use of the cash flow statement to reconcile the logic of the other two financial statements.

```
\ STATEMENT OF CHANGE IN FINANCIAL POSITION
\ (SOURCES AND USES OF FUNDS STATEMENT)

COLUMNS YEAR0, YEAR1, YEAR2, YEAR3, YEAR4, YEAR5
\

\ SOURCES:
FROM NET INCOME = 0, NET INCOME
ADD DEPRECIATION = 0, DEPRECIATION EXPENSES
SUBTOTAL FROM OPERATIONS = FROM NET INCOME + ADD DEPRECIATION
CHANGE IN ACCOUNTS PAYABLE = 0, ACCOUNTS PAYABLE - '
      PREVIOUS ACCOUNTS PAYABLE
CHANGE IN ACCRUED WAGES = 0, ACCRUED WAGES - '
      PREVIOUS ACCRUED WAGES
CHANGE IN ACCRUED TAXES = 0, ACCRUED TAXES - '
      PREVIOUS ACCRUED TAXES
CHANGE IN SHORT TERM DEBT = 0, SHORT TERM DEBT - '
      PREVIOUS SHORT TERM DEBT
TOTAL SOURCES = SUM(SUBTOTAL FROM OPERATIONS .. '
      CHANGE IN SHORT TERM DEBT)
\
```

Figure 11-21 Cash Flow Statement Logic *(continued)*

```
\USES:
CHANGE IN CASH AND INVESTMENTS = 0, CASH AND INVESTMENTS - '
        PREVIOUS CASH AND INVESTMENTS
CHANGE IN ACCOUNTS RECEIVABLE = 0, ACCOUNTS RECEIVABLE - '
        PREVIOUS ACCOUNTS RECEIVABLE
CHANGE IN INVENTORY = 0, INVENTORY - PREVIOUS INVENTORY
\PERIOD DECISION VARIABLES:
PROPERTY PURCHASES = 0
EQUIPMENT PURCHASES = 0, 30000, 20000, 51000, 37000, 47000
LONG TERM DEBT PAYMENT = 0, 20000, 20000, 20000, 20000, 50000
TOTAL USES = SUM(CHANGE IN CASH AND INVESTMENTS .. '
        LONG TERM DEBT PAYMENT)
```

Figure 11-21 Cash Flow Statement Logic

PROPERTY PURCHASES, EQUIPMENT PURCHASES, and LONG TERM DEBT REPAYMENT appear as decision variables. That is, these amounts are specified as decisions from managers concerning their planned business activities each year. When decisions like these are made for each planning period that do not appear in the income statement, then the cash flow statement is usually the preferred location for period decisions. In most situations, managers usually specify changes in assets as purchases and/or dispositions rather than as balances.

Next, let's enter the cash flow statement:

To enter the cash flow statement:

❶   Verify that model FINPLAN is displayed in your currently active window. If it's not displayed, then access this model.

❷   Type the cash flow statement that appears as Figure 11-21. Do not enter the COLUMNS statement; it appears only for your reference. Review the logic and make any edits.

❸   Click **File**, click **Save** to save model FINPLAN that now includes the logic for the cash flow statement.

Model FINPLAN is nearly complete. The automatic borrowing logic needs to be included before the model is solved.

Automatic Borrowing and Repayment of Debt

The automatic borrowing and repayment of debt is a frequent focus of financial planning models. That is, one of the primary purposes of the model is to determine the amount of debt financing required for a particular business plan. How much borrowing is required? When does the borrowing take place? These are among the key questions addressed with the model. The **automatic borrowing and repayment of debt** encompasses appropriate logic *within* the planning model so that the expected amount and timing of any borrowing is calculated when the model is solved.

Logic that calculates the borrowing and repayment of debt as a model is solved frees managers to concentrate on the other planning issues, such as adjustments in expenses, revenues, inventories, and accounts payable. Business planning models constructed under the principles of the cash flow reconciliation approach and implemented with IFPS allow managers to quantitatively explore a variety of actions available to them, while monitoring short term debt and remaining confident in the validity of their model logic.

An example of the model logic that implements the direct calculation of changes in SHORT TERM DEBT as either BORROWING or REPAYMENT from the cash flow statement appears as Figure 11-22.

This logic is used in the same model with the prior example logic of Figures 11-18, 11-19, 11-20, and 11-21 for the integrated income statement, balance sheet, and cash flow statement.

```
\ CASH FLOW RECONCILIATION WITH AUTOMATIC BORROWING AND
\         REPAYMENT OF DEBT
COLUMNS YEAR0, YEAR1, YEAR2, YEAR3, YEAR4, YEAR5
\
PRELIM SOURCES = 0, SUM(SUBTOTAL FROM OPERATIONS .. '
        CHANGE IN ACCRUED TAXES)
BORROWING = MAXIMUM(0, (TOTAL USES - PRELIM SOURCES))
REPAYMENT = MAXIMUM(0, (PRELIM SOURCES - TOTAL USES))
```

Figure 11-22 Automatic Borrowing and Repayment of Debt Logic

The model logic in Figure 11-22 calculates the PRELIM SOURCES of cash and the TOTAL USES of cash from the cash flow statement. These are then used to calculated the expected amount of BORROWING and REPAYMENT. The MAXIMUM function is used to determine whether borrowing or repayment occurs. For any one column of the model, one of these two planning items is zero while the other is nonzero.

These values for BORROWING and REPAYMENT are used in the balance sheet to calculate the new balance for SHORT TERM DEBT. With the BORROWING and REPAYMENT calculated in the cash flow statement, the accounting identity of total assets equal to total liabilities plus equity is used to check the validity of the model logic. These calculations are central to the cash flow reconciliation approach.

Now let's complete entering model FINPLAN and solve it.

To enter the automatic borrowing and repayment of debt logic:

❶ Verify that model FINPLAN is displayed in your currently active window. If it is not displayed, then access this model.

❷ Type the automatic borrowing and repayment of debt logic that appears as Figure 11-22. Do not enter the COLUMNS statement that is for your reference. Review the logic making any edit corrections.

❸ Click **File**, click **Save** to save model FINPLAN that now includes the logic for the cash flow statement.

Next, the model is solved.

❹ Click the **Solve button** in the toolbar, then click the **OK button** to accept the solve defaults. Inspect the solution.

TROUBLE? If any undefined variable messages appear, then you need to correct these errors in entering your logic and repeat Step 4.

❺ Print both the solution and model for your reference.

The preceding integrated financial statement example includes only SHORT TERM DEBT as a built-in decision variable calculated by the model. Frequently, planning models also include INVESTMENTS as another planning item that is calculated by the model. When the SHORT TERM DEBT balance is zero, then INVESTMENTS take place that earn interest. The planning model contains logic that calculates the values for the four possible situations of an investment increase, an investment decrease, short term borrowing, or short term repayment. In any one time period, (1) an investment increase and short term repayment or (2) an investment decrease and short term borrowing may take place. That is, if the SHORT TERM DEBT is paid off, then any remaining funds are placed in INVESTMENTS, and similarly when additional borrowing is necessary and investments exists in the prior time period.

The income statement and balance sheet of the preceding example are modified to include INVESTMENTS as shown in Figure 11-23. The income statement logic calculates the interest earned on the investments, while the balance sheet contains INVESTMENTS as a new current asset planning item.

```
\ INCOME STATEMENT
COLUMNS YEAR0, YEAR1, YEAR2, YEAR3, YEAR4, YEAR5
\
               •
               •
               •
OPERATING EXPENSES = SELLING EXPENSES + '
      ADVERTISING EXPENSES + ADMINISTRATIVE EXPENSES + '
      INTEREST EXPENSES + DEPRECIATION EXPENSES
      INVEST INTEREST RATE = 0, 10%
INVESTMENT INTEREST = 0, PREVIOUS INVESTMENTS * '
      INVEST INTEREST RATE
INCOME BEFORE TAXES = GROSS PROFIT - OPERATING EXPENSES + '
      INVESTMENT INTEREST
               •
               •
               •
\ STATEMENT OF FINANCIAL POSITION
\
\ ASSETS:
CASH = 53000, PREVIOUS + 11000
INVESTMENTS = 0, PREVIOUS + INVESTMENT INCREASE - '
      INVESTMENT DECREASE
               •
               •
               •
TOTAL CURRENT ASSETS = CASH + INVESTMENTS + '
      ACCOUNTS  RECEIVABLE + INVENTORY
               •
               •
               •
\
\ LIABILITIES AND EQUITY:
               •
               •
SHORT TERM DEBT = 19000, PREVIOUS + SHORT TERM BORROWING - '
      SHORT TERM REPAYMENT
               •
               •
               •
```

Figure 11-23 Automatic Borrowing and Repayment of Debt with Investments Logic Changes for the Income Statement and Balance Sheet

Model FINPLAN can be modified to include the investment logic with the automatic borrowing and repayment of debt. Let's create the model FINPLAN2 as the model with the investments.

To modify a model to include investment logic with the automatic borrowing and repayment of debt:

❶　Verify that FINPLAN is displayed in your active Model window. If not, open the model as your active window.

❷　Click **File**, click **Save As** to display the Save As dialog box, type **FINPLAN2** in the Entity Name text box, then click the **OK button** to complete naming this model.

Now modify the logic for the income statement and statement of financial position.

❸   Edit model FINPLAN2 typing the new logic for INVEST INTEREST RATE, INVESTMENT INTEREST, INCOME BEFORE TAXES, CASH, INVESTMENTS, and SHORT TERM DEBT that appears as Figure 11-23. With SHORT TERM DEBT, two variable names are revised.

Next the revised model is saved.

❹   Click **File**, click **Save** to save model FINPLAN2 that now includes the modified logic for the automatic borrowing and repayment of debt with investments.

With the modifications finished for the income statement and statement of financial position, the cash flow statement is revised for the additions to the balance sheet. In the cash flow statement, a CHANGE IN INVESTMENTS planning item is added to the uses of cash. The revised logic for the cash flow statement appears as Figure 11-24. This is located above the CHANGE IN CASH planning item to facilitate the use of the SUM function in the automatic borrowing and repayment of debt calculations. Also, the CHANGE IN CASH planning item replaces the CHANGE IN CASH AND INVESTMENTS planning item.

```
\ STATEMENT OF CHANGE IN FINANCIAL POSITION
COLUMNS YEAR0, YEAR1, YEAR2, YEAR3, YEAR4, YEAR5
\
\ SOURCES:
                      •
                      •
                      •
\
\ USES:
CHANGE IN INVESTMENTS = 0, INVESTMENTS - PREVIOUS INVESTMENTS
CHANGE IN CASH = 0, CASH - PREVIOUS CASH
                      •
                      •
                      •
TOTAL USES = SUM(CHANGE IN INVESTMENTS .. '
        LONG TERM DEBT PAYMENT)
```

Figure 11-24   Automatic Borrowing and Repayment of Debt with Investments Logic Changes for the Cash Flow Statement

Now let's make these modifications in the logic of FINPLAN2.

To modify the cash flow statement to include investments as a separate planning item:

❶   Verify that model FINPLAN2 is displayed in your currently active window. If it is not displayed, then access this model.

❷   Edit model FINPLAN2 typing the new logic for CHANGE IN INVESTMENTS, CHANGE IN CASH, and TOTAL USES that appears in Figure 11-24. TOTAL USES is revised with the CHANGE IN INVESTMENTS. Review the logic making any edit corrections.

❸   Click **File**, click **Save** to save model FINPLAN2 that now includes the modified logic for the cash flow statement.

The cash flow reconciliation and automatic borrowing and repayment of debt with investments is expanded to calculate the four variables of INVESTMENT INCREASE, INVESTMENT DECREASE, SHORT TERM BORROWING, and SHORT TERM REPAYMENT as shown in Figure 11-25.   Both a PRELIM SOURCES and a PRELIM USES of cash are calculated as a transitional step in determining a CASH EXCESS or CASH DEFICIENCY from the cash flow statement. These two intermediate variables are used in determining whether changes occur in INVESTMENTS or SHORT TERM DEBT. Although the use of intermediate variables is not required, they greatly simplify implementation of the logic that calculates the INVESTMENT INCREASE, INVESTMENT DECREASE, SHORT TERM BORROWING, and SHORT TERM REPAYMENT. Furthermore, these intermediate values provide a ready means for reviewing the logic to verify that it correctly carries out the desired calculations.

```
\ CASH FLOW RECONCILIATION WITH AUTOMATIC BORROWING AND
\        REPAYMENT OF DEBT WITH INVESTMENTS
COLUMNS YEAR0, YEAR1, YEAR2, YEAR3, YEAR4, YEAR5
\
PRELIM SOURCES = 0, SUM(SUBTOTAL FROM OPERATIONS .. '
        CHANGE IN ACCRUED TAXES)
PRELIM USES = 0, SUM(CHANGE IN CASH .. LONG TERM DEBT PAYMENT)
CASH EXCESS = MAXIMUM(0, (PRELIM SOURCES - PRELIM USES))
CASH DEFICIENCY = MAXIMUM(0, (PRELIM USES - PRELIM SOURCES))
\
INVESTMENT INCREASE = 0, '
        IF CASH EXCESS .GE. 0 .AND. '
                PREVIOUS SHORT TERM DEBT .LE. CASH EXCESS '
        THEN (CASH EXCESS - PREVIOUS SHORT TERM DEBT) '
        ELSE 0
\
INVESTMENT DECREASE = 0, '
        IF CASH DEFICIENCY .GT. 0 .AND. '
                PREVIOUS INVESTMENTS .GE. CASH DEFICIENCY '
        THEN CASH DEFICIENCY '
        ELSE IF CASH DEFICIENCY .GT. 0 .AND. '
                        PREVIOUS INVESTMENTS .LT. CASH DEFICIENCY '
                THEN PREVIOUS INVESTMENTS '
                ELSE 0

\
SHORT TERM BORROWING = 0, '
        IF CASH DEFICIENCY .GT. 0 .AND. '
                PREVIOUS INVESTMENTS .LE. CASH DEFICIENCY '
        THEN (CASH DEFICIENCY - PREVIOUS INVESTMENTS) '
        ELSE 0
\
SHORT TERM REPAYMENT = 0, '
        IF CASH EXCESS .GE. 0 .AND. '
                PREVIOUS SHORT TERM DEBT .GE. CASH EXCESS '
        THEN CASH EXCESS '
        ELSE IF CASH EXCESS .GT. 0 .AND. '
                        PREVIOUS SHORT TERM DEBT .LT. CASH EXCESS '
                THEN PREVIOUS SHORT TERM DEBT '
                ELSE 0
```

Figure 11-25   Automatic Borrowing and Repayment of Debt with Investment Logic Changes for the Cash Flow Reconciliation

Now let's complete the revisions to model FINPLAN2 and solve it.

To modify the automatic borrowing and repayment of debt logic:

❶ Verify that model FINPLAN2 is displayed in your currently active window. If it is not displayed, then access this model and select its window.

❷ Edit the model entering the revised automatic borrowing and repayment of debt logic that appears as Figure 11-25. Do not enter the COLUMNS statement that appears for your reference. The BORROWING and REPAYMENT logic is replaced with the CASH EXCESS and CASH DEFICIENCY logic as these modifications are made. Review the logic making any edit corrections.

❸ Click **File**, click **Save** to save model FINPLAN2 that now includes the logic for automatic borrowing and repayment of debt with investments.

Next, the model is solved.

❹ Click the **Solve button** in the toolbar, then click the **OK button** to accept the solve defaults. Inspect the solution.

TROUBLE? If any undefined variable messages appear then you need to correct these errors in entering your logic and repeat Step 4.

❺ Print both the solution and model for your reference.

These and other automatic borrowing and repayment of debt alternatives are available for inclusion in a planning model. As you develop your own business models, you need to determine the extent of management involvement in these financing decisions. Then you can incorporate appropriate built-in decision making in your model. Regardless of the built-in financing logic, the cash flow reconciliation approach facilitates development of a valid model and provides a means for monitoring the validity of all subsequent revisions.

Simultaneous Equations in the Debt-Interest Problem

Although business-planning models are used for a multiplicity of purposes, a frequently occurring issue is the simultaneous solution of a model to determine the amount of debt financing required to maintain a minimum cash balance. Simultaneous equations occur when the short term debt balance at the *end* of a time period is used to calculate the interest expenses for that *same* time period. This is an implementation of the assumption that borrowing takes place at the *beginning* of the time period and that the interest expenses occur for the entire time period. With this assumption, a change in the amount of borrowing for the time period changes the amount of the interest expenses that reduces profits causing additional borrowing (Figure 11-26). This change in borrowing and interest expenses continues until the incremental change becomes negligible.

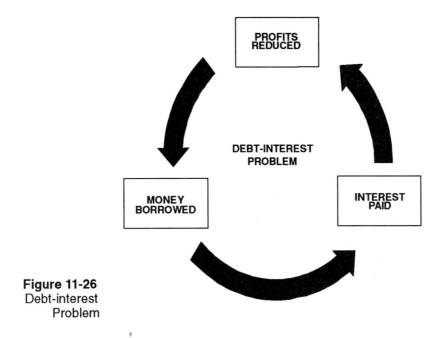

Figure 11-26
Debt-interest
Problem

The key factor that determines whether simultaneous equations occur in the debt-interest problem is the assumption of when debt borrowing occurs. If borrowing occurs at the *end* of the time period and the interest is expensed in the *following* time period, then the equations are *not* simultaneous. If borrowing occurs at the *middle* of the time period and interest expenses are calculated on the average short term debt balance, then the use of the ending balance in calculating an average results in simultaneous equations. The model logic for end of period borrowing, beginning of period borrowing, and average of period borrowing is illustrated in Figure 11-27. No modifications of model logic in the balance sheet or cash flow statement are required for the application of simultaneous equations for debt borrowing.

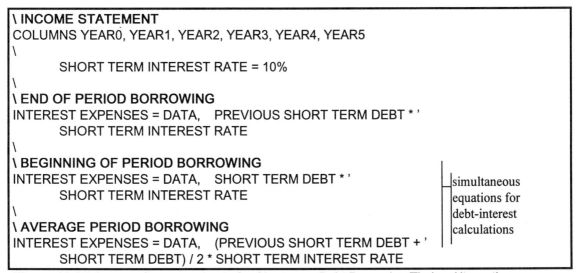

Figure 11-27 Income Statement Logic for Short-term Debt Borrowing Timing Alternatives

In Figure 11-27, the use of PREVIOUS determines whether the debt-interest equations are simultaneous. All you need to do is accidentally omit one PREVIOUS and you cause the occurrence of simultaneous equations in your model. Because this error is so easily committed, the appropriate strategy for building a planning model is a two-step process as follows:

(1)   Use PREVIOUS with SHORT TERM DEBT and other similar variables to build the model and validate the logic *without* simultaneous equations.

(2)   Remove PREVIOUS from those model variables that you want to be simultaneous when you solve the model and obtain the desired solution.

This strategy helps to assure that only your intended planning items are calculated using simultaneous equations. When modifications to your model logic are required, the process should be reversed. That is, insert the PREVIOUS to remove simultaneous equations and then modify and validate your logic revisions. Remove the PREVIOUS when you do the solve to obtain the desired solution.

In the income statement, INTEREST EXPENSES for both short and long term debt may be modified for the mid-year as shown in Figure 11-28. This causes simultaneous equations in the calculation of the short term debt.

\ INCOME STATEMENT
COLUMNS YEAR0, YEAR1, YEAR2, YEAR3, YEAR4, YEAR5
\
INTEREST EXPENSES = 26300, 10% * (PREVIOUS SHORT TERM DEBT + '
        SHORT TERM DEBT) / 2 + 12% * (PREVIOUS LONG TERM DEBT + '
        LONG TERM DEBT) / 2

Figure 11-28   Interest Expenses Logic with Mid-year Average Balance for Both Short and Long Term Debt

Let's modify the logic for calculating interest on short and long term debt so that the average balance outstanding is the amount on which interest is paid.

To modify the income statement to mid-year balances for interest expenses:

❶   Verify that model FINPLAN2 is displayed in your currently active window. If it is not displayed, then access this model.

❷   Edit model FINPLAN2 typing the new logic for INTEREST EXPENSES that appears as Figure 11-28.

❸   Click **File**, click **Save As** to display the Save As dialog box, type **FINPLAN3** in the Entity Name text box, then click the **OK button** to save this model that includes the modified logic for the mid-year average loan balances.

Next let's solve the revised model with simultaneous equations.

To solve a model with simultaneous equations:

❶   Click the **Solve button** in the toolbar to display the Visual IFPS/Plus message "Simultaneous equations encountered when solving model." Click the **OK button** to proceed with the solution. See Figure 11-29.

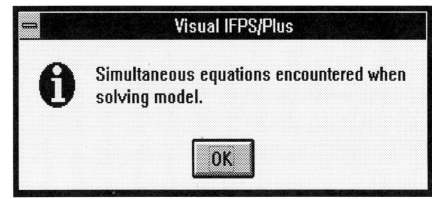

Figure 11-29
Simultaneous
Equation
Message

❷   Click the **OK button** in the Solve dialog box to request the default solution.

❸   Review the solution, then print both the model and its solution for your reference.

When Visual IFPS detects the existence of simultaneous equations in your model, a message box appears to indicate that simultaneous equations were encountered when solving the model. To have IFPS solve your model containing simultaneous equations *without* displaying the message box, the SIMULTANEOUS AUTO statement may be included in your model. This statement is placed on a separate line anywhere in your model. The bottom of a model is a convenient location for the SIMULTANEOUS AUTO statement. If you want to temporarily disable the simultaneous auto feature, make this a comment statement in your model. In this manner, it is easy to toggle the simultaneous auto on and off.

Let's add a statement to the model so the simultaneous message does not appear.

To automatically solve a model with simultaneous equations:

❶   Click the FINPLAN3 model window to make it active.

❷   Scroll to the bottom of the model since this is a convenient location for the simultaneous statement.

❸   Type **SIMULTANEOUS AUTO** to include this statement in your model.

❹   Click **File**, click **Save As** to display the Save As dialog box, type FINPLAN4 in the Entity Name text box, then click the **OK button** to save this model that includes the simultaneous statement.

❺   Click the **Solve button** in the toolbar, then click the **OK button** in the Solve dialog box to request the default solution.

❻   Review the solution. This is the same as the solution you produced without the simultaneous statement.

By assuming that debt borrowing or repayment occurs at the end of a period, a recursive model is readily constructed. With a recursive model, interest is paid on the outstanding debt from the prior planning period with any loan payments assumed to be made at the end of the planning period—precisely the way in which the interest on monthly loan is usually calculated.

The accuracy of the recursive planning model may satisfy the requirements of many business plans. When considering the potential inaccuracies in the other assumptions of a business plan, the additional accuracy achieved by using a simultaneous equation solution versus a recursive one is often minimal. A more straightforward recursive solution is frequently sufficient to provide the required accuracy. Why use a micrometer to measure debt when a yardstick was used to measure the sales or other planning items?

If the timing of debt borrowing and repayment is so critical to planning that a simultaneous solution is required to achieve the desired level of accuracy, then it is likely that you have not selected a short enough time period for the planning model. That is, attempting to achieve the accuracy of a monthly time period with a model that is based on an annual planning horizon.

Nonetheless, for planning situations that require simultaneous equations for debt financing, it is imperative that a valid model is constructed first. Once a model is validated, you can set a minimum cash balance and use simultaneous equations in IFPS to determine short term borrowing or investment purchases.

Questions

1.   A(n) _____ planning model is a vehicle for quantitatively expressing the goals and objectives of business.
        a. financial
        b. cash
        c. income
        d. business

2.   The most frequently observed method of articulating change in the revenues, expenses, and so forth into the future.
        a. growth rate
        b. linear change
        c. zero based budgeting
        d. planning zone

3.   The second most frequently observed method of articulating change in the revenues, expenses, and so forth into the future.
        a. growth rate
        b. linear change
        c. zero based budgeting
        d. planning zone

4.   The third most frequently observed method of articulating change in the revenues, expenses, and so forth into the future.
        a. growth rate
        b. linear change
        c. zero based budgeting
        d. planning zone

5.   The _____ method is a frequently used method of forecasting financial statement variables.
   a. percent of expenses
   b. percent of sales
   c. growth percent
   d. linear change

Case Problems

1. Good Morning Products

Frosty, Crush, and Kimberly reviewed the last model that you created from their data. They think that is does not clearly represent the company as a whole. They want a financial plan that includes the Balance Sheet, Income Statement, and Statement of Change in Financial Position. Using FINPLAN4 as an example model, Frosty wants you to change the data in Year0 to:

	YEAR0
INCOME STATEMENT	
SALES	3381400
ADVERTISING EXPENSES	79000
ADMINISTRATIVE EXPENSES	98000
INTEREST EXPENSES	64000
DEPRECIATION EXPENSES	102000
OPERATING EXPENSES	**
INVEST INTEREST RATE	0
INVESTMENT INTEREST	0
INCOME BEFORE TAX	**
INCOME TAX RATE	0
INCOME TAX	17600
NET INCOME	**
BALANCE SHEET	
ASSETS:	
CASH	76500
INVESTMENTS	0
AVERAGE DAILY REVENUE	0
DAYS RECEIVABLE	0
ACCOUNTS RECEIVABLE	90000
INVENTORY RATIO	0
INVENTORY	15750
TOTAL CURRENT ASSETS	**
PROPERTY	350000
PLANT AND EQUIPMENT	350000
ACCUMULATED DEPRECIATION	-200000
NET PP AND E	**
TOTAL ASSETS	**

** calculations from the FINPLAN4 model.

	YEAR0
LIABILITIES AND EQUITY:	
ACCOUNTS PAYABLE	70000
ACCRUED WAGES RATIO	0
ACCRUED WAGES	100000
ACCRUED TAXES RATIO	0
ACCRUED TAXES	13220
SHORT TERM DEBT	34715
TOTAL CURRENT ASSETS	**
LONG TERM DEBT	225000
COMMON STOCK	**
RETAINED EARNINGS	164315
TOTAL EQUITY	**
TOTAL LIABILITIES PLUS EQUITY	**
SHARES	1500

** calculations from the FINPLAN4 model.

Change only the information above, do not revise the period decision variable or any other variables in model FINPLAN4.

Now, for YEAR1 through YEAR5 make the following changes:

In the income statement:

Sales go up every year by 200,000, advertising expenses increases each every year by 1,000, administrative expenses goes up every year by 1,500, interest expenses goes up every year by 2,000, depreciation expenses increase each every year by 4,000. The invest interest rate is 10 percent for all of the years, income tax rate is 40 percent for all of the years. The following line items are calculated using the logic included in the FINPLAN4 model: operating expenses, investment interest, income before tax, income tax, and net income.

In the balance sheet:

Cash increases each year by 11,000, investments are calculated from the FINPLAN4 model. Average daily revenue is calculated from the FINPLAN4 model, days receivable are as specified in the FINPLAN4 model, accounts receivable is calculated from the FINPLAN4 model, inventory ratio is 22 percent for all of the years, inventory goes up every year by 1,500. Accounts payable increase each year by 20000. The accrued wages ratio is 5 percent for all of the years, accrued taxes ratio is 25 percent for all of the years. The following line items are calculated using the logic included in the FINPLAN4 model: total current assets, property, plant and equipment, accumulated depreciation, net PP and E, total assets, accrued wages, accrued taxes, short term debt, total current assets, long term debt, retained, total equity, and total liabilities plus equity.

In the statement of change in financial position:

The following line items are calculated using the logic included in the FINPLAN4 model: net income, add depreciation, subtotal from operations, change in accounts payable, change in accrued wages, change in accrued taxes, change in short term debt, total sources, change in investments, change in cash, change in accounts receivable, and change in inventory.

After making these revisions, print the model and the solution to the model.

2. The Woodcraft Furniture Company

Joe, Martha, and Ray examined the model you created from their data. They think that is does not clearly represent the company as a whole. They want a financial plan that includes the Balance Sheet, Income Statement, and Statement of Change in Financial Position. Using FINPLAN4 as an example model, Frosty wants you to change the data in Year0 to:

	YEAR0
INCOME STATEMENT	
SALES	12190100
COS PERCENT	0
COST OF SALES	8567372
GROSS PROFIT	**
ADVERTISING EXP RATIO	0
ADVERTISING EXPENSES	1210010
ADMIN EXP RATIO	0
ADMINISTRATIVE EXPENSES	675000
INTEREST EXPENSES	1836000
OPERATING EXPENSES	**
INVEST INTEREST RATE	0
INVESTMENT INTEREST	0
INCOME BEFORE TAX	**
INCOME TAX RATE	0
INCOME TAX	17600
NET INCOME	**

BALANCE SHEET	
ASSETS:	
CASH	100000
INVESTMENTS	0
AVERAGE DAILY REVENUE	0
DAYS RECEIVABLE	0
ACCOUNTS RECEIVABLE	200000
INVENTORY RATIO	0
INVENTORY	600000
TOTAL CURRENT ASSETS	**
PROPERTY	50000
PLANT AND EQUIPMENT	120000
NET PP AND E	**
TOTAL ASSETS	**

LIABILITIES AND EQUITY:	
ACCOUNTS PAYABLE	100000
ACCRUED WAGES RATIO	0
ACCRUED WAGES	250000
ACCRUED TAXES RATIO	0
ACCRUED TAXES	32275
SHORT TERM DEBT	47375
INSURANCE	60000
TOTAL CURRENT ASSETS	**
LONG TERM DEBT	228375
COMMON STOCK	**
RETAINED EARNINGS	176975
TOTAL EQUITY	**
TOTAL LIABILITIES PLUS EQUITY	**
SHARES	3500

** calculations from the FINPLAN4 model.

Change only the information above, do not revise the period decisions in the cash flow statement of FINPLAN4.

For YEAR1 through YEAR5 make the following changes:

In the income statement:

Sales goes up every year by 1,120,000, cos percent is 40 percent for all of the years, advertising exp ratio is 10 percent for all of the years, admin exp ratio is 8 percent for all of the years, administrative expenses goes up every year by 1,500. Interest expenses is calculated from the FINPLAN4 model except the interest percent for long and short term debt is 8 percent, operating expenses is calculated from the FINPLAN4 model, invest interest rate is 10 percent for all of the years, income tax rate is 40 percent for all of the years. The following line items are calculated using the logic included in the FINPLAN4 model: cost of sales, gross profit, advertising expenses, investment interest, income before tax, income tax, and net income.

In the balance sheet:

Cash goes up every year by 11,000, inventory ratio is 22 percent for all of the years, inventory goes up every year by 1,500, accounts payable goes up every year by 20,000, accrued wages ratio is 5 percent for all of the years, accrued taxes ratio is 25 percent for all of the years. The following line items are calculated using the logic included in the FINPLAN4 model: investments, average daily revenue, days receivable, accounts receivable, total current assets, property, plant and equipment, net PP and E, total assets, accrued wages, accrued taxes, short term debt, total current assets, long term debt, retained earnings, total equity, and total liabilities plus equity.

In the statement of change in financial position:

The following line items are calculated using the logic included in the FINPLAN4 model: net income, add deprecation, subtotal from operations, change in accounts payable, change in accrued wages, change in accrued taxes, change in short term debt, total sources, change in investments, change in cash, change in accounts receivable, and change in inventory.

After completing these revisions, print the model and its solution.

3. The Last National Bank

Carrie and J. J. reviewed the model you created from their data. They think that is does not clearly represent the company as a whole. They want a financial plan that includes the Balance Sheet, Income Statement, and Statement of Change in Financial Position. Using FINPLA4 as a model, Carries wants you to change to data in Year0 to:

	YEAR0
INCOME STATEMENT	
REAL ESTATE MORTGAGES EARNINGS	**
INSTALLMENT LOANS EARNING	**
COMMERCIAL LOANS EARNINGS	**
OTHER INVESTMENTS EARNINGS	**
TOTAL INTEREST EARNINGS ON ASSETS	**
REGULAR SAVINGS EARNINGS	**
INTEREST PLUS CHECKING EARNINGS	**
MONEY MARKET EARNINGS	**
OTHER BORROWED FUNDS EARNINGS	**
TOTAL INTEREST EXPENSE	**
INTEREST MARGIN	**

** calculations from the Tutorial 1 Case Problem 3 model.

BALANCE SHEET

	YEAR0
ASSETS:	
PRIME INTEREST	15%
REAL ESTATE MORTGAGES	35000
REAL ESTATE INTEREST	10%
INSTALLMENT LOANS	1000
INSTALLMENT LOAN INTEREST	**
COMMERCIAL LOANS	25000
COMMERCIAL LOAN INTEREST	**
OTHER INVESTMENTS	2000
OTHER INVESTMENT INTEREST	**
TOTAL CURRENT ASSETS	**
TOTAL ASSETS	**
LIABILITIES AND EQUITY:	
REGULAR SAVINGS	1000
REGULAR SAVING INTEREST	5.5%
INTEREST PLUS CHECKING	15000
INTEREST PLUS CHECKING INTEREST	6%
MONEY MARKET CERTIFICATES	4000
MONEY MARKET INTEREST	**
OTHER BORROWED FUNDS	5000
OTHER BORROWED FUNDS INTEREST	**
TOTAL CURRENT LIABILITIES	**
RETAINED EARNINGS	38000
TOTAL EQUITY	**
TOTAL LIABILITIES PLUS EQUITY	**

** calculations from the Tutorial 1 Case Problem 3 model.

Change only the information above, do not revise the period decisions in the cash flow statement of FINPLAN4.

For YEAR1 through YEAR5:

In the income statement:

The following lines items are calculated by multiplying the loans with the interest for than loan:

Real estate mortgages earnings, installment loans earnings, commercial loans earnings, other investments earnings, regular savings earnings, interest plus checking earnings, money market earnings, and other borrowed funds earnings.

In the balance sheet:

Prime interest goes up 3 percent for year1 and year2, falls 10 percent in year3, increases 7 percent in year4, then falls 8 percent in year5. Real estate mortgages goes up 2,000 for year1 and year2, falls 9,000 in year3, increases 7,000 in year4, then falls 4,000 in year5. Real estate mortgages interest goes up 3 percent for year1 and year2, falls 10 percent in year3, increases 7 percent in year4, then falls 5 percent in year5. Installment loans goes up 2,000 for year1 and year2, falls 9,000 in year3, increases 7000 in year4, then falls 4,000 in year5. Commercial loans goes up 2000 for year1 and year2, falls 9,000 in year3, increases 7,000 in year4, then falls 4,000 in year5. Other investments goes up 2,000 for year1 and year2, falls 9,000 in year3, increases 7000 in year4, then falls 4000 in year. Regular savings is the same for all 6 years. Regular savings Interest goes up 3 percent for year1 and year2, falls 10 percent in year3, increases 7 percent in year4, then falls 8 percent in year5. Interest plus Checking goes up 2,000 for year1 and year2, falls 9,000 in year3, increases 7,000 in year4, then falls 4,000 in year5. Interest Plus Checking interest goes up 3 percent for year1 and year2, falls 10 percent in year3, increases 7 percent in year 4, then falls 8 percent in year5. Money Market Certificates goes up 4,000 for year, 2,000 for year2, falls by 9,000 in year3, increases by 7,000 in year4, then falls by 5,000 in year5. Other Borrowed Funds goes up 2,000 for year1 and year2, falls 10,000 in year3, increases 7,000 in year4, then falls 4,000 in year5.

In the statement of change in financial position:
The following line items are calculated using the logic included in the FINPLAN4 model: from interest margin, subtotal from operations, total source.

4. Harvest University

The chief financial officer reviewed the model created from the data. You think that is does not clearly represent the university as a whole. You want a financial plan that includes the Balance Sheet, Income Statement, and Statement of Change in Financial Position. Using FINPLAN4 as a model, you want to change the data in Year0 to:

	YEAR0
INCOME STATEMENT	
STUDENTS	20000
CREDIT HOUR RATIO	32
AVERAGE FULL TIME FACULTY SALARY	3500
AVERAGE PART TIME FACULTY SALARY	10000
FULL TO FTE RATIO	90%
TUITION PER CREDIT HOUR	80
LAB FEE PERCENT	20%
CREDIT HOURS	**
TUITION	**
LAB FEES	**
ENDOWMENT INCOME	250000
OTHER INCOME	100000
TOTAL REVENUES	**
ADMINISTRATIVE SALARIES	4550000
SECRETARIAL SALARIES	3250000
FTE FACULTY	**
FULL TIME FACULTY SALARIES	**
PART TIME FACULTY SALARIES	**
TAS SALARIES	285000
OTHER SALARIES	1050000
TOTAL SALARIES	**
FRINGE BENEFITS	**
UTILITIES	2200000
OTHER OPERATING EXPENSES	800000
TOTAL EXPENSES	**
NET INCOME	**

** calculations from the Tutorial 1 Case Problem 4 model.

BALANCE SHEET

	YEAR0
ASSETS:	
CASH	153000
INVESTMENTS	0
ACCOUNTS RECEIVABLE	20900
INVENTORY RATIO	0
INVENTORY	21000
TOTAL CURRENT ASSETS	**
PROPERTY	100000
PLANT AND EQUIPMENT	350000
NET PP AND E	**
TOTAL ASSETS	**
LIABILITIES AND EQUITY:	
ACCOUNTS PAYABLE	12400
ACCRUED WAGES	1000
SHORT TERM DEBT	19000
TOTAL CURRENT ASSETS	**
LONG TERM DEBT	200000
RETAINED EARNINGS	412500
TOTAL EQUITY	**
TOTAL LIABILITIES PLUS EQUITY	**

** calculations from the FINPLAN4 model.

Change only the information above; do not revise the period decisions in the cash flow statement of FINPLAN4.

For YEAR1 through YEAR5:

In the income statement:

Students goes up 500 every year, average full-time faculty salary goes up 10,000 every year, average part time faculty salary goes up 10,000 every year, tuition per credit hour goes up 4 every year, lab fee percent goes up 2 percent each year, endowment income increases 10,000 each year, other income increases 10,000 each year, administrative salaries increases 500,000 each year, secretarial salaries goes up 5,000,000 each year, TAS salaries goes up 1,000,000 each year, other salaries goes up 1,000,000 each year, utilities increases 1,000,000 every year, and other operating expenses increases 100,000 every year. The following line items are calculated using the logic included in the projected income statement model created in Tutorial 1: tuition, credit hours, lab fees, total revenues, fte faculty, full-time faculty salaries, part time faculty salaries, total salaries, fringe benefits, total expenses, and net income.

In the balance sheet:

Cash is 165,000 in year1, 195,000 in year2, 197,000 in year3, 207,000 in year4, and 208,000 in year5; accounts receivable increases 10,000 each year; inventory ratio is 22 percent for all of the years. The following line items are calculated using the logic included in the FINPLAN4 model: investments, inventory, total current assets, property, plant and equipment, net PP and E, total assets, accounts payable, short term debt, total current assets, long term debt, retained earnings, total equity, and total liabilities plus equity.

In the statement of change in financial position:

The following line items are calculated using the logic included in the FINPLAN4 model: from net income, subtotal from operations, change in accounts payable, change in accrued wages, change in short term debt, total sources, change in investments, change in cash, change in accounts receivable, and change in inventory.

Make these revisions to a copy of the FINPLAN4 model, then print the model and its solution.

5. Midwest Universal Gas

Mary, Francis, and Petro reviewed the model you created from their data. They think that is does not clearly represent the company as a whole. They want a financial plan that includes the Balance Sheet, Income Statement, and Statement of Change in Financial Position. Using FINPLAN4 as a model, Frosty wants you to change the data in Year0 to:

	YEAR0
INCOME STATEMENT	
SALES	216000
COS PERCENT	0
COST OF SALES	8567372
GROSS PROFIT	**
SELLING EXP RATIO	0
SELLING EXPENSES	311042
ADMIN EXP RATIO	0
ADMINISTRATIVE EXPENSES	162500
INTEREST EXPENSES	60999
DEPREC EXP RATIO	0
DEPRECIATION EXPENSES	103544
OPERATING EXPENSES	**
INVEST INTEREST RATE	0
INVESTMENT INTEREST	0
INCOME BEFORE TAX	**
INCOME TAX RATE	0
INCOME TAX	17600
NET INCOME	**
BALANCE SHEET	
ASSETS:	
CASH	195000
INVESTMENTS	0
AVERAGE DAILY REVENUE	0
DAYS RECEIVABLE	0
ACCOUNTS RECEIVABLE	300000
INVENTORY RATIO	0
INVENTORY	75000
TOTAL CURRENT ASSETS	**
PROPERTY	265000
PLANT AND EQUIPMENT	800000
ACCUMULATED DEPRECIATION	-100000
NET PP AND E	**
TOTAL ASSETS	**

** calculated from the FINPLAN4 model.

	YEAR0
LIABILITIES AND EQUITY:	
ACCOUNTS PAYABLE	250000
ACCRUED WAGES RATIO	0
ACCRUED WAGES	30000
ACCRUED TAXES RATIO	0
ACCRUED TAXES	59483
SHORT TERM DEBT	139333
TOTAL CURRENT ASSETS	**
LONG TERM DEBT	402000
COMMON STOCK	**
RETAINED EARNINGS	204184
TOTAL EQUITY	**
TOTAL LIABILITIES PLUS EQUITY	**
SHARES	9000

** calculations from the FINPLAN4 model.

Change only the information above, do not revise the period decisions in the cash flow statement of FINPLAN4.

For YEAR1 through YEAR5:

In the income statement:

Sales goes up every year by 240,000, cos percent is 40 percent for all of the years, selling exp ratio is 14.4 percent for all of the years, admin exp ratio is 8 percent for all of the years, interest expense is calculated from the FINPLAN4 model with 12 percent as the short term debt interest rate and 9 percent as the long term debt interest rate, depreciation expenses ratio is 8.6 percent for all of the years, invest interest rate is 10 percent for all of the years, income tax rate is 40 percent for all of the years. The following line items are calculated using the logic included in the FINPLAN4 model: cost of sales, gross profit, selling expenses, administrative expenses, depreciation expenses, operating expenses, investment interest, income before tax, income tax, and net income.

In the balance sheet:

Cash goes up every year by 11,000, inventory ratio is 22 percent for all of the years, inventory goes up every year by 1500, accounts payable goes up every year by 20,000, accrued wages ratio is 5 percent for all of the years, accrued taxes ratio is 25 percent for all of the years. The following line items are calculated using the logic included in the FINPLAN4 model: investments, average daily revenue, days receivable, accounts receivable, total current assets, property, plant and equipment, accumulated depreciation, net PP and E, total assets, accrued wages, accrued taxes, short term debt, total current assets, long term debt, retained earnings, total equity, and total liabilities plus equity.

In the statement of change in financial position:

The following line items are calculated using the logic included in the FINPLAN4 model: from net income, add depreciation, subtotal from operations, change in accounts payable, change in accrued wages, change in accrued taxes, change in short term debt, total sources, change in investments, change in cash, change in accounts receivable, and change in inventory.

Revise a copy of FINPLAN4, then print the model and its solution.

6. General Memorial Hospital

Berry and Gloria reviewed the model you created from their data. They think that is does not clearly represent the company as a whole. They want a financial plan that includes the Balance Sheet, Income Statement, and Statement of Change in Financial Position. Using FINPLAN4 as an example model, Berry wants you to change the data in Year0 to:

	YEAR0
INCOME STATEMENT	
SALES	12647000
ADMINISTRATIVE EXPENSES	250000
INTEREST EXPENSES	22000
DEPRECIABLE ASSETS	500000
DEPRECIATION EXPENSES	**
OPERATING EXPENSES	**
NET INCOME	**
BALANCE SHEET	
ASSETS:	
CASH	0
INVESTMENTS	0
AVERAGE DAILY REVENUE	0
DAYS RECEIVABLE	0
ACCOUNTS RECEIVABLE	20000
INVENTORY	21000
TOTAL CURRENT ASSETS	**
PLANT AND EQUIPMENT	500000
ACCUMULATED DEPRECIATION	-60000
NET PP AND E	**
TOTAL ASSETS	**
LIABILITIES AND EQUITY:	
ACCOUNTS PAYABLE	12400
ACCRUED WAGES RATIO	0
ACCRUED WAGES	1000
SHORT TERM DEBT	19000
TOTAL CURRENT ASSETS	**
LONG TERM DEBT	200000
COMMON STOCK	**
RETAINED EARNINGS	148600
TOTAL EQUITY	**
TOTAL LIABILITIES PLUS EQUITY	**
SHARES	2000

** calculations from the FINPLAN4 model.

Change only the information above, do not revise the period decisions in the cash flow statement of FINPLAN4.

For YEAR1 through YEAR5:

In the income statement:

Sales is 11,694,000 for year1; 10,805,000 for year2; 99,750,000 for year3; 9,202,000 for year4; and 8,481,000 for year5; administration expenses goes up every year by 100,000; interest expenses is 19,800 for year1; 17,600 for year2; 15,400 for year3; 13,200 for year4; and 11,000 for year5; depreciable assets decrease every year by 50,000; depreciation expenses is calculated by taking depreciable assets and dividing it by 6. The following line items are calculated using the logic included in the FINPLAN4 model: operating expenses, net income.

In the balance sheet:

Cash is 65,000 for year1; 95,000 for year2; 97,000 for year3; 10,700 for year4, and 108,000 for year5; accts pay ratio is 12 percent for all of the years; accounts payable compounds each year by the accts pay ratio as its growth rate; accrued wages ratio is 5 percent for all of the years. The following line items are calculated using the logic included in the FINPLAN4 model: investments, average daily revenue, days receivable, accounts receivable, total current assets, accumulated depreciation, net PP and E, total assets, accrued wages, short term debt, total current assets, long term debt, retained earnings, total equity, and total liabilities plus equity.

In the statement of change in financial position:

The following line items are calculated using the logic included in the FINPLAN4 model: from net income, add depreciation, subtotal from operations, change in accounts payable, change in accrued wages, change in short term debt, total sources, change in investments, change in cash, change in accounts receivable, and change in inventory. There is no equipment purchases or property purchases, so these amounts are set to zero.

Make a copy of model FINPLAN4 and revise it for these changes. Print the model and its solution.

7. River City

Lisa and Frank reviewed the model you created with their data. They think that is does not clearly represent the city as a whole. They want a financial plan that includes the Balance Sheet, Income Statement, and Statement of Change in Financial Position. Frank agrees that SALES can be treated as an equivalent to the city's tax revenues. So they can use the FINPLAN4 model in preparing their projections, they agree to leave the INCOME TAX calculation in the model, but to set the values to zero. Using FINPLAN4 as a starting point, Frank wants you to change the data in Year0 to:

	YEAR0
INCOME STATEMENT	
SALES	23745000
ADMIN EXP RATIO	0
ADMINISTRATIVE EXPENSES	52000
INTEREST EXPENSES	26300
DEPREC EXP RATIO	0
DEPRECIATION EXPENSES	32000
OPERATING EXPENSES	**
INVEST INTEREST RATE	0
INVESTMENT INTEREST	0
INCOME BEFORE TAX	**
INCOME TAX RATE	0
INCOME TAX	17600
NET INCOME	**
BALANCE SHEET	
ASSETS:	
CASH	53000
INVESTMENTS	0
AVERAGE DAILY REVENUE	0
DAYS RECEIVABLE	0
ACCOUNTS RECEIVABLE	20900
INVENTORY RATIO	0
INVENTORY	21000
TOTAL CURRENT ASSETS	**
PROPERTY	100000
PLANT AND EQUIPMENT	350000
ACCUMULATED DEPRECIATION	-60000
NET PP AND E	**
TOTAL ASSETS	**

** calculated from the FINPLAN4 model.

	YEAR0
LIABILITIES AND EQUITY:	
ACCOUNTS PAYABLE	12400
ACCRUED WAGES RATIO	0
ACCRUED WAGES	1000
ACCRUED TAXES RATIO	0
ACCRUED TAXES	3900
SHORT TERM DEBT	19000
TOTAL CURRENT ASSETS	**
LONG TERM DEBT	200000
COMMON STOCK	**
RETAINED EARNINGS	148600
TOTAL EQUITY	**
TOTAL LIABILITIES PLUS EQUITY	**
SHARES	2000

** calculations from the FINPLAN4 model.

Change only the information above, do not revise the period decisions in the cash flow statement of FINPLAN4.

For YEAR1 through YEAR5:

In the income statement:

Sales is 3.785.000 for year1, 38.266.000 for year2, 3.866.000 for year3, 3.907.000 for year4, and 3.949.000 for year5; administration expenses ratio is 8 percent for all of the years; interest expense is calculated from the FINPLAN4 model with 10 percent as the short term debt interest rate and 12 percent as the long term debt interest rate; depreciation expenses ratio is 9 percent for all of the years; investment interest rate is 10 percent for all of the years; income tax rate is zero for all of the years. The following line items are calculated using the logic included in the FINPLAN4 model: administrative expenses, depreciation expenses, operating expenses, investment interest, income before tax, income tax, and net income.

In the balance sheet:

Cash is 65.000 for year1, 95.000 for year2, 97.000 fore year3, 107.000 for year4, and 108.000 for year5; inventory ratio is 22 percent for all of the years; inventory compounds each year by the inventory ratio which is its growth rate; accounts payable ratio is 12 percent for all of the years; accounts payable compounds each year by the accounts payable ratio which is its growth rate; accrued wages ratio is 5 percent for all of the years; accrued taxes ratio is 25 percent for all of the years. The following line items are calculated using the logic included in the FINPLAN4 model: investments, average daily revenue, days receivable, accounts receivable, total current assets, property, plant and equipment, accumulated depreciation, net PP and E, total assets, accrued wages, accrued taxes, short term debt, total current assets, long term debt, retained earnings, total equity, and total liabilities plus equity.

In the statement of change in financial position:

The following line items are calculated using the logic included in the FINPLAN4 model: from net income, add depreciation, subtotal from operations, change in accounts payable, change in accrued wages, change in accrued taxes, change in short term debt, total sources, change in investments, change in cash, change in accounts receivable, and change in inventory.

Make a copy of the model FINPLAN4 and revise it to include these changes. Print the model and its solution.

Tutorial 12

Validating and Revising a Financial Statement Model

Introduction to Model Validation and Revision

Once you have developed a business planning model, you can use it to explore a variety of what-if alternatives. These alternatives can be simple changes in planning assumptions that require only changes to data, or they may be complex changes that result in modifying model logic. Throughout these interrogations, it is important to verify that the correct logic is included in the model. **Model validation** is the process of verifying that a model contains the desired and correct logic. In particular, validation focuses on insuring that correct accounting formulas are included in the model. As models are revised in exploring various alternatives, the model must be continuously validated. Historical data and formulas built into a financial statement model are used in validating model logic.

Historical Data

Historical data are most useful in validating the logic of the balance sheet. The solution matrix organization requires an opening balance sheet. These opening balances are used to calculate the subtotals and totals for the assets and the liabilities plus equity. If total assets are *not* equal to total liabilities plus equity, that indicates that an error occurred in either entering the opening balance amount or in the formulas used to calculate the various subtotals and totals in the balance sheet. Furthermore, the total assets and total liabilities plus equity calculated by the model can be compared with the actual financial statements from which the opening balances are obtained to verify them.

When historical data are entered in the income statement, these data values are used to validate the logic for the subtotals and totals in this statement. These calculated values are compared to those from the actual income statement that provided these data. In general, the process is one of entering the data from the historical statements and calculating subtotals and totals that are compared to the data source.

Checking Accounting Relationships

A variety of formulas are used to calculate many planning items in the projected columns beyond the opening balances. When a model is constructed based on the cash-flow-reconciliation approach, model validation is carried out by independently calculating total assets and total liabilities plus equity. Then, if they are not equal, *an error is signaled*. A **check account**, used to detect errors, is calculated as total assets minus total liabilities plus equities. If this account is *not* zero, it indicates that one or more errors have occurred. Because balance-sheet-error cascade frequently occurs (that is, errors accumulate across the planning periods), a convenient error detection account that is calculated is the check change account. The **check change** is the difference between the check account amount last period (t-1) and the check amount in the current period (t). The check change is the amount of error that occurs in any one planning period. With valid accounting logic, the check and check change amounts are zeros. When the check and check change are *not* zero, these values are used to perform a "search for familiar numbers" on the model solution. That is, rather than reading the logic to locate an error, the solution is scanned to find a number that matches the check or check change. Since an error amount is easily doubled, the check half and check two amounts are calculated and used in locating an error. The logic for these check accounts are *included in the model* so they are calculated with each solution (Figure 12-1). This is preferred to manually calculating these values.

```
\ BUSINESS PLANNING MODEL VALIDATION
\
CHECK = TOTAL ASSETS - TOTAL LIABILITIES PLUS EQUITY
\
CHECK CHANGE = CHECK - PREVIOUS CHECK
\
CHECK HALF = CHECK CHANGE / 2
\
CHECK TWO = CHECK CHANGE * 2
```

Figure 12-1 Validation Check Logic

Besides these check accounts, a check nine can be included in the model that is calculated by dividing the check change account number by nine. A division by nine is applied in tracking down transposition errors. Although this check is useful in verifying historical data, it does not provide checking for the calculated values that comprise a majority of the planning model. As a result, the inclusion of this calculation in your model is optional.

Check accounts signal the occurrence of an error when they are not zero (Figure 12-2). However, these accounts do not indicate the location of the error in the income statement, balance sheet, or cash-flow statement. The error could be in any of the three financial statements, although it is calculated as the difference between total assets and total liabilities plus equity. You need to locate the source of the error within your planning model.

```
\ BUSINESS PLANNING MODEL VALIDATION
\
CHECK          0.00    822.22    836.22    891.22    919.22    974.22
\
CHECK CHANGE   0.00    822.22     14.00     55.00     28.00     55.00
\
CHECK HALF     0.00    411.11      7.00     27.50     14.00     27.50
\
CHECK TWO      0.00  1,644.44     28.00    110.00     56.00    110.00
```

Figure 12-2 Check Accounts Signal Error

Let's include these check accounts for validating model logic in FINPLAN4.

To include the check accounts in a business planning model:

❶ Verify that model FINPLAN4 is displayed in your currently active window. Access the MRBCS Models and Reports file and this model, as necessary.

❷   Type the check account logic that appears as Figure 12-1 at the bottom of the model.

❸   Click **File**, then click **Save As** to display the Save As dialog box, type **FINPLAN5** in the Entity Name text box, then click the **OK button** to rename the model as you save it.

Next the model is solved.

❹   Click the **Solve button** in the toolbar, then click the **OK button** to accept the solve defaults. Inspect the check accounts. They should all display zeros.

❺   Print the model for your reference.

Now let's include an intentional error in model FINPLAN5 by incorrectly using a SUM function so you can see how the check accounts signal the occurrence of an error.

To introduce an intentional error caused by a SUM function in a planning model:

❶   Verify that model FINPLAN5 is displayed in your currently active window.

❷   Locate the formula that calculates TOTAL CURRENT ASSETS.

❸   Edit the formula so TOTAL CURRENT ASSETS is calculated as **SUM(CASH .. INVENTORY)**

❹   Click the **Solve button** in the toolbar, then click the **OK button** to display the default solution.

❺   Locate the check accounts in the solution. These accounts now display nonzero values similar to those shown previously in Figure 12-2 and signal the occurrence of an error in the model.

❻   Click the Model window's Control Menu box to close this window, then click the **No button** so the intentional error is not saved.

Once an error is detected with the check accounts, it needs to be located and corrected. Before exploring strategies for locating and correcting errors, let's consider alternative forms of the cash-flow statements and additional check accounts that may be used in your planning model.

Alternative Cash Flow Statements

In Tutorial 11, a statement of change in financial position is used as the cash-flow statement for the cash-flow-reconciliation approach of model construction. Other arrangements of cash-flow statements may be used with the cash-flow-reconciliation approach. These cash-flow statements may readily take one of three arrangements as follows:

- Sources and uses of funds
- Cash receipts and cash disbursements
- Sources and uses of working capital

Model FINPLAN5 and its predecessors all contain a sources and uses of funds statement or a statement of change in financial position as the cash-flow statement. For cash-flow reconciliation, the particular form of the cash-flow statement is *not* important. What is important is that your planning model includes a cash-flow statement. The cash-flow statement you select should present this information in a form most readily understood and used for decision making. A statement of cash receipts and cash disbursements focuses on the impact of all transactions on cash and presents this information in a form most useable to many small business owners and managers. Receipts and disbursements readily shows those activities that generated cash and those that consumed cash. A sources and uses of working capital statement focuses on changes that affect working capital rather than cash. **Working capital** is the difference between the current assets and the current liabilities. Working capital is affected by changes in inventories and payables. This is a more comprehensive view of current assets and current liabilities, rather than just focusing on cash, investments, and short-term debt.

Cash Receipts and Cash Disbursements

An example of a statement of cash receipts and cash disbursements appears as Figure 12-3. This cash-flow logic replaces that for the Statement of Change in Financial Position in model FINPLAN5. However, the same logic is used to calculate the INVESTMENT INCREASE, INVESTMENT DECREASE, SHORT-TERM BORROWING, and SHORT-TERM REPAYMENT for the automatic borrowing and repayment of debt with investments. The same logic is still used for the check accounts in the model.

```
\ STATEMENT OF CASH RECEIPTS AND CASH DISBURSEMENTS
\(CASH FLOW STATEMENT)
COLUMNS YEAR0, YEAR1, YEAR2, YEAR3, YEAR4, YEAR5
\
BEGINNING CASH = 0, PREVIOUS ENDING CASH
\
\CASH RECEIPTS:
CASH SALES = 0 , SALES - ACCOUNTS RECEIVABLE
RECEIVABLES COLLECTED = 0, PREVIOUS ACCOUNTS RECEIVABLE
OTHER INCOME RECEIVED = 0, INVESTMENT INTEREST
TOTAL CASH RECEIPTS = 0, CASH SALES + RECEIVABLES COLLECTED + '
       OTHER INCOME RECEIVED
\
\CASH DISBURSEMENTS:
COST OF SALES PAID = 0, COST OF SALES - ACCOUNTS PAYABLE - '
       PREVIOUS INVENTORY
ACCOUNTS PAYABLE PAID = 0, PREVIOUS ACCOUNTS PAYABLE
INVENTORY PURCHASES = 0, INVENTORY
OPERATING EXPENSES PAID = 0, OPERATING EXPENSES - '
       DEPRECIATION EXPENSES - ACCRUED WAGES
ACCRUED WAGES PAID = 0, PREVIOUS ACCRUED WAGES
INCOME TAXES PAID = 0, PREVIOUS ACCRUED TAXES + '
       (INCOME TAX - ACCRUED TAXES)
\PERIOD DECISION VARIABLES:
PROPERTY PURCHASES = 0
EQUIPMENT PURCHASES = 0, 30000, 20000, 26000, 37000, 47000
LONG-TERM DEBT PAYMENT = 0, 20000, 20000, 20000, 20000, 50000
TOTAL CASH DISBURSEMENTS = 0, SUM(COST OF SALES PAID .. '
       LONG-TERM DEBT PAYMENT)
\
```

Figure 12-3 Cash Receipts and Cash Disbursements Logic *(continued)*

```
\FINANCING:
\(AUTOMATIC BORROWING AND REPAYMENT OF DEBT)
SUBTOTAL ENDING CASH = 0, BEGINNING CASH + TOTAL CASH RECEIPTS - '
        TOTAL CASH DISBURSEMENT
PLANNED CASH = 0, CASH
CASH EXCESS = 0, MAXIMUM(0,(SUBTOTAL ENDING CASH - PLANNED CASH))
CASH DEFICIENCY = 0, MAXIMUM(0,(PLANNED CASH - SUBTOTAL ENDING CASH)
\
                    •
                    •
                    •
        (same logic for INVESTMENT INCREASE, INVESTMENT DECREASE,
            SHORT-TERM BORROWING, and SHORT-TERM REPAYMENT)
                    •
                    •
\
ENDING CASH = CASH, BEGINNING CASH + TOTAL CASH RECEIPTS - '
        TOTAL CASH DISBURSEMENTS - INVESTMENT INCREASE + '
        INVESTMENT DECREASE + SHORT-TERM BORROWING - '
        SHORT-TERM REPAYMENT
```

Figure 12-3 Cash Receipts and Cash Disbursements Logic

This statement contains two balances: BEGINNING CASH and ENDING CASH. All other planning items are flows that are grouped as cash receipts, cash disbursements, and financing. Cash receipts and cash disbursements focus on the cash that is generated and consumed in the operation of the business. The calculations of CASH SALES and RECEIVABLES COLLECTED are typical of the formulas used throughout this statement with complementary logic applied in their calculation. The timing differences in making a sale and collecting the cash for that sale are a primary focus of these calculations. CASH SALES are those sales made and collected in the current period, whereas RECEIVABLES COLLECTED are the credit sales from the prior period that are collected in the current period. Similar calculations are used for OTHER INCOME RECEIVED, COST OF SALES PAID, ACCOUNTS PAYABLE PAID, INVENTORY PURCHASES, OPERATING EXPENSES PAID, ACCRUED WAGES PAID, and INCOME TAXES PAID.

Period decisions that require cash are included in this statement similar to their application in the sources and uses of funds statements. The SUBTOTAL ENDING CASH is an intermediate calculation of the cash balance before any automatic borrowing and repayment of debt. This is used to calculate the CASH EXCESS or CASH DEFICIENCY that subsequently determines the INVESTMENT INCREASE, INVESTMENT DECREASE, SHORT-TERM BORROWING, and SHORT-TERM REPAYMENT.

Model FINPLAN5 is modified to include the statement of cash receipts and cash disbursements in place of the statement of sources and uses of funds (change in financial position). This is accomplished by removing the old cash-flow statement logic and replacing it with the new logic. Let's do that.

To modify a model to include a statement of cash receipts and cash disbursements:

❶   Verify that model FINPLAN5 is displayed in your active window by accessing this model as necessary.

❷   Edit model FINPLAN5 by deleting the old cash-flow statement and typing the revised cash-flow statement that appears in Figure 12-3. Do not enter the COLUMNS statement that is for your reference. The logic for the variables INVESTMENT INCREASE, INVESTMENT DECREASE, SHORT TERM BORROWING, and SHORT-TERM REPAYMENT should remain in the revised cash-flow statement. Review the logic and make any edit corrections.

❸   Click **File**, click **Save As** to display the Save As dialog box, type **CASH** in the Entity Name text box, then click the **OK button** to save the model with the revised cash-flow statement.

Now the model is solved.

❹   Click the **Solve button** in the toolbar, then click the **OK button** to accept the solve defaults. Inspect the solution. Verify that the check accounts are all zeros.

TROUBLE? If the check accounts are not all zeros, you made a mistake in revising the model. Review the logic you entered and make the necessary corrections, then repeat Step 4.

In this manner, the cash-flow reconciliation approach to business modeling is implemented with the statement of cash receipts and cash disbursements. The model validation remains based on the same application of the check accounts to signal errors.

Sources and Uses of Working Capital

An example of a sources and uses of working-capital statement appears as shown in Figure 12-4. The excess of current assets over current liabilities is the amount of working capital. Working capital represents assets financed with long-term capital sources that do not require near-term repayment. Therefore, the greater the working capital, the greater is the cushion of protection available to short term creditors and the greater is the assurance that short-term debt will be paid when due. Changes in the long-term sources and uses of working capital determine the amount of working capital generated in the current period. This working capital change then appears as changes in the current asset and current liabilities planning items. So, the long-term sources and uses of working capital are equal to the net change in current assets and current liabilities. To reflect these changes, the statement is organized in the section of working capital sources, working capital uses, and changes in working capital.

```
\ STATEMENT OF CHANGE IN FINANCIAL POSITION
\(SOURCES AND USES OF WORKING CAPITAL)
COLUMNS YEAR0, YEAR1, YEAR2, YEAR3, YEAR4, YEAR5
\
\WORKING CAPITAL SOURCES:
FROM NET INCOME = 0, NET INCOME
ADD DEPRECIATION = 0, DEPRECIATION EXPENSES
SUBTOTAL FROM OPERATIONS = FROM NET INCOME + ADD DEPRECIATION
INCREASE IN LONG-TERM DEBT = 0, MAXIMUM(0, '
       LONG-TERM DEBT - PREVIOUS LONG-TERM DEBT)
SALE OF COMMON STOCK = 0, MAXIMUM(0, COMMON STOCK - '
       PREVIOUS COMMON STOCK)
TOTAL SOURCES OF WORKING CAPITAL = '
       SUM(SUBTOTAL FROM OPERATIONS .. SALE OF COMMON STOCK)
\
```

Figure 12-4 Sources and Uses of Working Capital Logic *(continued)*

```
\WORKING CAPITAL USES:
PROPERTY PURCHASES = 0
EQUIPMENT PURCHASES = 0, 30000, 20000, 26000, 37000, 47000
LONG-TERM DEBT PAYMENT = 0, 20000, 20000, 20000, 20000, 30000
TOTAL USES OF WORKING CAPITAL = SUM(PROPERTY PURCHASES .. '
        LONG-TERM DEBT PAYMENT)
\
CHANGE IN WORKING CAPITAL = TOTAL SOURCES OF WORKING CAPITAL - '
        TOTAL USES OF WORKING CAPITAL
\


\CHANGES IN WORKING CAPITAL:
CHANGE IN INVESTMENTS = 0, INVESTMENTS - PREVIOUS INVESTMENTS
CHANGE IN CASH = 0, CASH - PREVIOUS CASH
CHANGE IN ACCOUNTS RECEIVABLE = 0, ACCOUNTS RECEIVABLE - '
        PREVIOUS ACCOUNTS RECEIVABLE
CHANGE IN INVENTORY = 0, INVENTORY - PREVIOUS INVENTORY
CHANGE IN ACCOUNTS PAYABLE = 0, PREVIOUS ACCOUNTS PAYABLE - '
        ACCOUNTS PAYABLE
CHANGE IN ACCRUED WAGES = 0, PREVIOUS ACCRUED WAGES - '
        ACCRUED WAGES
CHANGE IN ACCRUED TAXES = 0, PREVIOUS ACCRUED TAXES - '
        ACCRUED TAXES
CHANGE IN SHORT-TERM DEBT = 0, PREVIOUS SHORT-TERM DEBT - '
        SHORT-TERM DEBT


\
CHANGES IN WORKING CAPITAL = SUM(CHANGES IN INVESTMENTS .. '
        CHANGE IN SHORT-TERM DEBT)

                        •
                        •
                        •
```

Figure 12-4 Sources and Uses of Working Capital Logic

If they occur, an INCREASE IN LONG-TERM DEBT and the SALE OF COMMON STOCK are sources of working capital. The uses of working capital are the period decisions that affect long term assets and liabilities. These are input in the same manner as that used in the other arrangements of the cash-flow statement.

For changes in working capital from the current assets and current liabilities, working capital is increased by an increase in an asset or by a decrease in a liability. The CHANGE IN ACCOUNTS RECEIVABLE and CHANGE IN ACCOUNTS PAYABLE illustrate these calculations. If an asset balance decreases, then a negative amount is calculated that represents a decrease in working capital. So, for the changes in current assets and current liabilities, negative values indicate a decrease in working capital for that particular planning item.

In Figure 12-4, the CHANGE IN WORKING CAPITAL represents the long-term sources and uses, while the CHANGES IN WORKING CAPITAL reflects the changes in the current assets and current liabilities. Here, the difference between "CHANGE" and "CHANGES" is important in specifying two distinct planning items with their individual methods of calculation. If the logic is correct, these two planning items should produce the same result. However, they need to be calculated separately.

For the automatic borrowing and repayment of debt, the logic is modified for calculating the CASH EXCESS and CASH DEFICIENCY (Figure 12-5). The PRELIM CHANGES is an intermediate variable that calculates the changes in the current assets and current liabilities without the changes in investments or short-term debt. Once again, these amounts are then calculated from the CASH EXCESS and CASH DEFICIENCY using the same logic for the INVESTMENT INCREASE, INVESTMENT DECREASE, SHORT-TERM BORROWING, and SHORT-TERM REPAYMENT.

\ STATEMENT OF CHANGE IN FINANCIAL POSITION
\(SOURCES AND USES OF WORKING CAPITAL STATEMENT)
COLUMNS YEAR0, YEAR1, YEAR2, YEAR3, YEAR4, YEAR5
\
             •
             •

\(AUTOMATIC BORROWING AND REPAYMENT OF DEBT)
PRELIM CHANGES = 0, SUM(CHANGE IN CASH .. CHANGE IN ACCRUED TAXES)
CASH EXCESS = 0, MAXIMUM(0,(CHANGE IN WORKING CAPITAL - '
     PRELIM CHANGES))
CASH DEFICIENCY = 0, MAXIMUM(0,(PRELIM CHANGES - '
     CHANGE IN WORKING CAPITAL)

             •
             •

    (same logic for INVESTMENT INCREASE, INVESTMENT DECREASE,
      SHORT-TERM BORROWING, and SHORT-TERM REPAYMENT)
             •
             •

Figure 12-5 Automatic Borrowing and Repayment Logic for Working Capital Statement

---

Model FINPLAN5 is modified to include the sources and uses of working capital statement in place of the statement of changes in financial position. This is accomplished by removing the old cash-flow statement logic and replacing it with the new logic. Let's make these changes.

To modify a model to include a sources and uses of working capital statement:

❶   Verify that model FINPLAN5 is displayed in your active window by accessing this model as necessary.

❷   Edit model FINPLAN5 by deleting the old cash-flow statement and typing the revised cash-flow statement that appears in Figures 12-4 and 12-5. Do not enter the COLUMNS statement, which is for your reference. The logic for the variables INVESTMENT INCREASE, INVESTMENT DECREASE, SHORT-TERM BORROWING, and SHORT-TERM REPAYMENT should remain in the revised cash-flow statement. Review the logic and make any edits.

❸   Click **File**, click **Save As** to display the Save As dialog box, type **WORK** in the Entity Name text box, then click the **OK button** to save the model with the revised cash-flow statement.

Now the model is solved.

❹   Click the **Solve button** in the toolbar, then click the **OK button** to accept the solve defaults. Inspect the solution. Verify that the check accounts are all zeros.

TROUBLE? If the check accounts are not all zeros, you made a mistake in revising the model. Review the logic you entered and make the necessary corrections, then repeat Step 4.

The concept of a check account as a built-in test for model logic can be extended to include a check for the working capital statement (Figure 12-6). Like the other check accounts, the desired values are zeros. As you create and modify your planning models, you should consider including other appropriate tests like these as variables calculated in the model. Remember, with an IFPS report definition, you can select the desired row for inclusion in your final report. So, if you do not want to print any of the check accounts, then don't include them in your IFPS report definition.

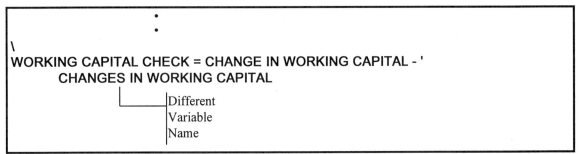

Figure 12-6 Working Capital Check Account

Let's include this check account in the model with the sources and uses of working capital statement.

To include another check account in a model:

❶   Verify that model WORK is displayed in your active window by accessing this model as necessary.

❷   Edit model WORK by adding the logic for calculating the WORKING CAPITAL CHECK as shown in Figure 12-6.

❸   Click **File**, then click **Save** to save the revised model.

Now solve the model.

❹   Click the **Solve button** in the toolbar, then click the **OK button** to accept the solve defaults. Inspect the solution. Verify that the new check account displays zeros in all columns.

This completes the modification of the cash-flow statement as a sources and uses of working capital statement. Although you may include more than one arrangement of the cash-flow statement in your planning model, this or one of the other two arrangements is adequate for the cash-flow-reconciliation approach that assists in validating model logic.

Ratio Analysis

When you use financial ratio analysis to evaluate the expected financial results, the calculation of these ratios is included in your business planning model. Several ratios described in Tutorial 11 are selected for inclusion in the model (Figure 12-7). Of course, you could include other ratios in your model as well.

```
\ FINANCIAL RATIO ANALYSIS
COLUMNS YEAR0, YEAR1, YEAR2, YEAR3, YEAR4, YEAR5
\
CURRENT RATIO = TOTAL CURRENT ASSETS / TOTAL CURRENT LIABILITIES
INVENTORY TURNOVER = 0, COST OF SALE / ((INVENTORY - '
        PREVIOUS INVENTORY) / 2)
RETURN ON SALES = NET INCOME / SALES
RETURN ON ASSETS = NET INCOME / TOTAL ASSETS
RETURN ON EQUITY = NET INCOME / ((TOTAL EQUITY + '
        PREVIOUS TOTAL EQUITY) / 2)
EARNINGS PER SHARE = NET INCOME / SHARES
DEBT RATIO = (SHORT-TERM DEBT + LONG-TERM DEBT) / TOTAL ASSETS
```

Figure 12-7 Projected Financial Ratios

Let's add the ratio analysis to model FINPLAN5 for evaluating the projected financial results.

To include the ratio analysis in a business planning model:

❶   Access model FINPLAN5 as your active entity.

❷   Type the financial ratio logic that appears in Figure 12-7 at the bottom of the model.

❸   Click **File**, then click **Save As** to display the Save As dialog box, type **FINPLAN6** in the Entity Name text box, then click the **OK button** to rename the model as it is saved.

Now solve the model.

❹   Click the **Solve button** in the toolbar, then click the **OK button** to accept the solve defaults. Review the calculated ratios.

❺   Print the model and its solution for your reference.

These ratios are a convenient means for quickly evaluating the overall financial plan in determining the desirability of an alternative.

What If and Continuous Validation

What-if alternatives often focus on changing data values and modifying logic. For example, the SELLING EXPENSE RATIO data value may change from 10 percent to 12 percent. Alternatively, new debt financing can be arranged, such as BANK LOAN, that requires new logic. Data changes seldom cause errors in the model logic, whereas adding new planning items frequently causes errors. The check accounts provide a mechanism for continuously monitoring the validation of your planning model. Whenever a change is made and you solve the model, you should inspect the check accounts to verify they are all zeros. Although you can skip this step for simple data changes, such as that for the SELLING EXPENSE RATIO, you should inspect the check accounts for any other data changes or logic modification. In this manner, the check accounts allow you to *continuously monitor* the validity of your model.

Tracking Down Errors

An error condition is signaled when the check accounts are *not* all zeros. What strategy can you follow in tracking down the location of an error so you can correct it? Actions that you can take in locating errors include the following:

• Use both model logic and the output solution numbers.

Sometimes an error is located by reading the logic. Sometimes an error is spotted by reviewing the solution. By laying out the logic and solution in a side-by-side arrangement and reviewing both the logic and its result, you can often discover the source of an error. Also, the ANALYZE command is useful in displaying the logic and solution values together.

• Review the logic for errors by reading through the model and carefully considering each formula.

Verify that correct growth rate and ratio variables are used in your calculations. Confirm that the cash-flow statement contains the appropriate variables for your income statement and balance sheet, and that complementary logic is used in their calculations. Review SUM functions to insure that only the desired variables are added.

• Use the check accounts to determine the amount of the error(s) and apply the "search for familiar numbers" technique to spot numbers that are the same magnitude as those for the check accounts.

The check accounts provide an indication of the magnitude of an error. If the check change is 43, then an income statement amount of 1000 is not likely to cause this error. Use the check accounts to focus your attention on solution values of approximately the same amount as those calculated for the check accounts.

• Work from left to right across the solution in obtaining a balance with check accounts of zero.

Balance-sheet errors accumulate across the planning periods. The leftmost or first column of the model usually contains the opening balance sheet. You should focus on correcting this error before proceeding to other errors in later time periods. This removes the affect of the error accumulation and allows you to focus on the error in a particular time period.

• Watch for patterns in the check accounts, such as a check change that goes to zero after several periods of being nonzero.

Patterns in the check accounts are frequently caused by conditional logic calculated using the IF-THEN-ELSE in IFPS. When a pattern of nonzeros followed by zeros occurs, you should inspect the logic and solution values for this conditional logic.

• When only one error remains undetected, usually the numbers displayed for one or more of the output solution variables will exactly match the check or check change account pinpointing the location of the error.

In most situations, when only one error remains in a model, there is an exact match between the solution values for one of the check account variables and one of the other variables. The error is frequently located somewhere in the logic that references that variable. The particular variable may not be the cause of the error. It could be that the variable was used incorrectly with complementary logic in one of the other financial statements. However, somewhere in the chain where that variable is used in a calculation you will find the logic error.

•When all check accounts are zero in all columns, review the output for reasonableness.

Through a variety of creative accounting formulas, the check accounts may all be zeros and the model logic still contains an error. For example, the logic could be correct for paying a loan, but eventually the loan balance may become negative because the loan payment is continued after the loan is paid off. A review of the solution for reasonableness should spot these errors. The ratio analysis provides a quick overall summary for your reasonableness check.

•The *last resort* is to review the logic and place a check mark by each balance sheet account that appears in the cash-flow statement and each cash-flow account that occurs in the balance sheet. Then apply check marks in a similar manner for the income statement accounts. All accounts using complementary logic should have check marks. Any accounts without check marks from this process indicate an error in reconciliation.

The cash-flow statement is used to reconcile the logic from the balance sheet and income statement considering how each account affects cash. Complementary logic is used in linking these financial statements. As a result, the check mark procedure should isolate any accounts that were omitted in these calculations.

•When all check accounts are zero and your solution output passes the reasonableness test, produce your final solution for evaluation.

Several solutions may be required in reaching a solution with valid model logic. You should use the check accounts and inspection for reasonableness until you are confident that a good solution exists.

With IFPS, you can print your model and its solution and then manually search through them to spot potential sources of your error. However, with the analysis feature of IFPS, you can let IFPS help you with your search as you review logic and search for familiar numbers. Let's create an intentional error and then see how you can track it down and correct it. The error you will introduce in your model is in the LONG-TERM DEBT in the opening balance. Although you know what the error is, you will gain experience in using the check accounts for model validation.

To include an intentional error in the opening balance sheet:

❶   Access model FINPLAN6 as your active entity.

❷   Locate LONG-TERM DEBT and change the opening balance from 200000 to **20000**, that is, remove one of the zeros.

❸   Click **File**, then click **Save As** to display this dialog box, type **ERROR1** in the Entity Name text box, then click the **OK button** to rename and save the model.

Next solve the model and examine the check accounts.

❹   Click the **Solve button** in the toolbar, then click the **OK button** to accept the solve defaults. Scroll the solution to display the check accounts. See Figure 12-8. Because the CHECK is nonzero in the first column, you know there is an error in the opening balance sheet.

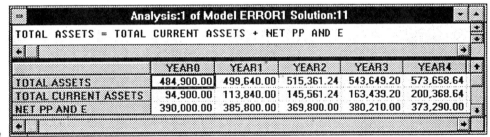

Figure 12-8
Check Accounts
Signal Error

Error in opening
balance sheet

Once an error condition is detected, you can use Analyze to assist you in locating the error. Analyze allows you to view both selected logic and solution values in the same window. Let's use analyze to locate the balance-sheet error.

To use analyze to review model logic and solutions values in locating potential errors:

❶   Verify that the solution is your active window.

❷   Scroll the solution and click **TOTAL ASSETS** to select it.

❸   Click **Analysis**, then click **Analyze** to display the logic and the solutions values of all the variables used in calculating TOTAL ASSETS. See Figure 12-9. Review these values. They all appear correct so you need to continue the search.

Figure 12-9
Analyze Displays
Logic and Solution
Values for
Related Variable

Analysis:1 of Model ERROR1 Solution:11					
TOTAL ASSETS = TOTAL CURRENT ASSETS + NET PP AND E					
	YEAR0	YEAR1	YEAR2	YEAR3	YEAR4
TOTAL ASSETS	484,900.00	499,640.00	515,361.24	543,649.20	573,658.64
TOTAL CURRENT ASSETS	94,900.00	113,840.00	145,561.24	163,439.20	200,368.64
NET PP AND E	390,000.00	385,800.00	369,800.00	380,210.00	373,290.00

❹   Select the solution window, scroll the solution and click **TOTAL LIABILITIES PLUS EQUITY** to select it.

❺   Click **Analysis**, then click **Analyze** to display the logic and related solution values for TOTAL LIABILITIES PLUS EQUITY. See Figure 12-10.

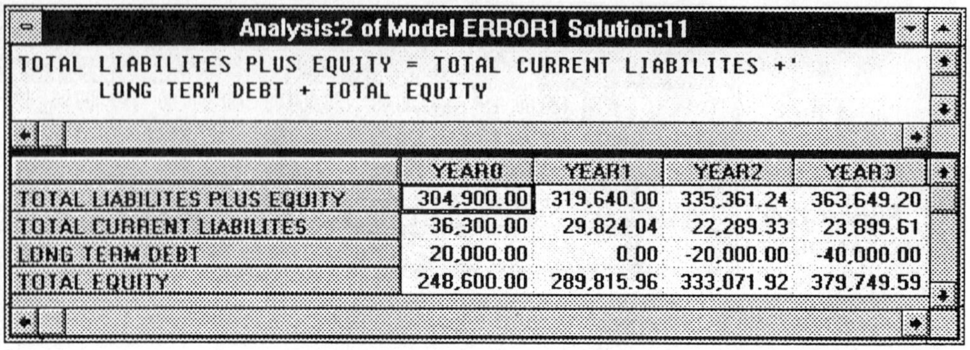

Analysis:2 of Model ERROR1 Solution:11

TOTAL LIABILITES PLUS EQUITY = TOTAL CURRENT LIABILITES +'
LONG TERM DEBT + TOTAL EQUITY

	YEAR0	YEAR1	YEAR2	YEAR3
TOTAL LIABILITES PLUS EQUITY	304,900.00	319,640.00	335,361.24	363,649.20
TOTAL CURRENT LIABILITES	36,300.00	29,824.04	22,289.33	23,899.61
LONG TERM DEBT	20,000.00	0.00	-20,000.00	-40,000.00
TOTAL EQUITY	248,600.00	289,815.96	333,071.92	379,749.59

Figure 12-10 Analyze Displays Logic and Solution Values for Related Variable

❻ Review these values and notice that the LONG-TERM DEBT balance is zero in column YEAR1 and becomes negative after that. Because the balance is negative, this appears as the error condition. Also, if the check account error amount of 180000 in each column is added to the opening balance then this would not produce a negative result. You conclude you found the error and are ready to correct it.

❼ Select the Model window and change the opening LONG-TERM DEBT balance from 20000 to **200000** by adding the missing zero.

❽ Click the **Solve button** in the toolbar, click the **OK button** for the default solution, and scroll to the check accounts to verify they are now all zeros and the error is corrected.

Sequential Model Revision Technique

Sequential model revision is the step-by-step process of making a series of modifications to model logic. Suppose you need to add several new planning items to a model that is complete with all check accounts producing zeros. When making these modifications, follow two fundamental procedures. First, make all the changes to the model at one time, adding all the new planning items. Then solve the model and inspect the check accounts. Second, you could *add the logic for each planning item one at time;* this method is called *sequential model revision*. As each planning item is included in the model, you solve it and inspect the check accounts. If no errors are indicated, continue by including the next planning item.

With sequential model revision, the number of potential statements in your model where an error may occur is usually limited to only three or four. You can readily focus on the logic in these newly added statements as you locate and correct the error. This is much easier than attempting to track down an error that may be caused by a much larger number of statements that you added to your model all at one time.

Sequential model revision requires a business planning model with a complete income statement, balance sheet, and cash-flow statement that includes the check account logic. However, this model can have a very limited number of planning items in each statement. For example, the income statement may include only one or two different expenses other than depreciation and interest. Once the basic model its validated, then additional expense items could be included. And, similarly for assets and liabilities. Starting with a complete, but simplified, integrated financial statement model and expanding it using sequential model revision is a **top-down approach** to model development. The top-down approach is a good strategy for developing a complex business planning model that starts with a valid model and uses continuous model validation to insure the integrity of your model logic.

Simultaneous equations can cause a problem in making model revisions. If your model contains simultaneous equations, how do you know they are caused by your debt-interest calculation and not by another, incorrect formula?. You should follow a three-step process in modifying a model that contains simultaneous equations and whose solution you indeed want calculated simultaneously. The process is:

1. Insert PREVIOUS for those planning items that you want calculated as simultaneous and disable your SIMULTANEOUS AUTO statement by making it into a comment statement.
2. Add new logic to your model using sequential model revision and validate all your logic changes.
3. Remove PREVIOUS and enable the SIMULTANEOUS AUTO before you solve the model and obtain the desired solution.

This procedure helps to insure only those variables that you intend to calculate using simultaneous equations are indeed calculated that way. Because inserting and removing PREVIOUS is so easy in IFPS, this procedure is the quickest means of obtaining a solution with valid model logic.

Sequential model revision is explored by revising model FINPLAN6 to include PREPAID EXPENSES and DIVIDENDS with DIVIDENDS PAYABLE. The first revision is to include PREPAID EXPENSES as a new current asset. The second revision is adding DIVIDENDS with DIVIDENDS PAYABLE as a new current liability. In preparation for modifying the model, the simultaneous equations are disabled. Let's do that.

To disable the simultaneous equations:

❶   Access model FINPLAN6 as your active entity.

❷   Click **File**, click **Save As**, type **REVISE1** in the Entity Name text box, then click the **OK button** to rename your model before making the revisions.

❸   Locate the INTEREST EXPENSES formula and insert **PREVIOUS** for both the SHORT-TERM DEBT and the LONG-TERM DEBT.

❹   Locate the INVESTMENT INTEREST formula and insert **PREVIOUS** for the INVESTMENTS to remove the last simultaneous variable from your model.

❺   Locate the SIMULTANEOUS AUTO statement and place a \ (backslash) as the first character on this line to make it a comment statement, which disables this feature and completes the temporary removal of simultaneous equations from the model.

❻   Click the **Solve button** in the toolbar, then click the **OK button** for the default solution. Inspect the check accounts and verify they are zeros.

The model is now ready for making modifications. If any simultaneous equations are encountered, they indicate an error condition that requires correction. The first modification is the inclusion of the new PREPAID EXPENSES variable as a current asset. Because this is a balance-sheet variable, it also requires a modification in the sources and uses of funds statement. Whenever you add or delete any planning items from your model you need to determine if other planning items must also be modified. Let's include PREPAID EXPENSES in model REVISE1.

To add a new asset variable to the balance sheet:

❶   Verify that model REVISE1 is your active entity.

❷   Locate the INVENTORY variable and add this logic immediately below it:
PREPAID RATIO = 0, 0.03
PREPAID EXPENSES = 0, PREPAID RATIO * SALES

❸   Modify the calculation of TOTAL CURRENT ASSETS by adding:
+ PREPAID EXPENSES

❹   Locate CHANGE IN INVENTORY and add this logic immediately below it:
CHANGE IN PREPAID EXPENSES = 0, PREPAID EXPENSES - '
       PREVIOUS PREPAID EXPENSES
Note that the CHANGE IN PREPAID EXPENSES is summed in the TOTAL USES so no change is required in its calculation.

❺   Click **File**, then click **Save** to save these revisions.

❻   Click the **Solve button** in the toolbar, then click the **OK button** to display the default solution.

❼   Inspect the check accounts, they should all be zeros.

❽   Scroll the solution window and click **TOTAL CURRENT ASSETS**, then click **Analysis** and click **Analyze** to display the logic and solution values that includes the PREPAID EXPENSES. These are reasonable solution values, so this part of the revision is complete.

If the check accounts are not all zeros and the solutions values appear incorrect, then you would need to examine your changes to discover your error. However, in doing this you would only need to focus your attention on the planning items modified for including the PREPAID EXPENSES. This is a small set of the variables included in the entire model.

Now you are ready to continue with the next revision to the model, which is the inclusion of DIVIDENDS and DIVIDENDS PAYABLE. DIVIDENDS PAYABLE is added to the model because the dividend declared at the end of the year is not paid until the beginning of the next year. Let's make these modifications to the model now.

To include the planning items for dividend payments in the model:

❶   Locate the NET INCOME variable and add this logic below it:
       DIVIDEND PER SHARE = 4, PREVIOUS + 1
DIVIDENDS = 8000, DIVIDEND PER SHARE * SHARES

❷   Locate the ACCRUED TAXES variable and add this logic below it:
       DIVIDEND PAY RATIO = 0, 0.25
DIVIDENDS PAYABLE = 0, DIVIDEND PAY RATIO * DIVIDENDS

❸   Modify the calculation of TOTAL CURRENT LIABILITIES by adding:
+ DIVIDENDS PAYABLE

❹   Modify the calculation of RETAINED EARNINGS by including:
- DIVIDENDS
That is, when dividends are declared, they cause a reduction in the retained earnings.

❺   Locate CHANGE IN ACCRUED TAXES and add this logic below it:
CHANGE IN DIVIDENDS PAYABLE = 0, DIVIDENDS PAYABLE - '
       PREVIOUS DIVIDENDS PAYABLE

❻   Modify the calculation of PRELIM SOURCES so it is:
PRELIM SOURCES = 0, SUM(SUBTOTAL FROM OPERATIONS .. '
        CHANGE IN DIVIDENDS PAYABLE)
That is, CHANGE IN ACCRUED TAXES is replaced by CHANGE IN DIVIDENDS PAYABLE as the last planning item in the group that is summed.

❼   Click the **Solve button** in the toolbar, then click the **OK button** to display the default solution. Inspect the check accounts and note the amount of the error is equal to that for the DIVIDENDS. Because DIVIDENDS is a use of funds, it must be included as such in the sources and uses of funds statement.

❽   Locate CHANGE IN PREPAID EXPENSES and add this logic below it:
DIVIDEND PAYMENTS = 0, DIVIDENDS
Note this is included in the SUM function for calculating the TOTAL USES, so that summation does not need to be modified.

❾   Click the **Solve button** in the toolbar, then click the **OK button** to display the solution. Inspect the check accounts and verify they are all zeros.

❿   Scroll the solution window and click **TOTAL USES**, then click **Analysis** and click **Analyze**. Review the logic and solution to conclude the results appear reasonable.

Once the revisions are complete with the check accounts displaying all zeros and the solution passes the reasonableness test, the simultaneous equations are enabled and the final solution obtained. Let's do that.

To enable simultaneous equations and produce the final solution:

❶   Locate the INTEREST EXPENSES formula and remove the **PREVIOUS** you insert for the SHORT-TERM DEBT and the LONG-TERM DEBT.

❷   Locate the INVESTMENT INTEREST formula and remove the **PREVIOUS** you inserted for INVESTMENTS.

❸   Locate the SIMULTANEOUS AUTO statement and remove the \ (backslash) to activate it.

❹   Click **File**, then click **Save** to save these revisions.

❺   Click the **Solve button** in the toolbar, then click the **OK button** for the default solution.

❻   Print the model and its solution for your reference.

Using sequential model revision, you successfully modified the financial statement model. You should use this procedure whenever new planning items are added to the model to insure the integrity of its logic. The model is ready for evaluating any additional what-if alternatives or printing a management-style report using an IFPS report definition. In this manner, the validity of a financial statement model is continuously maintained as various business situations are explored to support decision making.

Questions

1. _____ validation is the process of verifying that a model contains the desired logic.
    a. Solution
    b. Model
    c. Financial
    d. Cash

2. A _____ account is calculated as total assets minus total liabilities plus equity.
    a. Saving
    b. Check
    c. Cash
    d. Model

3. _____ model revision is the step-by-step process of making a series of modifications to the model logic.
    a. Sequential
    b. Order
    c. Line
    d. Saving

4. This model revision has a top-down approach.
    a. Sequential
    b. Order
    c. Line
    d. Saving

Case Problems

1. Good Morning Products

Frosty, Crush, and Kimberly would like you to add the check account logic in Figure 12-2 to their planning model. Are all the check accounts zero? If they are not, what are they off by? What could you change in the model to get them to be zero? Now they would like you to add the ratios in Figure 12-7 to the model you created for them in Tutorial 11, Case Problem 1. Once you have solved the model Frosty, Crush and Kimberly would like your interpretation of what the ratios mean to their company's future. Write a paragraph that reviews these ratios.

2. The Woodcraft Furniture Company

Joe, Martha, and Ray would like you to add the check account logic in Figure 12-2 to their planning model. Are all the check accounts zero? If they are not, what are they off by? What could you change in the model to get them to be zero? Now you need to add the ratios in Figure 12-7 to the model you created in Tutorial 11, Case Problem 2. Once you have solved the model, Joe, Martha, and Ray would like your opinion of what the ratios mean to their company's future. Write a paragraph that reviews these ratios.

3. The Last National Bank

Carrie and J. J. would like you to add the check account logic in Figure 12-2 to their planning model. Are all the check accounts zero? If they are not, what are they off by? What could you change in the model to get them to be zero? Now they would like you to add the ratio CURRENT RATIO in Figure 12-7 to the model you created for them in Tutorial 11. Once you have solved the model, Carrie and J. J. would like your interpretation of what the ratios mean to their company's future. Write a paragraph that evaluates these ratios.

4. Harvest University

The chief financial officer would like you to add the check account logic in Figure 12-2 to their planning model. Are all the check accounts zero? If they are not, what are they off by? What could you change in the model to get them to be zero? Now the chief financial officer would like you to add these ratios from Figure 12-7: Inventory turnover, ratio on tuition, return on assets, return on equity, and debt ratio to the model you created in Tutorial 11. One you have solved the model, the chief financial officer would like your interpretation of what the ratios mean to their university's future. Write a paragraph that evaluates these ratios.

5. Midwest Universal Gas

Mary, Francis, and Petro would like you to add the check account logic in Figure 12-2 to their planning model. Are all the check accounts zero? If they are not, what are they off by? What could you change in the model to get them to be zero? Make these changes. Now they would like you to add the ratios in Figure 12-7 to the model you created for them in Tutorial 11. Once you have solved the model, Mary, Francis, and Petro would like your interpretation of what the ratios mean to their company's future. Write a paragraph that evaluates these ratios.

6. General Memorial Hospital

Berry and Gloria would like you to add the check account logic in Figure 12-2 to their planning model. Are all the check accounts zero? If they are not, what are they off by? What could you change in the model to get them to be zero? Make these corrections to the model. Now they would like you to add the ratios in Figure 12-7 to the model you created for them in Tutorial 11. The ratios they want to include are all the ratio except for the inventory ratio. Once you have solved the model, Berry and Gloria would like your interpretation of what the ratios mean to their hospital's future. Write a paragraph that evaluates these ratios.

7. River City

Lisa and Frank would like you to add the check account logic in Figure 12-2 to their planning model. Are all the check accounts zero? If they are not, what are they off by? What could you change in the model to get them to be zero? Now they would like you to add the ratios in Figure 12-7 to the model you created for them in Tutorial 11. The ratios they would like to include are all the ratios except for the inventory ratio. Once you have solved the model, Lisa and Frank would like your interpretation of what the ratios mean to their city's future. Write a paragraph that evaluated theses ratios.

8. Good Morning Products

After reviewing the model solved in Problem 1, Frosty realizes that SALES for YEAR0 should be 3400000. Do a what-if calculation on the model from Problem 1 for SALES and solve the model. What has happened to the model? Write a letter to Frosty explaining the changes in the model.

9. The Woodcraft Furniture Company

After reviewing the model solved in Problem 2, Joe realizes that CASH should be 150000 in YEAR0. Do a what-if calculation on the model from Problem 1 for CASH and solve the model. What has happened to the model? Write a letter to Joe explaining the changes in the model.

10. Last National Bank

After reviewing the model solved in Problem 3, Carrie received additional information from the accounting department that indicates the RETAINED EARNINGS for YEAR0 should be 19000. Do a what-if calculation on the model from Problem 3 for RETAINED EARNINGS and solve the model. What has happened to the model? Write a letter to Carrie illustrating the changes in the model.

11. Harvest University

After reviewing the model solved in Problem 4, the CFO realizes that ACCRUED WAGES for YEAR0 should be 2000. Do a what-if calculation on the model from Problem 4 for ACCRUED WAGES and solve the model. What has happened to the model? Write a letter that describes the changes in the model.

12. Midwest Universal Gas

After reviewing the model solved in Problem 5, Mary realizes that ACCOUNTS PAYABLE should be 450000 in YEAR0. Do a what-if calculation on the model from Problem 5 for ACCOUNTS PAYABLE and solve the model. What has happened to the model? Write a letter to Mary explaining the changes in the model.

13. General Memorial Hospital

After reviewing the model solved in Problem 6, Gloria realized that ACCRUED WAGES for YEAR0 should be 2000000. Do a what-if calculation on the model from Problem 6 for ACCRUED WAGES and solve the model. What happened to the model solution? Write a letter to Gloria illustrating the changes in the model.

14. River City

After reviewing the model solved in Problem 7, Lisa received additional information for the accounting department that indicates the RETAINED EARNINGS for YEAR0 should be 185600. Do a what-if calculation on the model from Problem 7 for RETAINED EARNINGS and solve the model. What happened to the model? Write a letter to Lisa describing the changes in the model.

APPENDIX

Installation of VISUAL IFPS/Plus

The Student Version of Visual IFPS/Plus is a WIN32s application. The Client and Server may be installed on a 386 PC(or better) with at least 8 meg of memory, running Windows 3.1 with Microsoft's WIN 32s Support installed or with Windows95 installed.

Hardware/Software Requirements

Specific hardware/software requirements are:
- a 100% IBM-compatible, 386 or 486 personal computer (PC) with a hard disk and a floppy drive;

- 8 MB RAM (16 MB RAM recommended if other applications will be run simultaneously);

- VGA or higher screen resolution;

- WINDOWS 3.1 or Windows95;

- 10 meg of free disk space;

- Microsoft's Win32s Support installed for Windows 3.1.

- Key Codes: **1252711082**
             1252547498
             1252479530
             1013160000

Theses Key Codes will need to be entered during installation of IFPS/Plus. You will need to retain these numbers in case you ever need to reinstall the product.

Student Version Limitation

The Student Version of IFPS/Plus has the following limitations:

- Modeling - a maximum of 120 variables or 60 columns can be defined.
- IFPS Database - maximum of 500 rows or 40 fields, per relation
- Universal Consolidation - Maximum of 3 levels deep and no more than 15 nodes.

Overview of Installation

The installation process has three steps.
1. Installing WIN32 Support
2. Installing Server
3. Installing Client

CAUTION ALERT!

> You need to install IFPS/Plus Student Version in the sequence indicated above.

Installing Win32s Support

If you are using Windows 3.1 and do not already have Win32s support installed on your PC, you will need to do so before installing IFPS/Plus.

To install Win32s Support to your PC:

❶   Place the **WIN32S Support** disk (Disk 1) in your disk drive.

❷   Select **RUN** from the program manager's file menu.

❸   In the Command Line prompt, type:
a:setup or b:setup
(whichever is appropriate for your disk drive)

❹   When asked to do so, place Disk 2 in the floppy drive.

This will install or update the Win32s support on your PC.

Installing the Server

The files on your IFPS/Plus installation diskettes are packed to save space. You will need to run **setup** to unpack and build the files on your PC.

To install the IFPS/Plus Server to your PC:

❶   Select **Run** from the Program Managerfile menu.

❷   Place **Server** Disk 1 in your disk drive.

❸   Type **a:setup** (or **b:setup** if your disk drive is b)

❹   You will be prompted for the directory where you want IFPS/Plus to be installed. Press the **OK button** to accept the default of **C:\IFPS**. You can specify a different directory (limit of 8 characters) for installation by replacing the default value in this dialog box prior to pressing the **OK button**. See Figure A-1.

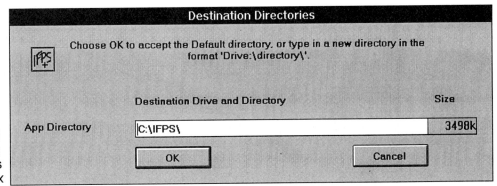

Figure A-1
Destination
Directories
dialog box

❺   You can choose either a full installation or an update only. If you are installing the product for the first time. you will need to select **"Full Installation."** If you select **"Update Files,"** only modified files will be installed.

TROUBLE? During the installation process, various files are written to your Windows directory. If one of these files already exists, you can **Copy Over** the old file, **Rename** to old file, **Skip** the update of this file, or **Exit** without completing the installation. Check the date of the file. If the old file has a more recent date, select **Skip**; otherwise, select **Copy Over**.

❻   You will be prompted for the Coordinator ID's and four Key Codes. Leave the Coordinator ID's blank and enter the four Key Codes supplied on the first page of this appendix. During the setup process, the Key Codes will be updated in the file SYSPROF. If you do not enter them during the install process or enter them incorrectly, you can edit the file SYSPROF (in your IFPS installation directory) with a text editor.

Installing the Client
After the Server installation is completed, you will need to install the Visual IFPS Client.

To install the Visual IFPS Client to your PC:
❶   Select **Run** from the "Program Manager" file menu.
❷   Place **Client** Disk#1 in your disk drive.
❸   Type **a:setup** (or **b:setup** if your disk drive is b).
❹   You will be prompted for the directory where you want IFPS/Plus to be installed. Press the **OK button** to accept the default of **C:\IFPS**. You may specify a different directory (limit of 8 characters) for installation by replacing the default value in this dialog box prior to pressing the **OK button.**
❺   You will have a choice of either a full installation or an update only. If you are installing the product for the first time. you will need to select **"Full Installation"**. If you select **"Update Files"**, only modified fields will be installed.

TROUBLE? During the installation process, various files are written to your Windows directory. If one of these files already exists, you **Copy Over** the old file, **Rename** to old file, **Skip** the update of this file, or **Exit** without completing the installation. Check the date of the file. If the old file has a more recent date, select **Skip**; otherwise, select **Copy Over.**

If you select "**Full Installation**" for both the Client and Server, the setup program will create a new program group (**Visual IFPS/Plus**) on your Window's desktop. If the program group already existed, you will be asked whether to *Replace* or *Add* any program items. Setup attempts to add to this group if it already exist.

The following program items replaced in this group:

IFPS/Plus Server   Doubleclicking on this icon will activate the IFPS/Plus Server.

Visual IFPS/Plus   Doubleclicking on this icon will activate Visual IFPS/Plus.

IFPS/Plus Help   Doubleclicking on this icon will display the on-line Help for Visual IFPS/Plus. All user documentation for Visual IFPS/Plus is provided in the on-line Help.

If doubleclicking on this icon produces a message from windows stating that there is no application associated with this file, you will need to start up **File Manager**. Next, select **Associate** from the **File** menu. In the Associate dialog box, enter **.hlp** in the "Files with extension:" box and **winhelp.exe** in the "associate with:" box. Press the **OK button** to save this setting and close the dialog box.

Now, you are ready to turn to the first Tutorial and start learning how to use Visual IFPS.

Index

Task Reference

Visual IFPS/Plus Release 5 for Windows

TASK	MOUSE	MENU	KEYBOARD
Close active window		Click File, click Close, or doubleclick the control-menu box	
Copy a highlighted selection		Click Edit, click Copy	CTRL+C
Cut a highlighted selection		Click Edit, click Cut	CTRL+X
Diagram a variable		Click Analysis, click Analyze	
Exit Visual IFPS		Click File, click Exit	ALT + F4
Explain result from a variable	Click the Explain button or Doubleclick the cell in the solution	Click Analysis, click Explain	
Goal Seek	Click the Goal Seek button	Click Analysis, click Goal Seek	
Graph data from solution	Click the Graph button	Click Analysis, click Graph	
Help screen access		Click Help, click Contents	
New model, report, datafile, and so forth	Click the New button	Click File, click New	
Open model, report, datafile, and so forth	Click the Open button	Click File, click Open	CTRL+F12
Outline a variable		Click Analysis, click Outline	

TASK	MOUSE	MENU	KEYBOARD
Paste		Click Edit, click Paste	CTRL+V
Print the active window		Click File, click Print	CTRL+F12
Save the entity in the active window		Click File, click Save	SHIFT+F12
Save the entity in the active window with a new name		Click File, click Save As	
Set the default directory	Click the Context button, Select the text in the Directories text box, Type the disk drive letter, and press the [Enter] key	Click File, click Set Entity Context, Select the text in the Directories text box, Type the disk drive letter, and press the [Enter] key	
Solve a model	Click the Solve button	Click Analysis, click Solve	
Switch to the IFPS server	Click the Server button	Click Server, click Command Session